Praise for Leigh Montville's

STING LIKE A BEE

"A book that belongs in the top tier of Ali literature."

—Booklist

"A dramatic, pleasing tale of a sports iconoclast fighting for his rights." *—Kirkus Reviews*

"Meticulously researched. . . . The inventory of Ali books is indeed long. But put this one on the short list." *—Newsday*

"Montville has given fans and boxing historians a thoroughly enjoyable and informative read."

—Library Journal (starred review)

"Revealing. . . . With dry humor, Montville portrays the central figures of Ali's life." *—Publishers Weekly*

LEIGH MONTVILLE

STING LIKE A BEE

Three-time *New York Times* bestselling author Leigh Montville is a former columnist at *The Boston Globe* and former senior writer at *Sports Illustrated*. He is the winner of many sports journalism awards, including the 2016 Red Smith Award, and was inducted into the National Sportswriters and Sportscasters Hall of Fame in 2009. Montville is the author of *Evel, The Mysterious Montague, The Big Bam, Ted Williams, At the Altar of Speed, Manute,* and *Why Not Us?* He lives outside of Boston, Massachusetts.

STING LIKE A BEE

A BEE

MUHAMMAD ALI vs.
THE UNITED STATES OF AMERICA
1966–1971

LEIGH MONTVILLE

ANCHOR BOOKS
A Division of Penguin Random House LLC
New York

FIRST ANCHOR BOOKS EDITION, APRIL 2018

Copyright © 2017 by Leigh Montville

All rights reserved. Published in the United States by Anchor Books, a division of Penguin Random House LLC, New York, and distributed in Canada by Random House of Canada, a division of Penguin Random House Canada Limited, Toronto. Originally published in hardcover in the United States by Doubleday, a division of Penguin Random House LLC, New York, in 2017.

Anchor Books and colophon are registered trademarks of Penguin Random House LLC.

The Library of Congress has cataloged the Doubleday edition as follows:
Names: Montville, Leigh, author.
Title: Sting Like a Bee : Muhammad Ali vs. the United States of America, 1966–1971 / Leigh Montville.
Description: First edition. | New York : Doubleday, 2017.
Identifiers: LCCN: 2016056528
Subjects: LCSH: Ali, Muhammad, 1942–2016. | African American boxers—United States—Biography. | Boxers (Sports)—United States—Biography. | African American Muslims—Biography. | Vietnam War, 1961–1975—Conscientious objectors—United States. | BISAC: SPORTS & RECREATION / Boxing. | BIOGRAPHY & AUTOBIOGRAPHY / Political.
Classification: LCC GV1132.A44 M66 2017 | DDC 796.83092 [B]—dc23
LC record available at https://lccn.loc.gov/2016056528

Anchor Books Trade Paperback ISBN: 978-0-307-95032-1
eBook ISBN: 978-0-385-53606-6

Author photograph © Robin Moleux
Book design by Michael Collica

www.anchorbooks.com

Printed in the United States of America
10 9 8 7 6 5 4 3 2 1

For Linda

Contents

STING LIKE
A BEE

Introduction

The hearse was a Cadillac, black and long and shiny, which figured because Muhammad Ali always was a Cadillac man. The first money he ever spent as a professional boxer went to West Broadway Motors in downtown Louisville to buy his mother a pink Eldorado. The second money went to buy an Eldorado for himself.

He roared through a string of Cadillacs in his early life, one replacing the other. He liked them flashy, too. He had one Cadillac that contained two phones so he could call two people at once if he wanted. A Cadillac was a sign of success. Wasn't it? He showed up one day in Chicago with a new Cadillac low rider that was so flashy a friend told him it was embarrassing just to travel with him.

"You should be in a classier ride," the friend suggested. "A Rolls or a Bentley."

"What's a Bentley?" the heavyweight champion of the world asked.

This final Cadillac was a 2016 XTS, which had been modified into a hearse somewhere in Ohio. The driver was thirty-three-year-old Chase Porter, whose family owns A. D. Porter & Sons, the funeral home that also buried Ali's mother and father. Ron Price, another funeral home employee, rode shotgun. Muhammad rode in the back in a $25,000 mahogany box.

The day—June 10, 2016—was filled with schedules and grand moments and famous people. The hearse would take a trip of slightly over twenty-three miles to cover a ceremonial route that would include a couple of highways and then travel down Muhammad Ali Boulevard, which once was Walnut Street. It would go past the Andrew Young

Center, which is very close to the Muhammad Ali Center, past the Beecher Terrace housing complex and past Central High School and past the Kentucky Center for African American Heritage and past 3302 Grand Avenue, Muhammad Ali's boyhood home, which has been restored as a museum. The procession would continue past all kinds of memories, big and small, would accompany the famous man straight down Broadway past various public buildings that were important in his life. The finish would be Cave Hill Cemetery.

Former heavyweight champions Mike Tyson and Lennox Lewis and actor Will Smith, who played Ali in a movie, would be among the pallbearers at the private graveside service. A public memorial then would be held at a fifteen-thousand-seat arena named after a string of fried chicken restaurants, the KFC Yum! Center, maybe the first memorial service ever held in a building with an exclamation point in the middle of its name. Tickets for this event had disappeared in the blink of a civic eye, every seat filled. Former president Bill Clinton, comedian Billy Crystal, and news host Bryant Gumbel would be among the speakers. Senior advisor Valerie Jarrett would read a statement from President Barack Obama, who had to attend his daughter's high school graduation in Washington, D.C.

ESPN and TV One and Bounce TV all would carry the proceedings live. Millions would watch. Millions more, maybe billions around the world, would see at least a part of what took place on news reports. People in Louisville would stand and stare, laugh and cheer, maybe cry a little bit as the procession passed. Flowers would be thrown. Affection would be public and unforced.

This was the send-off from this mortal coil that a head of state would receive. The funeral of a top-level movie star, a pop singer, might contain some of the same elements. Michael Jackson came to mind. A boxer had it here. A boxer. There hadn't been a funeral for an athlete in America this big probably since the one for Babe Ruth, who lay in state for two days and nights at Yankee Stadium in 1948. This was special. This was different. This was Muhammad Ali.

The first rose landed on the windshield of the 2016 Cadillac XTS almost as soon as the procession began. Chase Porter tried to sweep it off with his windshield wipers. A streak was spread across the glass. Roses would be a problem for the entire trip.

"Windshield wipers aren't to remove flowers," Porter said later to the writer from the *New York Times*.

The *New York Times*.

This was not about a boxer at all.

This was much bigger than that.

He was not an extremely old man when he died, seventy-four, same age as Bernie Sanders, who still was running for president, but it seemed as if Muhammad Ali had been old for a long, long time. Disease does that. He had begun to be compromised in the last two fights of his career. He was thirty-nine when he retired. That meant he had been sick, getting sicker, for more than thirty-five years.

The Parkinson's disease gave him a tremor, a shake, that only grew worse with time. His movements became more and more restricted until the last few years when he hardly could move at all. The slur in his voice became worse and worse until he could not talk.

The only part that grew larger, better, was his aura.

There was no stopping his aura.

Sweet Jesus, there wasn't.

The years passed and he became a secular saint. He was a postmodern Mother Teresa, shuttled around the world to minister to the masses. He lit the torch at the 1996 Summer Olympics in Atlanta, and there were quiet sighs mixed with cheers in every time zone on earth. He negotiated with despots to free hostages, didn't even have to say a word; just his presence was a convincing argument. He was a symbol of unity and possibility.

Everyone can get along. That was the unspoken message assigned to him in his later years. He was the black man who didn't disrupt the most segregated neighborhood. He was the Muslim who didn't want to blow up anything except injustice. There was a universal acceptability to him. Is that the word? Acceptability? He was a night light in what often seemed to be a very dark room.

"Ali did more to normalize Islam in this country than perhaps any other Muslim in the history of the United States," Sherman Jackson, a Muslim scholar, said when he spoke at the Jenazah, the Muslim funeral service held a day before the large service. "Ali made being a Muslim cool. Ali made being a Muslim dignified. Ali made being a Muslim relevant. Ali put the question of whether a person can be a Muslim and an American to rest."

"He dared to love black people at a time when black people had a problem loving themselves," Reverend Kevin Cosby, a Louisville pastor, said at the big service. "He dared to affirm the beauty of blackness."

His silence in his later years allowed him to say more than he ever said in those rapid-fire pronouncements of his youth. He could be anything and everything people wanted him to be. His inactivity kept him out of trouble. There were no more divorces, no more controversial headlines. He couldn't be found in Las Vegas in his declining years with young women and champagne and strange chemicals in the glove compartment of a rental car. He was on an island of purity, clean as everyone hoped an idol and role model would be. His most noted indulgence for the longest time was performing amateur magic tricks, pulling a coin from some adoring kid's ear.

The $80 million Muhammad Ali Center, opened eleven years earlier, was a monument to this perfect life. It resembled a presidential library, a patriotic or religious shrine. Boy Scouts and 4-H club members and busloads of inner-city kids could be shuffled through exhibits that preach the power of positive thinking. He did it! You can, too! Get working! The motto for the center was "Be great. Do great things." Mentioned often were "The Six Core Principles":

Confidence—Belief in oneself, one's abilities, and one's future.
Conviction—A firm belief that gives one the courage to stand
    behind that belief, despite pressure to do otherwise.
Dedication—The act of devoting all of one's energy, effort, and
    abilities to a certain task.
Giving—To present voluntarily without expecting something in
    return.
Respect—Esteem for, or a sense of the worth or excellence of,
    oneself and others.
Spirituality—A sense of awe, reverence, and inner peace
    inspired by a connection to all of creation and/or that which is
    greater than oneself.

Who could argue with any of that? Who?

"This bolt of lightning, this combination of power and beauty . . . ," the comedian Billy Crystal said in a well-received eulogy. "We've seen still photographs of lightning at the moment of impact. Ferocious in its strength. Magnificent in its elegance. And at the moment of impact, it lights up everything around it so you can see everything clearly. Muhammad Ali struck us in the middle of America's darkest night, in the heart of its most threatening gathering storm. His power toppled the mightiest of foes and his intense light shined on America and we were able to see clearly injustice, inequality, poverty, pride, self-realization, courage, laughter, love, joy, and religious freedom for all. Ali forced us to take a look at ourselves, this brash young man who thrilled us, angered us, confused and challenged us ultimately became a silent messenger of peace who told us life is best when you build bridges between people not walls."

Wow.

He had been on Facebook pretty much until the day he died. Well, someone had been on Facebook for him. Every third or fourth day, a message would be sent through the electronic air. Sometimes it would be the commemoration of an event—fifty years, say, since he starched Henry Cooper for the second time—but usually it would be a piece of advice for modern living.

"In the ring I can stay until I'm old and gray because I know how to hit and dance away."

"Eyes on the prize."

"The fight never stops."

"Outrun the people who stop because of despair."

"If my mind can conceive it, and my heart can believe it—then I can achieve it."

"Give everything your best shot."

"Team work makes the dream work."

"It's hard to be humble when you're as great as I am."

"Love is the net where hearts are caught like fish."

Wow.

—

The rough-edged, controversial character at the core of all this devotion was hard to glimpse through the haze of adoration in the days after his death. Flaws are not usually chiseled in marble. The time when he was loud and confident and half crazy with energy, when he startled and threatened his country, when he became known around the world, seemed like it happened long, long ago. There were constant mentions of it, for sure, stories that were told, black-and-white video clips that were shown, but when the clips were finished after a fuzzy minute or ninety seconds, the cameras returned to the pixilated present, sharp and clear on the screen.

The past could not compete. Jim Brown, the football great, or Kareem Abdul-Jabbar, the basketball great, would tell a story, make an observation. Pictures of the Thrilla in Manila or the Rumble in the Jungle or some other moment—there he is with the Beatles—would be shown. Ali himself would shout outrageous stuff, funny stuff, straight into the camera. It was all interesting, great, but black-and-white and dated. He could have been Winston Churchill talking about D-Day, Jimmy Stewart talking about the banking business in Bedford Falls, New York. The news or SportsCenter or whatever was the program of the moment would return sharp and crisp, digital, perfect color, today.

There was no context.

There was no urgency.

There was no frame of reference.

The fighters from his time pretty much were gone. Joe Frazier was gone. Sonny Liston was gone. Ken Norton. Floyd Patterson. Henry Cooper was gone. Ernie Terrell. Cleveland (Big Cat) Williams. Archie Moore. Jerry Quarry. Oscar Bonavena was long gone. Ron Lyle. Jimmy Young. A bunch of fighters were gone. A bunch of sparring partners. Big Mel Turnbow. Jimmy Ellis. Eddie (Bossman) Jones. Gone.

The people who had been around him were gone. The cook, Lana Shabazz. The little guy, Sarria, who gave him rubdowns. The guy who guarded his body, the guy who found him entertainment in the night, the guy who carried the water bucket. Gone. Bundini Brown, noisy and unforgettable, gone for a while. Trainer Angelo Dundee, the voice of reason, was gone. The eleven white businessmen from Louisville who backed an eighteen-year-old Cassius Clay at the start of his career, who negotiated his course to the title, were gone. All eleven of them.

Malcolm X, of course, had been gone for a long time. The Honorable Elijah Muhammad was gone. Herbert Muhammad, Elijah's son, who became Ali's manager and confidant, was gone. Howard Cosell was gone. People today didn't even know who Howard Cosell was. Don Dunphy was gone. The entire layer of famous sportswriters who criticized Ali mightily—Red Smith and Jimmy Cannon and Jim Murray and Dick Young and the rest—was gone. The talk show titans who loved him, easy money, easy conversation, Johnny Carson and Merv Griffin and Mike Douglas, the guy from Philadelphia, had been gone for a while. Norman Mailer, who was fascinated by him, was gone. Budd Schulberg was gone. Alex Haley was gone. Sinatra! Sinatra loved him. Sinatra was gone. Elvis was gone. James Brown and Sam Cooke.

Stokely Carmichael and Martin Luther King and H. Rap Brown and Lester Maddox and J. Edgar Hoover and Richard Nixon and Lewis B. Hershey, head of the Selective Service. Gone. The judges from all his cases were gone. All nine of the judges from the Supreme Court who decided on his case were gone. The members of all those important boxing commissions who made all those important decisions were gone.

A bunch of the places from his time were gone. The 5th Street Gym in Miami was gone. The old Madison Square Garden was gone. The old Yankee Stadium was gone. The Houston Astrodome, the Eighth Wonder of the World, was vacant and falling down. A case could be made that boxing was gone, probably an overstatement because boxing always will survive in some elemental fashion, the cockroach of organized sport, but the heavyweight division certainly had been gone for a long while in the United States.

The Vietnam War was gone. Dusty history. President Obama had walked down the streets of Hanoi less than three weeks earlier, walked with some of those remaining Viet Cong, who were pretty old now. The civil rights problems were gone, replaced with other civil rights problems, no doubt about that, but water fountains and restrooms and restaurants and hotels and schools and public transportation and voting booths and a whole bunch of other stuff now were protected by law from discrimination. The talking points were gone, the talking points from Ali's time.

A whole lot was gone.

—

The trick to seeing him as he really was would be to bring back everyone. Set the people up again in the present tense. Have them return to where everything happened. Let them walk and talk their way through the same troubles. Live everything again.

For a stretch of time, five years, 1966 through 1971, the most turbulent, divided stretch of this nation's history outside the Civil War, Muhammad Ali was discussed as much as anyone who walked on the planet. He was part of arguments about race, religion, politics, war, and peace. Not to mention boxing. It was an unmatchable story.

Here was this kid, this athletic prodigy, who fell into the thrall of an offbeat religion, the Nation of Islam, not the Islam known around the world, the Nation of Islam, a racially based cult as curious as the Hare Krishnas, as suspicious as the Moonies or the Scientologists or any other group that rings your doorbell, ding-dong, and promises salvation as if it were as easy to purchase as a vacuum cleaner with three monthly payments. He fell for it, foolish and proud, young and impressionable, and he wound up in everyone's house. Ding-dong. Every house in the world.

Pretty much illiterate, he was supremely good-looking and supremely verbal at a time when television invaded everywhere and these qualities became more important. He could fight in a boxing ring in a way no one ever had seen, talk in an excited way no one really had heard. He was part boob, part rube, part precocious genius, boom, somewhat honorable, and could be really funny.

Five years.

He stumbled into his situation, said he didn't want to go to war because of his religion, put one foot in front of another, and came out the other end a hero. Controversy found him and surrounded him. He fought the U.S. government, history, a Gallup poll majority of the American public, and Joe Frazier. He somehow survived.

Five years.

Joe Namath was the quarterback of the New York Jets. The Beatles were bigger than Jesus Christ. Lyndon Baines Johnson and Richard Nixon were presidents of the United States. Martin Luther King was vibrant and alive. And then he was not. An unpopular war in a faraway country was a background to everyday life. Demonstrations and riots were commonplace. A powerful noise was everywhere, the sound of frustration and anger and civil discord. A boxer tried to stick and jab, land a haymaker against his own government.

Muhammad Ali, very much a human being, was in the middle of everything.

Right here.

Now.

This was the guy who drove the Cadillac. Not the saint who rode in the back.

1

Local Draft Board No. 47

The day moved slowly. Bob Halloran tried to keep the conversation going in the living room of the small concrete house at 4610 NW 15th Court in the worn-down section of Miami, Florida, that the residents called Brownsville, but after one hour passed, two hours, three, there wasn't much else he could say. The list of topics had been covered and covered again. He mostly sat and waited, a talkative man curiously out of words as Muhammad Ali puttered and fretted, went outside and came back, and sometimes watched cartoons on the black-and-white television set.

A worry squirmed in Halloran's chest that Ali would become tired of him and would send him home. Or would want to be with different people. Or something. What then? The twenty-nine-year-old local television sports reporter from WTVJ tried to be as inconspicuous as possible.

His cameraman had set up on the front lawn in the morning. The guy was still somewhere out there watching the equipment. Neighborhood kids also were out there, kids who came around Ali every day, kids who treated him as if he were one of them, another kid, ready for fun. Most days he was. This day he wasn't. A worry also squirmed in the chest of the heavyweight champion of the world.

Local Draft Board No. 47 was preparing to make its move in Louisville, Kentucky. The machinery already was in motion. Although a New York lawyer had been dispatched to plead Ali's case, there was little doubt what the result would be. The weight of the U.S. government would fall directly on top of the primary resident of this house.

Nobody knew for sure when it was going to happen, but rumors had been floating for a week that he was going to be made eligible for the military draft at any moment. The demand for soldiers had grown, more than doubled, with the escalation of the Vietnam War. The generals at the Pentagon now wanted more than 400,000 troops for the war effort.

Ali had failed the intelligence test twice, which resulted in a 1-Y classification, unfit for service, but under new standards, changed only three days ago, his score of 16 now passed. He not only would become 1-A, eligible, but at twenty-four years of age, newly single again, he would be at the top of the induction list for the next month's call. All indications—which included comments he had made in the past on the subject—were that he would challenge the order to report.

Halloran had received a tip that today, Thursday, February 17, 1966, was the day all this would begin. Thursday was the day that Draft Board 47 made its weekly announcements. The tip was that the news would come from Louisville later in the afternoon, but Halloran had wanted to make sure he was there for the moment. That was why he had arrived before anyone else. That was why he had been here so long.

Waiting.

Waiting.

Waiting.

Communication was a problem. The bulletin from Louisville would come across the wire machine in the newsroom, but there was no way the people at the station could reach Halloran here. There was no such thing as a cellphone. He had to call them. The only phone he could use was Ali's home phone.

As time stretched, the reporter became uneasy about breaking the mood periodically by standing and going to that phone. Any news? Okay, thanks. The movement, the words, seemed intrusive. He would shuffle back to his place to watch more cartoons.

The wait continued.

Ali was more than just another interview subject. Halloran had known the boxer since he was a nineteen-year-old kid, since he was Cassius Clay, back from the Olympics, training at the 5th Street Gym at the start of his professional career. Boxing was important in Miami. There were no other professional sports, unless you counted horse racing, which also was important. The University of Miami was important. The Miami Dolphins, the new football team, no doubt would be important when they finally opened for business in the fall. That was it.

Halloran needed material for two shows a night. He spent much of his week at 5th Street, upstairs in the heat and the sweat and the multicultural noise, talking with fighters and trainers and whoever might come through the door. Ali was at the top of the list, now the most known professional athlete in the world. Need words? Ali, Cassius, whichever name was used, would deliver them with style and emotion. Often they would be in rhyme.

In the early days, the beginning, Halloran sometimes would see him in the mornings, running from Brown's, the little hotel in the Central Naval District, to the gym in Miami Beach. The trip took him over the Causeway. Who ran over the Causeway? Halloran would pick him up, save him from being clipped by the traffic. They would go somewhere for breakfast.

On the crazy night when the kid took the title from Sonny Liston at the Convention Center, when Liston didn't leave his stool for the seventh round, Halloran was with him for the whole experience. Sat with him and Angelo Dundee and Sugar Ray Robinson and maybe Bundini Brown in the stands early in the night to watch Ali's younger brother, then called Rudy Clay, now Rahman Ali, win a ten-round decision over Levi Forte, who later became a crack bell captain at the Fontainebleau. Was in the locker room just before the fight, was there when Sugar Ray, known as the greatest fighter of all time, pound for pound, had to sit on top of Ali's chest to keep him from hyperventilating. Was in the ring seconds after the fight ended, first reporter to get to the new champ.

"I'm the king of the world!" the kid shouted, pretty much hyperventilating now in public. "I shocked the world. Shocked the world. I am the greatest. I'm a baaaaaaaaaaaaad man."

Halloran kept good field position as the chaos developed, as people came from everywhere to be in that ring. The words went into his WTVJ microphone in a rush. The kid moved and moved, side to side, climbed on top of the ropes in a neutral corner, shouted and shouted some more, celebrated and pranced. Halloran kept with him as much as possible until there was a tug from behind.

"Hey," a nasal New York voice said, "you've had your time. This is network television."

That was how he met Howard Cosell, the most prominent sports announcer in the country.

The two-year anniversary of that fight, that night, would arrive in eight days. The two years had passed in an unremitting rush of activity. The day after the fight, the new champ declared himself a member of the Nation of Islam, a disciple of the Honorable Elijah Muhammad. The news was greeted with public discomfort as he began his dialogue about the separation of the races, about white devils and slavery guilt. Four days later he was in New York at the United Nations with Malcolm X. Malcolm X! Radical! Revolutionary! Everything had unrolled from there as most of America winced.

"A rooster crows only when it sees the light," the new champ said. "Put him in the dark and he'll never crow. I have seen the light and I'm crowing."

The kid who ran across the Causeway free and easy moved at a much faster speed after his announcement. He changed his religion, changed his name to Cassius X, changed it again to Muhammad Ali, traveled across Africa on a triumphant tour, was married, beat Liston again in Lewiston, Maine, of all places, went to Europe to fight a few exhibitions, came back to the United States to humiliate Floyd Patterson in Las Vegas, then was divorced little more than a month ago. Every day seemed touched with notoriety, with adventure.

He cut a record in New York, ten backup singers and a six-piece band, the lyrics written for him by Sam Cooke. He visited the pyramids, where he rode a horse, then visited with Egyptian president Gamal Abdel Nasser, whom he called "one of the sweetest, most loving, humble men on the planet earth," which was not an opinion shared by the U.S. government. He had an operation for an inguinal hernia in Boston, which delayed the second Liston fight. He then used his personal bus that he named Big Red to bring sparring partners, cooks, friends, even media on the road to Chicopee, Massachusetts, to train for that fight when it eventually happened in Lewiston. (When the bus broke down in Fayetteville, North Carolina, he said, "Give me them buses. When they catches fire, it's not 30,000 feet to the ground.") He was the subject of a mammoth question-and-answer interview with Alex Haley in *Playboy*. He was on the cover of *Time* magazine, seemingly on the cover of half the magazines in the world. He was a twenty-four-hour news machine.

Never shy or intimidated, he seemed at ease no matter where he landed. He spoke with the bulletproof certitude of a fourteen-year-old, a teenager convinced he knew everything about all subjects. He talked politics with politicians, religion with theologians, anything with anybody. Doubt was never involved.

In a visit to the British Isles, in the birthplace of iconic Scottish poet Robert Burns, Alloway, a Scottish town outside Glasgow, he was his usual self. Seated in a famous wooden chair that had been built from the wooden presses that printed Burns's first edition of poems in 1786, prodded by reporters, Ali "composed" one of his own poems.

"I heard of a man named Burns," he said, "who's supposed to be a great poet. But if he was: How come I don't know it?"

The words, so basic, so formulaic, were straight out of an adolescent joke book. What level of bravado allowed him to say them here? He never thought twice. Reporters scribbled while he spoke. The "poem" went across the world, probably read by more people than ever read a single Robert Burns sonnet. Tom McMynn, curator of the Burns cottage, was not amused.

"I don't think Robbie would have thought much of his poetry," the curator said.

Moments like this happened with regularity. The young heavyweight champion of the world was a caricature, the American innocent dropped into one sophisticated situation after another. He survived because his curiosity was obvious and contagious. He was showman as much as he was boxer. Everywhere he went was part of the performance. His charm, when he used it, which was much of the time, could grab strangers of all ages, sexes, races, national origins. This could have been a continual, triumphant parade.

Except . . .

Except he was a member of the Nation of Islam.

Except he made a lot of people uncomfortable.

In a country that had begun to push and pull itself apart with the assassination of John F. Kennedy on November 22, 1963, voices and sects and constituencies all claiming a piece of the future, louder each day, Ali had become a figure of controversy, sitting on a position at the far, far end of the racial debate. He was no marcher from Selma, Alabama. He was no link to Schwerner, Goodman, and Chaney, the three slain civil rights martyrs in Philadelphia, Mississippi. The Nation of Islam under the Honorable Elijah Muhammad preached separation, not inclusion, closer to the teachings of the KKK than the work of the Reverend Martin Luther King. The NOI talked self-defense, not nonviolence, an eye for an eye, Jack, shut your mouth.

"When Cassius Clay joined the Black Muslims and started calling himself Cassius X, he became a champion of racial segregation and that is what we are fighting against," Reverend King said. "I think perhaps Cassius should spend more time proving his boxing skill and do less talking."

With the assassination of Malcolm X a year earlier—a murder perpetrated by members of the NOI at the Avalon Ballroom on February 21, 1965—Ali had become the most prominent Black Muslim in the country. Malcolm was threatened with death, then murdered because he had repudiated the "straitjacket world" of the NOI's black racism and called the Honorable Elijah Muhammad a "religious faker." Ali had stayed true to the religion and the man in charge.

He appeared on the stage of the Chicago Coliseum at the NOI national convention five days after the assassination, the same day Malcolm was buried in New York, and stood next to Elijah Muhammad, who said that Malcolm received what he deserved. ("Malcolm was preaching bloodbath . . . he got what he deserved.") The champ, by his very presence, agreed. Agreed? He fought a five-round exhibition against his brother that was the main entertainment of the afternoon.

Most major cities had an NOI temple in the ghetto, black men dressed in suits and ties and stern demeanors posted at the doors. The body language and the language from the pulpit both said that this was not a group to be dismissed lightly. White America certainly noticed.

"Cassius belongs to a meandering cadre of the community that calls itself 'The Fruit of Islam,'" columnist Jim Murray of the *Los Angeles Times* wrote. "History has shown this fruit is bitter and poisonous. It is the Gestapo in blackface. Its stock-in-trade is terror, its payoff is death. Cassius has enrolled in this despotism, the first heavyweight champion since Max Schmeling to be in bondage to a cancerous tyranny."

This view pretty much was a majority view. Clay or Ali or whoever he was had gone to a dark side. He had been brainwashed, bamboozled, led astray. Why was he complaining? He was the heavyweight champion of the world. This was an exalted position in American culture. He could have anything he wanted. What was the matter with this guy? Why couldn't he be happy? Be normal?

Aren't money and fame enough?

"The fact is that my being a Muslim moved me from the sports pages to the front pages," Ali boasted to Alex Haley in that interview in *Playboy* in October 1964. "I'm a whole lot bigger man than I would be if I was just a champion prizefighter. Twenty-four hours a day I get offers—to tour somewhere overseas, to visit colleges, to make speeches. Places like Harvard and Tuskegee, television shows, interviews, recordings. I get letters from all over. They are addressed to me in ways like 'The Greatest Boxer in the World, U.S.A.' And they come straight wherever they're mailed from. People want to write books about me. And I ought to have stock in Western Union and cable companies, I get so many of them. I'm trying to show you how I have been elevated from the normal stature of fighters to being a world figure."

The problem was, the part of the world where he lived was not impressed.

Halloran had checked in regularly with Ali during all these travels and changes. The young Miami reporter had wrangled the only television interview with Ali's wife, Sonji, who was now an ex-wife because the champ said she did not want to be a full-fledged Black Muslim. He had done an interview with Ali's mother, the sweet woman overwhelmed by the change in her son's religion. The relationship between boxer and reporter persevered through whatever happened. Even when Ali was flanked by his many Muslim associates, hard-looking men in suits, white shirts, and bow ties, he had a loyalty to familiar faces who had been there at the beginning. Ali had a tendency to adopt people. Halloran was on the adopted list.

Chicago was supposed to be Ali's home now, but that was just the rented apartment where he and Sonji had lived. He was here in Miami as often as he was anywhere. This was where he trained with Angelo, where he reassembled the pieces of his craft. He was here now to get back in shape for a defense of his title against the awkward Ernie Terrell, the six-foot-six challenger he had designated as "The Octopus." The fight was supposed to take place in six weeks, on March 29, 1966, in Chicago.

The little house in what the champ called "spooktown" served him just fine as a base of training operations. He walked the streets as a hero. The neighborhood didn't bother him. He could live anywhere because he never had to travel for entertainment. He *was* the entertainment.

"It is one of those houses that always seems stuffy, where the warm smell of dinner hangs around the next morning and you can reconstruct the previous night's menu by sniffing in corners," would be a description by writer Jack Olsen in *Sports Illustrated.* "In this house in a shabby section of Miami, there is the constant presence of Negroes, of too many humans for the size of the place, no matter whatever their color. They drift in and out: celebrity Negroes, little children Negroes, big sparring-partner Negroes, door-to-door salesman Negroes, neatly-dressed Muslim Negroes, quick-dollar Negroes, old Negroes in skinny yellow shoes, young Negroes in porkpie hats, affluent Negroes driving black Cadillacs. In this house, kept neat and tidy by three Muslim 'sisters,' there remains something of the atmosphere of the 'colored only' waiting room of the Florida East Coast Railroad."

Perfect.

This business with the draft was a surprise, certainly not part of the plans for the Terrell fight. When Halloran had approached him a night earlier, talking about the tip from Louisville, Ali had been stunned. He had not expected anything this soon.

He had awakened early in the little house this morning, crossed the Causeway, and run his roadwork around the golf course five times. Later he sparred three rounds apiece with three large sparring partners, all of them over six feet four, reasonable facsimiles of Mr. Terrell. Back across the Causeway, he found that other reporters had started to appear at the house. Word had begun to spread.

Two years ago, there had been a burst of controversy when Ali flunked the test before and then again after the fight in Miami against Liston. That had subsided. Headlines were diverted to other sports-page stories. His 1-Y status had become background, part of the general unease about him. The news from Louisville would return all this to the front.

The many, many veterans of World War II who had returned home were now in their late forties, their fifties and sixties. These were men who had much less celebrated lives interrupted at Ali's age for far more harrowing service. This was not a sympathetic group. It already had spoken when he failed those tests.

"Had I flunked math [as Ali did] I still could have peeled potatoes for the first two months of my Army service—which I did," Representative William H. Ayres, a Republican from Ohio, a private in World War II, had said. "Anybody that can throw a punch like Cassius ought to be able to throw a knife around a potato."

This was the type of opinion that awaited. This was the basic opinion.

Halloran decided to check with the office one more time. What else could he do? He stood up, walked to the phone. The voice at the other end said nothing had happened. Then, as Halloran started to hang up again, bells started ringing in the background at the station.

That was how the wire machines worked, the Associated Press, United Press International, Reuters, all of them. When a story arrived, a sequence of bells designated how important it was. UPI's sequence, for example, went from four bells for an urgent story, five for a bulletin, to eleven for a truly important story, a stop-the-presses "flash." When all the services sent a truly important story at the same time, all the bells on all the machines would ring, so many that all other business in newsrooms around the country would stop. That was the sound here.

There was no doubt about the story.

"That's from Louisville," Halloran soon yelled to Ali. "It's official. You're 1-A."

The broadcaster had the presence of mind, the competitive instinct, to leave the receiver to the phone on the floor instead of hanging up. That way the outside world could not intrude. Any competition would be behind in the chase. Also, any extra advisors would not be able to reach Ali to tell him not to speak to the press.

The broadcaster hurried the new 1-A draft candidate out to the front lawn, dodging whoever was there. Ali didn't want to say anything at first, a thought that lasted for about half a second. Sure, he'd talk. He'd always talk. He couldn't help himself. With the neighborhood kids in the background, with the knot of reporters growing larger with new arrivals by the moment, Ali talked about the possibility of being in the U.S. Army. As expected, the champ was not enthused. He adopted a "why me?" approach. These were words that he would repeat for all interviews for the rest of the day.

I can't understand how they do this to me. Why be anxious to take me—a man who pays the salary of at least 200,000 men a year—200,000 men, you hear?

I can't understand out of all the baseball players, all of the football players, all of the basketball players—why seek out me, who's world's only heavyweight champion?" he said. "Why are they so anxious pay me $80 a month—me, who in two fights pays for six new jet planes? I'm fighting for the government every day. I'm laying my life on the line for the government every day. Nine out of 10 soldiers would not want to be in my place in the ring. It's too dangerous.

For two years the Army told everybody I was a nut and I was ashamed. And now they decide I am a wise man. They embarrassed my parents. Everybody was asking them questions, asking them if I was a nut. Even my ex-wife was ashamed. Yeah, it bothered me a bit. Now, without ever testing me to see if I am wiser or worser than before, they decide I can go in the Army.

When the interview ended, Halloran went back into the house and returned the receiver to the phone. The machine began to ring and would not stop for a while. The broadcaster hurried to the studio to edit his tape.

Ali stayed in front of the house. He kept talking. Other stations, other reporters had arrived. Kids. Reporters. Cameras. Muslims. Neighbors. There was a low-grade pandemonium.

"Why are they so anxious?" he asked about the draft powers that seemed to be in control of his life. "Why are they gunning for me? All these thousands of young men who are 1-A in Louisville and I don't think they need but 30, and they have to go into the two-year-old files to seek me out."

Between interviews, he would fool with the neighborhood kids. He questioned a sixth-grade girl about her studies. Robert Lipsyte, a *New York Times* reporter, noticed that the champ also sang a little bit. Just background. The song was "Blowin' in the Wind," by Bob Dylan.

How many roads must a man walk down
Before you call him a man?

Perfect.

By six thirty, he was back in the dining room of the little house, sitting with assorted people around a table, interviews done, when the *CBS Evening News with Walter Cronkite* came onto the television screen. The group had been waiting for this, the set dragged into view. Cronkite rolled through the day's troubles—congressional debate on the war, possible nuclear tests by Communist China, new government in Italy, food crisis in India. A pair of battles in Vietnam were reported, 350 of the enemy confirmed dead in one, 126 in another, U.S. casualties listed as "light" in both. Correspondent Dan Rather was in Vietnam. He asked a soldier what his message to President Lyndon Johnson would be, and the soldier said, "I'd just like to let him know that I'm behind him." Commercials were played for Kent cigarettes, Gold Medal flour, and Wheaties cereal. There was a strike in the Dominican Republic and a riot at an Indiana girls school, and the flu was sweeping the country, bed rest recommended as the best cure.

The news finally moved to Miami, Florida. Cronkite said Cassius Clay had been reclassified as 1-A by his draft board in Louisville, Kentucky. He spoke with Bob Halloran of CBS's sister station WTVJ. Everyone kept quiet in a hurry.

"Was this a surprise?" Halloran asked.

"Yes, sir, that was a great surprise to me. It was not me who said I was classified 1-Y the last time."

The voice that had dominated the conversations in the dining room now came from a different direction. There was the recorded Ali, back on the front lawn in the afternoon sun, saying all those things he said. He was agitated all over again for the homes across America.

"Why me?" he said in conclusion. "A man who pays the salary of at least 50,000 men in Vietnam, a man who the government gets six million dollars a year from for two fights, a man who can pay in two fights for three bomber planes . . ."

Ali stood at the end of the report. Everybody in the room was talking. He asked if Lyndon Johnson had heard this interview. Did Johnson watch this news or the other one with Huntley and Brinkley? Someone said he probably watched both.

"Huh," the champ said.

At the WTVJ studios in downtown Miami, Halloran also watched the *CBS Evening News*. His report on the local news had run earlier and longer than the lead story. He felt good about his work. Here he was now, though, with Walter Cronkite doing the introductions.

Walter Cronkite. This was a first.

How about that?

The story had only begun. The drama that followed would cover the next five years, four months, and eight days.

2

Those Viet Congs

The famous quote did not come until a day later. The interviews on the lawn at 4610 NW 15th Street were long finished when Ali took a phone call in the morning from Tom Fitzpatrick, a thirty-nine-year-old sportswriter for the *Chicago Daily News*. The fight with Ernie Terrell was scheduled to take place in less than six weeks, March 29, 1966, at the International Amphitheatre near the Union Stock Yards in Chicago. Tickets had to be sold. There were reasons to talk to sportswriters from Chicago.

The *Daily News* was an afternoon paper, so Fitzpatrick was looking for a different angle, different words from what everyone would read over breakfast. He was not disappointed.

"I am a member of the Muslims and we don't go to no wars unless they are declared by Allah himself," Ali said into the phone. "I don't have no personal quarrel with those Viet Congs."

Bingo.

That second sentence, the one about the Viet Congs, would become the defining quote for all that followed for the heavyweight champion of the world. The initial rush of self-indulgent emotion recorded by Bob Halloran and the other reporters was enough to get America agitated about a man who talked too much, loved himself too much. The mention of the Viet Cong, first reported in the afternoon edition of the *Daily News*, then repeated on the wire services to newspapers across the country, brought a focus to that agitation, put all the anger into a convenient package.

Nothing against those Viet Congs? This was the hook. Was it dissent or was it treason? Common sense or sedition? No boldface or italics were needed. The words would jump off the page without help.

"We Muslims are taught to defend ourselves when we are attacked," Ali further told Fitzpatrick. "Those Viet Cong are not attacking me.

"These Viet Congs are fighting a very nasty war over there," he added. "There's a lot of people getting killed. Why should we Muslims get involved?"

Variations of "I don't have no personal quarrel with those Viet Congs" would be included in all future biographical stories about Ali. This would become his stand, his legacy: the ten words that changed his life. The quote would become part of American historical dialogue, stuff for schoolkids to remember. Who said "Give me liberty or give me death"? Patrick Henry. Who said "I don't have no personal quarrel with those Viet Congs"?

An added quote would be assigned to him later: "No Viet Cong ever called me 'nigger,'" but he did not say that. Not now, not for many, many years, if he ever did. The quote was said by other people—activist Stokely Carmichael, for one—but somehow was assigned to Ali in slippery history. His quote was, "I don't have no personal quarrel with those Viet Congs."

He would try later to give the words context. He would claim in his 1975 autobiography, *The Greatest: My Own Story,* that on his way back from the gym that day when he received the news, he had seen some kids throwing rocks at a little girl. He said he stopped and asked what was happening and the kids told him they were playing "army and Viet Cong" and the little girl was Viet Cong. The words made him flash to pictures he had seen in a magazine of a little girl walking among dead bodies outside Saigon. Troubled, he took this little neighborhood child in his arms and walked her home, away from the trouble. The incident was still in his head when he spoke later.

None of this happened. The autobiography would be filled with these little feel-good memories that were too good to be true, bedtime-story perfect, invented by the champ and ghostwriter Richard Durham. He never mentioned the little girl to any reporters on that day. He never even mentioned the Viet Cong until his late interview with Fitzpatrick.

The quote that became remembered was another part of his daily torrent of words. Captain Sam Saxon, the man who first introduced

Ali to the NOI in Miami, said he was with the champ at one point in the day and told him, "You got nothing against those Viet Cong," and the champ agreed, yes, he had nothing against those Viet Cong. Ali perhaps remembered and repeated the phrase in the interview, nobody really conscious of the impact. There was no plan; the words came out with all the other words. The difference was that these words landed in the catch basin of the national mind.

Those Viet Cong were killing more than eighteen American kids every day. The death total for 1965 had been 1,928 (double the casualties of any year in the Iraq War), and that would be tripled, to 6,350, in 1966 with the new escalation (more deaths in one year than in the entire Iraq War). In 1968, the height of the Vietnam War, 16,899 American kids would lose their lives. That would be forty-six per day.

Not being upset with the Viet Cong seemed much worse than not submitting to the draft or not wanting to be involved in the war. Graphic pictures of these dying American boys had begun to appear on the nightly news. The enemy was supposed to be the enemy.

"I don't want to scare anybody about it, but there are millions of Muslims around the world watching what is happening to me," Ali said to Fitzpatrick. "I'm not making a threat [that they'll get angry and do something]. I'm just saying maybe."

This was heavy stuff.

Ali was familiar with the role of villain. He had chosen it in the early stages of his professional career, tried it on as if it were a black hat and a scowl discovered in the back of a family closet. He kept it when he found that it brought increased attention and larger paydays.

His marketing idea was that bad was much more interesting than good, an approach that newspapers, the television nightly news, and the gossipy woman next door had adopted long ago. People were more interested in paying money to see Sylvester the Cat than Tweety, Tom more than Jerry, Wile E. Coyote more than that beep-beep Road Runner.

This approach was adopted when Ali returned from the 1960 Olympics with his light-heavyweight gold medal and found himself back at the beginning in the professional side of the sport, no more than another low-watt attraction fighting unheralded opponents named Terry Hunsaker, Herb Siler, Tony Esperti, and Duke Sabedong. Where was the money, the instant payoff for those hundred-plus amateur fights? (His amateur record has been recorded in various places with various numbers, ranging from 99-8 to 137-7.) Where was that joy the country felt when he stood on that podium in Rome, the "Star-Spangled Banner" played for the world to hear? He was in a hurry. What would make people notice again? The answer appeared on his television screen.

"Soon after I turned pro, I discovered that even though I won the Olympic title, I wasn't making any money," Ali said to Alex Haley in *Playboy*. "I was the only champion who didn't have no jack jangling in his jeans. . . . One night I was watching Gorgeous George on TV. He was jumping around making a lot of noise and threatening his opponents and I said to myself, 'this guy's on to something. I think I'll put some of that into my act.'"

Gorgeous George, whose real name was George Raymond Wagner, was an eighth-grade dropout from Nebraska who had become one of television's first stars in the fifties, as notable as Lucille Ball or Milton Berle or Bishop Fulton J. Sheen. He strutted into the ring in sequined robes and high-heeled shoes and had bleached-blond hair that looked as if it came from the same bottle Marilyn Monroe used. His personal "valet" preceded him, squirting perfume into the air. George was a sissified, exaggerated stereotype of a homosexual, effeminate to the ultimate, totally in love with himself. He also was a sneaky, dirty wrestler once the matches began. The combination was irresistible. People howled from the moment he was introduced. A ringside spectator named Hatpin Mary sometimes would stick said hatpin into George's grand backside somewhere during the proceedings, to everyone's amusement.

Ali, as Cassius Clay at the time, adopted pieces of this act—the villain was known as the "heel" in wrestling, the hero known as the "babyface"—and added some of his own. The adopted parts involved the self-important bluster, the constant confidence, the repeated declarations about how pretty he was, the demonization of every opponent. He became a shouter, eyes bugged out of his head, one of those people who always seemed to be ticking, ready to explode. The predictions, the rhymes, the nonsense were part of his act.

He was especially insufferable and comic in the buildup to the first fight with Liston. He called Liston "The Bear," and wore a light blue jacket that said "Bear Huntin" on the back. He went to Las Vegas, screamed outside the champ's house, confronted him in a casino, made his life miserable. He asked if that big bear was as "rangy and fast and pretty as me." Gorgeous George couldn't have done any better.

"[Clay] is light-hearted and breezy and has just enough twinkle in his eyes to take most of the obnoxiousness from the wild words he utters," Arthur Daley of the *New York Times* said before the fight. "When they are imprisoned in print, however, the twinkle is never captured and Cassius just becomes nauseous."

The twinkle made its last unadulterated appearance in the moments after Ali won the title. He was outrageous, comical, as he shouted in triumph from the ring at the sportswriters who picked Liston to win easily. He boasted about his looks, his ability, his battle plan for the odd fight that he had won when Liston refused to come out for the seventh round. No doubt about it, the night the young challenger captured the title he was a hoot. He made even his worst detractors admit they had been wrong about what would happen.

The change came the next day with his announcement that he was a member of the Nation of Islam. The comedy of the past was overwhelmed by the message of the present. The bigmouthed character became a Black Muslim. This was not what most of the paying public wanted to hear. The villain's words now meant something. The jokes took second place to personal philosophy.

"I don't have to be what you want me to be," Ali said at his press conference. "I'm free to be who I want.

"I go to a Black Muslim meeting and what do I see?" he said. "I see there's no smoking and no drinking and their women wear dresses down to the floor," he said. "And then I come out on the street and you tell me I shouldn't go in there. Well, there must be something in there if you don't want me to go in there.

"In the jungle, lions are with lions and tigers with tigers and redbirds stay with redbirds and bluebirds with bluebirds," he said. "That's human nature, too, to be with your own kind. I don't want to go where I'm not wanted."

The softness here was in contrast to the national image of the NOI and the Honorable Elijah Muhammad. For the white folk who had paid attention, not a large group at the start, this was a cult more than a religion, a theology that talked about white devils and spaceships and a black scientist named Jakub, who had an enormous head and created the white devils six thousand years ago to persecute the black man.

The Muslims had demands. What was it that Malcolm X always said? "Nobody can give you freedom. Nobody can give you equality or justice or anything. If you're a man, you take it." Most national stories about the faith mentioned the large number of convicted criminals who now were members.

At first there was the thought that Ali's conversion was a phase, a mistake by a twenty-two-year-old guy—twenty-two years, thirty-nine days at that—who had landed in a new situation with new levels of fame and economics. He had been brainwashed by some slick sales-men, sold this bill of curious religious goods. He would grow out of it soon enough. A Black Muslim? He would realize a heavyweight champ could have a much easier life.

"He's always been such a good boy," said his mother, Odessa Clay. "He's been taken in by these Muslim people. We pray he'll see the light—and we think he will."

"That Muslim stuff is a phony religion," said his father, Cassius Clay Sr. "They brag that they don't drink, smoke or fool around with women. That is only one commandment. There are Ten Commandments."

The depth of Ali's belief soon became established. If this was a brain-wash, it was a very good one. Standing at the side of the Honorable Elijah Muhammad after Malcolm X's death, the heavyweight champion of the world became a potential target for revenge. He never blinked.

As city after city rejected the idea that it should be the host for his rematch with Liston because of worries of Black Muslim violence, because of the potential for *his* assassination, his commitment never changed. As the fight finally landed in a hockey rink in Lewiston, Maine, and he trained in Chicopee, Massachusetts, trailed by five policemen every day as he went from his motel room to the converted banquet hall where he sparred, he laughed about the threat. As he was guarded by more than two hundred policemen on the night of the fight, with hourly reports of Malcolm X Muslims coming north from New York to kill him, he laughed some more. He then dropped Liston in one round with one "anchor punch," supposedly taught to him by old-time actor Stepin Fetchit, and as all of America wondered what the hell was going on, he exulted.

"Nobody wants to kill me," he said. "If they shoot, the gun will explode in their hands, the bullets will turn, Allah will protect me."

The Lewiston win was followed six months later with the twelfth-round TKO embarrassment of Floyd Patterson. Poor Floyd, thirty-one years old, was a gentle man, a practicing Catholic, a two-time heavyweight champ who had been knocked out twice by Liston in the first round, causing him to disguise himself in shame when he walked the streets after the fights. He was cast here as a classic babyface by Ali, drawn for the fight as "The Rabbit," as the white man's version of a good black man, yessir, nosir, Uncle Tom. Ali cast himself, of course, as the heel. He was the belligerent black man the white man feared in the night.

Booed during the introductions, booed during the lopsided fight, booed at the end, Ali converted the night into a morality play. True Black Man pummels Fake Black Man. He would use this plotline often during his boxing career, no one ever sure if he was kidding to hype the crowd or was as serious as could be. The answer was left to the observer to decide. Ali simply laid out the story.

His domination of Patterson was obvious. The challenger, who claimed he hurt his back in the fourth, didn't win a single round. Ali played with him, taunted him, called him "the white man's black man," said, "Come on, black man, fight for America." He seemingly could have knocked him out in any round, finally dropped him in the sixth, then finished him in the twelfth. Ali would claim that he was waiting for the referee to stop the fight all night, that he tried not to hurt Patterson, but the ringside view mostly was that he punished the challenger for insisting on calling him "Clay," not his Muslim name, in the prefight publicity whirl. Fake or real, the villain was in charge all the way.

"He's mean," legendary retired champion Joe Louis said. "He worked that poor Floyd over good. He handled him like a baby and he gave him more than he had to give him. I think he could have knocked him out from the first round if he wanted to, but he didn't want to. I think he just let him have it for fun."

"While we were fighting, Clay said maybe once or twice in the earlier rounds, maybe like in the third or fourth, 'What's my name?' and I said 'Cassius,'" Patterson said years later. "And finally, in the latter part of the fight, I'd say in the ninth, tenth or eleventh round, and I was really taking a really bad beating, suffering, he said 'Now what's my name?' I believe I said the same thing, 'Cassius Clay and that's what it's always going to be, regardless of the results of this fight. Cassius Clay.'"

"Round one, I said, 'What's my name?'" Ali said, some number of years later. "He didn't say nothing. So round two, round three, I hit him with my right hand. 'What's my name?' He said, 'Muhammad Ali, Muhammad Ali.'"

Either way, the fight was a showcase for Ali. This was how well he could box. The two bouts against Liston had been characterized by their strange conclusions. This fight was characterized by Ali's abilities. He had dazzle, flash, incredible speed. There never had been a heavyweight champ like this young guy. He danced and moved like a middleweight, but had the size and power of a heavyweight. He had told everyone before the fight that Joe Louis would have been too slow to beat him. Rocky Marciano would have been too short. Jack Johnson would have been too ugly. Jack Dempsey would have been too light and couldn't punch. That left him at the top. The Greatest. He looked the part against poor Patterson.

He said he didn't need love. He had talent.

"I'm not worried about those boos," he said. "Those were white people. I got all the black people, some white people, too, and the people of Africa and Asia."

That theory would be tested with his remarks about the draft and the Viet Cong. The volume became louder. Starting now.

"There is a patina of panic glazing his eyes as he talks compulsively in bursts of words . . . ," Gene Ward, a former Marine Corps correspondent at the battle for Tarawa, wrote in the *New York Daily News*. "The very thought of being drafted into the army makes him cringe, and his torment is the talk of the last resort of a man who is turning to jelly."

"Not since A. Hitler was stirring up a mess of trouble some 30 years ago has there been anyone to compare with our boy Cassius Clay when it comes to making enemies and having a bad influence on a lot of people," wrote Johnny Janes, executive sports editor of the *San Antonio Express and News*. "His eternal popping off as to his fistic prowess was bad enough and his hooking up with the Black Muslim movement was worse. . . . Now he has been re-classified 1-A by his Louisville draft board and he screamed so loudly and so long that it was suspected he had been robbed of his ego."

This was the message in most commentaries across the country. It didn't matter that athletes everywhere were diving into National Guard units, that college seniors were moving along to graduate degrees to keep their student deferments, that marriages were made in haste to stay away from that dreaded 1-A classification, that countless potential draftees limped and gimped to induction physicals, hoping that bad knees, flat feet, or a heart murmur would keep them home and safe from those Viet Cong. A game of bureaucratic hide-and-seek was taking place everywhere, winks and nods as rich kids stayed home and poor kids went, but Ali was not part of this. He had turned the Induction Follies game board upside down, the pieces falling on the floor. This was not respectable behavior.

One writer called him "the black Benedict Arnold." Another said if he was drafted, the perfect place for him to be sent was Fort Bragg. The Benton Harbor *News-Palladium* in Michigan ran an editorial that said Ali's appeal to be exempt from the draft because he was a member of the Nation of Islam "makes as much sense as exempting members of the Ku Klux Klan." The *Post-Crescent* in Appleton, Wisconsin, said that "Clay's remarks are an insult to true conscientious objectors."

The only place he seemed to have true support was from the United States' geopolitical enemy: the Soviet Union. TASS, the Soviet news agency, agreed with Ali, though not in an exactly complimentary way.

"Why is he being drafted now?" TASS asked. "Maybe Clay got smarter. No, this is not noticeable. The point is that the escalation of the dirty war [in Vietnam] is demanding ever more cannon fodder. Clay's intellectual development is the least of the worries for the shameless warriors."

The Nation of Islam was returned to the first page of the news with Ali's situation. The Honorable Elijah Muhammad had served four years in prison for refusing to fight in World War II. Didn't everyone line up to fight in World War II? Apparently not. Other Black Muslims also had gone to jail for the same reason. Was the Nation controlling

Ali here? Or was he making his own decisions? The curious religion became even more curious. Was this the start of some national insurrection? It seemed as though the Nation of Islam, hmmmmm, had this history of civil disobedience when called to service.

"The Muslim paper called *Muhammad Speaks* is full of praise for Nasser, Ho Chi Minh, Cuba and China," syndicated columnist Jim Bishop wrote. "The message is not lost any more than the unsigned cartoon showing a Negro enlisting and being told by a white sergeant with a forked tail: 'You have just sold your soul to the devil.'"

Syndicated satirical columnist Art Buchwald, who at the age of seventeen had found a bum to pose as his father so he could join the Marines after Pearl Harbor (because that was too young to enlist without parental consent), suggested that Ali would be used in the army to bore the Viet Cong to death. A fictitious general detailed the plan.

"What we plan to do is drop Clay into Viet Cong territory and leave him there for a week," the general said. "By this time he will have bored everyone in the area to death and we'll send in our regular troops to occupy the countryside. We'll then pick up Clay and drop him in another area and in a short time, Vietnam will be secured."

The *Chicago Tribune* led the charge in the Midwest. The conservative newspaper, with the motto "An American Newspaper for Americans" underneath a picture of the American flag on the front page every day, made the first call for the cancelation of the fight with Terrell. Even before the reclassification announcement, the *Tribune* had published an editorial titled "Sucker Bait" that questioned the necessity of a promotion that involved a man "considered too dumb to carry a musket and who has joined the Black Muslim hate group." Ali's well-quoted words from Miami turned this opinion into a cause.

"We haven't found anyone who is persuaded that Cassius Clay should be enriching himself at the expense of sucker spectators by fighting here on March 29 instead of doing his fighting in the army," an editorial said on Friday, a day after Ali's remarks. "We find it deplorable that so many Chicagoans are unwittingly encouraging him by their interest in a fight whose profits will go largely to the Black Muslims, upon whom Clay counts to rise up and save him from his duty to his country."

The next day, the circulation leader in Chicago was back with specific demands. It called on Illinois governor Otto Kerner, a World War II veteran and a former major general in the Illinois National Guard, to tell the appointed state athletic commission to kill the fight.

"He [Kerner] should let the commission know immediately—before any more suckers have a chance to buy tickets—that the scheduled fight is not only a discredit to boxing, but that it is a dishonor to the state and a flagrant insult to the many Illinois veterans," the American newspaper for Americans said. "The people of Illinois, and especially the veterans and the parents of those now in service, should let him know how they feel. His address is The Governor's Mansion, Springfield, Illinois."

Added pressure came from predictable directions. Kerner, Chicago mayor Richard Daley, the three members of the boxing commission, the local promoters Ben Bentley and Irv Schoenwald—everyone associated with the fight was put on the spot. The leader of the Illinois branch of the American Legion condemned the champ's remarks in forceful language. The Illinois fifth district of the Veterans of Foreign Wars passed a resolution urging Kerner and Mayor Daley to "intercede and instruct the Illinois boxing commission" to cancel the fight. Politicians stood in line to add their negative opinions to the pile.

"I landed at Normandy on D-Day in World War II," said State Senator Arthur Gottschalk (R–Park Forest). "I wasn't athletic and I was scared, but there wasn't a man in my landing craft who wasn't proud to be there. I'm sure I know what they all think of Clay."

"I think it is an insult to the people of this state to permit a man like Clay who swears allegiance to an admitted cult of violence [the Black Muslims] to reap a harvest of cash from the very citizens he has insulted with his whining attempts to avoid the draft," said Charles Siragusa, another veteran and the head of the Illinois Crime Investigating Commission. "What he has said is an affront to every American who ever wore the uniform of this country."

There were a lot of living Americans who had worn that uniform.

Ali was rattled by the uproar. Or so it seemed. Still in Miami, he backed away from his responses to those questions about the Viet Cong. He said he had not checked with the Honorable Elijah Muhammad before he talked. The words had been his own. Maybe he had said some things he didn't mean. When Governor Kerner—who said he was "disgusted" at the champ's statements after the *Tribune* ran a third editorial, one of fifteen stories about the situation in one issue—ordered the commission to revisit the license for the fight, Ali acted. He called the commission offices and was apologetic.

"I feel I made some statements that were wrong," he said.

He blamed newspaper reporters for making him go off "half-cocked," a basic defense for all celebrities caught in controversy for something they said that exploded in print. He apologized to the commission, to the promoters, to the public for his "big mouth." He said he was willing to do whatever was necessary to allow the fight to continue.

"From this point on, the newspaper writers will never maneuver and trick me on any subject about politics or the war in Vietnam," he said. "I'm not a politician. I'm the heavyweight champion of the world."

This humbled approach appeared to work. The three members of the commission indicated they were inclined to allow the fight to be held. At least they wanted to hear more. Ali proposed that he appear before them in four days, on Friday, before any decision would be made. The contrite champ already was scheduled to travel that weekend to Chicago for the Nation of Islam's Savior's Day convention, a major liturgical event in the religion. A public hearing would be his chance to further prove his contriteness.

"He apologized for his statement to the commission," chairman Joe Triner said after talking with Ali on the phone. "He apologized to the Governor. He apologized to the public for having his big mouth open to make these statements.

"He is willing to do anything to convince the public he is sorry for these statements. He asked to come in Friday before the commission and we agreed."

When Ali arrived late in Chicago on Thursday night, he was greeted at the airport by Ben Bentley. Bentley, who had encouraged Ali to call the commission in the first place, took out a piece of tape and put it across the champ's mouth, a gag picture for waiting cameramen. Ali said—before the tape was placed—that he wished he had thought of this before he spoke in Miami. He said no more.

Ali's lawyer was fifty-year-old Edward W. Jacko, who had been successful in a number of suits to allow members of the Nation of Islam to practice their religion while in prison. Known in the New York press as "Jacko the Giant Killer," he had an office on 125th Street in Harlem and also had been successful in a number of lawsuits against the New York police for brutality. Many of these suits involved members of the Nation of Islam.

After Malcolm X led a hundred or so Black Muslims from Harlem's NOI Temple No. 7 in military-style formation, followed by as many as five thousand onlookers to the precinct house on 123rd Street to protest the beating and arrest of three NOI members in April 1957, Jacko took the case. ("I'd have shot the nigger, but other cops kept getting in the way," one New York City patrolman allegedly said at the scene about thirty-one-year-old defendant Johnson Hinton.) Three years later, after a lot of publicity, Jacko wrangled a $75,000 settlement in damages from the city for Hinton. That was when he received his nickname of Giant Killer.

He had presented Ali's letter to Draft Board 47 in Louisville requesting a hearing prior to any reclassification, so was familiar with the situation. The letter listed Ali's different reasons for not being drafted—financial reasons because of payments for his divorce and for support of his mother and father, religious reasons from his conversion to the NOI, procedural reasons from his rejection twice earlier by the army—and was signed "Muhammad Ali / Slave Name Cassius M Clay Jr." The reclassification was Draft Board 47's negative reply.

Jacko now tried to orchestrate Ali's personal appeal to the Illinois Athletic Commission. He had advised Ali on what to say on the phone call, provided the conciliatory words. Before the lawyer flew from New York for the hearing, he composed a similar statement for Ali to read before the commission. It contained the same apologetic sentiments. The commissioners would nod publicly at these wise words. Commerce would resume. There once again would be time for a few poems about how fast the large Mr. Terrell would fall before the champion's punches.

"What he says and how he says it will affect my vote," Chairman Triner promised.

Easy. Everything would be easy.

"Clay is an irresponsible kid and he says things all the time that don't make sense and I think his comments about the draft were ridiculous," Mr. Terrell said from his training camp in Pleasantville, New Jersey.

"But they should not warrant the stopping of our fight. I've learned to just ignore the stuff he says. And I'm going to close his mouth in the ring on March 29th."

Easy.

The meeting was switched from the Athletic Commission office to a larger Commerce Commission hearing room in the State of Illinois Building at 160 North LaSalle Street. The scheduled starting time had been switched to 12:30 on February 25, 1966, but Ali arrived at noon, accompanied by Jacko, Louisville attorney Arthur Grafton, and Chauncey Eskridge, another high-profile attorney from Chicago who did work for both the NOI and for Martin Luther King. Football player Jim Brown, a friend and part of Main Bout productions, which held the television rights for the Terrell fight, was a blocking back for everyone. He held Ali's hand as they cut through the crowd outside the building.

An out-of-sync ungainliness was attached to the proceedings from the start. Everything seemed wrong. The layout of the hearing room was like a courtroom, but without the decorum. Cameras and yammering observers and an oversized police presence were everywhere. The three commissioners would sit in high-backed leather chairs on an elevated podium, same as trial judges. Ali would be cast in the role of petitioner, seated on the floor with his representatives. He would be looking upward at the people who would decide his fate.

Arriving early, he had to stand in the back of the crowded room for a half hour, then for fifteen minutes longer when the start of the meeting was delayed again until 12:45. He wore the unofficial NOI uniform: the dark suit and the white shirt and the bow tie. When he finally sat, the ungainliness was intensified.

Ali had gone to breakfast with Eskridge at the home of the Honorable Elijah Muhammad on the South Side of Chicago. He later said the meeting with the commission wasn't mentioned until he was ready to leave. Eskridge explained to the Honorable Elijah Muhammad that Ali was expected to apologize. Apologize? The leader gave his counsel.

"Brother, if you felt that what you said was wrong, then you should be a man and apologize for it," he said. "And, likewise, if you felt what you said was right, then be a man and stand up for it."

Ali considered the advice on the ride to the hearing. There was little internal debate.

The deal was off.

As attorney Jacko saw his careful typewritten words discarded, as he grabbed at Ali from behind, only to be brushed away and shushed as some outside nuisance, the champ blew up the meeting and blew up the projected fight. Thoughts about contrition were abandoned. The hell with these people. Ali returned to his original thoughts about the military draft and the U.S. government.

From the moment Chairman Triner addressed him as "Mr. Clay" and Ali responded with "My name is Muhammad Ali," the words touched with emotional ice, this was an adversarial relationship. The champ made it clear that he would not follow the predicted and prescribed path.

"First of all, I'm not here to make a showdown plea or apologize as the press has projected I will," he said. "My apology is only to apologize for what embarrassment and pressure may have been put on you, not me. I should have told these things to the government—the draft board—not the reporters. I didn't mean to insult anyone or the people with children, sons, in Vietnam."

He said he was sorry that the remarks had been public, that they had been stretched across the country's newspapers, and was sorry that this had brought pressure on the promoters of the fight, but not sorry about the sentiments inside those remarks. That was how he felt at the time. That was how he still felt. His situation would be determined in the future, "straightened out" with the draft board in Louisville.

"Then you are not apologizing for the unpatriotic statement you made?" Chairman Triner asked.

"I'm not apologizing for anything like that because I don't have to," Ali replied. "I'm apologizing just for what I said to the press."

The meeting dissolved from there. The room was filled with excitement mixed with consternation. Chaos. What was Ali doing? Why had he changed his mind? What would come next? Joe Robichaux, the one black member of the commission, a chairman of the 21st Ward of the city, a friend and appointee of Mayor Richard Daley, tried to bring some order.

"Mr. Clay . . . ," he said.

"Muhammad Ali," the champ replied.

"Mr. Clay . . ."

"Muhammad Ali . . ."

"You previously came before the commission and told us that you were the people's champion. Do you think you're acting like the people's champion now?"

Chaos.

As Ali tried to answer in the midst of the noise and activity, fellow commission member Lou Radzienda called for the meeting to be adjourned. As Triner said "No, I'm not satisfied with the answer," the champ and his lawyers and people stood. The meeting was done.

A half hour later, Illinois attorney general William G. Clark announced an opinion that the fight was illegal. The hearing might not have been necessary in the first place.

Two problems were listed: that a promotional corporation has to have fifty members, and this one, National Sports Promotions, had only two; and that the licenses for both Ali and Terrell were illegal because neither man met "standards of conduct" under state law. Neither of these was an oft-cited infraction. They had been dug out of the fine print for this specific situation. The governor did not want this fight to happen.

Clark had delivered his opinion to the commission before the hearing even started, presenting his case in private in that half hour while Ali waited in the crowded room. The commission was free to disagree and to vote to allow the fight to be held. The promoters also had a right to disagree. Under ordinary circumstances various courses could have been followed, the attorney general's office forced to decide a next legal move, but after Ali's appearance, the spirit seemed drained from all objections.

Mayor Daley agreed with the attorney general's opinion. Governor Kerner agreed. The athletic commission bumped along—even held a second hearing on Monday, Terrell in attendance this time, but no Ali—then gave its decision on Wednesday. Triner and Robichaux voted against. Lou Radzienda voted for. The fight was canceled.

The *Chicago Tribune* celebrated.

"For this happy outcome of an unpleasant dispute we owe thanks to Mayor Daley, Gov. Kerner and Atty. Gen. William G. Clark," the newspaper proclaimed. "All of them exhibited the leadership, common sense, and courage which are expected of elected officials. The attorney general's use of the powers of his office to right a wrong was in the best tradition of public service and the law profession."

The *Chicago Defender,* the city's newspaper published primarily for people of color, had a different reaction. The *Defender* was not a booster of the Honorable Elijah Muhammad, nor of Ali in his antidraft remarks. The paper still handed out its "Onion of the Day" award to the athletic commission.

"Had not Ali expressed a viewpoint at odds with the personal philosophies of the politicians, it is doubtful the fight would be in jeopardy," the *Defender* wrote. "As a human being, as an American, even as a 'Black Muslim,' Ali shares in the right of freedom of speech. Perhaps Voltaire said it best: 'I totally disagree with what you have to say but I shall defend to the death your right to say it.'"

Free speech had a price. That was the lesson here.

It had been just three weeks since Ali uttered his first words on the subject. The first tangible loss from his resistance to the draft had arrived promptly and with significant public outcry. Money was left on the bargaining table.

This was the most curious of boxing occurrences: a fight for the heavyweight championship of the world had no home.

3

Foreign Affairs

Montreal was the first choice. The day the fight was thrown out of Chicago, an application was filed to stage Ali-Terrell at the Montreal Forum, home of the Montreal Canadiens. The move seemed to make sense.

"Montreal is a good fight town of two million people, and there hasn't been a title fight here in eight years," said George Hanson, boxing writer for the *Montreal Star*. "I'd say the buffs are ready—really rather hungry—for another title fight."

That optimism lasted for twenty-four hours. Then, no, the deal was dead. The Forum was not available; Montreal was not available. The suburb of Verdun, Quebec, was mentioned as a possibility. Then, no, Verdun passed and then Sorel, Quebec, was listed as another possibility.

Louisville also was suggested. And Bangor, Maine. And Las Vegas. And Manchester, New Hampshire. And Huron, South Dakota. And Pittsburgh. And Miami. And . . .

One by one these possibilities fell apart. Politicians paraded to microphones to save their constituents from the prospect of viewing a potential draft dodger in short pants. It was an easy case to make.

"Cassius Clay should be held in utter contempt by every patriotic American," Governor John H. Reed of Maine declared in a representative explanation. "Maine's sons and daughters are fighting and dying in Vietnam and I don't think Maine people want our state to be used to further ambitions and gains of an individual of Clay's character."

New York had refused the fight even before Chicago did, due to alleged gangster ties involving Terrell's longtime manager, Bernard

Glickman. The allegation was that Glickman was a surrogate for a Chicago mobster, Tony Accardo, who had been banned from boxing. That part of the equation was forgotten for the moment. Ali was the one big issue.

He had spent the past weekend, as promised, at the Nation of Islam's convention in Chicago at the Convention Center. He was pictured in the uniform of the elite Fruit of Islam guards, an elaborate costume that was topped off by a fez with the initials "FOI" embroidered across the front. He looked as if he were a resident of some foreign country.

Men sat with men for the long day of speeches. Women, dressed in uniform and modest white robes, sat with women. The ten white reporters who were allowed into the convention crowd, estimated to be between three thousand (city) and six thousand (Nation of Islam), were searched five times. Chicago firefighters refused to be searched and did not enter the building.

Ali stayed near the Honorable Elijah Muhammad throughout the leader's speech, which lasted almost three hours. He shouted encouragements when the leader denounced the integration attempts by the Reverend Martin Luther King, shouted again when the leader said the Vietnam War was fueled by black soldiers while the sons of white leaders stayed home with college deferments. The leader also mentioned Ali's situation.

"You are robbing him [Ali] like you did Joe Louis," he said at one point. "Louis ate at my house. He is walking around like a bum—that's what he is. I could have cried. You want to make a bum, too, of Muhammad Ali, but you won't if he sticks with Elijah."

The search for a site for the fight finally ended two weeks after the Illinois Athletic Commission hearing, on March 8, 1966, in Toronto, where owner Harold Ballard offered the sixteen-thousand-seat Maple Leaf Gardens, home of the city's hockey team. A one-vote win in the Ontario parliament ratified the invitation. Mike Malitz, speaking for Main Bout Inc., the holder of television rights, said that he was pleased that someone "finally has looked at this as a sports event instead of something else," but here, too, there were problems.

Seventy-one-year-old Conn Smythe, the builder of the arena, former coach, general manager, and owner of the hockey team, and a Canadian hero from both World Wars, resigned from the board of directors and sold his remaining shares in the team in protest. He said management had put "cash ahead of class" and that he had been "traded for $35,000 and a Black Muslim minister."

"The Gardens was built for many things, but not for garbage disposal," Smythe said. "This fight has been kicked out of every place in the United States and we need all the friends we can get in the world today. If it's not good enough for Montreal, then by heavens it's not good enough for Toronto."

A bigger problem than Smythe's exit soon arrived. Ernie Terrell saw the details of the contract for the restructured fight. The new arena, new city, new country meant a new deal. The new deal stunk, in Terrell's opinion. ·

In Chicago, he said he had guarantees of $100,000 from the live gate and $50,000 from the television receipts and would receive $12,500 for training camp expenses. In Toronto, there were no guarantees, no expense money, and a clause had been added by the Maple Leaf Gardens people that if he won, he would have to defend his title against Canadian heavyweight champion George Chuvalo within two months at the arena. None of this made sense to Terrell. He already had fought Chuvalo, grinding out a fifteen-round decision fourteen months ago in a defense of his WBA title.

"Why should I fight him again?" Terrell asked. "I would give anything to fight Clay. . . . I'd fight him anywhere in the world for 50 cents. But with this new contract . . . it makes it impossible."

Terrell was out. Gone. The fight was dead.

Except it wasn't.

Enter the aforementioned Mr. Chuvalo.

He was twenty-eight years old, six feet tall, 216 pounds, a Cro-Magnon brawler who seemed to have stepped into the ring from a long-ago generation. He had a big head, a thick neck, and a definite lack of fear. The son of Croatian immigrants, he had grown up on the west side of Toronto, and put together a 34-11-2 record to become a heavyweight contender and a local favorite. Losses to Floyd Patterson and then to Terrell, both close decisions, had stalled his climb in the rankings, but he was still a legitimate opponent.

Everything here was done in a hurry. Chuvalo said that he received a call from Mike Malitz asking if he would fight Muhammad Ali at

Maple Leaf Gardens in seventeen days. Seventeen days? Chuvalo told
Malitz to wait a minute while he put in a call to his wife.

"Honey, are we doing anything on March 29, 17 days from now?" he
said.

"No," she replied, checking her appointment book. "Why do you ask?"

"Because you're going to go watch me in a fight that night."

"Who are you going to fight?"

"Muhammad Ali."

The match was made.

Ali had one stop to make on his way to Toronto. On the afternoon of
March 17, 1966, he appeared in front of Local Draft Board No. 47
in Louisville. He flew into the city in the morning from Miami and
arrived with his father, Cassius Marcellus Clay Sr., and with attorney
Jacko. Dressed in a black suit with a black bow tie, he looked nervous before entering the building. He was quiet, fidgeting, looked like
another young guy caught up in the legal system. He did not talk with
the gathered reporters.

The meeting lasted thirty-five minutes. This was not a formal appeal
but a review of his case. Ali restated the claims in Jacko's letter to the
board, a more restrained recital of his feelings. The hearing seemed
to be a pro forma exercise. The board quickly denied his request and
refused to change his classification. Ali would have a chance to file an
appeal of the decision within ten days, which Jacko indicated would
be done.

The one good bit of news was that Ali would be allowed to leave the
country during any appeal, which would enable him to fight Chuvalo.
This had been a final doubt in the saga of the championship fight, only
the third defense of his title.

"I'm not saying anything about the draft board," he said to the assembled reporters outside 1405 West Broadway. "I'm not saying anything
bad about the draft board. I just ain't talking about nothing but fighting."

The champ had to smile when he made this pronouncement, a slight
amazement, perhaps, at his own self-control. He joked with a few spectators, said that his life had been turned upside down with all this draft
business.

"This whole thing has been disturbing to me," he said. "I've broken camp three times and missed three days of training. It's too bad the fight won't be carried on too many stations because a lot of people want to see me beat. It's always a possibility, too, because I'm human.

"I may be the greatest, but I'm also human."

The idea that he might be vulnerable was the sales pitch that he took with him to Toronto two days later. He said he was fifteen pounds over-weight. He said he had a bruised knuckle that kept him from working on the heavy bag, the exact exercise he needed to fight Chuvalo. He said there were no predictions because he had never been in this situation, not physically ready to fight. When he was knocked down in a public sparring session by Jimmy Ellis, well, what do you think about that?

None of this was very convincing. He weighed 215 pounds when he took a physical during the week before the fight, only five more than he weighed in his last defense, against Floyd Patterson. His opponent, Chuvalo, also pointed out that this "out of shape" Ali had been in training for the bout against Terrell. Chuvalo said he had been sitting around the house until Malitz called. He felt now like a college kid cramming for a final exam at the last minute.

Ali and his Muslim entourage took up residence in a motor lodge on the edge of Lake Ontario. In this foreign environment, a small bit of normality was restored to his life. There were no reports of car-loads of assassins coming across the border, even as the well-publicized trial of three members of Mosque No. 7 in Harlem for Malcolm X's murder plodded, step-by-step, toward a guilty verdict in a New York courtroom. The air in Canada seemed more still. He was a boxer again getting ready for a fight.

The Vietnam business still was present, especially when he did interviews with the U.S. press, but the cloud of animosity did not hang outside his front door. Canadians didn't have the same views that Americans did.

"You don't need a federal investigation to reveal that Clay is one of the most conscientious champions in history," Al Sokol wrote in the *Toronto Telegram,* a viewpoint rarely put forth in the States. "He doesn't drink, smoke, swear, run around with women or associate with underworld figures. Cassius Marcellus Clay is as free today from criminal connection as he was the day he won the Olympic light heavyweight title in Rome six years ago.

"All Clay said was he didn't have any argument with the Viet Congs. You begin to wonder how hatred would be directed at Muhammad Ali if his name was John Doakes of the Ku Klux Klan."

The relaxed Ali sang "Here comes Peter Cottontail, hopping down the bunny trail" as Easter approached. He organized fifty-yard dashes among the kids who hung around his motel, awarding one-dollar prizes to the winners of the heats, ten-dollar prizes to the winners of the finals. He wore a cowboy hat when he talked with reporters, even though Toronto never had been known for an abundance of cowboys.

"I am the most popular fighter for women because I am so pretty," he declared, a voice from the comic past. "They don't like to hear my mouth and they want to see me get beat. So they drag their daddies to the fight. The old man, he wants to sit in front of the TV set and sleep, but the women, they are interested in me. That's another reason I am the most publicized sports person in history.

"I have a scrapbook in my room," he added, a voice from the not-so-comic present. "It's this thick. [A foot high.] On one side is the sporting write-ups. On the other side is the controversial write-ups. Those controversial write-ups are getting bigger than the sporting write-ups all the time."

There would be no big payday for this fight. That was a fact that became more evident every day. The seventeen-thousand-seat arena was scaled modestly, tickets ranging from $50 ringside to $7 in the rafters, but interest still was restrained. The odds were 6-1 in favor of Ali, and even that seemed low. In the United States, interest was almost nonexistent. Closed-circuit presentations had been banned in Boston, Miami, and San Antonio and the number of sites reduced in many other locations. Only seventy thousand seats were available across the nation in thirty-two cities.

The presence of Herbert Muhammad and the Nation of Islam in the promotion, especially as partners in Main Bout Inc., was not missed. Harold Sugarman, president of H&B American Corporation, a cable antenna firm servicing eighty-one thousand homes in California, said that H&B had carried a number of heavyweight championship fights in the past. It would not carry this one.

"I'm not waving a flag or screaming patriotism," Sugarman said. "I'm just being practical. The Muslims have half the action on the fight. It is their mission to extinguish the white race. If they do, they're going to do it without any help from me."

The Muslims added a behind-the-scenes mystery to everything. They clearly had replaced the Louisville Syndicate, Ali's first white businessmen backers from his hometown, as the major force behind his movements. The deal with the Syndicate would expire in October, and everyone pretty much expected the Muslims to take full control. ("We went into the group for fun; it's not fun any more," said advertising man Archie Foster, offering a common Louisville complaint.)

The Muslims already were part of Main Bout Inc., and Herbert Muhammad already was Ali's business manager. What would they do next? They were a new business force in the back streets of boxing. Even Chuvalo, running roadwork in the Toronto mornings near his house, wondered about the Muslims. He had constructed an elaborate explanation of how he had been tapped for this fight, of why Terrell had turned it down. It was a much different story from the one Terrell told.

Chuvalo said his own fight with Terrell over a year ago still rankled him. He had discovered that his manager, Irving Ungerman, was confronted at the chicken processing plant he owned by Terrell's infamous manager, Bernard Glickman, before the fight. The message was "if your guy wins you will wind up in a cement box at the bottom of Lake Ontario." Chuvalo also learned that the referee in the fight had been contacted, a similar message imparted. He figured the judges also must have received the same message. How could he win?

Chuvalo decided that Glickman must have made the same sort of threats to Herbert Muhammad and Ali's people. Glickman now was in the hospital under heavy police guard after being severely beaten. The news report was that he had run afoul of the mob, but Chuvalo didn't believe it. He thought that the damage had been delivered by a few of those Fruit of Islam guards.

"All Herbert Muhammad had to do was snap his fingers and all his Islamic guys are right there and bing-bam-boom, that's it," the fighter said, years later. "And that's why I got the fight."

There was no mention of any of this as the event approached. The days peeled away without any grand headlines.

Ali said he was not like old-time heavyweight champion Jack Johnson, who was scorned in the United States for his relationship with a white woman, because "Jack Johnson was an integrationist; I'm a segregationist." There was no uproar. Henry Bolton, Maple Leaf Gardens manager, dismissed worries about pickets as "old stuff" because Russian hockey teams and Alabama governor George Wallace had appeared at the arena, presumably on different nights. No big deal. Chuvalo grunted and worked, former champions Joe Louis and Rocky Marciano brought into his camp to give him advice. The world press, over 150 credentials issued, two even to the *Chicago Tribune,* prattled about the lopsided matchup.

A surreal quality hung over everything, this heavyweight title fight constructed in seventeen days' haste. There was even a debate about whether it was a true fight for Ali's crown. The WBC, the governing body, said it did not recognize the fight, but *Ring* magazine and most reporters said it was a fifteen-round fight and certainly it was for the heavyweight championship. Chuvalo would be seen as the king if he won. It was a championship fight.

"Clay risks the most valuable title in sports in a foreign country for peanuts with most of his fellow countrymen rooting for Chuvalo to stage one of boxing's greatest upsets," Fred Down of United Press International wrote.

The fight on March 29, 1966, the date when Terrell was supposed to have been the opponent in Chicago, followed a predictable course. Ali was in charge against the dull work of the challenger, clearly in another category of the sport, faster and stronger, just better, able to unload five, six, seven punches in a row without being touched. The challenger, also true to expectations, never went to the canvas. His eyes were almost closed by the eleventh round as spatters of his blood decorated the ring, but George Chuvalo was a tough cookie. He surely could take a punch.

There were no controversies; no mysterious anchor punches or accusations about unnecessary punishment being dispensed. This was an exercise completed without drama or conversation. The paid crowd of 13,540 people saw no more or no less than what was expected. The people who couldn't watch on television in the States did not miss much.

"We had a contest between a bull and a bumblebee at Maple Leaf Gardens—with the usual result," *Toronto Star* columnist Milt Dunnell said. "The bull came out of it with his face looking like a bucket of balls at a golf driving range."

Three days later, Ali was in New York in the ABC studios for *Wide World of Sports,* the network's highly rated weekly athletic grab bag, dissecting the fight with Howard Cosell. They had become a pair in the American mind, the nasal-voiced broadcaster and the talkative boxer. Cosell was almost singularly resolute among reporters and interviewers in calling the champion by his adopted name (although "Cassius Clay" was splashed on the screen under Ali's talking head on *Wide World*). Ali seemed appreciative, always ready to praise Cosell as a true bright light in a dim journalistic world. There was a vaudeville quality to their appearances, the forty-eight-year-old Cosell as the straight man, delivering serious-sounding and lengthy questions filled with multisyllabic words; Ali, half his age, whacked the questions out of the park. Showmanship, never a large part of sports interviews, was in abundance.

Cosell tried to make a big deal here out of referee Jackie Silvers's reluctance to penalize Chuvalo for low blows. He pointed out "11 to 13 low blows" in the third round alone. The announcer cranked up his level of outrage as if he were talking about a great moral injustice. Ali, who complained only once about low blows during the fight, seemed to take them for granted in a bout against a body puncher like Chuvalo.

"If I ever fight him again I'm going to have a cup made that is twice as thick," he said.

At the end of the fight discussion, Cosell visited the draft problem. He invited the champ to apologize for what he had said. Ali tried to say he wanted to talk only about boxing, but Cosell pressed the issue. He said "you owe it to the American people" to explain. He also said that Ali should talk directly into the camera.

The explanation (into the camera) was the same as Ali had given to the boxing commission in Chicago and everywhere else. He felt bad for the promoters, the ones who lost money on the fight, but that was it. He wouldn't take back anything he had said.

"I'd be less than a man to sit here and deny it," he said.

This seemed to satisfy Cosell. He stretched out his right hand.

"Take care of yourself," he said, shaking the boxer's hand.

"Same to you," the boxer replied.

A picture of Ali delivering yet another hard right to Chuvalo's hard head was on the cover of the following April 11, 1966, edition of *Sports Illustrated* as the magazine began a five-part series titled "Cassius Clay: The Man, The Muslim, The Mystery." Senior writer Jack Olsen, forty years old, white, had spent three months with and around the champ. His five accounts, which would be collected together a year later as the basis for a book called *Black Is Best: The Riddle of Cassius Clay,* were a first visit to a strange place for most Americans, a look inside the champ's life in the Nation of Islam. The sounds were different, the sights were different, the smells, thoughts, feelings, people were different.

Olsen, the writer, also found that he was different.

"It is next to impossible to explain something that I experienced in working on this story," he said in an introduction to the series, "but somewhere along the line, I learned what it is like to be a Negro. . . . I was around the Muslims for a couple of months, and they make you feel exactly the way some whites make the Negro feel. They don't insult you; they just act as if you aren't there. The shortest and quickest course a white man can take to learn about Negroness is to hang with the Muslims. Then he will understand the American Negro—the cloud of contempt in which he walks the streets, the feeling that he comes only as high as the white man's knee, the feeling that produces Uncle Toms at one end of the spectrum and Black Muslims at the other, the feeling of what it is to be considered dirt."

This series was the deepest examination of Ali's adjusted life to date. He had talked often about producing an autobiography, no doubt with a ghostwriter, but hadn't begun the process. This was a book-length project by the foremost sports magazine in the country. Money was spent.

Olsen stayed around and stayed around, awkward most of the time. He picked up nuggets of information and time with his man when he could. Ali never did remember his name, nevertheless tapped him for a quick loan of ten bucks the first time they met. Olsen painted a picture of a troubled and misguided twenty-four-year-old who had stepped away from both his family and his original backers, the ones who had tried to impart a financial strategy and direction for his career. The champ was now with the Muslims, controlled in both mind and body. The strange religion dominated his days and nights, his every decision.

Ali's mother and father lamented to Olsen about how little they saw their oldest son. Worse than that, they lamented about how little influence they had on him, none, as a matter of fact. Neighbors and friends said that Cassius Clay Sr. had fostered this antiwhite attitude in the beginning, suspicious of all dealings with white folk, argumentative, and—surprise—very talkative. Clay Sr. denied this. He thought his son was being brainwashed by new so-called friends. Odessa Grady Clay, the champ's mother, mostly fretted about the change that had taken place with both of her sons. She said the Muslims didn't like her because she had lighter skin, a perceived sign of weakness.

Ali was expansive in his thoughts about his different life. He read passages from the Honorable Elijah Muhammad's book *Message to the Blackman in America,* especially descriptions of apocalyptic scenes that could arrive as soon as right now, 1966, when Negroes would be taken to glory, whites finally dealt a cruel justice. He defended his Muslim name, degraded his slave name of Cassius Marcellus Clay. (His father said he thought Cassius was a wonderful name, Roman in origin, better and certainly older than the name Muhammad.) There was an evangelistic fervor when the champ started rolling, a cadence filled with alliteration and repetition and observation.

Olsen noted that the words of these supposedly extemporaneous messages, fresh the first time, soon seemed to come from the same package. They sounded like mental recordings, dropped onto a 45 rpm turntable at the appropriate moments. These were the arguments that drove Ali's family to despair.

Brainwashed. That was the family verdict.

"Why you have to be almost totally illiterate to be sold on that Muslim bill of goods!" Ali's aunt Mary Clay Turner said. "I'll just plain old give you the facts. *You have to be illiterate.* Cassius is about the cleanest thing in the whole confounded Muslim organization. All the rest of them have scars and smears on their names. If they haven't been hustlers, well, they're hustlers now! If they haven't been robbers, they're robbing now! This is it, you know I'm not lying! Practically every one of em's been in prison. Cassius falls for all that business about no drinking and no smoking, but he didn't know they drink behind the doors and cuss, and whip their mamas and do everything. And they'd kill you just as quick as they'd kill me, and don't you forget it!"

There were few quotes from Muslims in the stories, none from the Honorable Elijah Muhammad, none even from Herbert Muhammad. There were no descriptions of mosques and services. The background to Ali's life mostly was detailed by his family and by the Louisville business group and by the two white men in his entourage, trainer Angelo Dundee and Dr. Ferdie Pacheco.

Ali needed constant attention. That was an observation. He needed people to laugh at his jokes, to accommodate his whims. The whims could be anything at any time. He was out of control. That was another observation. He needed money because he gave it away to members of the Nation of Islam who asked. He didn't value money except when he needed it. He had no investments, no savings. He simply didn't listen to advice. He didn't even listen to advice about boxing. He wouldn't listen to sparring partners, wouldn't listen to Dundee, wouldn't listen to anybody. He was the greatest. He had begun to act the role.

The final thought from family and non-Muslim friends was that the heavyweight champion of the world was in trouble. Look at the hearing before the athletic commission in Chicago. Look at the problems with the draft. Look at how the most marketable fighter in the world now had to travel the world to make a devalued dollar.

"Cassius will just have to mature," Dr. Pacheco, the Miami physician who had attached himself to the champion's entourage, said toward the end of the final article. "It's not impossible. Some men mature late in life and some men mature in adversity. And boy! is he heading full-speed into adversity! For one thing, he's got to win every fight now either by knockout or by a big margin. Remember, if any boxer can stand on his feet for fifteen rounds against Clay in an American ring, why the American public is so desirous of lancing this boil on their rear end they just might lance him right out of the decision. They may give him the old zinger, boxing style. That's one of the adversities he faces: going into the Army as the ex-champion of the world."

Olsen compiled thirty-four one-hour tapes during his research. At the end of each interview, sometimes at the start of a new one, the writer would record his impressions of what he had seen or heard or what he felt. He would complain in his gravel voice about how Ali or the people in Ali's circle would make appointments and when Olsen arrived, tape recorder ready, they wouldn't be there or would walk away without a word. He felt it was a racial situation, a use of power, control over the white interloper on the scene.

"It's almost liking to twist white people around . . . ," Olsen said into his tape recorder. "Let's face it, a shoeshine boy at Hialeah doesn't have too many times to humiliate white people. Or at least inconvenience them. This is a different situation."

Olsen's view of Ali was complicated. The writer was around enough to see different sides of the young champ, "a jumbled up assortment of personalities, totally not integrated [with each other]." He never knew which personality would be waiting for the latest installment.

Shopping in a high-fidelity store, buying the biggest speakers available for his car, chatting up the Cuban salesgirl, the champ, the subject of all this controversy, all this angst, could have been a college kid, the all-American boy, wearing a blue sweater and paratrooper boots, carefree and enjoying life. ("If they all look like you in Cuba, I should move there.") Waving his hands, talking about the Nation of Islam, on the other hand, he was the religious fanatic, no other way to describe him. Talking about the next fight, the next attraction, he was the showman extraordinaire. ("I am the greatest.") Working at his craft, boxing, putting in the miles and hours, he was "the cold-blooded professional." Pushing around his friends, demanding things, he was the bully. Telling "his MF jokes, slapping you on the knee, repeating his punch lines," he was the joker.

He was all these people. He could even be a half dozen more.

"We're all jumbled assortments of personalities," Olsen said into his tape recorder, "but with this man, one personality will take over to the exclusion of all the others. For example, if he's explaining Islam to you, you're not going to get him out of that until he's finished, which may be two hours later."

—

An easy analysis—made first in Toronto by Chuvalo's manager, Irving Ungerman—was that the bizarre present course of Ali's life had been determined by his divorce early in the year from his wife, Sonji. The divorce instantly made him eligible for the draft because only single men could be called. No matter what their scores on intelligence tests, married men were exempt. Everything had followed from there.

If there had been no divorce, there would have been no chance for reclassification. If there had been no reclassification, there would have been no comments about the Viet Cong. If there had been no comments on the Viet Cong, the fight against Ernie Terrell would have taken place in Toronto and a next opponent would have been found for some site in America. If . . .

The divorce continued to be a problem for Ali. The ramifications were tangible.

The couple had been married less than a year before Ali filed papers in court, but still he was ordered to pay $1,250 per month in alimony for the next ten years when the case settled on January 7, 1966. He also had to pay Sonji's $22,500 attorneys' fees. The champ was delighted to be granted his freedom, on the grounds that his wife had failed to live up to pre-agreed Muslim standards of dress and conduct, but was staggered by the financial judgment in a Miami courtroom.

No payments had been made to Sonji by now. None. Four months had passed. Chuvalo had been dispatched already a week ago. Sonji's attorney, Lawrence Hoffman, said the single check written to Sonji had bounced. There had been no other attempts to fulfill the divorce agreement.

Ali also had skipped appearances in court, and when he skipped another one on April 5, Judge Harold Spaet ordered that the champ be arrested. Attorney Jacko, who flew in a hurry from New York to Chicago then down to Miami, offered Sonji two checks from a Black Muslim bank for $26,250 to pay for the attorneys' fees and the missing alimony, but she refused to accept them. The judge rescinded the arrest order and gave Ali two more days to pay.

The money arrived at the last moment, two days later, two hours before the deadline. It was delivered by a Miami attorney. He said the money had been wired from New York and Chicago from people he didn't know and "I don't want to know." Sonji celebrated, said, "I am now The Greatest." Ali made plans to make some more money.

Ten days later he signed a contract for a rematch with Englishman Henry Cooper. The fight would take place in thirty-five days in London, outdoors at Highbury, the home of the Arsenal soccer team. This would be the first heavyweight championship fight in Great Britain since February 10, 1908, when Canadian Tommy Burns knocked out Englishman Jack Palmer in four rounds. There were plans that Ali would have three fights in a row in Europe, maybe one per month.

If and if and if and if. The divorce had led him all the way to Europe and this strange schedule. Everything was in a hurry. The draft board might come calling at any moment, and he needed money. The future could not be trusted.

"We stayed in the Piccadilly Hotel for three weeks," promoter Bob Arum said years later. "Ali went running in Hyde Park every morning. The paparazzi were everywhere trying to get his picture. An American film crew was there filming 'The Dirty Dozen.' We had a riot. Angelo Dundee and I hung out at a casino rumored to be mob-connected. We had a helluva time."

London was another escape, an even better escape than Toronto. Nobody cared about Vietnam or the draft or the Muslims. The outrageous twenty-one-year-old character who had appeared in tails and spats three years earlier on the streets of London to fight Cooper at Wembley Stadium, bug-eyed and loud, challenging all critics, shouting out poems, was the character the Brits remembered. That was whom they saw now.

No matter that he didn't shout as much. No matter that he didn't have a poem to predict a round for Mr. Cooper this time. ("If Cooper gives me jive, I'll stop him in five; if he gives me more, I'll stop him in four," he had said three years ago before he won the first fight in, yes, five rounds.) This was the same guy they remembered. He was the heavyweight champion of the world now. He had stature, style, sparks that bounced around him.

His biggest frown emerged only when he talked about Jack Olsen's series in *Sports Illustrated*. He thought it was "bigoted and inaccurate and that like many so-called depth analysis of his character has tried to drive a wedge through him and those close to him," according to a report in the *New York Times*.

"The American press keeps me in shape," he said, "because if they do this to me now, when I'm world champion, I know how devilish they're going to be if I lose."

He was surrounded wherever he went. The requests for autographs would start in the hotel lobby, move with him into Piccadilly Circus, and continue for the rest of the day. The doors would be opened to his workouts at the White City Gym, free admission, and the crowds were so large he couldn't make his way to the speed bag or heavy bag and had to do most of his training in the ring. He estimated he signed his name over a thousand times per day.

A picture was taken after a morning run in Hyde Park, a stretch called Rotten Row. Mixed in with sparring partners was Jim Brown, acting in *The Dirty Dozen,* which was being filmed at nearby Markyate, Hertfordshire. Brown also was connected to the promotion by his stake in Main Bout Inc. The caption in the London *Times* read "Clay, surrounded by camp followers . . ." The best football player in America, the Hollywood actor, wasn't even noticed. The boxer was the star.

"No trouble here," trainer Angelo Dundee reported. "He's been talking fight talk, none of the other stuff. The press conferences are very pro the champ. One guy, an African, said, 'It is a black and white fight, isn't it?' And he said, 'No, you're more intelligent than that. It's just a fight.'

"A political guy asked him about the Muslim bit and everybody jumped him. 'Are you a sportswriter?' they asked. 'Are you at a political rally?' And then somebody said that the guy was a German, not an Englishman."

In the first fight, three years earlier, the square-jawed Cooper had dropped Ali with a left hook, the second time the American ever hit the canvas as a professional. The knockdown came with two seconds left in the round. Ali said the punch was so hard it even disturbed some of his ancestors in Africa. Much was made about a delay when Dundee found a split in Ali's glove between rounds and everyone had to stand and wait for the glove to be adjusted. Brief as the delay was, the seconds of extra rest allowed Ali's head to clear, and as predicted, he was able to stop Cooper on cuts in the fifth.

(The *Daily Mirror* reported that Ali was "Hanging on like a scared pickaninny" when he stood up after being knocked down and that his brother, Rahman, was "barking like some jungle savage" from the corner. Racial attitudes were not an exclusive property of the United States.)

The only real question about the rematch was whether Cooper could connect with another left hook, his best punch. The chances were not good. Ali had improved in the three years. Cooper, now thirty-two, mostly had grown older.

"The bookmakers make Clay, at 5-1, a clear favorite but so they did Liston when Clay took the title," John Rodda wrote in the *Guardian*. "If there is to be any logic about it all Clay will retain his title and win in a fashion similar to that three years ago."

This was exactly what happened. Cooper was a vision of boxing's static past as he imitated John L. Sullivan, hands high, jab and jab, look for the hook, one-two-three-four, a patterned tour around the ring. Ali was improvisation, jazz, hands down much of the time, flicking out a hand and flicking out another and then unloading drumbeat combinations.

In the sixth round, Cooper's face exploded. The two boxers went into a corner, the challenger forcing the action. Ali unloaded a rapid sequence of lefts and rights to the head. When the fighters came out of the corner, they both were covered by Cooper's blood. A cut over his left eye poured blood down the Englishman's face.

"You could hear it (the blood) come out and it just took everything out of me," Ali later said. "The referee put me on the spot by allowing it to continue. This hurt me too much and when I saw the blood, I did not feel like hitting him. I have celebrated all my fights, but not this one. I do not have anything to celebrate after this one."

"My eye went numb soon afterward," Cooper said as he blamed the cut on a clash of heads, "and with the amount of blood gushing out I knew it was a bad one. The referee, after his first look, said I could carry on, but I knew I hadn't got long . . . the blood was just streaming into my eye."

George Raft, Lee Marvin, and Sean Connery, all at ringside, seemed happy enough with the result. Cooper went to Guy's Hospital for twelve stitches. Ali, after a couple of days' rest, went to Cairo.

He had talked about visiting a string of African countries, but settled in the end for four days of adulation in Egypt. He toured an iron and steel plant, where he led over two hundred workers in prayer. An expensive edition of the Quran was presented to him by the Supreme Council of Islamic Affairs. He watched boxing tryouts for the Cairo team in the upcoming Nasser Cup. He attended a light show at the Giza pyramids. He visited with President Nasser for forty minutes, according to the president's spokesman. He sparred for six rounds with three Egyptian boxers at the Gezira Sporting Club, the place packed with five thousand people, music playing for all six rounds, dancing in the aisles. He went to Alexandria, where he had lunch with the commander of the Egyptian navy. He toured resort areas along the coast. He was busy, busy, busy, showered with praise, love, affection, wherever he went.

Wasn't this the way the life of a heavyweight champion was supposed to be? He had been asked in London if he thought about staying overseas, draft be damned. He had rejected the thought. He said that the United States was "my home."

"In Cairo you said that you were coming back to beat the draft," a reporter asked, first thing, at a press conference at JFK Airport in New York as the champ switched planes on June 2, 1966, on the way to Chicago.

"I never said that," Ali replied.

There was no easy patter. There was no fun.

He said, in answer to a question, that America was fine. He did not hate his country. He was treated fine in America, "like a king."

The king did not smile as he said this.

The Cooper fight had been shown in the United States on *Wide World,* live and free on a Saturday afternoon, Cosell in the front of the production. ("I think Muhammad is going to talk to us now. Muhammad . . .") The production was a hit, even though it was matched against the Preakness, the second leg of horse racing's Triple Crown; it attracted the largest sports audience of the year. The Nielsen rating was 22.5, which meant that 67 percent of the viewing audience was watching the fight. The Preakness had a 6.3 rating, 19 percent of the audience.

The fight was the first athletic event bounced from Europe on Intelsat 1, the Early Bird satellite that had been sent into orbit a year earlier to provide television, radio, and telephone communication between continents. The transmission worked so well that promoters were ready to use it again in a hurry. Markets were open now that never had been open. A fight in Europe could be sold, live, in the United States. There was proof.

In the last week of June, slightly over a month after his dispatch of Cooper, Ali signed to fight British brawler Brian London in London. The fight would take place in five weeks, on August 6. He also signed to fight Germany's Karl Mildenberger in Frankfurt a month after that on September 10. This clearly was an accelerated moneymaking schedule. Ali predicted that 560,000 people around the world would see these two fights, not to mention any number of characters from outer space.

"I am not only the world champion, I am the universal champion," he proclaimed. "Don't laugh. I know they're out there and I know who they are. Some people think it's swamp fire, but it's flying saucers. They saw my fight in Toronto and they were at Lewiston, Maine."

He spent only fifty-three days in the United States before he returned to London. He was in Chicago. He was in Louisville for a quick visit. He was in New York, where he went to a movie theater to watch Ernie Terrell defend the other half of the heavyweight title with a unanimous fifteen-round decision over Doug Jones. ("Terrell is the crossword puzzle fighter," Ali said, discounting the win. "He comes into the ring vertically and leaves horizontally.") His most public appearances were on *The Tonight Show,* where he appeared three times with Johnny Carson. He was loose, easy, charming.

"People keep asking me which is the real Clay, the one they read about or the one they watch on television," sportswriter Larry Boeck of the *Louisville Courier-Journal* said in a five-part series called "My Friend, Cassius." The writer had known Ali for over ten years.

"I get along with Johnny Carson," Ali said. "He speaks nice, he asks me nice questions, he treats me like a man, calls me by my name, Muhammad Ali. . . . I treat people like the Bible say, 'Do unto others what you want them to do unto you.'"

Boeck, who was white, also asked about the *SI* story: Did Ali really hate white people? Was his life that far out of control?

"I don't know what that man was talking about," the champ said. "I treat everybody right. I haven't done nothing you could find to show I hate anybody. Hate will run you crazy, going around hating everybody. I don't have no time to hate. I'm trying to make some money and get ahead and treat people like they treat me. . . .

"It takes a lot of nerve for somebody, mainly a white, to ask me do I hate. I haven't lynched nobody and hid in the bushes. I haven't deprived nobody of freedom; I haven't deprived nobody of justice; I haven't deprived nobody of equality. I haven't blowed up nobody, no churches. I haven't lynched nobody in 400 years. . . . We're victims of hate and I think a man is awful ignorant in front of the world asking a Negro do he hate. If someone of my kind do hate, he would be justified in hating the treatment he is getting and I do hate. If someone of my kind do hate—I hate the way I'm being treated, and I hate the way people like James Meredith walking down the highway trying to love and getting shot. I hate to see pregnant women kicked around the streets. I hate to see people shot and beat and killed. I do hate all that. I'm not wrong for that."

The shooting of Meredith had captured America's attention. The thirty-two-year-old activist, who had integrated the University of Mississippi four years earlier, protected by three thousand federal troops amid riots, had begun a publicized "March Against Fear" from Memphis, Tennessee, to Jackson, Mississippi, on June 5. On June 6, he was shot three times by a sniper, later identified as James Aubrey Norvell, a forty-one-year-old unemployed white hardware clerk. Only thirty miles of the 220-mile march had been covered.

The Reverend Martin Luther King and members of various civil rights groups quickly flew to Memphis and took Meredith's place. The nightly news now paid nightly attention as the days and miles passed and the number of marchers grew to fifteen thousand, the largest march in Mississippi history. Recovered sufficiently from his wounds, Meredith was able to return for the grand finish in Jackson on June 26. Four thousand residents had registered to vote during the march. A new and memorable term to the nation's racial dialogue also had been added.

"This is the 27th time I have been arrested and I ain't going to jail no more!" Stokely Carmichael of the Student Nonviolent Coordinating Committee (SNCC) said in Greenwood, Mississippi. "The only way we gonna stop them white men from whippin' us is to take over. What we gonna start saying now is 'Black Power.'"

Ali went back to London on July 23. The big news was that on the trip from Heathrow Airport to his hotel, he convinced the driver to let him take control of the bus. The switch was made at seventy miles per hour as passengers fretted. He was at the wheel when everybody arrived at the hotel.

Jackson, Mississippi, again was on the other side of an ocean.

The fight against London was a hard sell. The thirty-two-year-old challenger from Blackpool had been pounded two years earlier by Henry Cooper in a fifteen-round decision for the British Commonwealth heavyweight title. Cooper, of course, had been pounded by Ali for a second time. The commonsense math didn't work. It was pointed out that age, height, weight, reach, and record all went in favor of the champion.

The *Daily Mirror* tried to help by asking its readers to figure out a game plan for the brawling Mr. London (real name Brian Sydney Harper). How could he upset the overwhelming favorite? The best replies would win twenty-guinea seats to the bout at the nineteen-thousand-seat Earls Court Exhibition Centre.

"In London's corner is Danny Varey—his training advisor," the advertisement read. "As the seconds slip away, Varey is giving London the last few vital words of advice. Put yourself in Varey's position. What would YOU tell the 'Blackpool Bulldog' to do against the towering Negro? How would you take his championship belt away from him? Deprived of it, he would be just another handsome, talented, if somewhat eccentric, young Negro."

The winners of the contest seemed to have a common theme: Brian London should create mayhem in the ring. He should push and shove and taunt the champ. In the words of Mr. Hughes of Kirby, no first name given, London should "bait and hook him." The *Mirror*'s boxing writer said that if Ali was allowed to control the ring "like some dusky matador, the situation would be grave."

The challenger contributed a bad poem to the promotion about "two fists made for Clay and two feet that will dance on this day." The champion went the prose route with "Brian London would rather run through hell in a gasoline sports coat than dream he could beat me. He would rather take a chance shaving a wild lion with a dull razor." There were obligatory pictures of the champ doing roadwork, hitting the heavy bag at the Board of Control gymnasium at Haverhock Hill, posed against various London landmarks. He was one of the ninety-two thousand people at Wembley Stadium on July 30, 1966, who watched England win its first World Cup by beating Germany, 4–2. He admitted that he slept through most of the match because he was tired and because soccer was a sport played by "little gals" in the United States.

Fight night arrived. The expected happened.

London threw no more than two solid right hands as he was overwhelmed by Ali's speed and punching power. The knockout came at 1:40 of the third round as a final flurry of lefts and rights sent the challenger to the ropes and then to the floor, where he seemed to consider climbing back onto his feet then, no, fell back.

The crowd was estimated at eleven thousand, probably was less, as spectators rattled around the arena. There were some boos for London when he was done, but they were halfhearted. This was simply a night of business.

The most interesting note for the London tabloids came when a twenty-six-year-old "coloured" striptease dancer showed up in a blue sports car as Ali was leaving the country two days later. She had said a day earlier that Ali had given her a ring, but now denied it. She said they were just friends. Ali said he didn't remember her.

"Hundreds of girl fans have been around every day to our hotel," he said in the airport lounge. "There have been Egyptians, Arabians, Americans, English . . . so many! I can't place her, but I'd probably know her if I saw her."

Brian London returned by train to Blackpool. At the station, a welcoming committee of one girl was waiting. He signed her autograph book.

"Be friendly," he wrote.

4

The FBI

The Federal Bureau of Investigation had been at work while Ali was making money in Canada and London. A report by the agency was part of the legal process when someone asked to be classified as a conscientious objector. Since this was one of Ali's possible routes to challenge the draft, a thirty-one-page report on his situation was compiled and submitted to Local Draft Board No. 47 on July 9, 1966.

Thirty-five interviews were conducted with various sources, named and unnamed, in Louisville, Miami, Chicago, and New York. To qualify as a conscientious objector, any draft registrant had to show that he was opposed to war in any form and that this objection was based on religious training and that he was sincere in his belief. Ali obviously was a special case. The report was more extensive than anything most of the 170,000 applicants for conscientious objector status between 1965 and 1970 would ever receive.

The results were typed into long paragraphs—only seventeen paragraphs in the thirty-one pages of single-spaced text—that detailed Ali's life and conversion to the Nation of Islam. Behind the words was the image of various agents sitting on porches and in parlors, white men with trim haircuts and seersucker suits, maybe sharing a glass of lemonade as they asked people of color about the local boy who had grown into controversial fame.

The interviews did not seem hostile. People gave their opinions. The agents quoted the answers without comment. The result was a flat and easy narrative. The report began:

Registrant was born January 17, 1942 in Louisville, Kentucky. He is a member of the Nation of Islam.

(This was the shortest paragraph in the report.)

A representative of Central High School, Louisville, Kentucky, advised that the registrant entered Central High School on September 4, 1957, having completed the 9th grade at DuValle Junior High School. On March 31, 1958, the registrant voluntarily withdrew from Central High School. No reason for the withdrawal is shown on the records but records reflect that during the 1957–58 school year, registrant made poor grades. Registrant re-entered Central High School in September, 1958 and remained until he graduated on June 11, 1960. He ranked 376 in a graduating class of 391. His average grades for the 9th, 10th, 11th and 12th years were 72.7. Registrant's IQ test score in 1957 was below average. Registrant's attendance at school was rather irregular. Registrant was rated fair with respect to emotional control; he was rated fair as to leadership; above-average as to health; average as to intellectual ability, initiative, social attitude, effort, honesty, scholastic zeal. Registrant participated in tennis in 1958–59 and chemistry craft in 1959–60. This official advised that general information around the school was that the registrant was primarily interested in boxing and not in school. He was an amateur boxer at the time he was in high school and participated in Golden Gloves activities. A teacher advised that he considers registrant's family a fine family and was particularly commendatory concerning the registrant's mother. Registrant's grandmother exerted a strong influence on registrant's family and she was an outstanding woman. Registrant presented no disciplinary problems while attending Central High School. Registrant was a "happy-go-lucky" kid. Registrant's primary interest was in boxing. During registrant's school years there never was any reason to question his honesty and he was not the "pugnacious-type" individual. He had a likable personality and was well-liked and respected by other students. This teacher characterized the registrant as an extrovert and his brother to be an introvert. Registrant was considered to be average with respect to religion. This teacher believes registrant is sincere and honest with respect to his Islam beliefs and that "someone sold the registrant completely" with respect to the Islam religion. This teacher expressed the opinion that if the registrant has claimed that he is conscientiously opposed to military service this is a sincere claim and not for the purpose of avoiding military service. Another teacher recalled that during the high school years registrant was very well-liked by other students. During those years he was "a lovable boy—just a big good-natured kid." This teacher never observed any particular religious activities by the registrant. There was no indication that he was other than a normal high school student whose primary interest, however, was in boxing. This teacher advised that, in his opinion, the registrant has always been of good character with respect to matters of morals, integrity, and the like. He noted that during registrant's youthful years he was just a big good-natured boy and the teacher is convinced he would have remained so to this date if someone, say, "of the Black Muslims had not given him an injection of the hate stuff." This teacher expressed the view that the only way that he could give registrant credit for being sincere in a claim as a conscientious objector is to consider registrant as being exceedingly stupid. This teacher stated that he doesn't think registrant is that stupid and therefore concludes registrant is not sincere in his conscientious-objector claim. He stated that he could not reconcile registrant's profession as a heavyweight boxer with his conscientious-objector claim.

The FBI grammarians decided this was where the long paragraph should end. The report proceeded from there in the same style, same government language, largely stripped of nuance. This was a compilation of comments, not history. Background was missing. Explanations were missing. Everyday facts were taken for granted.

The local court officials who would read the report, for example, all would know that Central was the de facto segregated black high school in Louisville. The changes mandated by the *Brown v. Board of Educa-*

tion decision by the Supreme Court in 1954, when the registrant was in sixth grade, still had not reached Louisville when he started high school three years later. Despite Kentucky governor Lawrence W. Wetherby's declaration that the state would abide by the newly delineated law, a loophole kept the Louisville schools pretty much segregated as they ever had been. All students were allowed to transfer from the school where they had been assigned if room could be found at another school. Room always could be found for the white students in the white schools of Louisville. Nothing much changed.

Founded as Louisville Colored High School in 1882, funded at first only by taxes received from the African American community, Central had become a bulging urban educational institution when a new building was opened in 1952 at the corner of 12th and Chestnut Streets. The school had 1,400 students and fifty-seven faculty members.

There were no great marches or disturbances when Ali was there. One former student remembered going to a protest at a Louisville lunch counter, but said it was more a high school adventure than a real protest. Gerald Eskenazi, a reporter for the *New York Times,* interviewed the principal for Ali's time, who said that the champ's IQ was recorded at 78, which was 22 points below normal. The principal interjected that it wasn't unusual for black students to do poorly on a test geared toward white kids. He also said that Ali was a kid who became nervous when he had to take tests. Family members later claimed the champ was dyslexic.

The more famous Central High School at this time was in Little Rock, Arkansas, an all-white school where nine black students had been sent to integrate in September 1957. The ensuing riots and the delaying tactics of Arkansas governor Orval Faubus forced President Dwight Eisenhower to send in 1,200 men from the 101st Airborne to keep order. The troubles of the students, known as the Little Rock Nine, were played out in national headlines.

Closer to home, James Howard, who was the same age as Ali, was one of ten black students who tried in 1956 to integrate the all-white high school in Sturgis, Kentucky, which was 165 miles west of Louisville. The students were turned back on the first day by an angry mob, which caused Kentucky governor A. B. (Happy) Chandler to call out the National Guard and the state police. Integration in Sturgis, same as Little Rock, was accomplished only with a military escort.

Howard, thirteen years old at the time, came from a ghetto that was called Boxtown. The name came from the fact that most of the houses had been built from wooden boxes. Threats had been made that all of Boxtown would be burned to the ground if efforts at integration were pursued. Threats were sometimes accompanied by action.

"There were threats about, 'Oh, you niggers won't live to see another day if you live to come back to school here. Any niggers that have any—ah, have any kids out here won't have jobs if you continue to go . . . ,'" Howard said. "It wasn't just a case of my feeling that I was in physical danger: I was spit on. I had eggs thrown at me, tomatoes thrown at me, I was hit with rocks, I was kicked, I was pushed, I was shoved. So it wasn't just whether I felt I was in danger: it was real."

The front-page fate of Emmett Till, fourteen years old, six months older than Ali, was another reminder of how perilous life could be for black kids in the South. A visitor from Chicago to Money, Mississippi, a town five hundred miles from Louisville, Till made the alleged mistake on August 28, 1955, of flirting with a white woman, twenty-one-year-old Carolyn Bryant, the proprietor of a market for sharecroppers. Three days later his mutilated body was found in the Tallahatchie River, weighted by a seventy-pound cotton gin tied to his neck with barbed wire. The two men arrested and tried for the crime, one of them Bryant's husband, eventually were acquitted by an all-white jury after a sixty-seven-minute deliberation.

"If we hadn't stopped to drink pop, it wouldn't have taken that long," was the quote from one of the jurors.

The trial was front-page news. Outrage about the result was doubled, tripled, multiplied after the two defendants, unworried due to the protection of double jeopardy, were paid by *Look* magazine and confessed in an article a year later. This was one of the starting points of the civil rights movement in the United States. Rosa Parks said that she was thinking of Emmett Till three months later on December 1, 1955, when she refused to move to the back of that bus in Montgomery, Alabama.

Ali's boyhood was filled with these racial images, this combustion that had developed at last after historic silence. He said later in life that he was fascinated by Emmett Till at the time, studied Till's pictures in the newspaper, both alive and grotesquely dead. How could this other kid be killed? Just like that? It was a wonder.

The FBI report did not deal with any of this.

"A representative of the Louisville, Kentucky Department of Recreation recalled that when the registrant was about 12 years of age he began participating in the boxing program of the Department," the report continued. "This official stated that he was very closely associated with the registrant until the registrant was 18 years of age. He stated that during the time he was associated with the registrant, he was a good, honest, clean-living boy. He never smoked, drank, ran around with girls or used profanity. His whole life was boxing and becoming a boxing champion. During this period of time the registrant did go to church and, although not an overly religious boy, did believe in an Almighty Being and lived accordingly. This official stated that he did not believe the registrant can be sincere in any claim that he is conscientiously opposed to military service. Such a claim just didn't square with his knowledge of the registrant during the time that he was in almost daily contact with him. He recalled that when the registrant registered with Selective Service he made no statement indicating he was conscientiously opposed to such service. This person noted that he had heard that registrant's father disliked individuals of the white race."

The Nation of Islam was mentioned often in the report. Most of the former and present neighbors and business associates who were interviewed seemed to hover between wonder and dismay when they talked about Ali's religious conversion. They couldn't understand the change that had taken place with this fun-filled kid they once knew. They mostly felt as if he had been sold a strange product and they couldn't believe, still, that he had bought it. The strange product was the Nation of Islam.

The specifics of the religion were not detailed in this report, but they had been well covered in other FBI documents. The FBI had tracked the activities of the NOI for a long time.

Founder Wallace Fard Muhammad, an ephemeral and charismatic character, surfaced in Detroit in 1930. He claimed to have been born in Mecca and sold his religion door-to-door, preaching the Quran as an antidote to the Bible and the incivilities of the white man. His rise in Detroit—money was collected, a temple established—was well chronicled until he disappeared in 1934 as mysteriously as he arrived, never to be seen again.

The Honorable Elijah Muhammad, born Elijah Robert Poole, one of thirteen children of a lay Baptist minister in Sandersville, Georgia, was Fard's top student and inherited the role of leader. (He claimed that Fard had been "Allah in the flesh.") The major growth of the religion came directly through Elijah Muhammad's efforts. He left Detroit for Chicago, then Milwaukee, then Washington, D.C. He established temples at each stop. Sent to the federal correctional institution in Milan, Michigan, from 1942 to 1946 for evading the draft during World War II, he continued to preach behind bars, an environment inductive to converts, and began to establish an empire when he was released. The FBI followed every step.

A sixty-six-page report on the Nation of Islam filed eleven years earlier, in 1955, covered the history, organizational structure, and beliefs of this "especially anti-American and violent Cult." It said seventy members had been arrested for draft evasion during World War II, and "approximately 40" imprisoned. Members also had defied the draft for the Korean War.

Under the heading "Disloyalty and Disrespect for the United States Government," the FBI quoted the NOI newspaper, *The Final Call of Islam*. Little was left to doubt about the religion's view of the country.

"Of all the governments of the world there never existed one so wicked as America, which has misled the Holy People of Allah, and deceived them into worshiping a God they cannot see, nor hear, that is a God that does not exist," an unnamed NOI writer declared. "For this cause, Allah has stretched forth his hand against the wicked America to bring her down, even to dust and ashes, a country whose land is full of churches and in them wickedness is practiced beyond words to describe."

Elijah Muhammad's views on national flags during World War II were described. On the American flag, "the flag of the white devil," the white represented the white race, the red represented the blood that was lost by black men keeping everything safe for the white devils alone, the blue background and white stars represented justice for the white man but no one else. The Japanese flag, on the other hand, was "similar to our flag of Islam . . . because the Japanese are our brothers and they are the only ones who will give us justice, freedom and equality."

The NOI, the 1955 report concluded, was a treasonous, treacherous organization. With its demands to create a separate black nation and its philosophy that the black man was God's chosen person on earth, the report stated that the NOI was a threat to overthrow the government.

"Based upon an analysis of the rabid teachings of this group, it is definitely considered that these people present a threat to the internal security of the United States," the FBI concluded, "and would, with the right number of followers and the opportunity, be more than willing to perform acts which would subvert American principles and endanger the existence of the American nation as such."

Another report, ninety-two pages compiled a decade later in June 1965, after the assassination of Malcolm X and the conversion of Muhammad Ali, estimated that the NOI had "5000 cult followers who attended 37 numbered temples and 31 unnumbered groups, the majority of them in the East and Midwest." The NOI claimed much larger numbers, somewhere between twenty thousand and fifty thousand members.

Undercover agents had been sent to meetings to record the rhetoric for this report. Nothing had changed. If anything, the language had become more harsh. The Vietnam War and violent white reaction to the civil rights movement had stretched the boundaries of antagonism.

"We are told by the white man to bury the hatchet," one speaker said. "We'll bury the hatchet in his head."

"Why go abroad to fight?" another asked about the draft call. "Let's fight the devil, the white man, right here in this country."

In the middle of all this was Ali, who had become the most well-known face of the religion. He had been front and center with the Honorable Elijah Muhammad when Malcolm X was assassinated. He was on the talk shows. He was in the news. He presented the NOI's doctrine to far more people than the leader or anyone else ever had. He talked to people Elijah Muhammad and Malcolm X never could reach.

"Elijah recognizes the importance of publicity and uses it to aid recruitment," the 1965 report said. "In NOI member Muhammad Ali—

heavyweight boxing champion Cassius Clay—Elijah had a widely publicized athlete whose devotion to the NOI is exploited for recruitment
purposes."

The fact that Ali's apartment at 7083 South Cregier Avenue in Chicago was burned out in a fire on the same night Malcolm was assassinated in New York added to the drama. (The Chicago fire department
quickly ruled the fire accidental, the result of a dropped cigarette by a
downstairs neighbor when he fell asleep on a sofa. People still thought
what they wanted to think.) There had been worries that Malcolm's followers might seek vengeance, might attack Ali. Security was added for
his appearance in a boxing exhibition a week later at the NOI national
convention in Chicago. That was how important Ali was.

He was not one of the worriers.

"I walk the streets daily by myself," he told reporters. "I have no body
guards. I fear nobody. If anybody wants me, I'm not hard to find. . . .

"The white people have got all the airplanes and all the bullets and
I'm not afraid of them. Why should I be afraid of the black man?"

Assassinations? A religion that flourished in jails? Muslims? The kid
next door? This was the background to the conversations now with the
people who knew the heavyweight champion of the world. This was
why the people worried about him.

What was he thinking?

The FBI report quoted various unnamed "associates" who didn't
believe he was thinking at all. The term "brainwashed" was used often.
One associate said that Ali believed the world was going to end in 1966
and wondered what would happen when the world did not end. Another
associate said that in 1964 he told Ali that he would lose over a million
dollars by associating with the Muslims. Ali responded that his religion
was more important to him than any amount of money or whatever
people might think about him.

All the associates said the champ was "utterly sincere" about his
beliefs, a kind and gentle soul, but questioned his judgment. One said
he was "sincere, but foolish" and "weak-minded" in his relations with
the Muslims. Another called him "stupid" for joining the NOI and
another called him "incredibly stupid." One said he blamed Ali's father
for instilling a dislike of white people that led him to the Muslims.

Another, a neighbor, told a far different story about the father and the Muslims.

> The neighbor recalled that about a year ago the registrant's father arrived at the registrant's home, obviously intoxicated. He had a knife in his hand and started shouting about the registrant's membership in the Muslims and the fact that registrant's father's name was being ruined by the Muslims. He stated that he was going to kill all the Muslims around the registrant's house. The neighbor noted that the registrant got extremely upset at his father's statements and actions and he attempted to attack his father and had to be physically restrained from hurting him. While still being held, the registrant was attempting to kick his father. The neighbor feels that the registrant is basically "a stupid person" although he does have some native intelligence. He feels that the registrant's stupidity together with a quirk or flaw in his character, apparently developed through childhood environment, has made it possible for him to accept the teachings of Elijah Muhammad.

The agents visited the brick home at 7307 Verona Way that Ali had bought for his parents for $17,000 after he signed his first professional contract. The house was an upgrade from the two-bedroom middle-class home at 3302 Grand Avenue where he lived from first grade through high school. The house was nice, but far from grand, part of another all-black neighborhood. The agents probably noticed the two Cadillac Eldorados in the driveway, the pink one and the convertible, also purchased by the champ.

All this was part of his plan. He had talked as a kid with his mother, Odessa, forever about this, daydreamed about the money he would make and the things he would buy for her. He also had talked with the local Cadillac dealer as a kid, told him he would be back when he signed a contract. The words were sweet at the time, boyish adolescent ramblings on summer afternoons, but they all had come true. He had bought everything he promised and more.

There was, alas, a price: the material things had replaced the son.

He was in Chicago. He was in Miami. Hell, he was in Europe,

Africa. He seldom was in Louisville. The last time he came to the house, this house where he never lived, he was accompanied by Joe Louis. The present heavyweight champion was showing the legendary former heavyweight champion his hometown. They sat in the living room, talked for no more than twenty-five minutes, and left. The cab had waited for them on the street, meter running. That was how short the trip was. The meter ran for the entire time.

Life had changed forever when Ali turned professional and went to Miami to train with Angelo Dundee. That was the opinion of the father, Cassius Clay Sr. Their son was a kid who never was alone, a kid who had to be with people, an audience, every minute of every day. He had no audience in Miami. Angelo was good, worked with him in the ring, but Angelo went home at the end of the workouts. The son was by himself.

Until he met the Black Muslims.

They had taken control, the Muslims had. The one Muslim, Sam Saxon, had been in the room day and night. The other Muslims had followed. They were everywhere now, the Muslims. They were his family now.

When the son came back to Louisville as champion after beating Sonny Liston, the parents met him at the airport. Odessa had made a cape for the new king to wear. Cassius Sr. carried a homemade crown. The son refused to wear either one. They didn't fit into his new life, his new religion. The parents stood on the stage, embarrassed.

"I'd like to meet this Elijah Muhammad some time, hear what he says," Cassius Sr. had said to his son once, trying for conversation.

"When you're talking to me, you're talking to Elijah Muhammad," his son replied. "I say what he would say."

This was the feeling of loss the agents tapped in their visit.

The registrant's mother and a reference advised that the registrant lived at home with her in Louisville until he turned a professional boxer in about 1960. Since becoming a professional boxer, he has spent most of his time in Chicago or Miami. At the time the registrant registered with the Selective Service he made no objection to registering and said nothing about being opposed to military service. In about 1960, the registrant changed his religion to that of Islam. He became connected with this faith by attending a mosque in Miami, Florida. In 1964, at the time the registrant was ordered to take a physical examination by his draft board, the registrant told his mother that his religion taught him that one could not engage in violence or kill any human being or take part in any war. He told her he sincerely believed thus and that his conscience would not permit him to serve in the Armed Forces of the United States or any other country. Since 1964 the registrant has told his mother that he could not take part in anything related to war, as it would be against his religion and his mother expressed the conviction that the registrant is sincere and honest in his beliefs regarding military service. The registrant's mother noted that although the registrant has not lived continuously at home since becoming a professional boxer, she maintained frequent contact with him. She has no doubt whatsoever that his claim of being conscientiously opposed to participating in any military effort is a sincere one and a deeply seated conviction held by him. She feels that this conviction occurred after the registrant became a member of the Islam faith. She noted that she had raised the registrant in the Baptist faith but after he left home he became interested in the Islam faith. She thought the registrant had been influenced most in accepting the Islam faith by the leader of that faith, Elijah Muhammad. The registrant always has been "a good boy." He has never been in violation of the law except in connection with traffic violations. She stated that she could not recall the registrant ever having engaged in any physical fights with anyone during his youth other than supervised amateur boxing.

Missing here, of course, were the parental memories of the energetic, always-moving, always-talkative boy at home before he left and became famous and a Muslim. The good memories.

Cassius Marcellus Clay Jr. ran everywhere, even when he was small, ran off ahead of everyone. He raced the school buses after he started training to box. Raced those buses every day. When he did slow down to walk, he always walked on his toes, maybe the reason he could move so well for a large man in the ring. What kid walks on his toes? This one did. He chased chickens and dogs in the backyard, terrorized those chickens and dogs. Every day. He was a bottle baby. He loved to eat so much that he ate his bag lunch on the way to school. Every day. When Odessa tried to stop this by giving him money for the cafeteria lunch, he bought the neighbor kid's bag lunch every day. Ate that on the way to school.

So big at the age of three that his mother had to pay a fare for him on the bus (normal age: five), he always played with older kids. Not only played with them, but organized them, was the boss. He called the other kids his "babies."

When he was only six months old, lying in the crib, he swung and hit Odessa in the mouth, loosened two teeth, which later had to be removed. She said now that she was his first knockout victim. She found her elder son to be a hoot. The younger one, Rudy, Rudolph Valentino Clay, okay, now Rahman, was quiet. Cassius was always doing something. He had one of those scooters kids love and pumped and rode it so hard that he wore out his right shoe about every three weeks. Drove her crazy. What kid needs a new right shoe every three weeks?

He would cover himself in a white sheet and jump out from behind a door to scare her. He would tie a piece of string to the draperies and move them while she tried to read. That would scare her some more. Always something. He loved to climb, would climb every tree in the backyard, over and over. He was a Boy Scout, a member of the YMCA, went away to Camp Sky High when he was old enough. He cut grass, shoveled snow, worked at the branch library, where the librarian would find him shadowboxing in the stacks. He loved sweets. He was so good-looking as a little kid that other mothers always said he should have been a girl. He was no problem, never, always had respect for everyone. Yes, he did.

His name was Gi-Gi, because that's what he said, standing in his crib when he was a baby. Everybody called him that at home. Gi-Gi. When he started boxing he said what he was trying to say as a baby, just couldn't get it out, was "Golden Gloves."

Now he was Muhammad Ali.

"Rudy wants me to change my name to Muhammad Ali, too," Cassius Sr. said. "I say 'I've spent 50 years building up this name. I'm not going to lose all that.'"

Now fifty-four years old, Clay Sr. was much smaller than his son, but no less lively. He was a sign painter and an artist, a hustler and a talker, a pepper pot of a man bursting with opinions and bits of knowledge, proclamations about the approach of Armageddon, visions of ancient Egypt, Cleopatra coming down the Nile on a barge. Drinking had brought some trouble into his life at times, but he was a resilient character. He always had plans for the future. The plans were uniformly grand.

Cassius Clay Enterprises was the name of his latest possibility. The enterprises involved were still to be determined, but the name was a definite. If his son wasn't going to use it, the father said he would be proud to take advantage. Yes, he would.

An agent also talked to Ali's ex-wife, Sonji. Details of the failed marriage had been revealed in the divorce proceedings in Miami in January. It was the tale of a hasty union, encouraged by the Muslims at first because they thought this attractive woman would keep their champion away from nightlife and outside sexual temptation, discouraged in the end because Sonji wouldn't conform to stringent Muslim principles in dress and conduct for a woman.

She was twenty-six, two years older than Ali, variously described as a former model, former cocktail waitress, or former singer. She had worked for five years at the Archway Supper Club as a bartender in Chicago before Herbert Muhammad, the business manager, the son of Elijah Muhammad, hired her as a model and introduced her to Muhammad Ali at the Roberts Motel in Chicago. Twenty days later in Miami she became Ali's common-law wife by sharing vows in a motel.

"I was the heavyweight champion of the world," he said. "I couldn't be seen committing adultery."

The common-law couple took off in his Cadillac on a trip across the country to California, then back to Chicago. They were officially married on August 14 in Gary, Indiana. This was not a conventional marriage.

"Did you love her?" an attorney asked during the divorce trial.

"The onliest reason I married her was that she agreed to do everything I ordered her to do," Ali replied.

Among her marital mistakes, mentioned in his petition for divorce, was a tight denim pantsuit she wore to a news conference at his training camp in Chicopee, Massachusetts, when he was preparing for his second fight against Sonny Liston. Ali did not like this pantsuit.

"You could see all of her, the seams of her underwear . . . ," he told the court. "Tight pants around all those men was wrong."

Sonji told the judge she still loved Ali, but he did slap her once in New York after she objected when he put his arms around another woman. She said she had given up lipstick when she married him and had been forbidden to smoke or drink alcohol. She said she had worn knee-length dresses, many of them picked out by her husband, until the Muslims demanded that she wear longer and longer dresses.

In mild defiance, she wore a tight red dress to the divorce court and smoked in the ladies' room during a recess. Her lawyer asked Ali on the stand what he thought of Sonji's red outfit. Ali said he did not approve. The lawyer asked why.

"Because all her arms are out and her knees are showing," the champ said. "And it's too tight."

When she talked with the FBI, Sonji described where this kind of thought originated.

The registrant's former wife advised that she was married to the registrant for eleven months and resided with him in Louisville, Miami and Chicago until August 1965. She knew him for one month prior to their marriage. She knew that he was a member of the Nation of Islam when she met him and during their period of marriage she attended the Nation of Islam Mosque, primarily in Chicago on a relatively weekly basis, on Sundays. She is of the opinion that the registrant is sincere in his acceptance of the teachings of the Nation of Islam, as known to him through Elijah Muhammad, whom she thinks is the registrant's only spiritual advisor. She believes that the registrant blindly follows the teachings and precepts of the Nation of Islam, in that the registrant does not smoke, drink, or eat foods forbidden by the teachings of Muhammad. She expressed the opinion that she would still be married to the registrant if it were not for the influence exerted on his thoughts and actions by Elijah Muhammad and other members of the Nation of Islam. She recalled that she had attempted to comply with the instructions of the Nation of Islam regarding her dress, but since it was not in her heart to hate any person she was not acceptable to the Muslims and she expressed the opinion that the registrant was directed by influential active members of the Nation of Islam to disassociate himself from her, which he did. She noted that the Nation of Islam attorneys in Chicago had provided her attorneys with a check which bore the notation "Return of charitable contributions" in connection with her divorce settlement with the registrant. She stated that the registrant is controlled in his boxing career by the Nation of Islam through a firm owned and operated by the Nation of Islam. She noted that neither the registrant's mother or father is a member of the Nation of Islam and are not in sympathy in any way with the tenets of this movement. The registrant's former wife stated that she believes the registrant is sincere in his convictions with the qualification in her mind regarding his participation in a "savage sport" which to her is in opposition to the expressed teachings of the Muslims. She stated that the registrant is sincere in his conscientious objection to military service based upon his adherence to the teachings of the Nation of Islam, in that she believes he has been advised by Elijah Muhammad and other leaders of the Nation of Islam that such service is against the teachings of the Nation of Islam. She noted that she would still be married to the registrant if it were not for her failure to be accepted by the leaders of the Nation of Islam as the wife of the registrant.

The report ended with quotes from various newspaper stories. The Viet Cong quote was prominent. A quote from Ali in the NOI newspaper *Muhammad Speaks* said that the reason he had trouble in the fight with Chuvalo was because he relied on his own natural ability rather than placing his "faith, prayers and reliance" on Elijah Muhammad.

A quote from the *Chicago Sun-Times* had him saying that he always thought of himself as an American and always would. A quote from the *Miami News* said he was ready for jail.

"Let them put me in jail," he said in the story. "How big would that make me? Damn the fights, forget the money, let them put me in jail."

The report would not lie unread for long. On August 23, 1966, only two weeks after his return to the United States from the Brian London fight, Ali would appear in a Louisville courtroom before special judge Lawrence Grauman to plead his case as a conscientious objector. The report would be submitted by the FBI as the cornerstone of the government's side of the case. This was another step in the legal process. Grauman would deliver a nonbinding judgment to the U.S. Department of Justice, which would then submit its opinion to the Kentucky Board of Appeals, which would rule on the case.

This was Ali's chance to testify, to talk his way out of trouble. As the FBI report noted, talking was one of his strengths.

5

Judge Grauman

The appearance before the sixty-six-year-old retired judge, Lawrence Grauman, appointed as the hearing officer for the case, started at two o'clock on the afternoon of August 23, 1966. Ali carried copies of the Quran (Maulana Muhammad Ali's English translation) and Elijah Muhammad's *Message to the Blackman* as he arrived at the site, the formidable United States Post Office, Court House, and Custom House, a five-story Greek Revivalist structure of columns and limestone that had been built during the WPA thirties and covered a city block at Broadway and Sixth Street.

The books were props. He had a new lawyer for the hearing. The lawyer had told him to carry the books. They would be entered into evidence, exhibits B and C. There was a new approach with the new lawyer.

His name was Hayden C. Covington. Edward Jacko, the early defender of Malcolm X, Harlem's "Jacko the Giant Killer," last seen unsuccessfully trying to make Ali sit down and stick to the planned apology at the hearing in Chicago to rescue the Terrell fight, no longer was part of the operation. The new lawyer was a heavyset fifty-five-year-old white man whose tastes tended toward flamboyant suits and flamboyant speech, a Clarence Darrow character out of Texas whose career had been linked forever with the Jehovah's Witnesses religious group and its struggle against the U.S. government. He was probably as un-Muslim, un-black as a lawyer could be.

"This boy does not believe in participating in the war in Vietnam as a combatant or noncombatant," the lawyer, hired less than two weeks ago, said before entering the hearing. "He is sincere in this belief."

The reason for the change in legal representation was not complicated. Covington was a specialist in appeals. In twenty-six years with the Witnesses, from 1937 to 1963, he had sent 111 petitions and appeals to the Supreme Court. Forty-four cases were heard. He won thirty-seven of them. In 1943 alone he argued fourteen cases before the court. Never part of the well-bred, well-schooled Washington legal establishment, his style demeaned by the people who were, he still was the most successful lawyer ever to appear before the U.S. Supreme Court.

A number of his cases with the Witnesses had involved draft resistance. Since its inception in Pittsburgh in 1870, the group had refused to fight in wars, refused to recite the Pledge of Allegiance, refused to place country on a pedestal as high as God. The Witnesses believed that Exodus 20:3–5—"You shall have no gods before me. You shall not make for yourself a graven image, or any likeness of anything that is in heaven above, or that is in the earth beneath, or that is in the water under the earth, you shall not bow down to them or serve them"—told them what to do.

During World War I, Covington's mentor, Judge Joseph R. Rutherford, and the entire governing board spent two years in prison for sedition. During World War II, eight thousand Jehovah's Witnesses asked to be excluded from the draft. Half were granted their wish while the other half went through the appeals processes and court. More than 2,500 Witnesses were put in prison during World War II as draft resisters.

(The group had worse troubles in Nazi Germany. Half of the ten thousand members in the country were imprisoned for refusing military service, including two thousand who were sent to concentration camps, where an estimated 1,200 died.)

Covington was involved directly or indirectly in most of the Jehovah's Witnesses' cases before U.S. courts. He knew so much about the draft and its many regulations and nuances he published a thirty-page pamphlet about the subject in 1953. Titled "Procedure of Jehovah's Witnesses Under Selective Service," it told resisters what to do and how to act at each step of the appeal process. For the same hearing Ali faced, the resister was told to cover thirty-one different facts in his testimony. The first was:

1. The facts of his personal life that bear upon his sincerity, his conscientious opposition to participation in war between the nations of the world, his training for the ministry in the home and at Kingdom Hall and his activity as a minister . . .

Everyone was a minister in the Witnesses faith, everyone a proselytizer. Covington would contend that this was the same case with the NOI. Ali was a minister simply by being a member.

The chance to defend the champ was a return to prominence for the attorney. Despite all his success, he had been disfellowshiped by the Witnesses in 1963 for excessive drinking, a problem he said had developed as an answer to the pressures of his many court appearances. He still drank, as members of the NOI quickly noticed.

A decision was made by Covington and Ali at the beginning of the hearing to exclude the press in District Courtroom No. 2. If the job was to convince the judge, then this could be done without fanfare. There were no spectators, only officers of the court and Ali's legal team and whatever witnesses he might want to bring. This was not a trial. There was no spokesman for the government, only the FBI report. John L. Smith, an assistant U.S. attorney, was present, but did not speak. The only cross-examination would come from Judge Grauman. This basically was a hearing to allow Ali to present his case.

Covington called four witnesses to start. The first was Chauncey Eskridge, who was Ali's forty-nine-year-old tax attorney from Chicago. Eskridge occupied a unique position in the national black community. Not only was he Ali's attorney, he had done work for the Honorable Elijah Muhammad and the NOI for the past fifteen years. He also was the Reverend Martin Luther King's tax attorney and did work for the Southern Christian Leadership Conference and the NAACP. Somehow he moved easily between the conflicting visions for the black man's future, eloquent and steady.

Asked by Covington to give examples of Ali's commitment to the NOI faith, Eskridge first listed the divorce from Sonji. Her lack of belief had doomed the marriage. Ali said so, she said so, everybody said so. The lawyer from Chicago then noted the different economic opportunities Ali had rejected because they conflicted with his religion. He had turned down endorsements, turned down a film role. Wasn't this different from the way most athletes handled success? Ali had a "humbleness" that was different. He lived his religion, lived by a strict code that the religion imposed.

"The code of conduct requires that a man is looked that—as if he—he's sure of himself," Eskridge said. "That is to say, he is clean; his shirt is white; his tie is dark maroon or dark blue; he is clean-shaven; his hair is cut close; his language is circumscribed; his conduct is circumscribed; he does not eat deleterious foods which have pork products in them; he doesn't engage in the drinking of alcohol or the taking of nicotine; and to the women, they do not wear cosmetics."

Captain Samuel X. Saxon, thirty-four years old, the Muslim assistant minister and captain of Muhammad's Mosque No. 29 in Miami, was the next witness. He was generally credited with drawing Ali to the faith, starting with a chance meeting on Second Avenue in 1961. He described how he was selling copies of *Muhammad Speaks* and Ali came up to him and began to ask questions. They wound up in Ali's rented room, where he showed Saxon his Amateur Athletic Union trophies and Olympic gold medal. Everything progressed from there. Ali fell in love with the religion.

"Have you ever heard him say anything about his objections to serving in the Army, either combatant or non-combatant?" Covington asked.

"Yes, sir," Saxon replied. "He believes as I believe. I mean from me and him talking to one another, he believes as I believe, that he shouldn't take part in no war."

The next two witnesses were Ali's parents. They repeated their dissatisfaction with their son's choice of religion. They both said that yes, he was so committed to the NOI that he would die for it. There was no doubt about that.

"How did that subject come up?" Judge Grauman interjected while Cassius Clay Sr. testified.

"Well, we keep trying to hammer him out of it, you know," the father replied. "And he just says, 'You all think I'm kidding.' He says, 'I'll die for this thing.'"

Covington called "the next and last witness, Muhammad Ali, known also as Cassius M. Clay Jr., Registrant," to the stand. The boxer stood.

There was no pledge to tell the truth, the whole truth, nothing but the truth, because this was an informal hearing.

The words came in a controlled rush when Ali finally spoke in his own defense. No histrionics were involved. Covington asked two preliminary questions about name and age, place of residence, basic information for the stenographer, and then opened the real testimony with a well-rehearsed softball. The reply tumbled out of the champion's mouth.

Q. Now tell Judge Grauman—we have heard about your being raised up as a Baptist—how it was that you got acquainted with the faith of the Nation of Islam.

A. It's true that I was raised as a Baptist and while being raised as a Baptist I never understood the teachings of the Christian preacher and I never understood why Heaven was in the sky and I never understood why Hell was under the ground and I never understood why the so-called Negroes had to turn their cheeks and have to take all the punishment while everyone else defends themselves and fought back.

I never understood why our people were the first fired and the last hired.

I never understood why when I went to the Olympics in Rome, Italy, and won the Gold Medal for great America and I couldn't go in a downtown restaurant, and I always wondered why everything in it was white.

I always wondered these things and I am saying this to tell you why I accepted the religion of Islam the minute I heard it while in 1961 I was walking down the streets of Miami, Florida, a Muslim walks up to me and asked me would I like to come to Muhammad's Mosque and listen to the teachings of Islam and listen to why we are the lost people and listen to why—what my true religion was before we were made slaves and this sounded interesting and, by me being a person of common sense, I went to the Mosque to listen and immediately, on entering the Mosque—I would say the first half hour after being there, I immediately wanted to know what I could do to become a member, and I started to say that the Minister of the Mosque was preaching on the subject of why we are called Negroes. He said that the Chinese are named after China and the Cubans are named after Cuba and the Russians are named after Russia and Hawaiians are named after Hawaii and Mexicans are named after Mexico and Indians are named after India.

So, he said, what country is named Negroes and he said why are we called Negroes, and this made sense to me and I had to check into it.

I asked questions and he gave me good answers and he also said that we do not have our own names and all intelligent people on earth are named after their people of their land and their ancestors. He said the Chinese have names such as Chang-Chang, and Cubans have names such as Mr. Castro, and Russians have names such as Mr. Khrushchev and Africans have names such as Lamumba. We call ourselves Culpepper, Mr. Tree, Mr. Bird, Mr. Clay, Washington, and he said these were names of our slave master, and by me being an intelligent man and the Lord blessing me with five senses, I have to accept it because there have been write-ups in the Louisville papers where my father and me were named after a great white slave father named Cassius Marcellus Clay.

So, I had to accept this, and he also told us that the proper name of God is Allah and that the Honorable Elijah Muhammad was taught by Allah for three and one half years to teach the so-called Negroes the true knowledge of his God, the true knowledge of his religion, true knowledge of his names and his future and not to force himself on whites and not to beg whites to clean up the rats, but to clean up our own neighborhoods, respect our women, do something for ourselves, quit smoking, quit drinking and obey the laws of the land and respect those in authority.

Immediately, I had to check and see who is Elijah Muhammad because Elijah Muhammad taught and I asked all the press who he is and they said he was a self-styled leader and I had to find out what self-styled meant and I found out that everything that he taught then he had to style it his self.

So, common sense just told me that a man can't stand here in the middle of America preaching the things he's preaching and no government, no lawyers, no doctors, no theologists, nobody would challenge him or as much as even mention his name in public.

So, after finding out who he was, and I had to convince myself that he was a divine man from God because I knew that I would have to give up a lot and now that I have accepted the religion of Islam, I turned down at least one million, eight hundred thousand in movies.

I have turned down a two million bout with Ernie Terrell, and I have—I just put up fifty thousand cash yesterday to pay alimony fees on my wife only because she would not wear the proper dresses and be a Muslim.

All of this is why I am a Muslim and I really sincerely believe it and as my father and mother have said, I'll die right now in this courtroom, because I know this is the truth I'm talking.

This tone was exactly what Covington wanted, sincere and forthright.

A large part—the largest part—of Covington's successful defenses of the Witnesses over the years had been based on the fact that every member of the religion was considered a minister. Many of the cases involved members being arrested for speaking on street corners or knocking on doors or trying to sell the Witness newspaper, *Awake*. Much of the language in the speeches and the papers was inflammatory, directed against different organized religions, especially the Catholic Church, which was often referred to as "The Whore of Babylon." This often brought friction and noise.

Covington developed particular cases to be brought to the court system, especially the Supreme Court. He often prepared the defense before the crime was committed. These were First Amendment cases fighting against restrictions placed on the Witnesses by local laws or courts. He was the first lawyer to use this strategy, which now had been adopted by Thurgood Marshall and NAACP lawyers challenging civil rights laws across the United States. (Marshall and the NAACP would replace Covington and the Witnesses as the most successful appellants to the Supreme Court.)

Covington always emphasized that his clients were ministers of their religion, entitled to the right of free speech.

"If you do secular work," he once wrote, "explain that your primary occupation or vocation is the ministry as one of Jehovah's witnesses and that you engage in secular work during the week to support yourself and to 'provide things honest in the sight of all men' (Rom 12:17) . . ."

He wished to present the same defense for Ali. The champ's previous lawyer, Jacko, had challenged the draft board decision strictly as a case of conscientious objection. Covington said Ali was a minister in a religion, not simply a conscientious objector. This became a different First Amendment situation. He wanted to begin a different appeal process while this one was completed. The idea was to have as many points of appeal as possible, more chances to win a deferral.

"I don't know why this wasn't done in the first place," the lawyer said. "It's been hidden under a bushel basket and it's my duty to bring it to the light of day."

"This boy has as much right to a ministerial deferment as any minister in the United States. And I am confident he will get it."

The witness stand in front of Judge Grauman was a first place to put this defense on the record. Covington pressed both Chauncey Eskridge and Sam Saxon to explain how Ali functioned as a minister. ("You say he is a minister?" Judge Grauman asked Eskridge, somewhat startled when the claim first was made. "Yes," Eskridge replied. "M-I-N-I-S-T-E-R?" the judge asked again. "Yes.") Eskridge detailed work Ali had done with youth gangs in Chicago. Saxon said that Ali was directly responsible for the conversion of Muslim brothers Eddie2X and Robert4X and Robert5X and always was encouraging black men to come to meetings. He spoke at meetings in Miami, was an attraction.

Ali expanded on the theme. After questions about how and when he had become a Muslim (Miami, 1963) and why he had changed his name (didn't want a slave name), Covington explored the depth of Ali's faith and his commitment to proselytizing, which the NOI called "fishing," searching for new members.

Q. Now, what, if anything, did you do about your belief (after your conversion) that—did you just quietly sit and say nothing to anybody about it, or did you get up and do something about it?

A. Well, Almighty Allah is my witness now, as I sit on this stand, about one hour after I first heard the teachings of the Honorable Elijah Muhammad, immediately I would run up and down the streets shouting it to other Negroes thinking they all would accept it and love it whenever they heard it, but I found out later that many of them are dead to the knowledge of the truth and they are hard to talk to and the Captain would have to stop me a lot and tell me to quit preaching and hollering down the streets too loud because all of these people heard about it before me.

They have had a chance to accept it, but they wouldn't, but now I'm a little more mellow in my approach on people constantly—but answering your question, I would at least—at least six hours of the day I'm somewhere, calling and talking or going to schools or colleges all over the country, Muslim temples, and there are some fifty mosques all over the country that I am invited to minister at right now, and constantly—in Chicago I have this thirty passenger bus that, daily, we go out bringing in busloads of people to the Mosque, and now I'm talking to the Blackstone Rangers, which is the worst Negro group in the wilderness of North America who have killed at least one hundred boys since they've been in Chicago, and the police—nobody could handle them and I was blessed with, all praise due to Allah, I was lucky enough to round up the twenty-one of the ring leaders and take them to *Jet* and *Ebony* magazine and where the write-up will come out in *Ebony* and *Jet* magazines sometime this week on the confessions they have made, how they say they are ashamed for the way they have been shooting and killing and how I've convinced them to come together, and this will be out soon. So this is what I do as far as ministering and talking is concerned.

Q. All right.

A. It's daily, all the time, but not only to blacks, but to many whites, on television, [like] the Les Crane Show, Johnny Carson, and the Irv Kupcinet Show in Chicago and Jack Brickhouse on his radio show where people call in—constantly defending the faith and teaching it, and we have to do more talking daily because these American, so-called Negro leaders are coming to our headquarters and they are coming to me and they are asking us more about our side of the program, so really, I'm planning to go full-time after this fighting is over, which I hope is in another year.

Q. But as a matter of fact, you put in about a hundred and sixty hours a month in it now: isn't that right?

A. Something like that; maybe a little more; yes, sir, but when I'm really in training and in camp for fights, a week or two before the fight I don't have time, not too much time, because I really burn a lot of energy debating and answering questions, so during training we don't do too much ministering.

Q. Right; now tell the judge what you have done in your fishing work as compared to what other Muslims—and we are not saying this to brag or anything, but just to state the facts—as to numbers that you have been able to bring in at the various places?

A. Yes, sir; I understand. First of all, I'd like to say that many people say that the reason I am so successful in my accomplishments as far as fishing great numbers of people is because I'm the heavyweight champion of the world and if I wasn't the heavyweight champion of the world I wouldn't draw the people, but the reason I can so strongly walk by all of this is because I, myself, know that it is the teachings of Islam that taught me to really restrain from cigarettes, women of all races that at least many Negroes run to in opposition to the teachings of Islam, and this is the onliest thing now keeping me out of night clubs and places that serve alcoholics like liquor and demonstrations where I could become popular in leading people.

So therefore, it's the teachings of Islam that has given me

the proudness and boldness to say, "I'm the Greatest," and lift my chin and which has enabled me to be one of the most popular athletes on earth. So, therefore, when they tell me that if I were not—"If you were not a Muslim; if you were not heavyweight champion; you would not have—you would not draw these people." So I know that it was Almighty God, Allah, through the teachings of the Honorable Elijah Muhammad that enabled me to be strong, plus to keep going once I—my mother and father raised me from a little boy to the age of eighteen to be strong and healthy, but after receiving fame and leaving the city, the teachings of my mother and father, the teachings of the Christian Church, that couldn't put enough fear into me to stay out of night clubs and couldn't put enough fear into me to dodge the English ladies and American white ladies and Negro ladies that chased me daily.

So, therefore, when they say that "You would not bring in five hundred people," inasmuch as I do sometimes, "You could not bring these five hundred people if you were not the champ," well, if it was not for Allah and the teachings of the Islam, I would not be champ and I would not hold my title so strongly after being the champion, so I would say that the average Muslim, answering your question, that the average Muslim is doing good if he brings three people on average a night to the Mosque and my average, all praise to Allah, with my title, I've been able to bring in, at the most, in three days' time my record in Detroit, Michigan, and that was about five hundred and fifty people and on the average it's thirty people a night.

Q. Now, have you devoted time not only to fishing, but also to teaching and preaching in the Mosques and temples and various—in the various parts of the United States in the Nation of Islam?

A. Yes, sir; and I'm due to be in an Atlanta, Georgia Mosque next Friday, but it will not be possible because I have to go to Germany for this bout, but much of my time is spent in the mosques on whatever city—there's not a city in the United

States where there's a mosque that I don't visit when I'm in the city, Muhammad's Mosque, and I have invitations to come to various Muslim groups and I will be speaking and lecturing to about ten thousand people the 28th of this month in Chicago at the international amphitheater where the Honorable Elijah Muhammad is addressing all of the press and the Negro leaders and Muslims plus all of the Negroes that are not Muslims, so we expect a crowd of about maybe ten thousand where I will be, I hope and pray Allah, one of the major speakers.

Q. All right. Now, I want to ask you whether or not it is true as stated in your conscientious objector form, and in other papers that are on file, that you have honest, sincere convictions and conscientious objections to the performance of military service, combatant and non-combatant; is it true that you do have these convictions sincerely?

A. Well, sir; I would not—and I say this before the Judge and the many here and Almighty Allah himself, who I'm sure is looking, wherever we talk, but I would not just say this just to get out of the Army—I have, I would say, caught more hell for being a Muslim, even before the Army talk came up, with my wife and boxing, and the movie rights that I turned down, the advertisements, the TV commercials, the royalties and endorsements that I have had to turn down and I have done all this before the Army came up and it's not just saying that I would not participate in war, but we actually believe it and feel it.

We fear—we fear the wrath of Allah once we come into the knowledge of Almighty God, and once we understand who the Honorable Elijah Muhammad is and his mission—then we fear Allah; we fear what will happen to us if we go astray of his teachings in any way.

So, therefore, we are awful serious in anything we say about fighting a war, adultery, or fornication, or drinking alcohol, cursing, using profanity, or anything that is against the teachings of the Holy Qur'an and the Honorable Elijah Muhammad, and Allah is who we really fear.

Covington guided his client past whatever bumpy spots the FBI report may have covered. One was the purchase of a gun in Miami Beach. Ali explained that the purchase was a joke, a whim. He was looking in a thrift store for a record player and found a collection of guns, including one that "Marshal Dillon" might have used. He bought a one-shot derringer, ninety-plus years old, cheap, maybe $40, to hang on his wall as a decoration. Captain Sam had spotted the decoration, said "We can't have this," and disposed of the weapon in the Atlantic Ocean.

The newspaper clippings the FBI included in its report, many of them flat-out wrong, others lacking context, were tackled one by one. No, he never said that he would quit the religion if every Negro in America hadn't joined in two years. No, he never tried to join the U.S. Army Reserve in Nebraska. Yes, he was sorry he had talked about relying on his natural ability, not the guidance of Allah, in the Chuvalo fight. No, he never claimed to have seen God, nor talked to God.

No, he did not hate white people. He hated some things white people had done. That was brought out in a question about a quote in a story:

Q. March 8, 1964 issue of the *Courier Journal,* Louisville, Kentucky, reported you as saying that you didn't—you don't hate anybody and, "I know the Muslims don't teach hate. If they did, I won't be with them." That is correct, isn't it?

A. That's true; we do not. Many people confuse the teachings of the Honorable Elijah Muhammad with the teachings of hate and the onliest hate I know, as far as the teachings of the Honorable Elijah Muhammad is concerned, and that is we hate the way that we've been treated for four hundred years. We hate the way that our pregnant women are kicked around the streets; we hate the way the innocent Negroes have been shot and lynched and killed outright, but the killers are not—never been caught—we hate that we're the first fired and the last hired and we hate the way we have served so faithfully for the country in all wars and have spent three hundred and ten long years enabling America to have fifty of the richest states on the planet and yet still we are subjected to treatment which cannibals and Africans are treated better.

He said that white people and black people had different natures, saw situations differently. He said that the Rev. Elijah Muhammad always taught that if a lion showed up right now in this courtroom, everyone would run. Why? Not because everyone hated the lion, but because they knew he had a different nature. That was the black man's situation with the white man. A different nature. That was why the black man should be separate.

"So, we do not hate white people," Ali concluded. "We want to go for ourselves and get some of this earth that we can call our own like other intelligent civilized humans do on the planet Earth. So, this is the press, distorting the teachings of the Honorable Elijah Muhammad, this is the press trying to turn Negroes against those teaching and brainwashing the world to the truth of the Honorable Elijah Muhammad. We are not haters. He teaches us to love. We don't break no laws. We are not in no riots, no demonstrations. We pray five times a day. We fast three days a week and we constantly worship at the Mosque three times a week. We are peaceful people and we are not haters, but we are the victims of hate."

Covington included the *Chicago Daily News* story by Tom Fitzpatrick, the one that started all the trouble, the one with the quotes about the Viet Cong, as he finished his questions. Ali came as close to apologizing as he ever would. He cited the Islamic teaching "He who holds his tongue will save his life" and said that Elijah Muhammad had "condemned" him for making "such a wild, boastful statement." He said he was "excited at the time" and "disturbed" and "I have paid greatly for it."

Judge Grauman now had the opportunity to ask questions. A lifelong resident of Louisville—the other side of Louisville, the white, gentry side—he was known as a lawyer's lawyer, a no-nonsense character who demanded punctuality and always brought at least two bulging briefcases with him to court for instant reference. Retired in 1964 after fourteen years as a judge of common pleas for the Fifth Division of Jefferson County, he had returned to private practice and had been named Outstanding Lawyer of the Year in May by the Kentucky

Bar Association. He had been given a silver pitcher at the Kentucky Hotel.

"It's going to be under 16 degrees if he's wearing a topcoat," another lawyer said, describing Grauman's approach to life. "I don't think he even owns a hat."

His questions came at a businesslike clip. He appeared to be concerned with when and how Ali had decided to become a conscientious objector.

JUDGE GRAUMAN: All right, sir; did you ever at any time until you were reclassified from deferred service so that your classification would subject you to be called for service, did you ever advise the Board that you were a conscientious objector?

THE WITNESS: You don't mean in 1960 when I was eighteen; you mean the first time—

JUDGE GRAUMAN: (Interrupting.) No, I mean when—how many times were you called?

THE WITNESS: The first time is when I was turned down.

JUDGE GRAUMAN: Yes, sir.

THE WITNESS: You mean at that time?

JUDGE GRAUMAN: Yes, sir; and what year was that?

THE WITNESS: I think that was sometime around 1964 when I was training for the Liston fight; about '64—a few weeks before the Liston fight, I think.

JUDGE GRAUMAN: Yes, sir.

THE WITNESS: I didn't tell them I was a conscientious objector, but I did have a discussion with the local Miami official where I wrote Cassius X on the paper. He asked me why that was and I explained it and the religion, I wrote Islam instead of Christianity, and the nationality, I wrote Asiatic Blackman instead of Negro, and he called me to the back room and he gave me a list of about three hundred something which looked like lists of organizations and said, "Do you belong to any of these? They are subversive groups," or something like that, and I said, "I don't belong to none of them. I'm a Muslim," but he didn't have Islam on the list.

JUDGE GRAUMAN: Yes, sir; but did you go through the physical examination and did you give them whatever information they requested of you at the time you were called for your physical examination?

THE WITNESS: I answered everything that the law required me to answer, but as I said earlier, the name, the religion and everything was different.

JUDGE GRAUMAN: Why didn't you tell them at that time if you were conscientiously a conscientious objector, why didn't you tell them that you were—under the law, couldn't be called into the military service if you were a conscientious objector?

THE WITNESS: Well, I've been told by my attorney, Mr. Hayden Covington, that that was a mistake, that I should have then, but at the time I was about two weeks from the Liston title fight and my manager, Angelo Dundee, Chris Dundee, Milt McDonald who had invested about $650,000 in the fight, plus many closed circuit TVs were sold out throughout the country, and it was arranged as the biggest fight in all history with Sonny Liston, and I was so disturbed, and working under pressure training for the fight, until I just—all I had on my mind was to obey the law, fill it out, and what they had for me to do, and still, I put my name down Cassius X and I put down I was a Muslim, and I put for religion I was a Muslim—Islamic; I'm no longer Christian, but at the time I saw no need to, being truthful, and immediately after that, I'm sure that millions of whites and people who had invested—not me, I fear nothing for money, but they had lost, or they would have lost at least three or four million dollars if I did that, looking back on it, but at the time this wasn't in my mind, at the time I did it, and I was under—just under the strain of the fight and I just filled the thing out and then walked out.

JUDGE GRAUMAN: Did you understand that if you passed the physical examination that you would be called into military service?

THE WITNESS: Yes, sir.

JUDGE GRAUMAN: But you said you were under such a strain that you didn't think of calling to their attention at the time you were a conscientious objector?

THE WITNESS: Well, I immediately—I didn't have much time to worry because they said immediately that I had failed the test, but a reopening was going to be held here in Kentucky, which I failed again.

JUDGE GRAUMAN: Immediately; how long after you took the test?

THE WITNESS: I believe a week or so, two weeks it seemed like—it was a little after I had beat Liston.

JUDGE GRAUMAN: Yes.

THE WITNESS: I heard that I failed the test.

JUDGE GRAUMAN: But after you beat Mr. Liston, were you under any pressure or tension?

THE WITNESS: Yes, sir; because I announced to the world that I was a Muslim then. It was unannounced to the world [until] then. It was just told to the Board of Miami at the time. They knew I was, but it was quiet.

JUDGE GRAUMAN: Did you make any announcement that you were a conscientious objector?

THE WITNESS: No, sir.

JUDGE GRAUMAN: When is the first time that you ever made an announcement that you were a conscientious objector?

THE WITNESS: I never announced not even up to the date yet that I was a conscientious objector. It was only found out when it was told here in Louisville when my lawyer Edward Jacko filed the papers and then it was the Board who talked then, and Mr. _____ I forget his name, but he is the one who said it. I've never outright disrespected the American Government or my draft board by blasting off and bragging and hollering that I'm a conscientious objector. I've never done that.

JUDGE GRAUMAN: But didn't Mr. Jacko, acting as your attorney under your authority and direction, didn't he present to the draft board and also to the appeals board the claim that you were a conscientious objector?

THE WITNESS: Yes, sir, he did.

JUDGE GRAUMAN: Well, that was all done with your approval?

THE WITNESS: Yes, sir.

JUDGE GRAUMAN: Well then, that's what I am trying to get at because the whole question is the sincerity of your claim. I'm trying to get the fact—the first time that there ever was any statement made with reference to your being a conscientious objector—the first time the statement was ever made to the board was after you were reclassified; is that right or wrong?

THE WITNESS: Yes, sir; let me see; the first time I failed I had no need to say anything. They said I wasn't fit. The second time—excuse me; I took the test in Kentucky and they advised me and said I wasn't fit. Then, when they reclassified me I came out with that outburst that was controversial and then my lawyer went in with the conscientious objector bit and then it was known then.

That was the first time it was known was when he put it in, but I have no need—excuse me, I have no need the first two times that I was called up to, because they never accepted me, but I'm sure that if they had I—as a matter of fact, Allah is my witness here that if they had called me when I was in Miami and I had passed the test then I would have had to do—just say I'm a conscientious objector, but I know nothing about the law and if I knew the right procedures at the time I would have moved accordingly, but I'm new—I'm learning each day about how this appeal and things go, but I didn't know at the time. I had no idea how they worked.

The judge also was curious about how a man could fight in the ring and refuse to fight outside it. How did the champion reconcile violence in boxing with pacifism in daily life? Ali said he never considered himself a violent fighter because he never lost his head in the ring. He said there were violent fighters, but he was not one of them. He always tried to be calm and cool. He said that football was a violent sport and no one complained. Why did they complain about boxing? He said there is a difference in intent between boxing and war. In boxing, the intent is not really to hurt anyone, but to win the fight. In war, the intent is to kill.

Judge Grauman also was worried about violence within the NOI. He wondered about the religion's preparations for trouble, preparations for the Armageddon that the religion imagined would happen soon. Ali tried to explain that there was no great conspiracy involved with his religion.

JUDGE GRAUMAN: Now, Mr. Covington has asked you with reference to certain things in the resume of the F.B.I. report. Now on page twenty-three there is a statement that the Nation of Islam was characterized as an all Negro organization which was originally organized in 1930 in Detroit. Members believed that they were the so-called Negro slaves of what was referred to as white devils in the United States. Is that correct?

THE WITNESS: Is that correct what?

JUDGE GRAUMAN: That members believe they were so-called Negroes or slaves of the white race, referred to as white devils in the United States.

THE WITNESS: Well, we do believe, taking your question like you gave it to me, first of all, member wise, we do believe that the so-called Negroes are now economically and mentally slaves of the white race and we do believe that the so-called Negroes, physically, mentally and economically, a hundred or four hundred years ago, and for the last three hundred of those years we were physically slaves and history shows and proves it. White literature. That it's true. Then, as far as the devil is concerned, I answered that a minute ago by saying that it's not just from what I understand from the teachings of the Honorable Elijah Muhammad, it's not just the color of a man's skin that makes him a devil. It is the deeds and work that he do, and our leader teaches us that the way the so-called Negro has been treated, lynched, burned, raped, tarred and feathered for four hundred years and today, still being shot and killed in front of news medias, and the people who are practicing those acts upon us are doing the works of a devil. So, that's what he teaches us and the Honorable Elijah Muhammad is the teacher of Almighty God, Allah, who taught him that these certain natured people who were oppressing his people were devils and that is not me. I'm not—I didn't know it six years ago, and the Honorable Elijah Muhammad teaches us that you do not know until the coming of Allah and I think that if anyone is a judge of kinds of white devils it should be Honorable Elijah Muhammad and he should be brought before the American Government in Washington, or on nation-wide TV and made to prove it, but I—that part of his teachings is just a grain of sand in a desert compared to what he teaches, but we believe all he has taught and this happens to be one segment of what we believe, but he is the preacher of it and he is the one I think should be confronted on why does he teach it to be proven wrong. I'm just a follower and believe what he teach.

JUDGE GRAUMAN: Now, the practices which have heretofore been mentioned, the Muslim engages in military drill and in judo training; do you approve of those practices?

THE WITNESS: Well, I think the Captain explained that we—that this is a part, and I would like to add to what he said—that this is a part in the Holy Bible that teaches that though I dwell in the shadow of the valleys of death I fear no evil; and we are taught by the Honorable Elijah Muhammad that though one dwells more in the shadow of death and the so-called Negro is here in the wilderness of North America, so therefore, by Allah, God, teaching the Honorable Elijah Muhammad, and by Allah teaching us to be peace-loving people, and by Allah teaching our leader to teach us not to be aggressors but to defend ourselves if attacked, so therefore, since we are so-called Negroes, the same as Martin Luther King's followers, the same as Adam Clayton Powell's followers, the same as Ralph Bunch's followers, and Roy Wilkins, James Meredith, and since we all look alike, we can easily be mistaken for one and attacked. So, by our teaching and by believing in God, whose law is self-preservation, we are taught not to be an aggressor, but defend ourselves if attacked and a man cannot defend himself if he knows not how, and we are taught that not only America, but all countries, all civilized government have armies and have guns around their shores, not necessarily to attack or to be the aggressor, but to defend America or our country or whatever it may be if we are attacked. So, we, the Muslims, to keep in physical condition, we do learn how to defend ourselves if we are attacked since we are attacked without justification for the past four hundred years.

JUDGE GRAUMAN: Now you heard the statements here about preparation for the War of Armageddon; what is your viewpoint as to why you are preparing for that war?

THE WITNESS: Well, the Honorable Elijah Muhammad teaches us and I heard him tell Martin Luther King at his dinner table and I have heard him tell Stokely Carmichael at his dinner table and I've heard him tell representatives of Clayton Powell, and representatives of them all that when you are talking about violence you are talking about taking law into your own hands and he says it is impossible for a slave to prepare for a war with his master. It is impossible for us to prepare for Armageddon since we don't make bullets, we don't make guns, we don't make—we don't control no food. If we had weapons, if we had machine guns, or that, but we can only fight for so long because we don't control the food factories, so it's foolish for us, or for an intelligent Government to think that we, the ten per cent of America, is hiding in some secret little meeting places in this country preparing to fight these atomic bombs, these jets, these helicopters and all type guns that you have that haven't been revealed to the public yet. So, we are not preparing in the way that whoever wrote that is trying to make it look. We are only preparing for the war of Armageddon divinely. We talk that the battle will be between good and right, truth and falsehood, and we are taught that the battle will be between God and the Devil and therefore we hope and pray that we are still here in good standing with the Honorable Elijah Muhammad, for when that hour and day come that we can be told what side to go to. We are trying to be prepared where we can go to the right side, whether it is leaving the country in a helicopter or whether it's leaving the country on a ship, or whether it's leaving the country in one of those flying saucers that they see over America, and we just hope that we are spiritually and physically and internally and mentally and morally able to get on the side of Allah and the honorable Elijah Muhammad when Armageddon starts, be we can't as much as—our damage, physically. As far as putting it out in a war would be like a bean shooter against a big German tank, so we are only preparing for Allah in spirit—in a spiritual way.

The hearing was done. It had lasted for three and a half hours. Ali went to the U.S. marshal's office in the building to meet with the small group of print and television reporters who awaited. He sat in the marshal's chair, leaned back, and pretended he was now the president of the United States.

"As the first Negro in the White House," he said in an important voice, "I'm having trouble getting this tax bill passed."

It was a kid's kind of joke, a reminder of how young he was despite all the noise around him. The teacher's out of the room! What can we do for a joke?

He refused to report on what had happened in the courtroom because "it would be disrespect for the American Government to say what happened." He said the hearing was "run just like I was in a courtroom," but there was no decision. He would have to wait for that.

Covington announced that he had filed a separate appeal with the draft board asking that Ali be deferred for being a minister in the Nation of Islam. He denied that this was a ploy to string out the judicial process.

"If Muhammad is a minister," the lawyer said, "he is entitled to be treated like one."

Ali was careful to repeat the important parts of this new approach. He told the reporters that, yes, he was a minister, that he spent 90 percent of his time on religion, and that he traveled around the country trying to recruit people. He said that his religion had become his "whole life."

On the steps of the courthouse, more television cameras were waiting. There also was a small crowd of fans and onlookers, maybe seventy-five people. He shook hands with an army private, who smiled.

"How are the home folks doing?" Ali asked, again playing the role of politician.

He ate dinner that night in a downtown cafeteria. Larry Boeck of the *Louisville Courier-Journal* reported that he had a "hefty dinner of a cheese sandwich, country fried steak, lima beans, a salad and lemonade." This was finished with two desserts: a piece of butterscotch meringue pie and a dish of pudding. He never did eat the vegetable soup he ordered because he was afraid there might be pork in it.

"Nobody puts pork in vegetable soup," one of his companions said.

"Well, in Negro restaurants, lots of times, they sneaks pork into vegetable soup," Ali said.

"But this isn't a Negro restaurant," the companion said.

The champ wouldn't budge, still wouldn't eat. It was as if he were making his case one more time to Judge Grauman.

See? Didn't eat the soup.

6

1-A

Ten a.m., August 23, 1966. Same day, four hours before the proceedings began in the courtroom in Louisville. The heartbeat of America seemed to flip and pound on the corner of Fifty-Fourth Street and Sixth Avenue in New York City. The speed of the flipping and pounding was quite fast for so early in the morning.

At the New York Hilton, right there on Sixth Avenue, Secretary of Defense Robert McNamara had walked onto the stage in the ballroom to deliver an important address on the draft and the war to the bleary-eyed delegates at the national convention of the Veterans of Foreign Wars. At the Warwick Hotel, across Sixth Avenue and just around the corner from the Hilton on Fifty-Fourth, the Beatles were in residence, scheduled for an evening of music at Shea Stadium. Crowds had assembled outside the hotels for both visitors.

Members of the group Youth Against War and Fascism, anywhere between sixty and one hundred of them, were kept behind police barricades on the Hilton side of the street. They held signs that said "McNamara Secretary of Aggression" and "Bring The GIs Home Now," which matched the chant "Big firms get rich, GIs get killed" that was a sound track for the morning. The Beatles crowd, four or five times larger, mostly female, also was noisy, kept behind different barricades on the other side of the street. The shouts here were for an appearance by John, Paul, George, or Ringo, preferably all together, but any one of the four would do.

Though Muhammad Ali was not mentioned by either of the groups, he was part of all this. McNamara's speech covered the changed situation with the draft. If the secretary of defense had his way—and it appeared there was no opposition in the government—thousands of young Americans who had flunked their draft tests would join Ali, eligible again and quickly inducted into the service. The secretary of defense envisioned that more than forty thousand extra troops would be added this way by the end of the year, a hundred thousand next year.

"I do not believe that the qualifying standard for military service should now be lowered," McNamara said in fine Pentagon doublespeak. "What I do believe is that through the application of advanced educational and medical techniques we can salvage tens of thousands of these men, each year, first for productive military careers and later for productive roles in society."

Though Congress had refused to fund a similar program a year earlier—the added soldiers called "the moron corps" by detractors of the bill—this program would be part of the general military buildup for the escalating situation in Vietnam. McNamara envisioned it as a great advance for draftees from "poverty encrusted environments," kids who had been seen as "low aptitude students." They would receive an education and a new life with time in the service. The bad part—the fact that they probably also would be sent to the war—was not mentioned. More than 600,000 young men flunked either their physical or the mental test every year. Now most would be eligible.

"Too many instructors look at a reticent, or apathetic, or even hostile student and conclude: 'He is a low-aptitude learner,'" the secretary said. "In most cases, it would be more realistic for the instructor to take a hard, honest look in the mirror and conclude: 'I am a low-aptitude teacher.'"

There was no reaction from the Beatles about this proposal—in Britain, it could have been another way out of Liverpool—but they had made their feelings known about the war at a serious and sober Monday press conference. Talking after they arrived in the city, they said they not only were against the war, but felt threatened on this visit in the United States.

"We don't like war," each of the singers mumbled. "War is wrong."

They no doubt would have expanded these comments on other trips, but they were cautious now. Six months earlier, John Lennon had said "We're more popular than Jesus now" in an interview with the *Evening Standard* in England. The quote, reproduced in context in the newspaper, part of a series, had come and gone without incident.

An American magazine for teens, *Datebook,* then purchased the interview. It ran the Jesus quote on the cover of the August issue that was released in the last week of July. The words turned out to be flammable in the United States. The Beatles had become the subject of sermons across the South, controversy across the country. More popular than Jesus? Bonfires had been held to burn their records. Radio stations had refused to play their songs. The whole thing was a mess.

Lennon had apologized in Chicago at the start of the seventeen-city tour, but the controversy was a tin can tied to the group's every move. In Memphis, the southernmost stop, the Ku Klux Klan had nailed a Beatles record to a cross, and when a firecracker was thrown toward the stage during the evening show the band thought it was the start of gunfire.

That had happened three days before they arrived in New York. That was why they didn't have a lot to say about the war or anything else that might be controversial. They were jumpy.

"What we say would not be misinterpreted in England the way it would be here," Paul McCartney said at the press conference. "You can say things like that in England. People listen a bit more. In America, they hold everything you say against you."

"There are more people in America so there are more bigots also," Lennon said. "You hear more from American bigots."

The group clearly did not like this change in atmosphere. The Beatles left New York and played in Seattle, Los Angeles, and then at Candlestick Park in San Francisco on August 29. They never played again in concert, except for one unscheduled appearance on the roof of Apple Records in London three years later.

Judge Lawrence Grauman went home to 3939 Napanee Road in Louisville at the end of this day to begin to formulate his decision. There was no grand rush. He would be given the 129-page transcript of everything he had heard. He would sit inside the complicated stew of modern life—What's that about Robert McNamara and the Beatles?—and weigh what he heard against his interpretations of the law. He would then send his recommendation along to Washington.

He was known as a hardworking man, often as much as eighteen hours a day, a stickler for the law. He was an FDR Democrat, carried into the county attorney's seat in the thirties when Franklin Delano Roosevelt finally swept the state away from the Republicans. He was Jewish in a heavily Christian state, but a solid part of the power structure. He was a thirty-third-degree Mason. He had taught Sunday school for twenty-six years at the Adath Israel Temple. He once had been president of the Louisville Bar Association.

His relationships with the black people of his city were mostly at the same distance that Ali's relationships with white people had been. He had made money in real estate, mostly rental homes he owned in black neighborhoods. There was a good chance he even owned some houses near the little pink house at 3302 Grand Avenue where Ali had been raised.

He had two sons. The eldest, Lawrence Jr., remembered the time he brought a black friend home one day when he was young. They played in his room, ate in the kitchen. His father told him that night after his friend had gone home that this was never to happen again. It never did.

"This was the South," Lawrence Jr. said. "This was what my parents knew."

This didn't work for Lawrence Jr. He had been a forerunner to the questioning kids of the sixties, gone from home at sixteen, sent to a sequence of prep schools, where he found trouble at one after another. He had straightened out his life in college and now was an English professor at Kenyon College in Ohio and the new editor of the *Kenyon Review*.

He said a family moment arrived when he earned a master's degree from the University of Chicago. His father and mother came to the graduation, held in the Rockefeller Chapel on campus. His father was stunned when he saw the number of black and brown faces that came down the aisle. These were graduates at the University of Chicago?

"Look," he said, nudging his wife each time a dark face passed. "There's another one."

"A black person, someone from India, whatever they were," Lawrence Jr. said. "Every time he saw one, he made a comment."

Now the same person was a judge in this publicized case of this publicized black man fighting against induction into the army. Did the publicized black man have a chance? Could a judge from this background hear the black man's arguments? Could he not hear the noise of public opinion, served daily to his ears?

The next day, Representative Paul A. Fino (R-NY) announced that he not only backed the reclassification of draft-eligible men, but wanted the standard dropped even lower. He said he had filed what he called a "draft the punks" bill.

"I am glad to see that the Army is going to take some of the educationally deprived that it so far has rejected," Fino said on the floor of Congress. "While many of these men are deprived . . . there are a good number that are nothing but punks. It is about time the American punk population got a free holiday in Vietnam where they will have a chance to demonstrate the combat ability that has frustrated tens of thousands of police. . . .

"I also hope very much that Cassius Clay will fight his next championship in a rice paddy under this program."

Representative L. Mendel Rivers (D-SC), chairman of the House Armed Services Committee, vowed two days later to make sure that result happened. As the final speaker at the VFW convention back in New York, he promised a change in the draft laws if Ali was deferred.

"If that theologian of Black Muslim power, Cassius Clay, is deferred by that board in Louisville, you watch what happens in Washington," Rivers told the cheering veterans. "We are going to do something if that board takes your boy and leaves him [Clay] home to doubletalk."

It was in this atmosphere that Judge Grauman would make his decision.

Ali would not be idle while his future was decided. Within a week of the hearing in Louisville, he was on a plane to Frankfurt, Germany, for his September 10 fight with Karl Mildenberger. This would be his fourth title defense in seven months, all four in foreign countries.

He arrived in Frankfurt on August 31 tired, cranky from the long flight, not wanting to do the expected verbal calisthenics for the press at the airport. Angelo Dundee made the excuse that his man had been in almost constant training since the run-up to the fight with Henry Cooper. Rest was the first priority upon arrival.

"Apparently you don't read the papers," Ali said, his only comment to the reporters. "I don't have to talk anymore. I don't have to make predictions. I am the champion of the world and that's all I'm going to say."

This was a business trip. He made that fact certain from the beginning. He had brought his mother along, and this could be a vacation for her. He was here for the win, the money, thank you very much, and a quick trip home.

Mildenberger, the twenty-eight-year-old southpaw who awaited him, had a 49-2-3 record on paper, which looked very good, but the facts behind those numbers were a forecast for trouble. He never had fought outside Germany, not once. His three draws, all against American contenders—Zora Folley, Amos Johnson, and Archie McBride—were seen as suspicious hometown decisions. Even though he was the European heavyweight champion, third in the world in the *Ring* magazine rankings and unbeaten in three years, he was a 10-1 underdog. The German public and press didn't give him a chance.

"I will give Clay a fight he never will forget," he said in response to that. "Compared with what he will get on Saturday, all his fights so far have been mere exhibitions."

Training in an open-air boxing ring in the resort town of Bad Soden, where Tolstoy wrote books and Mendelssohn composed symphonies, he attached a life-size photo of Ali to a nearby post and would stare at it between rounds in his sparring sessions. Most of his opponents in those sessions were light heavyweights, brought onto the scene to try to simulate Ali's speed. Mildenberger, two inches shorter at six feet one, eight pounds lighter at 194 pounds, with a four-inch deficit in reach at seventy-five inches, would need to try to match speed with speed against Ali. It was not a great prospect.

His big hope was his left-handed style. Ali never had fought a left-hander in the pros, but had lost twice to lefties in the amateurs. Mildenberger was a strange version of the species. He was right-handed in everything he did daily, from opening the door to writing a check. This meant his stronger hand was his right, which he would use to jab. His big plan, though, was to drive a left hand deep into Ali's liver. That was a weakness he thought he had found.

"Negro boxers always have trouble with my southpaw style," he said. "They're instinctive people and find it hard to adapt themselves to a different stance."

This was the first heavyweight world championship bout ever held in Germany, but it brought back echoes of the last fight between a German and an American black man for the crown. That was the famous rematch between Max Schmeling and Joe Louis, June 22, 1938, at Yankee Stadium. Schmeling had knocked out Louis in the twelfth round in a nontitle upset two years earlier, a result that was enjoyed mightily by Nazi leader Adolf Hitler. The world was on the edge of war, talk about "the master race" in the background, when Louis knocked out the German in the rematch in 124 seconds before Clark Gable, Douglas Fairbanks, Gary Cooper, J. Edgar Hoover, and seventy thousand other spectators. It was the most famous fight in boxing history.

Louis and Schmeling both were brought to Frankfurt to publicize the Ali-Mildenberger fight. Louis was part of the ABC television broadcast. Schmeling had become successful in Germany as a Coca-Cola distributor. The two were friends now and laughed easily about their past.

The fight was in the massive Waldstadion (Forest Stadium), which could hold eighty thousand people for boxing. Ali kept saying that the stadium would be sold out, but there was little chance it would be as much as half full. The residents of Frankfurt knew the odds.

"If I lose on Saturday, I will retire," Ali said, refusing to call a round, "but I don't believe a human on earth can mark my face. I never think of losing a fight. I always think of winning. If you get tagged, you get tagged.

"I don't see anybody who can whip me as long as I stay in shape. It's not easy training for all these fights. Every day that I get older, it gets a little harder to get up in the morning and run."

There was no rancor, little showmanship before the two men stepped into the ring. Mildenberger very carefully addressed Ali by his Muslim name; Ali thanked him for that. Ali did say something about sending this nice German boy to the moon, and the nice German boy suggested Ali might need a couple of people to help, but that was that. All nice. All business.

The fight followed the expected pattern—if knockdowns of the challenger in the fifth, eighth, and tenth rounds and a technical knockout at 1:30 of the twelfth round were parts of the expected pattern. Mildenberger's swollen face was covered in blood from giant cuts around both eyes. That was why the fight was stopped.

The crowd filled less than half the stadium. Schmeling and Louis sat next to each other, not too far from Jean-Paul Belmondo and Ursula Andress. Ali did what he was supposed to do, though probably not as fast as he was supposed to do it. Mildenberger lost, though probably not as fast as everyone had anticipated.

In the eighth round, pressing, pressing, he did connect with one left hand to the liver that made Ali wince. That was Mildenberger's major moment. If only he could have connected with another . . . he still felt good about himself. He fell down but got back up three different times. He was a warrior. The fight was stopped because he couldn't see anymore, not because he couldn't fight.

"I was not disappointed," he said years later to writer Stephen Brun in *Facing Ali*. "People gave me three or four rounds and I went 12 with the loudmouth. If I had not had any cuts, I could have gone 15. I proved to myself and I proved to him that I could stand up to the loudmouth."

"No marks," Ali said, checking his face in the locker room mirror. "This was a tough fight, and only the first Liston fight and the one against George Chuvalo were harder."

He was on a plane back to Chicago the next day. Included in his luggage was a cuckoo clock that he brought back for Hayden C. Covington. Just business.

The most notable part of the Mildenberger trip was that it marked the end of Ali's involvement with the Louisville Sponsoring Group (LSG). This was the collection of eleven local blue bloods who had backed and managed his career for the past six years, a period that started three days before his first professional fight, a six-round decision over Tunney Hunsaker at Freedom Hall on October 29, 1960.

The group had been marginalized since the arrival of Main Bout Inc., the television production group headed by Herbert Muhammad, for the Chuvalo fight. Ali wanted more Muslims, more friends, more black faces he saw every day to handle his career.

"I feel more at ease and am better able to communicate with certain of my friends and associates who have been with me during the past year . . . ," the champ said in his press release announcing a change in management. "It is these friends and associates to whom I will look in the future for guidance and advice."

There was no public animosity involved. The relationship had sort of worn down on each side, Ali ready to leave and his tired, all-white country club investors ready to let him go. The ride had been different from what any of them had imagined, louder and bumpier and down some unexpected paths.

"We were babes in the jungle but we survived," said forty-year-old lawyer Gordon Davidson, the most public face of the group. "And the scars don't bleed anymore."

Davidson, who had been a law clerk for Supreme Court justice Stanley Forman Reed and did research in the *Brown v. Board of Education* case, handled the contracts and the money. He and Bill Faversham, a vice president at Brown-Forman Distillers Corporation, makers of Jack Daniel's and other intoxicants, were the two investors involved directly with Ali. The rest (the entry price was $2,800) mostly followed the action in hopes of fun or profit or both.

The group had hired Angelo Dundee as a trainer, purchased the little three-bedroom house in Miami, charted Ali's course to the heavy-weight title. There had been assorted problems with the client. Cassius Clay Sr. repeatedly had warned his son that no black man ever received fair treatment from a white man. Ali had balked at his slow progress financially at the start, threatened to retire at different times, screamed to fight Liston for a payday before anyone else thought he was ready. He was a wonderful, engaging kid who sometimes could be a pain in the ass. The group also had been brought into a black militant Muslim world it never even knew existed.

"When did you first learn that Ali had become a Muslim?" Davidson was asked on writer Jack Olsen's tapes.

"The people from NAACP in Louisville actually were the first ones to bring it to our attention," he said. "They had been trying to get Clay to do a number of things and he wouldn't do any of them. Then there was something they really wanted him to do and he turned them down and gave a quote to the newspapers about how he was an athlete, wasn't political. That made them mad. They came to us and said, 'there's something you should know. This boy is hanging around with the Nation of Islam.'"

That message was early, well before the first Liston fight, well before Malcolm X had appeared on the scene. The LSG investors went through all the changes, all the adventures, tied to their excitable client.

Davidson remembered hanging around, riding and eating with the champ and Angelo, comments made, then adapted to the promotion of fights. The poems? The one-liners? He said they often were a collaborative effort. If something sounded good, it was there on the table. The champ was a master at delivering the result with animation and conviction.

"You'd say something and you wouldn't think he was listening," the lawyer said. "The next day he would repeat what you said. The day after that he would act like he invented it."

"'I said I was the greatest, I didn't say I was the smartest,'" Davidson said, repeating a familiar Ali line about flunking the test for the draft. "If I say it, it's not funny. If he says it, it's funny."

The weigh-in for the first Liston fight in Miami: that had been a moment. Davidson had gone to the dressing room to warn Ali that the boxing commission said there would be a $2,500 fine if he created a scene at the weigh-in. LSG would not pay the fine. Understand? Ali would have to pay the fine. Ali said he understood. He was relaxed, calm, perfect. Davidson walked with him down the hall. Calm. They turned the corner to the site of the weigh-in. Lights. Cameras. People. Ali went crazy.

With Bundini Brown behind him, he shouted and preened, yelled about floating like a butterfly, stinging like a bee, rumble, young man, rumble. He tried to get at Liston, but was held back by Sugar Ray Robinson. He said, "Someone is going to die at ringside tonight." His blood pressure registered at 200/100. His heart rate was 120 beats per minute, twice as fast as normal. Dr. Alexander Robbins, the chief physician for the Miami Boxing Council, determined that Ali was "emotionally unbalanced, scared to death."

"How'd I do?" Ali asked Davidson, back at the dressing room. He was calm again.

"You're fined the $2500," Davidson said.

"That's nothing."

The curious part of the relationship was that Ali never had taken any financial advice from the group. The investors had been successful in oil, real estate, and various other enterprises and were eager to point out places where he could grow his money. He never was interested. Money arrived, money left. He liked to spend his money. He always seemed to need more.

"He never did anything nefarious with it," Davidson said. "I don't think he gave it to the Muslims. He just spent it."

Earnings were supposed to be split 50-50 between Ali and the group, 60-40 in favor of Ali in the last two years, but a clause in the contract said all expenses would be taken out of the LSG share. This had proved to be an expensive concession. The champ could rack up expenses. No fortunes had been made by the investors. No money had been lost, but speculation in the stock market would have brought a bigger return.

The worry in the beginning was this kid from Louisville would be corrupted by the dark forces of boxing, by the behind-the-scenes mobsters who had controlled the sport for a long time. The LSG had been formed to stop that from happening, and it had. The goal at the beginning also was to win the heavyweight championship of the world. The LSG had been formed to make that happen, and it had. There had been more noise and combustion than anyone expected, but results were results.

An unlikely marriage pretty much had been a success.

"We wanted to help the kid," Gordon Davidson would say years later. "It wasn't like a bunch of Southern gentlemen buying a gamecock or anything."

One night after the agreement with the LSG officially ended, Ali returned to Louisville to box a six-round exhibition against Doug Jones for the Children's Hospital Foundation. It was an easy night, executed with sixteen-ounce gloves and headgear. Jones had given a young Ali a stern test in Madison Square Garden that ended in a controversial decision in 1963, but that was ancient history now. Ali simply played with him for six rounds, then took the microphone in the ring at the end, made a five-minute speech, and brought a number of local people to the ring for introductions. Davidson and Faversham were two of them.

"They handled me real nice," the champ told the crowd.

Management now belonged to Main Bout and Herbert Muhammad.

Herbert resigned as head of Main Bout and became Ali's manager of record. John Ali, another member of the Nation of Islam, became the head of Main Bout, which still handled television and all ancillary aspects of Ali's business. Bob Arum, television producer Mike Malitz of New York, and Jim Brown remained partners in the company.

The first major act of the new management was to bring Ali's career back to the United States. Time and television had softened Ali's image enough to reopen the domestic market. Main Bout scheduled a fight for November 14 against veteran Cleveland (Big Cat) Williams in the Houston Astrodome. The bout would be on closed-circuit television in theaters around the country. The three fights in Europe, broadcast on Saturday afternoons on *Wide World of Sports,* Ali in conversation with Howard Cosell, had created a demand. The heavyweight champion of the world was still controversial, but also an attraction again.

Gordon Davidson had one parting word to the new management. He didn't like the matchup with Cleveland Williams.

"If I had been running things, there would be no fight," he said. "The risk to Clay doesn't equate what the fight will produce in money."

This was debatable.

The Big Cat was an interesting opponent. He had a well-drawn body, at six feet three, 210 pounds, that could have been clipped from some superhero comic book. He had gold caps on his teeth. He had served three years in the U.S. Army. He wore cowboy clothes that included black hats, black boots, black jeans, and black shirts, which fit well in Houston, his adopted hometown. He had a 65-5-1 record that included an eye-catching fifty-one knockouts. Fifteen of those knockouts had been in the first round.

He also had a story.

On the night of November 28, 1964, while he was established and highly ranked in the heavyweight division, Williams and a friend were stopped on a highway outside Houston. Officer Dale Witten tried to arrest both men, Williams for driving while intoxicated. Somewhere in the process, words became heated. There was an altercation. Details were debated, but somewhere in the altercation Witten drew his .357 Magnum and somewhere in the scuffle Williams grappled for the gun and Williams was shot in the stomach. Williams said that somewhere in the aftermath he heard one of the patrolmen say, "I don't want to take this nigger to the hospital and get his blood all over the car." Then Williams passed out.

He did reach the hospital and wound up staying for a while. He lost a kidney, underwent operations for other internal problems, and weighed 155 pounds when he was released. He still had the bullet in his right hip. His return to full health eventually took place on the farm of his fast-talking manager, Hugh Benbow. The boxer lifted hay bales, plowed fields, lived a no-frills life. His body returned to its previous size and condition.

Four subsequent fights, all wins, had brought him back into the role of contender. Was he really back? Had his knockout punch returned? How good was he? These were intriguing questions.

"You're not so tall when you take off that hat and those boots," Ali said when the two men first met.

"I'm tall enough," Williams said.

The still-new Houston Astrodome, which developer Roy Hofheinz modestly called "the Eighth Wonder of the World," was an attraction in itself. Open for a year and a half, home of the Houston Astros and the Houston Oilers, filled to the skybox rafters for a Billy Graham crusade, half filled for a Judy Garland concert, the domed stadium featured an exploding scoreboard, theater-style seats, and, most important of all in a perpetually muggy environment: air-conditioning. The weather was guaranteed to be perfect indoors.

"When it's raining and miserable from New Orleans to El Paso and from Amarillo to the Rio Grande Valley," Hofheinz declared at the opening, "people are going to say, 'Let's get away from the drudgery, let's go on up to the dome, see the game, eat in the fine restaurants, sit on the upholstered seats.'"

This was the first boxing event in the building. Local promoter Earl Gilliam predicted a solid crowd. The fight also was a return to closed-circuit television for Ali, available in more than a hundred theaters around the country. The number was far different from the previous closed-circuit telecast, the long waltz with Chuvalo seven and a half months earlier, which was shown in only about twenty theaters due to the protests about the champ's antidraft comments. With no word on his appeal, only the city of Miami made a show of banning the broadcast of this fight. On November 14, 1966.

Ali promised an addition to his repertoire for the event. He called it "the Ali Shuffle," a little dance move he said he used as an amateur in the Golden Gloves and Olympics. Pow. Pow. Duck. Duck. Pow. He demonstrated. He moved his feet as if he were on an invisible treadmill that was going very fast.

"It's confusin' and works beautiful in a corner . . . ," he said. "With the Ali Shuffle I'll give Williams the quick, flashin' feet and I can throw combinations off it. Once I'm out of the corner I'll go back with the stick (the jab)."

By contract, Ali would receive $405,000 for his night's work. Williams was supposed to receive much, much less. On the night of the fight, that second figure changed even more dramatically. Williams's wife, Rita, heard a knock on the dressing room door, which she thought probably came from a fan who wanted to wish her husband good luck. She opened the door. A process server handed her legal papers that said Big Cat's earnings were going to be garnished for $67,615 to pay for his hospital bills after the shooting two years ago.

K. S. "Bud" Adams, owner of the pro football Oilers, had instituted the proceedings. Along with Hugh Benbow he had owned Williams's contract before the shooting. That company now was dissolved. Williams always thought insurance, maybe from the Oilers, had paid his bills. The idea that he now owed this money was a shock.

He told Bonnie Gangelhoff of the *Houston Press,* years later, that his wife said, "They've taken our money. They've taken our money. You're not going to get paid for this fight." Benbow, who also was surprised by the legal papers, said Williams "almost turned white." The idea that he was fighting for nothing quickly overwhelmed him. Biggest fight of his life. Heavyweight championship of the world. He would get nothing?

Williams's wife said Ali heard about the situation and told her husband if he didn't want to fight he didn't have to fight, but Williams rejected that idea. Moving like a man heading toward his execution, he went to the ring. He never shadowboxed, loosened, made himself ready. He never started to sweat. He proceeded to be destroyed.

Ali measured him for the first half of the opening round, then began to shake him with combinations in the second half. In the second round,

Williams was dropped to the floor three times, the last one at the bell, which saved him from a knockout. In the third, he was dropped again. Referee Harry Kessler stopped the fight at 1:08 of the round.

"I couldn't get myself together," Williams told Gangelhoff. "I could have done better without getting served. I believe I would have beat him . . . it shook my confidence. I was fighting for nothing."

The fight was seen as Ali's masterpiece. His punching power had been questioned in other fights, opponents slow to fall, but not this time. He dismantled this physical specimen of a fighter. He moved and moved. The Ali Shuffle was a wonder. Who had ever done something like this? The performance made him look as great as he always said he was. This wasn't the mysterious anchor punch against Liston. This wasn't the grim exhibitions against Chuvalo and Cooper, London and Mildenberger, success against outclassed pluggers. This was against Cleveland Williams.

"No longer does Cassius ask to be acclaimed as the 'greatest,'" said columnist Arthur Daley, one of his critics. "He's now ready to settle for being good. He's good, all right. He's awfully good."

"The greatest Ali ever was as a fighter was against Williams," Howard Cosell would say, years later. "That night he was the most devastating fighter who ever lived."

Was he? Or had the process server helped?

"Williams dies with his boots on," said Benbow, the challenger's manager. "He's a good old boy. . . . I'm not going to let him fight again. He won't put a glove on again. He's going to work like everybody else."

(Williams would fight again, twenty times in the next six years, with thirteen wins and seven losses. He also would lose a lawsuit to keep the $67,615 from being garnished from his purse against Ali.)

The champ exulted in interviews. The fight made a lot of money, 35,460 people setting an attendance record for an indoor fight. The closed-circuit was a surprising bonanza, especially in cities with a large African American population. There was a radio broadcast. Main Bout sold rights for telecasts and films in forty-two countries. The Muhammad Ali franchise suddenly looked much stronger.

Ernie Terrell appeared on the scene at the end of the fight to tee up the inevitable next fight. There was little doubt that this also would be at the Astrodome.

"This is truly an eighth wonder of the world, just like Judge Hofheinz says," said Herbert Muhammad, the new manger of Ali's fortunes. "Yes, I'd like to see my father [Elijah Muhammad] here some day. If the judge has a good price on a convention, we'll make him an honorary brother."

Judge Grauman had spent two weeks making and writing his decision, shipping it to Washington in the first week of September. The people at the Department of Justice, which could accept or reject his advice, spent almost three months reviewing the materials. A sixteen-page letter finally was sent on November 25, 1966, to the chairman of the Appeal Board for the Western District of Kentucky Selective Service System at 1405 West Broadway in Louisville.

Grauman's decision was included. He was called "the Hearing Officer" in the document.

"The Hearing Officer reported that the registrant stated his views for about one hour in a convincing manner," the letter said, "that he answered all questions propounded to him forthrightly; that there was no evidence of trying to evade the Hearing Officer's questions; and that he was impressed by the registrant's statements."

Grauman had liked Ali's testimony. There it was. He had found it believable. He also had liked the testimony of Chauncey Eskridge, which gave Ali's religious beliefs a time frame and sincerity. He had liked comments from the FBI report by the lawyer for the Louisville Sponsoring Group (which had to be Gordon Davidson) and an unidentified member of the group (no doubt Faversham). He knew Davidson, "a man of impeccable character," and was familiar with Faversham. The fact that neither of them would make any further financial gain from Ali's career was important.

Davidson had pointed out that he told the champ there was a route, already established, to enter the Army Reserve or National Guard, which would allow him to keep fighting. Why lose all this money by taking this stand? Ali had replied that money was not nearly as important to him as his religion. That seemed to be an important statement.

Grauman was convinced.

"The Hearing Officer concluded that the registrant is sincere on religious grounds to participation in war in any form," the letter said, "and he recommended that the conscientious-objector claim of the registrant be sustained."

There it was. Against odds and predictions by everyone involved, Ali had won in a court of law. He had stood before a judge, rolled out his thoughts in well-chosen words, not an excitable rush, and the judge had been convinced. The judge's son, Lawrence Grauman Jr., at odds with his father for most of a lifetime, was thrilled by the news. His father, the ultimate lawyer, the no-nonsense disciplinarian, the resident Southerner, despite all the noise, had found that the law favored this famous black man who did not want to fight in the army. Hallelujah.

Wait a minute.

Hallelujah?

There was more to consider.

The decision by Grauman was reported on page seven of the letter to the Appeal Board. There were nine more pages. The Justice Department had its own views of the FBI report and the hearing. Grauman's decision, remember, was only advice. The Justice Department could accept or reject that advice.

Noted were Gordon Davidson's comments in the report that he "could not be sure how deep any human conviction goes with the registrant" and that he wouldn't be surprised "if a year from now the registrant becomes disenchanted with the Muslims and voluntarily joins the United States Marines." Noted was Faversham's thought that Ali had been brainwashed "first by his father and then by the Muslims." Noted was the NOI belief that the white man was its enemy and that its members should disassociate themselves from the U.S. government and all its institutions. Noted were the different appeals Ali had made for deferments for financial hardship. Noted was the lack of a conscientious objector appeal when he first was given a physical. Noted were his comments about the Viet Cong.

The comments about the Viet Cong were always remembered.

"Neither the fact that he has 'no personal quarrel' with the Viet Cong nor his related objection to the Black Muslims getting involved in the Vietnam war constitute an objection which the Act recognizes," the letter said. "To qualify for exemption as a conscientious objector, the registrant's objection must be a general scruple against 'participation in war in any form' not merely an objection to participation in a particular war. (United States v. Kauten, 133 F.2d 703.)"

There was little doubt, as a reader turned the final nine pages, what the judgment would be. Ali had convinced the judge. He had won. The judge had not convinced the United States Department of Justice. Ali had lost. The great wheel of bureaucracy, fueled by unseen politics or passion or maybe simply a different interpretation of law, spun once more and delivered its product at the end of the letter.

> The burden of clearly establishing his conscientious-objector claim is upon the registrant. The Department of Justice concludes that this registrant failed to explain that burden.
>
> With due regard for the recommendation of the Hearing Officer, the Department of Justice finds that the registrant's conscientious-objector claim is not sustained and recommends to your Board that he be not classified in class 1-0 or 1-A-0 . . .
> Sincerely,
> T. Oscar Smith
> Chief, Conscientious-Objector Section

The shit had hit the fan. The Kentucky Court of Appeals took its time but, on January 10, 1967, supplied a unanimous 5–0 rubber stamp of approval on the Justice Department's recommendation. Two days later, Local Draft Board No. 47 rejected Ali's appeal as a Muslim minister. Covington announced various courses of appeal that were open, but his client right now was classified 1-A.

He could be called for induction at any time.

7

Ernie

The room was small, hot, stuffed. The long-established publicity office at Madison Square Garden Boxing was not made for this kind of publicity gathering. Two large desks, assorted reporters, cameramen, lights, cameras, filing cabinets, and winter coats made this a combustible scene from the start. Everybody was falling all over one another, uncomfortable, cranky.

Howard Cosell was a fine accelerant.

"I am surrounded at the moment by two massive men," the broadcaster, working this time for WABC-TV, began in his familiar New York cadence. "The gentleman at my left has just told me that he is the only man in the world that Muhammad Ali is afraid of. The gentleman to my left has to be Ernie Terrell. To my right is the author of a great new poem. He is the heavyweight champion of the world. He pretends that he will have an easy time of it February 6th at the Astrodome."

Three days after Christmas, December 28, 1966, was a fine time to get the promotional wheels moving for (as Cosell noted) the February 6, 1967, fight from the Houston Astrodome. Ali versus Terrell. At last. This was a press conference to announce the Garden as the prime New York location for the closed-circuit broadcast, a forty-foot screen promised for the event. The participants for that event, after the false starts in Chicago and Toronto, now stared at each other from the sides of the self-important announcer. They did not disappoint.

"I would like to say something," Terrell began. "Cassius Clay is—"

"Why do you want to say Cassius Clay when Howard Cosell and everybody else is calling me Muhammad Ali?" Ali interrupted. "Why do you of all people, someone who's colored, keep saying Cassius Clay?"

"Uh, Howard Cosell's not the one who's going to fight you," Terrell countered. "I am."

"You're making it pretty hard on yourself now. Why don't you call me my name, man?"

"Well, what's your name? You told me your name was Cassius Clay two or three years ago."

"I never told you my name was Cassius Clay. My name is Muhammad Ali. And you will announce it right there in the center of the ring if you don't do it now. You are acting like another old Uncle Tom. Another Floyd Patterson. I am going to punish you. Back off."

There was some closer physical contact here as the two men stared at each other. Maybe their chests bumped against each other.

"Why you calling me Uncle Tom?"

"Back off. Back off."

Here was where handlers tried to pull the men in different directions. The pulling was only half successful as insults continued to be thrown, especially by Ali. Cosell closed off the interview.

"And so, ladies and gentlemen, as the two contestants prepare for another battle right now . . . ," the broadcaster said, "another interview has been recorded for posterity as the two gentlemen continue to promote the fight."

Ali slapped Terrell. Ali tried to slap him again. Terrell tried to get to Ali. Handlers intervened. The little room was filled with manufactured chaos.

Cosell shouted to his cameraman.

"Keep shooting," he said.

The old dance had returned.

In the midst of his legal troubles and with the prospect of an induction call looming closer and closer, the beleaguered young champion reverted to his old moneymaking approach: he became the comic villain again. Hate me, hate me, buy a ticket. Established now as a real-life villain in the public mind, his old comic role took on even more significance.

"When he answers the bell, Terrell will catch hell" was the return to poetic prediction that had been missing from those various out-of-country title defenses.

"Sssssssss" was the predominant national reaction.

This postponed fight with the six-foot-six scuffler from Chicago had a chance to be a real moneymaker, best of Ali's career. Terrell was the World Boxing Association heavyweight champion, winner of an elimination fight with tough Eddie Machen, followed by defenses against George Chuvalo and Doug Jones. The title had been declared vacant when Ali went ahead with his rematch with Sonny Liston instead of fighting the highest-ranked WBA contender.

Ali held every other available crown, was unanimously seen everywhere as the rightful titleholder, but this still could be billed as champ against champ. This was a certified attraction. The promoters called it "The Fight of the Century," a touch of hyperbole that forgot a long list of important fights.

After he established the dance in the New York press conference, Ali followed the necessary promotional steps from the moment he arrived in Houston on January 10, 1967. He admitted, okay, maybe Terrell wasn't an Uncle Tom, but the man did say the wrong name, Cassius Clay, whenever he talked. A fearsome price would be paid for that. There would be no quick knockout. There would be no one saved by the bell. Punishment would be delivered in large and concentrated amounts. Remember Floyd Patterson? He also used that name. He also paid.

"That Terrell, he's done talked too much," Ali said. "He's got me mad. I was planning to knock him out, but that would be too good for him. I'm just gonna spank him. I'm gonna humiliate him. You might say I'm planning a Floyd Patterson whipping for Mr. Terrell."

This was the message he tried to impart to Mr. Terrell every day. Both fighters worked in a ring set up at the Astro Hall, an exposition space across the street from the dome. Ali worked at one p.m., usually before a full house of 1,400 fans at a dollar per head. Terrell worked at three, the crowd not as big at the end of his session, but packed at the start. That was when Ali would be there, hanging around on most days simply to yell at Terrell. Shades of Sonny Liston. Terrell was "The Octopus." Terrell was "The One-Armed Bandit," all left-hand jab and nothing else. Terrell would be toast.

Ali was in top physical condition. He had fought so often that he never had time to fall out of shape between opponents. He ran three miles in the morning through Memorial Park. He sparred in the afternoon. There was time to give speeches at both the University of Houston and Rice University. ("What do you think about the draft?" a kid asked at Wiess Commons at Rice. "I'm not cold," the champ replied. "Somebody feel cold?") There was time to appear at a department store. His weight was 212 pounds. He was a mature man at the top of his physical game. He turned twenty-five during training and was presented with a 578-pound cake by the promoters that was so large he thought maybe Terrell had been stuffed inside. He did not eat a big piece.

"My legs and back will never be the same," Angelo Dundee reported after he took a walk with his fighter. "That's the longest hike since I quit the Boy Scouts."

Ali's home away from home for the fight was a three-room suite, Room 1235, at the America Hotel, but he also established his actual home in Houston. After Hayden Covington filed more appeals that summarily were turned down in Louisville, the lawyer suggested that the battleground should be shifted to a new site. This was something that was legal to do. A man could move and switch draft boards. Covington said Houston was a place where appeals had been treated more kindly than in many cities. Ali and his Muslim advisors rented an apartment in the Ardmore Arms at 5962 Ardmore Street, Houston, Texas, 77021.

He told reporters—"in a big announcement that will shock and surprise you"—that he was moving to Houston because the people were nice to him and the press had been nice to him and that he planned to work with the local black population to try to uplift people "mentally, morally and every other way." There was no mention about a more lenient draft board. None. He put out a call to local real estate agents to find him a home to purchase for over $100,000.

"If there aren't any $100,000 homes here in colored or integrated neighborhoods, we'll just have to build one," he said. "I want this house to be something plush and fabulous."

To complete the picture for the draft board of the NOI minister newly arrived to preach to his flock, he appeared at Mosque No. 45, a former office and warehouse for a lumberyard, at 3400 Polk Street one day before the fight. A half-dozen white reporters were allowed into the hall after being patted down and searched. They were allowed to watch the first fifteen minutes or so of his speech.

He reportedly went into more harsh language after the reporters were removed, decrying the white man and the things the white man had done, but he spent most of his time before they left talking about the horrors of eating the pig, the hog, pork ("solid maggots") of any kind. He also talked about the glories of following the Honorable Elijah Muhammad. He talked a lot about Elijah Muhammad.

"I enjoy talkin' to you about this man," he told his congregation, most of it gathered solely to see the heavyweight champion of the world, "more than I will whuppin' Terrell's head."

Terrell thought he could beat Ali. That was his biggest strength coming into the fight. He had three inches in height, four inches in reach, and almost three years of experience on this guy. He had the good left hand—yeah, yeah, the one Ali always talked about—but more than that he had confidence. He was not afraid.

All the yapping, all the grim predictions did not matter. That stuff was nonsense.

"This time none of it will work," Terrell said. "I will not freeze like Cleveland Williams or panic like Sonny Liston or melt like Floyd Patterson. He's been trying to psych me and psyching is an indication of a lack of confidence. If Cassius is going to beat me up as bad as he says he is, he should keep quiet or I might not show up."

Ali made it sound like he was the first black man who ever lived, the first to fight through injustice. Uncle Tom? Terrell said he would compare hard roads to the Astrodome with this guy any day of the publicity week. He grew up in Inverness, Mississippi, one of ten children. His parents were sharecroppers. His father got a factory job in Chicago when Terrell was in his teens, so everyone headed to the cold north. He was a professional boxer two years before he graduated from Farragut High School. There were no press conferences when the first contract was signed.

What was the difference between his career and Ali's career? He never had the sharp management, the buzz around him of an Olympic gold medal winner. He never had the carefully planned list of opponents. His style was bang and hold, bang and hold, hit with the left and then hold with the right and grind around the ring. He was a defensive fighter, a neutralizer. There were no easy cheers for a fighter like that. He had no dazzling speed, no shuffle. He was a survivor. Ali had been able to swim only on the surface of this profession. Terrell had worked his way up from the bottom, holding his nose and banging away most of the obstacles in front of him. His record was an honest 39-4, and he hadn't been beaten in five years.

He had a history with Ali, had seen him around the Golden Gloves at the beginning, had eaten with him, talked with him, traveled in a car with him. He even had been a sparring partner for him in Miami in 1962 when Ali was training for a guy named Don Warner. How did that go? Jimmy Jacobs, the handball champion and fight film historian, was in Houston with a two-round clip of a sparring session at the 5th Street Gym. What did that look like? Ernie Terrell was banging the younger, lighter Ali around the ring with that left hand. Anyone could see.

"I wasn't the same fighter then," Terrell told Tex Maule of *Sports Illustrated*. "I didn't have the left hand I have now. I couldn't hurt people with it. He was a punk then and he's a punk now. He wasn't a complete fighter then and he's not a complete fighter now. He's where he is because of management. They made sure he never fought a tough fighter."

The tall man never thought twice before using the name "Clay." That was whom he had met, whom he had sparred against, whom he knew. If the name made *Clay* upset, that was fine. This was a prizefight. Wasn't *Clay* saying a lot of mumbo jumbo to make him upset? It was all nonsense.

Terrell demonstrated early in the promotion that he wanted respect. Upset that the billing on posters for the fight had his name listed in a smaller typeface than Ali's name, he said that he would pull out of the fight if this was not changed in forty-eight hours.

"In some cases my name looks like the fine print on an insurance policy," he said. "In other cases, the letters on my name are no bigger than the cheapest price for a ticket. I have an 89-year-old grandmother and she knows better than to do something like that."

The posters were changed.

Two nights before the fight, Terrell appeared on *Hollywood Palace*—ABC's lower-rated variety-show answer to *The Ed Sullivan Show*—with his group, Ernie Terrell and the Heavyweights. Terrell had a strong baritone voice, and performed regularly in the Chicago area. His sister Jean, part of the group though not a true heavyweight, later would become the replacement when Diana Ross left the Supremes. *Hollywood Palace,* which aired at 9:30 on Saturday nights, after the *Lawrence Welk Show* at 8:30, was where both the Rolling Stones and the Jackson Five made their U.S. television debuts. Unlike Sullivan's show on CBS, the *Palace* used a rotating roster of guest hosts that ranged in 1967 from Bing Crosby to Joan Crawford to Sid Caesar to Jimmy Durante.

Venerable comedian Jack Benny was the host when Terrell appeared. Benny, a successful refugee from radio, was famous for his understated delivery and perpetual stinginess. He looked small next to the six-foot-six Terrell as they did their rehearsed routine.

JACK: You know, Ernie, that Astrodome where you're going to fight
    Clay is quite a place. That dome is magnificent. Have you
    seen it?
ERNIE: No. I'll let Cassius tell me about it.
JACK: What?
ERNIE: He'll get a better view from his back.
(Canned laughter.)
JACK: If you have that much confidence, I'll bet two or three dol-
    lars on you.
(Canned laughter.)
JACK: Two dollars.
(Louder canned laughter.)

Ernie then proceeded to sing a song he had written about "Clay." He looked dapper in his midnight-blue tuxedo jacket and bow tie. The tune was stolen from "Billy Bailey, Won't You Please Come Home?" and detailed "Clay's" travels abroad to fight Chuvalo and Cooper, London and Mildenberger. The refrain was the best part:

"Ain't it a shame, you changed your name.

"I'll change your features, too."

(Canned laughter.)

This was not exactly what happened forty-eight hours later.

The fight was what Ali said it would be: a road company performance of *The Humiliation of Floyd Patterson*. Mr. Terrell, in the role of Mr. Patterson, took the same slings, arrows, and beatdown that Mr. Patterson did. He survived the fifteen rounds, a loser on a unanimous decision as opposed to the merciful TKO in the twelfth in the Patterson fight, but received the same physical battering and the same degrading verbal assault. Mr. Ali, in the role of Mr. Ali again, was—to steal the words of New York columnist Red Smith—"graceful and graceless" at the same time.

Terrell never could fight his fight. The champ was too fast to be caught, too elusive to be hit with that pawing left jab. Terrell attributed much of his problems to a left eye that suffered a broken blood vessel in the third round. He said the injury came from an illegal thumb stuck into the eye and that he was troubled by double vision for the rest of the fight. This could have been a factor, to be sure, but Terrell was the dirtier fighter in the bout and the skill of Ali was still the biggest factor.

He pummeled Terrell, the job easier and easier as the fight progressed. By the eighth round, in absolute control, he taunted Terrell, exactly as he said he would.

"What's my name?" he asked.

Bam-bam-bam.

"What's my name?"

Bam.

He became a schoolyard bully once again. All pretense that boxing was in any way a gentleman's game was dropped. The idea here was to make the overwhelmed opponent look foolish. This was what Ali had promised to do during the buildup. It also was what he had promised to do at the start of the fight when the two men were receiving their instructions from referee Harry Kessler, according to Terrell's trainer, Sam Solomon.

"Clay said, 'You're nothing but a white man's nigger,'" Solomon said. "Then he told Ernie, 'You love white folks, so I gonna beat your ass.'"

The reaction to the show, witnessed by a crowd of 37,321, a record for an indoor fight but well below the sixty thousand spectators the promoters had hoped would attend, was predictably not favorable. Ali compounded his words by not bothering to shake Terrell's hand after the decision was announced and called him "a dog" in a postfight interview. The cheers were for the plucky guy who took the punishment, not the egotistical character who administered it.

The press was not happy. The fallout was more dramatic than the fight.

"In my book, Clay fell headlong down the scale of sportsmanship," wrote George Whiting of the *Evening Standard* in London. "To half-paralyze your opponent with punches, to slash ugly slits over and under his eyes, to reduce him to a game but impotent wreck, these things may be ugly, but they come within the rules of the trade.

"Less forgivable was the cocky, arrogant manner in which Clay sneered and snarled and taunted—and even on occasion spat at the feet of the poor wreck of Terrell."

"Clay revealed himself as a good prize fighter, as a less-than-admirable human being, and as totally unworthy of the adulation he seeks," Shirley Povich wrote in the *Washington Post*. "Fine persons have traveled through boxing's history. Cassius Clay is not one of them."

"The 'sport' becomes downright degrading when a man sneers and belittles and bedevils a man he is systematically bleeding to death," Jim Murray wrote in the *Los Angeles Times*. "If you did it to a dog, they'd lock you up."

Ali tried to step back a day later in a quiet press conference at his hotel. He said he sometimes was carried away by his emotions when he fought. He sometimes said some things he shouldn't say. Terrell was a fine man. The words were all part of the promotion. The champ (of all federations now, including the WBC) added that his manager, Herbert Muhammad, had advised him to take this apologetic approach. Herbert Muhammad had squirmed a bit, too, at what happened in the ring.

Not that it was all that bad.

"They usually kill people in wars for attacking a man's religion," Ali said. "I just gave Terrell a little spanking. Some day I'll convert him. Ernie will be a Muslim, too."

By Saturday, when he appeared with Cosell on *Wide World of Sports,* he had become less apologetic, more defensive. He couldn't do anything right. People were picking him apart. White people. There was no way he could have made white people happy in his fight against Terrell unless he had lost.

"If I put him away in one round, it's bad," Ali said. "If I put him away in three rounds, it's bad. If I talk to him, it's bad. If I whip him clean, it's bad. I'm just wrong if I do it, wrong if I don't."

One month from the day he beat Terrell he was in New York City, checking in to the Loews Midtown Motor Inn, getting ready to put his title on the line forty-four days after he had beat Terrell. Things were moving fast in his life.

He had talked of going to Mecca after his victory, but that never happened. The trip was delayed until his draft status could be resolved. That meant he was free to fight thirty-four-year-old Zora Folley in Madison Square Garden. The contract was signed nine days after the Terrell fight while Terrell was still in the hospital, recovering from surgery to repair a "blowout fracture" to the bone structure behind that left eye.

There seemed to be a slapdash urgency to everything. The Garden had been pushing to host a fight, outbid the last two times by the Astrodome, and here was an opportunity. Ka-ching. The old arena on Eighth Avenue would close at the end of the year, move to a new site above Penn Station on Thirty-Third Street. This would be the first heavyweight championship fight in the old building since Ezzard Charles beat Lee Oma in 1951. It also probably would be the last.

Since closed-circuit wouldn't be a big draw, the Garden and RKO General formed their own network to show the fight directly in homes. Ka-ching. Since Folley wasn't a top-level draw, a onetime fearsome contender now past his shelf life, he accepted a 15 percent share of the live gate against Ali's 50 percent. Ka-ching. Folley was overjoyed simply to have the chance after being ducked by champions for his entire career.

The idea was to get the fight done. Ka-ching. An invisible clock was working now against Ali. Stories appeared every third day about another appeal filed or rejected as Hayden Covington worked his different angles against the Selective Service bureaucracy. The lawyer kept saying there was time, more time, more places to appeal, but one by one they were disappearing. The sooner this fight happened, the sooner the checks were cashed, the better everyone would feel.

No grand publicity buildup would be involved. The fighters were supposed to train in the Catskills, Ali at Kutcher's and Folley at Grossinger's, an homage to the New York boxing past, but sixteen inches of snow in the mountains ended that. Training for both men now was in the cramped basement of the Garden, with roadwork in Central Park.

Folley was a quiet, understated workman. He came from Chandler, Arizona, had nine kids, and was something of a hero from the Korean War, where he received five battlefield honors. The army was where he had found his profession. He forged his birth certificate when he was sixteen to enlist. While he was stationed at Fort Ord, California, his platoon sergeant had to pull out of a fight for the base heavyweight championship. The sergeant requested a volunteer to replace him. Folley fought, lost, but caught the bug. He had a bunch of fights in the service, turned pro when he became a civilian.

There might have been a glimmer of promotional possibility in his history—army hero versus draft dodger—but that wasn't Folley's style. Asked about Ali's situation, the challenger said he understood.

"I don't think he's a slacker," Folley said. "I've met several more people that way, some Jehovah's Witnesses. I can tell you about my religion— I'm a Baptist—but I don't judge the next guy. If he wants to be called Muhammad Ali and says that's his name, I'll call him that."

Thud.

Ali decried the fact that there were no possibilities here for public relations outrage. He liked this guy who even called him by his right name. The worst he could say was that Folley was "not a threat." Would people pay money to see Ali fight "not a threat"? He said that he had to find some personal motivation.

Local Draft Board No. 47 suddenly provided it with a letter.

The first word was "Greetings."

John F. X. Condon, the publicity man for Madison Square Garden, delivered the message on March 15, 1967, a week before the fight. Ali was eating dinner, sitting down. Condon placed a hand on his shoulder and told him that he had been drafted. His induction day was April 11 in Louisville. Ali was stunned.

He grabbed Condon's elbow and walked him outside into an alley. Could Condon repeat what he just said? Condon repeated the words. Ali stood there. He was chewing on a toothpick. He jiggled it up and down. He didn't speak for the longest time.

"If what you say is true, this is gonna be my last fight," he finally said. "All those people who want to see the greatest heavyweight who ever lived better come see me now.

"I don't want to say anything more. I don't want to talk to nobody. I'm gonna go to a movie and think about things."

He couldn't believe what had happened. This was the first of a string of moments he had tried to avoid.

The threat to his livelihood now had form and substance. A date. A place. Covington and the other lawyers still were at work—they had filed a federal suit just that morning to declare Draft Board 47 and all the draft boards in Kentucky invalid because of "racial imbalance," a lack of black members relative to the black population—but a date and a place were serious. The champ was on a list to go to basic training.

An appeal to have his induction site switched to Houston might buy a few days, but without some favorable court decision somewhere his moment would arrive. Would he take the step forward? Would he take the oath? Would he go? The hypotheticals had been ground down to realities.

What would he do?

"My decision is made," he said when he talked to reporters the next day, "but I have to answer to the government, not to no reporters."

He said the Honorable Elijah Muhammad would not tell him what to do. Elijah simply teaches the religion and the laws. The responsibility of the members of the Nation of Islam is to follow those laws. That was what he tried to do.

"I'll die for what I believe," he said. "I gave up $8,000,000 I could have made in endorsements, movies, records and other things because of my beliefs. I gave up the prettiest Negro lady in the country because she wouldn't wear long dresses. The government follows its laws, the Army obeys its laws. I follow Allah's laws."

"There are Muslims in the Army," a reporter suggested.

"The jails are full of Muslims who didn't go in the Army," Ali replied.

There was no doubt that his predicament was being followed by Muslims and sports fans and a lot of people around the country and around the world. A newspaper in Accra, Ghana, addressed an editorial to the U.S. government. The paper, *The Pioneer,* said that the people of Ghana suspected that the government wanted to draft Ali because of his color and religion and the fact that he was not "a likable person" to most Americans.

"It is suspected that the last days of this great fighter are drawing inexorably to a premature end," the editorial said. "Should he be goaded to death like this, all lovers of boxing and the numerous fans of Ali will know where to put the blame."

In England, Norman E. Lewis of 115 Harrowby Road, Birkenhead, Cheshire, wrote to Local Draft Board No. 47 in Louisville and asked to serve in the military in Ali's place. He gave two reasons:

> The first is that I consider it a great shame that thousands of sports-men in countries all over the world may be deprived of seeing in person the man who in my opinion is the greatest heavyweight boxer of all time.
>
> The second reason is that it grieves me when I see interviews on TV with young American soldiers serving in Vietnam. Once again, these boys are the salt of the earth. I am not being unpa-triotic to my country to say this. These things go in cycles and England has had a very good run.

Lewis did admit that he was fifty-four years old, but said that he had military experience. He had spent six years slogging through Italy during World War II and fourteen more in the Royal Auxiliary Air Force. He added that on his fifty-second birthday he parachuted out of an airplane for the first time and rode a motorcycle at over one hundred miles per hour.

In New York, Ali admitted that his situation certainly had brought a focus to the business at hand. He said on second thought that the fight with Folley might not be his last—his lawyers said he might have four months, due to appeals, and he could fight three more times, the first against Oscar Bonavena in Tokyo—but there was always the possibility that it would be. He would be ready.

He compared his situation with the troubles of New York congressman Adam Clayton Powell, another black man under duress. Powell, charged with financial and other indiscretions, had been unseated by the members of the House on March 1. He called the 307–116 vote against him "the end of the United States of America as the land of the free and the home of the brave." He urged his supporters to "keep the faith, baby."

"When the money is on the table and the stakes are down, you see a different me," Ali said. "A little mix-up like this makes me more vicious and mean. To get me off guard, everything's got to be rosy and nice. I've got a lot riding behind my fight. The tenseness is in the air, the same with [Adam Clayton] Powell. I represent the freedom of the Negro; they're all behind me. I strive on challenge. What I have to go through outside the ring is child's play compared to inside it."

The outside trouble obviously bothered him. The night before the fight with Folley he called Sugar Ray Robinson at eleven o'clock and asked him to come to the suite at the Loews Midtown. That was what Robinson said in *Sugar,* his 1994 autobiography written with Dave Anderson of the *New York Times.* Robinson made the trip from Harlem, wondering what the problem was so late at night, the heavyweight title at risk in less than twenty-four hours.

He said he found Ali alone in the room, something different right there. The champ was frazzled about the impending army business. He said he couldn't go into the army because Elijah Muhammad wouldn't let him go. Elijah Muhammad? Robinson thought Ali should be making his own decision.

He reported the dialogue as he remembered it.

"I don't care what [Elijah] Muhammad told you," I said, "but I do care about you. If you don't go in the Army, you'll go to jail. When that happens, they'll take your title away. When you come out of jail, you won't be able to fight. Do you realize you're forfeiting your entire career?"

"Well," he [Ali] stumbled, "Muhammad told me."

"But if you go to jail, none of those other Muslim leaders are going to jail with you. I know you respect your religion, but at the same time, you must live by the law of the land—wherever you live, you must live by the law."

"But I'm afraid, Ray. I'm real afraid."

"Afraid of what?" I said. "Afraid of the Muslims if you don't do what they told you?"

Robinson said that Ali did not answer the question.

The fight was the one-sided show it was expected to be. The champion dispatched the not-a-chance contender at 1:49 of the seventh round. He could have done the job in the fourth, when he dropped the contender and bloodied his nose, but the contender's survival instincts kicked into action. They did not kick in very well in the seventh.

"Are you playing with me?" Folley asked to start the seventh after Ali relied on stiff jabs for most of the fifth and sixth rounds.

"No—I'm not playing," Ali said.

He then proceeded to close the show with a flurry of lefts and rights, the final right on a downward route to Folley's chin. The fight seemed to please the 13,708 patrons, a crowd that included Sammy Davis Jr., Woody Allen, Ursula Andress, and Jean-Paul Belmondo, but, alas, not visiting supermodel Twiggy, who was hosting a party on the other side of Manhattan. Ursula Andress was quoted as saying that Ali reminded her of "a kitty cat."

The biggest story of the night was still the draft. What would happen next? Was this Ali's last fight for a while? Forever? No one could say for sure. Ali, before he left New York for Chicago to see Elijah Muhammad, seemed to close out all doubt about what he would do if called.

"Those who know my past assume that I will go to jail rather than the Army . . . and they know I never have deviated from my path," he said. "Common sense tells them that Muhammad Ali will not go into the Army, he'll go to jail. Common sense is not wrong. If I thought going to war would help 22,000,000 American Negroes get freedom, justice and equality, you would not have to draft me. I would join."

One small picture of a possible future had been captured during the buildup to the fight. At one of Ali's workouts, always packed to capacity at three hundred spectators, he had called a young boxer into the ring for an introduction. The boxer had simply appeared at the side of the ring.

"Joe Fraaaaaaazier," Ali said. "Come up here and talk to me."

Frazier, two years younger, was this Philadelphia kid who was following Ali's road map to the top of the heavyweight division. After he won the 1964 Olympic gold medal, he had signed a contract with Cloverlay Inc., a corporation of 159 investors who planned out his future. His record was 13-0, soon to be 14-0 with a sixth-round knockout of Doug Jones, the veteran who had given Ali trouble long ago.

His potential was easy to see, but Yancey (Yank) Durham, his trainer, said to remember that Frazier still was "only in high school." Ali was in college. The strategy was to "let Joe finish high school. Then we go to college."

"When Clay's legs slow down a little, he'll have to be a little more of a tiger," Durham said. "And he's not a tiger. He's a boxer. That's when we'll fight him. It could be six months or six years. But we'll be ready."

Ali clowned with Frazier now in the ring. Fooled around with his sports coat. Made fun of his suspenders. Said a few things. Frazier said a few things back.

"Two more years," Ali said.

"I'll be ready," Frazier said.

8

Civil Rights

The most famous photograph of Muhammad Ali was taken at the second Liston fight in Lewiston, Maine, on May 25, 1965, by Neil Leifer of *Sports Illustrated*. Destined to grace the covers of magazines, promotional materials, fat coffee-table books, printed products of all dimensions, it showed Ali standing over his fallen foe, snarling, yelling for Liston to "Get up and fight, Sucker." The composition was perfect. Ali's power, passion, physical beauty were displayed, click, in one shot.

The second-most-famous photo was taken today, March 29, 1967. None of that stuff was shown. The names of the photographers—the shot taken by various people, each a step away from the other—really did not matter. This was a news picture, not an artistic expression. Ali was in a jacket and tie, talking into three microphones held by two white hands. He was captured in mid-sentence, no different from a billion other pictures of a man who never was shy about talking.

The difference was the person standing next to him today. That person was Dr. Martin Luther King Jr.

They never had met in public before the day of the picture. They never would meet in public after the picture. This was their one public moment, captured in a brief press conference at a Louisville hotel after they met and talked in private for an hour and a half. This was the only picture there ever would be.

Ali was in town for a hearing before Judge James F. Gordon in federal district court on two motions that would allow him to stall his induction appointment. Dr. King was in town for a meeting of the directors of the Southern Christian Leadership Conference (SCLC). Opportunity, as much as anything, made the meeting happen.

"What we talked about is our business," Ali said, then added that when John F. Kennedy, Nikita Khrushchev, and other white leaders met it was "old stuff," but when two Negro leaders met "everybody considers it a big thing."

The meeting was, indeed, news because in all their time on the national runway, these two famous black men—the two most famous black men in America—had existed at opposite ends of the ideological map. They were the segregationist and the integrationist, the Black Muslim and the Christian, the friend of the violent and the proponent of the nonviolent. They were symbolic figures in the racial unrest that swept across the nation, but no two approaches to the same problem could be any more different.

"This was a renewal of our friendship," Dr. King said. "We are victims of the same system of oppression. Although our religious beliefs differ, we are brothers."

"We're all black brothers," Ali said. "We use different approaches to our everyday problems, but the same dog that bit him bit me. When we go out, they don't ask you if you are a Christian, a Catholic, a Baptist, or a Muslim. They just start whupping black heads."

Dr. King, thirty-eight, was thirteen years older than Ali. He had been famous since 1955 when he was a leader in the Montgomery, Alabama, bus boycott that began when Rosa Parks was arrested for refusing to surrender her seat to a white passenger. His philosophy of nonviolence, with its plan to use the emerging power of television to bring the shame of segregation into the nation's living rooms, had worked in Birmingham, Alabama (with the help of police chief Bull Connor and his water jets and police dogs); St. Augustine, Florida; and certainly in Selma, Alabama. His famous seventeen-minute speech at the 1963 March on Washington, started with the words "I have a dream today, my friends," was the most eloquent plea for civil rights ever made. He was awarded the Nobel Peace Prize in 1964.

King once had courted Ali, had sent a telegram to him early in his boxing career, back when he was preparing to fight Duke Sabedong in his seventh professional fight at the Las Vegas Convention Center on

June 26, 1961. Ali was nineteen years old at the time, still Cassius Clay, not a Muslim, fighting outside Miami or Louisville for the first time as a pro. He was so young he was still putting his act together.

As part of the promotion for the fight, he appeared on a radio show with Gorgeous George, the wrestler. This was the character who became his model as a villain. Gorgeous George talked about how pretty he was, how wonderful, and how the Convention Center was sold out for his appearance the next night. Ali, whose appearance was far from sold out two nights later, went to see the wrestlers the next night, felt the passion and excitement in the building, and adapted what he saw.

YOUR YOUTHFUL GOOD HUMOR, PHYSICAL PROWESS AND FLIPPANT CHARM HAVE MADE YOU AN IDOL TO MANY AMERICAN YOUNG PEOPLE, Dr. King wrote in his telegram to Las Vegas. MAY GOD PROTECT YOU AND YOUR OPPONENT IN THE COMING CONTEST. I LOOK FORWARD TO TALKING WITH YOU SOMETIME IN THE FUTURE.

There had been other communications between the men, as FBI wiretaps would disclose ("C. told MLK to take care" and "watch out for them whites" in one wiretap), but their philosophies had been too different for a close friendship, even though they did share the same lawyer, Chauncey Eskridge. (The lawyer, after talking with Dr. King, passed the phone to Ali for that wiretapped conversation.) Ali had criticized the idea of integration, of wanting to be near a white someone who really didn't want a black man near him. King had criticized Ali for his criticism, said he should stick to boxing, not engage in political discussions.

They would be linked forever as black icons for social change, but the picture was the one actual link, this one time the two men met in public. Probably the one time they ever met. Though nothing was explained about their discussion, some interesting developments happened after it took place. These developments began almost immediately.

A situation had become stressful in Louisville. Dr. King's latest struggle in Chicago had been for open housing. The goal of open housing was to strike down exclusionary practices against black home buyers and renters, to open up the marketplace for better housing opportunities. Resistance in Chicago had been mighty, white home owners and real estate agents fighting the idea, citing the right of a man to sell or rent to whomever he wanted.

This same fight now had begun in Louisville. An ordinance was in front of the Board of Aldermen to set up fines against sellers or rental agents who discriminated for race, religion, or national origin. The same arguments from Chicago had arisen, this time with a Southern accent. The words were not pretty.

One of the leaders of the Louisville protest was Dr. King's brother, Reverend A. D. Williams King, pastor of the West Chestnut Street Baptist Church. The SCLC had been involved from the beginning as confrontations and challenges unfolded nightly. Dr. King was scheduled to speak at his brother's church the next night and lead a protest march. Muhammad Ali—the foe of integration, the member of the Nation of Islam—after meeting Dr. King today would speak this night at the Antioch Baptist Church. A protest march would follow.

It was a curious event. Ali stood in the pulpit of a religion he didn't believe and talked to people involved in a cause he didn't believe was worth their time and effort. He was not afraid to tell them they were wrong.

"Black people should seek dignity and self respect before seeking open housing," he told the black people who were gathered together to seek open housing. "Ghettos don't make slums, people make slums.

"The condition our people are in now, if you gave them a $93 million [housing] project, they'll make a slum out of it in 24 hours . . . but intelligent people can turn a slum into a paradise."

He bobbed and weaved as if he were a Sunday morning revivalist. He grabbed at the lapels on his suit coat to make a point. In the house of Jesus, he talked about the Honorable Elijah Muhammad. He said that Elijah Muhammad's message had allowed him to find "the plain truth." He didn't mention Jesus, except when he moved into his boilerplate talk about race.

Why is white always pictured as good and black always pictured as bad? That was the familiar question.

"In church we see a white Jesus," he said. "The angels we see are white. . . . The good cowboys ride white horses. When we go to heaven we go to a white milky way, Mary had a little lamb, its fleece was white as snow. We have the White House. . . ."

The Reverend Ralph Abernathy, vice president of the SCLC, followed Ali to the pulpit. He admitted that he didn't share many of the heavyweight champion's beliefs, but said that freedom was the goal for everyone. Freedom for him would include freedom of housing.

"I don't want to move to Boston," Reverend Abernathy said. "It's too cold. I don't want to move to California. That's too far away. I want to be free in the South. If we can get freedom in Kentucky, Georgia, Alabama and Mississippi, I'd be happy as a jaybird."

Three buses then took 150 protesters, Ali not among them, from Antioch Baptist in the predominantly black West End of Louisville to DeSales High School in the predominantly white South End. The protesters marched to the house of Joseph Miller Krieger, the head of the opposition Concerned Citizens Committee. They chanted and sang freedom songs for half an hour. He did not appear until they were leaving, when he came out of the house and told reporters he was "amused."

The next day at a press conference at the SCLC meetings, Dr. King made a step in Ali's direction. Never in favor of the war in Vietnam, he mostly had kept out of the debate until recent months in fear of splitting support for civil rights. The increased body counts and increased civil disobedience had drawn him into the fray. It was not a popular decision in some usually liberal households, but he had come out against the war in a couple of speeches and led an antiwar march of five thousand demonstrators in Chicago a few days before he flew to Louisville.

The SCLC, his organization, now was officially against the war. A resolution condemning the war had been passed. Dr. King read the organization's five objections to what was happening in Vietnam. They differed a bit from Ali's reasons for resistance, but also covered much of the same ground:

- The money spent in military and pacification programs in Vietnam could be better spent aiding the ghetto and rural Negro.
- The war has confused the public and drowned the Negro's cry for equal rights.

- A "racially exclusive" Selective Service System discriminates against the poor and places Negroes in the front lines of combat in disproportionately high numbers.
- To win the world to the cause of freedom, this nation must practice at home what it preaches abroad.
- Engaging in a morally and politically unjust war undermines the nonviolence philosophy of the United States.

"Rather than have the American Dream slain in the jungles and swamps of Vietnam," Dr. King said, "we pledge ourselves to do everything in our power to end that war."

He gave a fiery speech about the local open-housing situation that night at his brother's Baptist church. News had arrived that eighteen pickets at a meeting of the Concerned Citizens Committee at Memorial Auditorium had been arrested. Dr. King preached the doctrine of civil disobedience one more time.

"We still have our marching shoes," he said. "The day of the demonstrations will be over the day that injustice is over in America. There is no better way to dramatize and expose social evil than to tramp, tramp, tramp."

Five buses then took three hundred demonstrators to Memorial Auditorium to protest the arrests. Dr. King was in the lead. The arrests that night were the first civil rights arrests in Louisville in three years. The SCLC was going to make a stand in the city.

Ali's trip to the courtroom had not been as successful as his visit with Dr. King. A day earlier a federal appeals court in Cincinnati had refused a request for a temporary restraining order that would have postponed his induction call. In U.S. district court in Louisville, he watched as Judge James F. Gordon denied his two different appeals.

One was a challenge of the racial composition of Draft Board 47. Only one black member of the board, recently added, gave the group any diversity. That was determined by Judge Gordon to be an issue that could be debated only after Ali had gone through the induction process. Denied. The second was the same request that had been made in Cincinnati, a three-judge panel to determine whether the lack of black people on Draft Board 47 made this a case of racial discrimination. Also denied.

Hayden Covington said that draft boards were supposed to be composed of neighbors. If Ali had been before a neighborhood board, there would have been a lot of black faces on it. The late addition of one black man was almost an insult.

"Bringing this man out of the woodpile is a confession of error," the lawyer said.

"This is a routine case," Fred Drogola of the Justice Department argued, denying any bias against Ali. "It is this man's turn to go and he has had his day before the Selective Service System."

The decision sent Ali's new draft board in Houston, Draft Board 61, into action. The letter was in the mail before Ali shook Dr. Martin Luther King's hand.

ORDER FOR TRANSFERRED MAN
TO REPORT FOR INDUCTION

From: The President of the United States
To: Mr. Cassius Marcellus Clay Jr.
AKA Muhammad Ali
5962 Ardmore Street
Houston, Texas 77021

Greetings:
    Having heretofore been ordered to report for induction by Local Board No. 47, State of Kentucky, Louisville, Kentucky, which is your draft board of origin, and having been transferred upon your own request to Local Board No. 61, State of Texas, Houston, Texas, which is your Local Board of Transfer for delivery to an induction station, you will therefore report to the last named Local Board at 3rd Floor, 701 San Jacinto St., Houston, Texas 77022 on April 28, 1967 at 8:30 A.M.

This appeared to be a final date. The air remaining in his challenges seemed just about spent. The champ had saved seventeen days by switching draft boards.

Covington said there was still hope. He had filed two appeals with the Supreme Court that were soon rejected. He then filed two more. Any approach might work. He was indefatigable, matched against a Justice Department that he said was being forced by public opinion to speed the case through the courts. The Supreme Court, always hardest to figure, was his hole card.

"At the time I started arguing the draft case of the Jehovah's Witnesses during World War II, the German general Rommel was chasing Montgomery across Africa," he said. "Things weren't good for the Allies, so we got a negative ruling from the Supreme Court. When the case came back again, Montgomery was chasing Rommel back across the desert—we were winning—so the judges came out with a decision exempting the Witness from service."

While waiting for whatever might happen—miracle or the expected— Ali tried to make a last bit of money. He signed a hurry-up fight before induction. Floyd Patterson was dragged out from the past as the opponent. Floyd had a bad back when they first met, remember? There was all that talk about humiliation, remember? Floyd had knocked out Henry Cooper and two lesser lights in the past seventeen months. Floyd would be a solid opponent, wouldn't he?

The papers were signed by the two parties at the Americana Hotel in New York on April 4, 1967. The fight would be on April 25 at the Las Vegas Convention Center and shown on closed-circuit outlets around the country. This would be Ali's real good-bye, off to the army or jail three days later in Houston. Step right up. Everything would happen fast while Covington pushed his appeals in Washington.

"I want the people to come out and see this living legend," the living legend said. "I don't say I'll never fight again, but it will be the last one for quite a while. You will see the fighting sensation, the greatest machine since automation."

Six days later the fight was canceled by the Nevada Athletic Commission. Done.

The major force behind the rejection was Governor Paul Laxalt. The governor said he had watched the first Ali-Patterson bout and "never felt emptier" at the conclusion. He feared a repeat would give the state of Nevada a bad name.

"If Clay should win after he admitted packing Patterson for eight rounds in the last fight, then everybody will feel it is just one of those things," Laxalt said. "If Floyd wins, it will create suspicion throughout the world."

The decision was announced the same day Ali arrived in Vegas to begin training. He had a brief press conference, then turned around and went home. In his good-bye, he did not forget the wrestling lessons he had learned in the gambling city in his youth.

"Tell all the fans and all the people that their idol, the living legend—they may be looking at him for the last time," he said. "It will be sad from here on out. Watching two flat-footed heavyweights slugging and butting each other. There'll be no more poems, no more Ali shuffle. You can take this game to the graveyard.

"Look and look close and remember me."

For a moment, Pittsburgh surfaced as a possible site, but Pennsylvania governor Raymond P. Shafer followed Laxalt's lead and rejected the event. Herbert Muhammad said from Chicago that the fight officially was canceled. He also said that racial and religious prejudice were the causes.

"If the champion was a white man, there'd be a fight," Herbert Muhammad said. "No doubt about it."

The open-housing situation in Louisville had grown worse while all this was happening. The Board of Aldermen, as expected, had voted against the measure, 9–3. The demonstrations, as expected, had begun immediately and continued for a week. The confrontations had grown uglier each night. On Monday night, three demonstrators had been hit by rocks thrown by hecklers. Twenty hecklers were arrested, mostly teenagers.

On Tuesday, Ali returned to the scene.

"I'm here to be with my people," he said. "The whole world is watching Louisville and I'm worried about what my people are doing."

Again, he said he did not see the point of the marches.

"What is the use of fighting and dying so you can live next door to the white man who doesn't want you there?" he asked.

He spoke at another Christian church, the Quinn Chapel AME, said "I never have been so moved" by a situation, but the situation would grow worse. More protesters would be arrested each night as they marched on white neighborhoods. More hecklers would confront the protesters, some carrying signs that read "White Power" or "Back to Africa." Two members of the American Nazi Party from Chicago would be arrested. A police cruiser would be overturned. It was an interracial mess.

Ali gave a press conference in his hotel room before he left the city. There were two situations he wanted to address. The first was the trouble on the streets. He couldn't believe what was happening in his hometown.

"As world heavyweight champion, I know the difference between a fair fight and a foul one," he said. "And this fight with cowardly white hoodlums, partly supported by the police, against peaceful black people, who seek only what should be given to every human being, is a foul one."

The second situation was more personal. He wanted to announce that he would not be going into the army on his induction date or any other date. This was not exactly news after all the things he had said in the past, but it was a measured distillation of his thoughts and reasons. Louisville and the current troubles were included. He would appear for the induction, but he would not go. He had a prepared statement that he read sitting down:

Why should they ask me to put on a uniform and go 10,000 miles from home and drop guns and bullets on brown people in Vietnam while so-called Negro people in Louisville are treated like dogs and denied simple human rights? No, I'm not going 10,000 miles from home to help murder and burn another poor nation simply to continue the domination of white slave masters of the darker people the world over. This is the day when such evils must come to an end. I have been warned that to take such a stand would cost me millions of dollars. But I have said it once and I will say it again. The real enemy of my people is here. I will not disgrace my religion, my people or myself by becoming a tool to enslave those who are fighting for their own justice, freedom and equality. . . . If I thought the war was going to bring freedom and equality to 22 million of my people, they wouldn't have to draft

me, I'd join tomorrow. I have nothing to lose by standing up for my
beliefs. So I'll go to jail, so what? We've been in jail for 400 years.

This was a literate extension of "I got nothing against those Viet Congs."
It wasn't written by him, no doubt about that, but it was read by him.
Presidents have speechwriters. These were his thoughts, his reasons.
Louisville was a final voice in the argument. The words that he blurted
out, half thinking, intoxicated by the sound of his young voice, four-
teen months earlier, had been sanded and bent into a sturdier shape.
He sounded much better than he did as an unblinking member of the
Nation of Islam.

"The situation in Louisville has a lot to do with my decision not to go
into the Army," he said, "but it's not the main reason."

Then again, he still was a member of the Nation of Islam.

The demonstrations in Louisville would continue to grow larger and
nastier for a while. The events of Kentucky Derby week in May were
canceled due to the protests. Threats were made to shut down the
Derby. Counterthreats were made by the Ku Klux Klan to defend
the Derby. Martin Luther King was forced to return and work a deal
with Derby officials, scheduling a protest march on the deserted streets
of Louisville while the race was being run.

A change of strategy eventually occurred for the marchers. The
march ended, but voter registration efforts began. Allied with the
Kentucky AFL-CIO and the Democratic Party, the SCLC was able to
replace eleven of the twelve aldermen in the November elections. The
open-housing law was passed in December.

Ali went from Louisville to Washington, D.C. The champ arrived
at Friendship Airport in Linthicum Heights, Maryland, on Friday,
April 21, 1967. He had a busy schedule ahead of him.

He would give a speech at Howard University on Saturday. He would
give a speech at the Lorton Reformatory and Youth Center in Lorton,
Virginia, on Sunday. Speeches at the Workhouse at Occoquan and the
city jail might or might not happen. He definitely would speak at the
Sunday service at Muhammad's Mosque No. 4, located in a large white

house at 1519 4th Street NW. He would be everywhere in the Washington, D.C., area.

"Another professor at the school, Dr. Lonnie Shabazz, was a minister of the Nation of Islam," Dr. Nathan Hare of Howard remembered years later. "He asked if we were interested in having Muhammad Ali speak to the students. I said that we'd love it, but funding was very low. He said there was no fee involved."

Howard University was the foremost African American institution of higher learning in the land. Hare, thirty-four, was an assistant professor of sociology, an activist teacher in an activist time. The Howard campus was exploding with thoughts of black pride, black power, black rage against the status quo. Hare had called for "the overthrow of the Negro college with white innards" in order to "raise in its place a black university relevant to the black community and its needs." He was not a favorite of the university administration.

In the past week, students had burned effigies of Howard president James Nabrit Jr., director of the Selective Service Lewis B. Hershey, and liberal arts dean Albert Cassell. The idea of Muhammad Ali's rhetoric added to the mix was not seen as a great idea. The administration refused to allow the speech to be held in an indoor venue.

"I myself went to the audio-visual department and checked out a sound system," Hare said. "I set it up on the steps of Frederick Douglass Hall. There was the threat of rain. Outdoors. You wondered how many kids would come. Saturday morning after Friday night on a college campus. A lot of kids thought it was a joke. Muhammad Ali wouldn't come here. They just didn't believe it."

The reason Ali was in Washington was that two last appeals had been sent to the Supreme Court. The nine judges all lived in the D.C. area. They all presumably had television sets and read newspapers. Was the heavyweight champion of the world really a minister? They would see and hear for themselves. The thought would be fresh in their minds on Monday, when their decision to consider or reject the appeals presumably would be announced.

The strategy had the touch of Hayden Covington all over it. The nonresident resident of Houston (Ali) would arrive at just the right time to do his good work in a city (Washington) that never had been one of the stops on his normal itinerary. One more angle would be played.

Hare traveled with two or three local members of the NOI to pick up the celebrated visitor at the airport. Ali said he had "five or six" speeches that he usually gave, but would do something special for Howard. Hare was intrigued by the conversation that took place next in the car. Ali and the Muslims worked on a poem. Everyone contributed, offered suggestions, but Ali made the choices of what he wanted. Was this the way he wrote all his poems?

Dinner was also interesting. Hare was not a member of the NOI, but had been around members both in Chicago and in Washington. The Muslims said they ate only one meal per day, but never explained how large that one meal could be. Especially for Ali.

"He ordered 12 eggs," Hare said. "He ordered four and five servings of different items on the menu. What would be a meal for you or me was an appetizer for him. I never had seen anyone eat so much."

The boilerplate speech was all it was supposed to be. More. It later would be called "The Black Is Best" speech at Howard. Kids came from all directions once they heard this really was happening. Local residents came. If this had been a weekday, classes in session, the crowd would have been enormous. It still was a thousand people, probably more, everyone packed as close as possible to the steps.

"All you need to do is know yourself," Ali said, his amplified voice bouncing off the buildings. "We don't know who we are. We call ourselves Negroes, but have you ever heard of a place called Negroland?"

"Black dirt is the best dirt," he said. "Brown sugar causes fewer cavities. The blacker the berry, the sweeter the juice. . . ."

This was familiar material in unfamiliar surroundings. He never blinked.

He sang a version of "A White Man's Heaven Is a Black Man's Hell," the NOI hymn first recorded by Louis Farrakhan in 1955. He held a copy of *Message to the Blackman* high in the air and said it contained the truth. (Copies available from my brothers passing among you.) He said one more time that he would refuse to be inducted into the army "under any circumstances."

The kids loved it all. A bunch of them were chanting "Hell no, we won't go," Stokely Carmichael's slogan, at the end. One kid, William Battle, from 1444 W Street NW, volunteered to take Ali's place in the army for $1,000.

"No, brother," the champ said. "Your life is worth more than $1,000."

This was Ali's most publicized speech at a college campus since his troubles began. He seemed to enjoy it as much as the kids did. He signed copies of *The Messenger* at the end. The paper had a cartoon that showed a black man telling Uncle Sam that he would rather go to jail than go to war. The headline on the front page was "Justice on Trial!"

"The notes that he had for the speech were written in big, big letters," Hare said. "I never forgot that. I've never seen it with any other speaker. Each letter was, I don't know, maybe an inch high."

Hare went with him the next day to the reformatory in Lorton and to the NOI meeting. (Permissions to visit the Workhouse and the city jail were denied.) Ali told a crowd of 350 juvenile inmates in Lorton, "The day is here to change the old rugged cross for the golden star." He told a crowd of five hundred at the mosque, an overflow of 150 listening outside, that "this is one nigger they're not going to get."

He had to see now if the Supreme Court—along with all these other people—had been listening. If they had listened, fine, but if they also happened to read any of the hundred-plus newspapers that published the columns of syndicated sportswriter Red Smith, they also had a counterpoint to consider. Red saw the Muslims as the villains in the piece.

"There are draft dodgers in every war and Clay isn't the only slacker in this one," Smith wrote. "Reading the papers, though, you would think he was. This isn't the fault of the papers. It is his position as heavyweight champion of the world, presumably the best fighter in the world, that he is pacifist, that's news. When he demands deferment as a minister, that's also news, especially to anybody who has heard him preach. I have heard him preach and he does not fit my notion of a man of the cloth.

"When he hired a lawyer to charge that he is a victim of racial discrimination, to challenge the constitutionality of the Selective Service, to sniff out every loophole and fling up every possible obstacle in a tireless effort to controvert the law—well, you wonder who's really behind it all."

—

Ali was resting in his room at the Washington Hilton Hotel, tired by his weekend activities, when the Supreme Court announced on Monday morning that it would not review his case in either of the two appeals. This meant that his induction day still was Friday and he would be required to appear. A reporter from the *Washington Post* delivered the news to his door.

"Did they do that?" Ali said about the decision not to review. "I expected it. There isn't any justice for me. They didn't even give a reason for turning me down. They're hypocrites. I can't get justice but they want me to go thousands of miles to get justice for somebody else. They want me to get shot at."

He seemed subdued, resigned. There would be other appeals, other avenues to try, no doubt, but this trip was done.

On that same day the court also overturned a conviction of a Midland, Texas, man because an involuntary confession was admitted into evidence; supported a lower court decision that gave a small frozen pie company in Salt Lake City a judgment against three larger frozen pie companies; and declined to rule on twenty-one other cases. The decision on Ali was the one that made national headlines.

The phone began to ring—didn't it always?—and he rolled into his familiar pronouncements.

"If Allah thinks I should sacrifice everything for my religion, I'm ready," he said. "I don't care about boxing now. I must not care about it, because I am giving it up for my religion. I don't believe in killing people."

"What can I spend it on?" he said when asked about the money that no longer would arrive in great buckets. "I don't smoke or drink since I joined the Muslims. That is what made me champion. I only eat one meal a day. I don't gamble and I don't bother with girls any more, although they used to chase me. I can only wear one suit at a time, ride in only one car at a time. If I got to die, I got to die."

The course was set. He would go to Chicago for a couple of days, then go to Houston on Thursday and report to Local Draft Board No. 61 at 8:30 a.m. on Friday. The final rescue, the cinematic last call from somebody that would stop the process, had not arrived.

The phone rang again.

Howard Cosell was on the other end.

"I am making a prediction," Ali said to the sportscaster. "When my career ends you will die. You will dry up without me. I made you."

He laughed at his own joke.

"I will be at the Ardmore Arms," the champ said, when Cosell asked where he could be found in Houston on Thursday, the night before induction. "In a humble apartment in the ghetto."

There were no more options.

9

No

The moment turned out to be less momentous than he thought it would be. There were no riots around the world, not in Cairo or Accra or Cleveland or Louisville or anywhere else. If you took away the news media, which turned out in human and technological force, cameras and people bashing into one another when the drafted man made his entry and exit, when he made any small move, there was little disturbance in Houston at the gray four-story U.S. Custom House on San Jacinto Street.

The Armed Forces Examining and Entrance Station was on the third floor. Ali and his three lawyers—Covington, Eskridge, and Quinnan Hodges, a Houston attorney added for local connections—cut through the gathered reporters and cameramen without comment. They filled an elevator. At the third floor, Ali went beyond a barrier by himself, joining thirty-five other draftees who were scheduled for induction. He was the only one who had brought three lawyers with him.

"I kind of feel sorry for the old guy," twenty-two-year-old John McCullouch of Huntsville, Texas, one of the inductees, pushed to the side of the elevator by the group, said about the twenty-five-year-old Ali. "He can't get away from all this mess."

The champ was gone for almost five hours, the tests and physical examinations and the moment of reckoning all taking place away from the public hoo-ha. The military public information office did issue a string of memos detailing the results of his physical tests. Ali did not have to retake the mental tests. One memo said that as a Muslim he did not eat the ham sandwich in the box lunch handed to all inductees. Stop the presses.

The media, left to await his return, found other diversions.

"He could have gotten out any time he wanted," Chauncey Eskridge told reporters. "I'm a colonel in the Illinois National Guard and I offered to put him in my regiment, but he didn't want that."

"He will never serve a day in jail," Hayden Covington declared.

"See that black man over there?" Raymond X, minister of Houston Mosque No. 45, asked as a draftee passed. "He's got two babies, his back's half broken, and Uncle Sam wants him. Give me liberty or give me death! Where's the Negroes working in this building? Only one here and he's pushing the Red Cross coffee pot."

The news photographers, finding the few protesters available outside, instigated a demonstration. Seventeen kids with hastily made signs walked around in a circle and sang "I want to be a Mau Mau." Somebody burned a piece of paper and said it was a draft card.

Ali was loose and friendly during most of the day, the other draftees reported before they boarded a bus to Fort Polk, Louisiana, and their new lives. He fooled around, did the Ali Shuffle in his underwear. He was pleasant. They said someone asked him if he really was afraid to go to Vietnam. Ali pretended he was holding a rifle and looked around, back and forth. He said he'd be more nervous about the people on his side in Vietnam than he was about the other side.

"The Viet Cong don't scare me," he said. "If they . . . don't get me, two guys from Georgia would. I'd have to watch for the Viet Cong and the guys behind me, too."

The jokes stopped when the induction ceremony took place. Ali was among eight candidates brought into a room. They were lined up in two rows of four. Ali was third from the left in the second row. Lieutenant S. Steven Dunkley was behind a lectern at the front.

"You are about to be inducted into the Armed Forces of the United States in the Army, the Navy, the Air Force or the Marine Corps, as indicated by the service announced following your name when called," he read from a piece of paper. "You will take one step forward as your name and service are called and such step will constitute your induction into the Armed Forces indicated."

Dunkley had a stack of cards. He read one name from each card. The seventh name was "Muhammad Ali."

"Was he tense?" a reporter asked McCullouch, the draftee, later.

"Everybody was tense," the new soldier said. "You have to realize, it was a big step for us to take, too. It looked to me like he was nervous.

"The officer said, 'Muhammad Ali, would you step forward' . . . and then there's just silence. I saw the officer take his card and put it on the desk."

Dunkley asked three times. Ali never moved. The other draftees—now members of the Armed Forces—were led out of the room. Navy lieutenant C. P. Hartman arrived and escorted Ali to another room. Hartman explained the ramifications of refusal. This was a felony punishable by five years in prison and a $10,000 fine. Did Ali understand all this? Ali said he did.

He was led back to hear Dunkley ask the question again. Ali refused again, was asked to write "I refuse to be inducted into the Armed Forces of the United States" and sign his name. He then was released, free to leave. The legal action now would move to the courts.

The pressroom in the Custom House was soon filled with disappointment and chaos when he arrived. Accompanied by his lawyers, he announced that he would not speak. After all the waiting by the reporters, he would be silent. There really was no need for the forest of assembled microphones. A prepared press release would do his talking. No, he wouldn't read it.

"How were you treated?" a reporter asked.

"Respectable," Ali replied.

That was all he said.

He handed out the press release himself. If he came to someone he didn't recognize, he asked, "Who are you?" If the name and publication in answer seemed authentic, he handed the person a copy.

There would be no mention of those Viet Congs. There would be no rat-a-tat takedown of the day, the military, or the U.S. government. The lawyers and the Honorable Elijah Muhammad had preached some obvious sense. Verbal gymnastics would not help anything right here. The press release would do the job, though the presentation would not be as colorful as if it were done in Ali's voice. The sound of lawyers typing dominated the words.

It is in the light of my consciousness as a Muslim minister and my own personal convictions that I take my stand in rejecting the call to be inducted in the armed services. I do so with the full realization of its implications and possible consequences. I have searched my conscience and I find I cannot be true to my belief in my religion by accepting such a call.

My decision is a private and individual one and I realize that this is a most crucial decision. In taking it, I am dependent solely on Allah as the final judge of these actions brought about by my own conscience.

I strongly object to the fact that so many newspapers have given the American public and the world the impression that I have only two alternatives in this stand: either I go to jail or go to the Army. There is another alternative and that alternative is justice. If justice prevails, if my Constitutional rights are upheld, I will be forced to go neither to the Army nor jail. In the end I am confident that justice will come my way for the truth must eventually prevail.

I am looking forward to immediately continuing my profession.

As to the threat voiced by certain elements to "strip" me of my title, this is merely a continuation of the same artificially induced prejudice and discrimination.

Regardless of the difference in my outlook, I insist upon my rights to pursue my livelihood in accordance with the same rights granted to other men and women who have disagreed with the policies of whatever administration was in power at the time.

I have the world heavyweight title, not because it was "given" to me, not because of my race or religion, but because I won it in the ring because of my boxing ability. Those who want to "take" it and hold a series of auction-type bouts not only do me a disservice, but actually disgrace themselves. I am certain the sports fans and fair-minded people throughout America would never accept such a "titleholder."

The stripping already had begun. Both the New York Athletic Commission and the World Boxing Association, an alliance of thirty state commissions, had been planning to take his title for weeks. The moment he didn't take that step, he became a former champ to those organizations. Other states, notably California and Texas, had indicated they would follow. The president of the British Boxing Council, also a vice president of the European Boxing Union, indicated those groups also would follow.

Ali's title would be vacated. Proposals already were being made for an eight-man tournament, featuring a string of people he had beaten, to select a replacement champion. Ali would be out of the picture.

"His refusal to enter the service is regarded by the commission to be detrimental to the best interests of boxing," said Edwin Dooley, head of the New York commission.

There apparently was no apparatus for appeal. The most attractive, most famous athlete in the country—in the entire world—could not make a buck at what he did. His job had been taken away from him as well as his title.

U.S. attorney Mort Susman said that Ali would not be indicted for "30 to 60 days." He also said that with appeals, the champ—okay, the former champ—would not face prison for another eighteen months or two years. He said nothing about where or how Ali would work during all this. Ali, again, said nothing.

When he returned to his suite at the Hotel America after his long day, not the Ardmore Arms, as promised, Howard Cosell was waiting.

"As you know, the heavyweight champion of the world has just made his decision," Cosell said into the camera for the ABC news. "He has rejected induction into the military forces. It is also his personal choice at this time to issue no statements, to talk to no one, though he has consented to sit here in front of this camera with this reporter."

The former champ did, indeed, sit in front of the camera next to the broadcaster. He didn't smile, didn't talk. Had there ever been a network news interview as curious as this one? Cosell kept talking as if he had landed an important moment with an important person. The man who did not take the ceremonial step was the man who did not say a word, not even "no" or "comment."

It was an interesting end to an interesting day.

—

The machinery of war—it should be noted—kept grinding while this sports page drama was played out in Houston. At about the same time Ali was telling the other draftees that he was more afraid of being shot by the two guys from Georgia than he was by the Viet Cong, General William Westmoreland, the commander of U.S. forces in Vietnam, addressed a joint session of Congress. This was an extraordinary moment, the first time in American history a battlefield commander addressed Congress while hostilities were taking place.

It also was red-white-and-blue theater.

"Backed at home by resolve, confidence, patience, determination and continued support, we will prevail in Vietnam over the Communist aggressor," the general declared to a standing ovation, one of nineteen he received during the speech.

Tall, slender, gray around the temples, Westmoreland was Lyndon Johnson's publicity man for the war. He stood stiff and straight like a general, talked like a general, looked like a general. He wore seven rows of campaign ribbons on his chest and four stars on each shoulder, saluted his audience in three directions: left, right, and center. He was there to sell tickets. His presence was a sign that the war was going to get bigger before it got smaller, that the recent increases in bombing raids were only a start.

"For months now we have been successful in destroying a number of main force units," he said. "We will continue to seek out the enemy, catch him off guard and punish him at every opportunity."

There were now 438,000 U.S. troops in South Vietnam. Expectations were that this figure would be increased to 470,000 or 480,000 in the next few months. The chances that those thirty-five new recruits headed from the Custom House to Fort Polk would eventually land in Vietnam were very good.

"Developments during the past several weeks, the increased bombings and other things all point to a much wider war," Senator William Fulbright, an opponent of the war, said after the speech. "The general was preparing the ground for it."

"The immortal words of Stephen Decatur, 'My country, right or wrong,' could never be truer," said Congressman L. Mendel Rivers, a longtime proponent of the war. "It's too late to question whether it's right or wrong."

The Selective Service in Washington released some war numbers during the day, about the same time Ali turned down that ham sandwich. One number of interest was the 101,332 men who were classified 4-D, which meant they were ordained ministers or seminarians or divinity students at "recognized theological schools." Someone with a 4-D exemption, which was the primary designation that Ali sought, was not involved with the military in any way. Ali was not asking for a designation that was obscure or rare.

The number of men in conscientious objector status, 1-A-0 or 1-0, was 21,673. This was the classification Ali first attempted to receive, but changed when he learned the conscientious objectors still were required to serve in noncombat roles in the military. The total number of draft registrants as of April 1, 1967, was 34,056,393. The Selective Service said that the number of conscientious objector classifications remained a constant percentage of .05 or .06 of the entire draft pool.

Only 353 men had been convicted in the last fiscal year for failing to step forward at induction, less than three-hundredths of 1 percent of the 1.1 million men classified 1-A. Ali would be trying not to be No. 354. A noteworthy statistic was that while black men accounted for only 11 percent of servicemen in Vietnam, they accounted for 22.4 percent of the deaths.

In the daily war news, strange Asian names and locations were rattled off as if they were on some military stock ticker: American pilots in F-105 Thunderbirds downed two MiG-17s over Hanoi, the forty-third and forty-fourth of the war. . . . American planes also attacked the Dan Phuong highway causeway with three-thousand-pound bombs . . . also attacked the railroad supply tracks and surrounding tracks outside Hanoi . . . also, farther south, attacked an oil storage dump in Vinh, a highway bypass bridge near Thanh Hoa . . .

A battalion of Marines in South Vietnam staged a combined amphibious and helicopter assault twenty-five miles south of Da Nang. The operation was called "Beaver Cage." . . . A company of the U.S. First Division found a large cache of arms forty-five miles northeast of Saigon that included nine hundred hand grenades, two hundred rounds of mortar ammunition, and thirty-five thirty-pound mines. . . . American helicopter gunships killed ninety Viet Cong in the U Minh Forest, 162 miles southeast of Saigon.

Agence France-Presse reported "some of the heaviest bombing of the war" in Hanoi. "It appeared hundreds of bombs crashed in the northern outskirts as wave after wave of attackers moved over the target area for 15 minutes." . . . Reuters reported that Hanoi claimed that four U.S. planes were shot down over the city. . . .

In a short, one-paragraph AP story, under the headline "Casualties Identified," the Department of Defense "identified today 20 United States servicemen killed in action." Names were not included.

Manzoor Ahmad Janjooa, a young Pakistani, squatted outside the United States embassy in Karachi and vowed to "fast until death" unless Ali was spared from the draft. Xinhua, the Chinese Communist press agency, cited Ali's refusal to be inducted as another indicator that "more and more African Americans are joining the ranks to oppose the United States' war of aggression" because "they would rather go to jail than go to South Vietnam to kill their brothers." The New York Civil Liberties Union rattled off a letter to the New York State Athletic Commission calling its action against Ali, taking away his title, "as unprecedented as it is unprincipled."

Reactions to the moment in Houston varied, sometimes along predictable lines, sometimes not. Defiance of the draft and opposition to the war had become ascendant movements in the country. Two weeks earlier, Dr. Martin Luther King had led a hundred thousand marchers to the United Nations building, where he called for the end of bombing in North Vietnam. More than two hundred draft cards were burned. This was a new but growing phenomenon. In San Francisco, the same day, Dr. King's wife addressed a crowd of fifty thousand at Kezar Stadium. A prominent sign at both marches was SNCC chairman Stokely Carmichael's extension of Ali's complaint into "No Vietnamese Ever Called Me Nigger."

The sports page reaction was mostly negative. Some sportswriters were angry, but more were sad or confused. They wondered how this talented young guy, who wouldn't have been sent to combat anyway, no doubt about that, could have made this decision. What was he thinking?

Red Smith, *New York World Journal Tribune*—"The only feeling the young man evokes here is one of sadness. He is a victim. He is one of thousands of young American males trying to dodge the draft, though the attention he commands as heavyweight champion of the world creates an impression that he is the only one. He is blatantly defiant."

Shirley Povich, *Washington Post*—"It is too bad he went wrong. He had the makings of a national hero."

Larry Merchant, *New York Post*—"Withal, the notion persists that Ali Baby is playing the old beat-the-draft game, that his various legal ploys are hardly consistent with the present theme that he is a minister. Probably this is true. But it is his right to play the game as much as, say, George Hamilton, or the many professional jockos who hide out in National Guard and reserve units."

Jesse Outlar, *Atlanta Constitution*—"Of course, Clay is entitled to his views. Certainly he doesn't have to agree that U.S. troops should be in Vietnam. But when you are drafted they don't ask whether you desire to serve. You either serve or face the consequences."

Jimmy Cannon, *New York World Journal Tribune*—"Clay has done it to himself. He is the assassin who killed the great heavyweight champion of the world. . . . There is no way to defend Clay. . . . If Clay doesn't go into the service, some other kid will be taken out of turn in his place."

One supporter of Ali was Bud Collins of the *Boston Globe*. Collins, who used "Muhammad Ali," never "Clay," in his stories, said that the country had better find some answers in a hurry because thousands of kids were going to be coming along who were going to say they "ain't got nothing against them Viet Congs." He said he respected Ali for his decision.

"People continue to moan that 'he could have been a wonderful person, loved by all, if the Muslims hadn't gotten him,'" Collins wrote. "But he wouldn't have been Ali. The Muslims had a religion that appealed and he went their way, devoutly, living above reproach. A man is still supposed to be able to practice any religion, however strange, if he doesn't hurt anybody."

The indictment came, as expected, ten days after Ali's arrest. A twenty-one-member federal grand jury in Houston, which included one black face, sent the case to trial court. There was little debate—Ali never took the stand—because the fact was obvious that he did not step forward when called. That was the only fact that mattered.

The most notable argument concerned his passport. Prosecutor Mort Susman argued that the passport should be confiscated. Hayden Covington argued that Ali needed the passport to fight overseas to make money to fund his defense. Possible fights were being negotiated for Stockholm, Tokyo, Germany, and Lebanon. Judge Ben C. Connally ruled Ali could keep his passport for now.

The formalities of the arrest procedure took place in the U.S. marshal's office in the courthouse. Ali was fingerprinted, had his mug shots taken, posted a $5,000 bond for bail. He was loose and easy through it all, cracking jokes with the policemen, but on the way out of the building he stopped to argue with a black woman who yelled to him that he was being foolish not to accept the draft.

"You got some bad advice from your attorney," she said. "Your attorneys want to take all your money and then they'll leave you. What are you doing this for, anyway?"

"For religion," Ali replied. "Have you got any religion?"

She said she did. Ali said he should be able to have his religion, too. That was the most important part of what he was doing.

"Are you serious?" she said.

"Yes, I'm serious," he said. "I'm ready to die for it."

This was an argument he would have to repeat three weeks later on June 4, 1967, in Cleveland when football's Jim Brown, basketball's Bill Russell and Lew Alcindor, and a number of other prominent black athletes arranged to meet with him. It was an unprecedented gathering of athletic talent to tackle a problem far outside athletics. The purpose of the meeting was to convince Ali to give up his fight against the draft.

At least that was what the stories said.

"Negro Stars to Urge Clay to Enter Army" was the headline. The UPI report, same as other stories, began: "CLEVELAND—Some of the nation's top Negro athletes will meet with Cassius Clay here Sunday to try and convince him to accept induction into the army."

Logic would work. That was the idea. Jim Brown would talk some sense into him. Bill Russell would. This group of people would. These men spoke the same language, the language of the elite black athlete. They not only had survived, they had prospered on the playgrounds of professional sport. They would be able to tell him how lucky he was to be where he was. Take the deal. Go ahead. That would be the message.

"The meeting was supposed to be secret, but word got out a little bit," said Cleveland sports photographer Tony Tomsic. "I remember I called *Sports Illustrated*. I told them about Ali, Brown, Russell, Alcindor. They said, 'Come on. If that was going on, we would have heard about it.'"

The consensus everywhere was that Ali should take a deal. Eskridge, the lawyer, had arranged a deal. Bob Arum had arranged a deal. Mort Susman, the district attorney, even offered a deal, even thought for a while that Ali would take it. The list of people who advised him to go ahead, go into the army, be like Elvis, perform for the troops, was long, getting longer. This meeting was the best chance that he would listen.

Even his manager, Herbert Muhammad, wanted this to work. That was a surprise.

"Herbert wanting Ali to go into the service was a shocker," Jim Brown told Branson Wright of the *Cleveland Plain Dealer* years later. "I thought the Nation of Islam never would look at it this way. But Herbert figured the Army would give Ali special consideration so he could continue his career. But he couldn't talk to Ali about that, so he reached out to me and I had the dilemma of finding a way to give Ali the opportunity to express his views without any influence. I never told Ali about my conversation with Herbert. I never told anyone, really."

Brown had called the meeting. He still was involved with Herbert and with Ali in business through Main Bout Inc. Retired from football for over a year, he also had started the Negro Industrial Economic Union, an organization to help black entrepreneurs.

The union planned to have offices in different cities around the country. Some of the athletes he called to the meeting would be involved. Among its ventures, the NIEU would handle the closed-circuit shows for Ali's fights in each of these cities. Ali would be a prime producer of revenue.

Most important for Brown, though, he was Ali's friend.

He had been around from the Cassius Clay beginning in Miami Beach. He liked the kid a lot. The business situation came out of friendship, not the other way around. (Ali introduced him one day at a Houston sparring session and boasted, "Jim Brown don't carry footballs no more. He carries briefcases.") The only thing he wanted Ali to do was whatever Ali wanted to do.

"People don't realize that the United States government was what we were fighting," Brown said. "And that's a very powerful force and they did want Ali [to go into the service] to make an example out of him and that was one of the reasons that I called the meeting because he was basically alone and this great force was going to try and bring him down and I conjured up this idea of bringing top athletes who were like-minded. Certain athletes did not get invited."

The meeting was held at the Negro Industrial Economic Union at 105-15 Euclid Avenue on the fringe of Hough, the Cleveland ghetto, where race riots had occurred within the past year. Brown, Russell, and Alcindor were joined by Willie Davis, defensive tackle for the Green Bay Packers; John Wooten, Sid Williams, and Walter Beach of the Cleveland Browns, Bobby Mitchell and Jim Shorter of the Washington Redskins; and attorney Carl Stokes, who would be elected mayor of Cleveland in November.

Brown had drawn up a guest list of open minds. The men he picked, some of whom had been in the military, arrived with different viewpoints, but they were all people Brown thought would listen to Ali. If Ali decided to backtrack, go into the army, they could say that they had convinced him. If he decided not to go, they could say that he had their blessing.

The meeting lasted two and a half, maybe three hours.

Ali won over his audience as if these famous athletes were a bunch of schoolkids from Howard University. There was no contest.

"I came there ready to talk him into going into the service," Bobby Mitchell said. "I actually felt that way. He whipped my behind pretty quick, because he can talk. But when it was all over, I felt pretty good walking out of there saying 'We back him.'"

"I'd been in the service," Willie Davis said. "But after I heard him talk, I was on his side."

Ali's passion about his religion was what shone through his words. He talked about how he was afraid of nothing, because his strength came through Allah. He said he walked around without bodyguards, no matter what the threat, because Allah would take care of him. He said, again, that he was ready to die for his beliefs.

How do you argue against that? The athletes realized early in the conversation that he knew more about the subject of the draft and the law than any of them. This was his life. How do you step in from the outside and try to change his mind? He was a lot smarter than any of those army tests ever indicated. This man could talk. There was never a chance his mind could be changed.

"The way this whole thing was promoted was false," Ali said after the meeting ended. "We're old buddies, friends. What we call soul brothers."

The group posed for a picture. Russell, Ali, Brown, and Alcindor, the superstars, were in the front. Everybody wore a suit jacket and tie. This could have been the picture of the announcement of a business deal, a grand political pronouncement, everything formal and proper. It was a singular moment in American sport, never to be repeated.

"We just wanted to get the facts on matters involved in this case," Brown told reporters. "After two and a half hours of friendly discussion we decided that he is sincere in his belief. He convinced us that his stand is based on that."

"I am still a Muslim," Ali interjected.

Racial relations in the country bothered the athletes more than anything Ali did or didn't do. That was the lesson the participants took away from the day. Brown and Russell already were active in social causes. Alcindor, who would become a Muslim in a renegade sect from the NOI and change his name to Kareem Abdul-Jabbar, would enter his senior year at UCLA. He also would become active in social causes.

"What I would rather have people concerned about are juries in the South that make a mockery out of our court system or a murderer acquitted in the South and writing a magazine article about how he did it," Brown said, evoking the memory of Emmett Till. "Such injustices are far more important to the future of our country than the draft status of Muhammad Ali—or, if you prefer, Cassius Clay.

"He's extremely religious and with people like that religion comes first. What do you do with a man's belief?"

Russell put his thoughts in a first-person article in *Sports Illustrated* that he wrote with Tex Maule. He said he had been stunned by Ali's faith. He suggested changing the word "Muslim" in any story about Ali to "Catholic" or "Baptist" or "Christian." The perception of this controversial character who didn't drink or smoke or chase women late into the night would be entirely different. Wouldn't it?

"The hypocritical and sometimes fanatical criticism of Ali is, it seems to me, a symptom of the deeper sickness of our times," Russell wrote. "I feel sorry for the court that tries him: it must be sensitive to public opinion and it cannot operate in a vacuum. If Ali is acquitted some people will say that they were afraid not to acquit him. If he is convicted the judge will have to give him the maximum sentence. That is because of the emotional climate of the country today."

Russell closed with a statement that any of the men at the meeting would have backed. A change of heart never was a possibility.

"I'm not worried about Muhammad Ali," Russell said. "He is better equipped than anyone I know to withstand the trials in store for him. What I'm worried about is the rest of us."

The trial opened on June 19, 1967, in federal court in Houston with jury selection. There was a delay at the start because the same pool of jurors was being used for the trial of some accused heroin smugglers. That jury was filled first.

Ali roamed the halls of the federal courthouse during the wait, singing and joking. He did not have the downbeat, anxious look of a normal criminal defendant. He talked with everyone, anyone. A woman handed him a Bible and asked him to autograph it.

"This Bible doesn't mention the word 'Negro,'" he said. "But when you read about Daniel in the lion's den, you're talking about Negroes and when you read about the lost sheep, you are reading about 22 million Negroes."

Percy Foreman, the famous trial attorney, was involved in the heroin smuggling case. Ali grabbed him when he passed in the corridor.

"Hayden, Hayden," he yelled to Hayden Covington, "you're fired. I got me a lawyer."

H. Rap Brown, chairman of the Student Nonviolent Coordinating Committee, who had been vocal and threatening about Ali's situation, was also in the corridor. At one point, earlier in the month, Brown had promised that thirty thousand Muslims would descend on the city for the trial. U.S. attorney Mort Susman, fearful of that situation, had taken Ali and his lawyers to lunch at the once-segregated Houston Club and asked for help. He was grateful when Ali agreed and told him not to worry. The thirty thousand Muslims had not arrived, but Brown was still making threats.

"If anything happens to Muhammad Ali, there will be retaliation by the Negro people," he said. "I think the whole corrupt America is on trial here."

If this was the case, it wasn't a very dramatic trial of corrupt America. The all-white jury was picked, six men and six women, and proceedings began immediately and ended the next day.

The fact that the government brought in a black assistant prosecutor was an interesting note, but not more than that. Carl Walker, forty-three years old, the first black assistant U.S. attorney in the South, had been assigned to handle the many draft-evasion cases that had begun to flood the office. More famous than the others, perhaps, this still was just another case.

He explained later in life that he was a fan of Ali, liked him personally, liked boxing, but his job was to prosecute. Ali certainly fought men he liked. This situation was no different. Business was business. The question was whether Ali had violated the law. His religious beliefs did not matter here.

"Sincerity is not the issue," he told the jury. "The issue is whether he refused to obey the law. It is our law, for all of us, regardless of what motivated him."

"This is an extraordinary case with an extraordinary man," argued Ali's Houston lawyer, Quinnan Hodges. "Never have I seen a more sincere, honest man."

The government called all its four witnesses before the trial was recessed at the end of the first day. All four were military officers who were on duty when Ali refused to step forward. Lieutenant Stephen

Dunkley said he called both "Cassius Clay" and "Muhammad Ali." There was no response to either name. He then called both names again.

"What happened?" Susman then asked navy lieutenant Clarence Hartman.

"Nothing," Hartman replied.

This was the only fact the government had to prove. Judge Joe McDonald Ingraham, sixty-three, told the jury the only fact that had to be considered was whether the accused had refused to be inducted into the armed services. Covington's arguments the next day about the racial composition of the draft board and his contention Ali was a minister did not matter. They would be heard during an appeal process.

The one comment Ali and his defense team found objectionable was when Susman, who also spoke, seemed to indicate that the Nation of Islam, the Muslims, were making Ali's decisions for him. Susman said he had studied the religion and found it "as much political as it is religious."

"If I can say so, Sir," Ali immediately interjected from the defense table, "my religion is not political in no way."

Ingraham told him this was not his chance to talk.

Covington said that Ali had not been under the influence of the Muslims in any way. The decision had been his own, an act of "sincerity and honesty."

The jury listened to the closing arguments and was directed to a room for deliberation. Twenty-one minutes later it gave its expected verdict: guilty.

Both sides argued for a reduced sentence. Susman noted that Ali's only previous troubles with the law had been driving offenses and that, yes, he had been an American hero when he won that gold medal in Rome in 1960. Covington and Hodges said that eighteen months would be an appropriate sentence since that seemed to be the average sentence other defendants in his situation received.

Judge Ingraham listened to neither side. He imposed the maximum penalty of five years in jail, plus a $10,000 fine. This would be interpreted by Ali's supporters as a signal that the Justice Department was in control, that it wanted to send a message to squeaky wheels everywhere, especially black squeaky wheels. Ingraham said the reason he gave the maximum sentence was that changes would be made during the appeal process. This was only a starting point.

"It's just what I thought," Ali said to reporters. "It bears out the teachings of the Honorable Elijah Muhammad and the mighty Allah."

He had spent a lot of his time in court drawing pictures while the lawyers did their business. He and his lawyers showed some of the pictures to the press. They were the drawings of a bored teenager—a plane flying into the rising sun, a boat passing through mountains, mystic symbols, busywork. One was a doodle with flourishes around his name. That was "Muhammad Ali."

In Louisville, the leaders of the open-housing campaign gave support to their friend. They wondered why no one else in the city was joining them.

"A few years ago when Muhammad Ali first won the championship, you couldn't say enough nice things about him in Louisville," said Hulbert James, director of the West End Community Council. "Now all of us by our silence have deserted him."

"This sentence is incredible," said Floyd McKissick, director of the Congress of Racial Equality. "Black America will certainly question a two-day trial in which an all white jury, six men and six women, took only 20 minutes to reach this verdict against Muhammad Ali."

The case now had an official name as it proceeded through the appellate courts: *Cassius Marsellus Clay, Jr.* [sic] *aka Muhammad Ali v. United States.* The spelling of his middle name, Marcellus, was wrong because he had misspelled it when he filled out his first form for Draft Board 47 in Louisville.

He was in Los Angeles three days later, on June 23, 1967. His conviction made him the foremost symbol of draft resistance in the country, and he was asked to be part of his first peace demonstration. He agreed and was dropped into—drove himself, actually, in a brown Rolls-Royce— the kind of raucous, chaotic situation he always had tried to avoid.

A crowd estimated at ten thousand had gathered at Cheviot Park. The idea was to hear some speeches, hear some songs, try out some antiwar chants, and then march down the Avenue of the Stars to the Century Plaza Hotel, where Lyndon Johnson, accompanied by his wife,

Lady Bird, was scheduled to speak at a $500-per-plate fund-raising dinner for Democratic high rollers. Eighty different antiwar groups were involved, demonstrators of all ages, sizes, and ethnicities. Picket signs were provided.

Ali arrived to cheers. He autographed what a newspaper said were "hundreds of draft cards" for male demonstrators, then stood on top of a garbage can to give his speech.

"Anything designed for peace and to stop the killing of people, I'm 100 per cent for," he said in his remarks. "I'm not a leader. I'm not here to advise you. But I do encourage you to express yourselves."

This was the closest to a red meat comment he ever would deliver to a group of demonstrators. He still pulled his punch. As he did in Louisville at the open-housing rallies, he stopped short of telling the assembled folk to "go get 'em." His fight against the draft was in a different framework. He was not an antiwar protester the same way these draft-card-burning, chanting kids were. He had a religious objection. He was a minister, remember?

H. Rap Brown, from the Student Nonviolent Coordinating Committee, was not as shy. He compared LBJ to Hitler.

"I can't believe Lyndon Johnson is more humane than Hitler," Brown said. "Hitler gassed people to death. Johnson bombs them to death."

Dr. Benjamin Spock, the baby doctor and pacifist, spoke. He said that the government was trying to divide the peace and civil rights groups from one another. Irving Sarnoff, chairman of the Peace Action Committee, said that America's violence in Vietnam was encouraging violence at home. He turned out to be more right about this subject than he knew.

When the march began, Ali was not part of it. Problems evolved in a hurry. Los Angeles law-enforcement forces had gathered en masse, 1,300 policemen, to deal with trouble. It was the largest local show of force since Paul Robeson sang at Wrigley Field in South LA in 1949, more than twice the number of policemen on the job at any one time during the Watts riots in 1965. Governor Ronald Reagan had let it be known that the National Guard also was ready if trouble began. An injunction had been issued in Santa Monica to keep the front of the hotel open to traffic, free from trouble.

Trouble, of course, happened with all this attention to stopping trouble. The law-enforcement people enforced the injunction by swinging batons when necessary, which seemed to be often. Some of the resisters resisted. The crowd was so large and in such a confined space that escape was inconvenient if not impossible. Many heads were opened, many torsos bruised. Fifty-one people were arrested.

This was one of the first big anti-Vietnam demonstrations for peace to run amok, demonstrators clashing with police. It was a preview of what would happen in the future across the country. LBJ, who worried that he would have to be hustled out of the banquet because of the disturbance, never did recover. His public appearances were curtailed in number, and limited to safe locations. Nine months later he would decide not to run for reelection. This demonstration set a standard for the future.

Two weeks later, Ali was forced to give up his passport, which ruined possibilities for a bunch of proposed nontitle foreign fights that he thought would cover his legal and living expenses. At the top of the list was a bout against Floyd Patterson in Tokyo. Judge Ingraham, making the decision at a hearing in Houston, cited the fact that Ali had been involved in antiwar activities in Los Angeles while on bail. He mentioned the autographs on the draft cards.

Ali would never take part in another peace demonstration. This was it.

10

Married

This was a surprise. In the midst of everything, his old life being dismantled piece by public piece, his boxing career on hold, his revenue source gone, the prospect of five years in prison looming over him like the shadow from a very large government building, the newly defrocked heavyweight champion of the world made a change in his personal status. He got married.

CHICAGO, August 18, 1967 (UPI)—Cassius Clay, the former heavyweight champion who faces a five-year prison term for refusing to be drafted, was married today to a 17-year-old member of the Black Muslim sisterhood.

The quiet ceremony combined the rites of the Muslim and Christian faiths. It was held in Clay's home on Chicago's South Side.

Herbert Muhammad, Clay's manager, served as best man and a Baptist minister officiated. Clay used his Muslim name, Muhammad Ali.

To thwart a swarm of reporters, Clay had the time of the ceremony moved up. His parents, who were on the way from Louisville, Ky., arrived too late to attend.

Clay's bride, Belinda Boyd, was schooled at the Black Muslim's University of Islam. She wore a floor-length white silk dress with a lace train. Clay wore a black silk suit.

The courtship had been taking place in curious fits and starts for an extended time. The groom was eighteen years old when the couple first met. The bride was ten years old. He was the famous boxer from Louisville, Cassius Clay, back from the 1960 Olympics with his gold medal. She was in fourth grade.

Her parents were strong members of the Nation of Islam, part of the inner circle of the Honorable Elijah Muhammad. Her father, Sandardee Ali, came back from World War II, listened to the street corner preachers from the NOI, read the literature, and liked the message, especially the part about finding strength in family. He joined and his wife came with him. His nine-to-five job was in the lithography department at American Can in Chicago and he worked a little bit on the side repairing televisions and radios, but he also became a confidant of the Honorable Elijah Muhammad.

Belinda was born into the religion. The NOI and the people in it dominated her young life. In her earliest memories, three years old, she was telling other kids what to do and what not to do under the laws of the religion. By the time she was eight or nine, she was babysitting for the Honorable Elijah Muhammad's grandchildren and waiting on the table at dinner when dignitaries came. She knew where to place the knives, the forks, the spoons of all sizes. She served coffee to Reverend Martin Luther King. She met leaders of African countries. She felt as if she were at the center of the world.

"You have to recognize that it was a special honor and a privilege to be where I was," she said years later, her name changed to Khalilah Camacho-Ali. "This was the royal family to us. We called them the royal family. These were the Kennedys. The Rockefellers. They get the respect. It is what it is. It was a blessing to be with the royal family."

Her school, the Muhammad University of Islam, was a total immersion in the religion. The day started with a pledge of allegiance to a flag that featured a sun, a moon, and a star and the words "Freedom, Justice, Equality and Islam." ("In the name of Allah, the beneficent, the merciful, let us give praise to Allah for giving to us a flag that represents the universe, the sun, moon and stars, and also means that we're free, equal and justified to all Mankind. The Honorable Elijah Muhammad, the Messenger of Allah. Amen.") This was followed by the school song. ("The University of Islam, Make our name forever ring. . . .") Everyone would sit and lessons would begin.

The school was seen as a prototype. The plan—never implemented—was that it would be replicated at every NOI mosque in the country, the same way Catholic schools were attached to parish churches. Boys went to school on one floor of the building, girls on another. Seldom did they meet, except at assembly, where they would sit on different sides of the hall.

In addition to normal subjects, students would learn Islamic history and black history. Books would include the *Books of the Caliphs, The 101 Amazing Facts of the American Negro, The Pictorial Book of American Negro History,* and *Black Gold,* a *Life* magazine book about the history of slavery in the United States. Teachers came from both the United States and Africa. Many also were university professors.

Belinda was a whirlwind at the school. She flourished in the structure of it, was a know-everything leader, the truest of true believers. She talked with anyone at any chance. She had opinions and confidence, not a lot of doubts. Why should she? She was a confidante of the royal family.

Word came down one day at school that this famous boxer from the 1960 Olympics would be coming to an assembly. She didn't know anything about boxing or the Olympics or about the famous boxer. She was not excited or impressed.

"All I knew was that this man wanted to see the empire of Elijah Muhammad because he saw Malcolm X teaching in the ghetto in Florida," she said. "That tripped him out. Malcolm X in the ghetto. So he came to Chicago. I think my teacher had made arrangements to have him come to the school. That particular day, I was an honor student in charge of putting everything up on the bulletin board. I was let out of class to do this."

She was in the auditorium, getting it ready, when she heard what sounded like heavy boots in the hall. She went to the door and peeked through a crack. She saw her principal and another man and a third man. She thought the third man, the one who made the noise with his boots when he walked, looked like a gladiator, a black gladiator. She had watched the movie *Hercules* only a night earlier. She thought this handsome, large black man was a black Hercules. A strange thought also entered her mind, simply appeared, a thought that scared her. The man looked like her.

"If I was a man . . . ," she said to herself. "If I had to be a man, this is what I would look like."

The thought was scary because only two weeks earlier, Sister Lottie had asked her to come to a charm class at the school to learn how a woman should act as a housewife. Belinda laughed and said she didn't need charm class because she never was getting married. Sister Lottie also laughed. She said of course Belinda would get married. Everyone did. Belinda said no, she was proud. She wouldn't marry anyone unless "he walk like me, talk like me, act like me." Which she knew was impossible.

Now here was this man who looked like her. Two weeks later. He stood in front of the assembly and showed his gold medal and said he was going to be heavyweight champion of the world before he turned twenty-one. He talked like her. He acted like her. He caused a commotion.

"Is that your brother?" Belinda's friend Charlene asked in the assembly.

"No," Belinda said.

"He looks like you. You're not related?"

"No."

"He sounds like you."

"No."

When the talk was finished, the students in the class lined up for autographs. They were arranged by height. Belinda was the tallest, so she was at the end of the line. She handed her piece of paper to the gladiator. He signed his name with a grand flourish. Cassius Marcellus Clay. Belinda, the honor student in the Nation of Islam school, was not impressed.

"You're proud of this name?" she asked the gladiator.

"I certainly am," he replied. "My mama gave me this. These are Roman names. You know what the Romans did? They ruled the world."

"This is a slave name," Belinda said. "You don't even know."

She tore up the paper with the autograph on it. She took the pieces and put them into the gladiator's big hand. She told him to take the paper and find out what his real name was. Then maybe they could talk.

Ten years old.

She walked away. Cassius Marcellus Clay? Huh. She was wearing the head scarf, but her hair was in a long braid that extended past the end. He watched her go.

"Who's the Indian girl?" he asked. "She just tore up my autograph."

That was what she became, the Indian Girl. He would notice her every time he came through Chicago. The Indian Girl. The one who tore up his autograph. She intrigued him, this little kid. He asked Wallace Muhammad, one of Elijah Muhammad's sons, who this girl was. Wallace said his father called her "The Princess of Islam."

"What's that mean?" the gladiator asked.

"It means she's never been tampered with," Wallace Muhammad said. "She's a virgin. She doesn't know anything about anything. She's a virgin and she's raised and grown and trained to be a wife and a mother and you can't touch her. And you can't mess with her because her father is my father's first lieutenant and you can't get to her unless you get through him. And that ain't going to happen."

The premonition that *I'm going to marry this man* seemed to fall apart when the gladiator, whose name was changed by now to a nonslave Muhammad Ali, married Sonji Roi a couple of years later. Marriage takes a man off the market. Belinda studied the pictures of the new bride and decided that she looked like Elizabeth Taylor. A black Elizabeth Taylor. Belinda loved Elizabeth Taylor in *National Velvet.*

The gladiator was, indeed, the heavyweight champion of the world now after beating Sonny Liston. Elizabeth Taylor should be able to keep the heavyweight champion of the world happy. The premonition had to be wrong.

Then Belinda met Sonji.

"You're the Indian Girl, aren't you?" Sonji asked when she came to the school with Ali. "You're so pretty. He talks about you all the time."

"Me?" Belinda said. "You've got to be kidding."

"No. You're the Indian Girl. Right?"

Oh, Lord, Belinda thought. Here we go.

She was thirteen years old now. Stories had surfaced about how the marriage had been arranged. Stories behind the stories. Sonji, the gossip went, was a hooker, a prostitute. Herbert Muhammad had talked her into a fast marriage with Ali. The Honorable Elijah Muhammad and other prime members of the NOI were worried that their young champion would be swept off his feet by some fast-talking, fast-moving woman. Maybe even a white woman. Probably a white woman. They weren't going to allow this to happen.

Sonji was the antidote. Belinda heard the stories but still liked her as a person until one day at the school when some character who looked like a pimp came to pick up Sonji at the school. This looked shady to Belinda. Why would Sonji go anywhere with this man? Maybe she didn't realize the possibilities in the man she had married. Maybe she didn't want to be married. Maybe she would not stay married. Maybe.

"Allah," Belinda said in her evening prayers, "if this marriage doesn't work, that's a sign to show he's mine."

She had become a fan of Muhammad Ali. She paid attention to his career. When he became a Muslim, changed his name, back before he won the title, he became more interesting to her. She was able to do a pretty good impression of him, getting the cadence down, the voice. She looked like him, talked like him! She began to write a poem for him as he approached the Sonny Liston fight in Miami. She had seen him, had a good conversation with him one night in Chicago after a service at the mosque.

"I'm serving bean soup, bean pie, in the restaurant and there's a long line," Belinda said. "He comes all the way to the front of the line and stops there. I said, 'what do you think you're doing?' 'I'm coming to see you,' he says. 'I have a Muslim name now.' I say, 'well, good for you, but you're not breaking the line, brother.' He says, 'the brothers and sisters all said it's OK.' I say, 'well, it's not OK, now go all the way to the back of the line.' And he went all the way to the back. Just stood there. Waited. Then he came all humble, respectful at the end. He said, 'I know who you are. I know your name. I know who your daddy is, who your mommy is.' I said, 'Boy, you are a smart young man.' He stayed and we talked until closing time."

She said she gave him the poem before he fought Liston. She said he memorized it and when she turned on television one night, there he was. . . .

This is the legend of Cassius Clay
The most beautiful fighter in the world today . . .

Her words tumbled out of his mouth. It was something to see. He spoke all twelve lines with grand emphasis and cadence. Mr. Iambic Pentameter. He described how the fight would unfold, what things he would do to the menacing Liston. The poor guy would be launched like "a spook satellite."

No one would dream when they put down their money
They'd see a total eclipse of the Sonny.

Fate would be in control.

Then he married Sonji and the premonition seemed dead. Then he fought Liston that second time in Lewiston and word arrived that he was not happy with Sonji. Hope returned. Four weeks after the fight, he announced that he wanted a divorce. Prayers from the young girl in the Nation of Islam had been answered.

The proposal came on the night of the senior prom. Actually, it came the morning after the night of the senior prom. Belinda was the class valedictorian. She went to the senior prom with Wali Muhammad because that was what she thought she was supposed to do. She had been raised with Wali as if they were cousins, so there were no romantic thoughts in her head. Wali's head was a different story.

"The prom was the first chance girls and boys had at the school to eat at the same table with each other, big whoop-dee-doo," Belinda said. "It was at the Top of the Rock at the Prudential Building. Everyone else was escorted by parents. I was allowed to go alone with Wali because we'd known each other forever. My father told him to have me home by 10 o'clock."

Wali had other ideas. He pulled the car into a park on the way home and said he had run out of gas, not exactly a novel prom-night approach. He tried to kiss Belinda. One of his legs already was in a cast from being broken in some athletic pursuit, and Belinda told him the other leg would be in a matching cast if he continued to try. She also told him he better have enough gas in the car to get her home or he was in serious trouble.

She arrived at midnight, worried about what her father would say. Muhammad Ali's flashy Cadillac was parked in the driveway. What was he doing here so late at night? Wali asked, "What's this nigger doing here?" Belinda said she didn't know.

She went to the back door. Her father was in the kitchen. There was no conversation about Wali. Her father said that Ali had been in the house for a while. He had something he wanted to say to Belinda. She said that he wouldn't be saying it now because it was midnight and she was tired. Men didn't come to the house at midnight to talk to women.

When she woke up in the morning, Ali was still there. He was sleeping on the couch. Her mother had brought him a pillow and some blankets. He soon woke up and asked her to marry him. Just like that.

"I'm there and my momma's cooking breakfast and my daddy's there and isn't this kind of personal?" Belinda said. "I'm nervous and I'm ready to say 'no,' because I never said 'yes' to any man."

The proposal was not a total shock because John Ali, part of Elijah Muhammad's inner circle and part of the Ali entourage, had sounded her out on the subject a few days earlier. What would happen *if* Ali asked? Belinda had said that the answer would be no. Of course it would be no. She was seventeen and headed for college.

Ali had heard this and devised a plan. He went through some logical reasons that the marriage should happen—"I like you and you like me, we're both Muslims, we're a lot alike"—and then delivered his knockout reason. Elijah Muhammad wanted this to happen. The Leader wanted her to marry Ali. Very much.

Belinda said yes. She felt she had no choice. The Honorable Elijah Muhammad had spoken. She knew this was true.

There was some more conversation between Ali and her dad, between Ali and her mother, back and forth, but none of that mattered to her. She said she had to do what Elijah Muhammad wanted.

"Daddy, will you give me your blessing?" she said to her father.

"This boy has no job," her father said.

"Yes he does. He's a fighter."

"Not now he isn't."

"He will be again," Belinda said. "I'm with him and I'll stick with him. I know those white men want their money. Trust me on this."

Her father gave his blessing.

They were married in a common-law arrangement as soon as permission was granted, the same way Ali had married Sonji. Belinda was in Houston for some of the court business in June before the formal wedding ceremony was held in August. She had never seen her man fight in person, never had been around the glory, so her first dances with his celebrity were these beleaguered trips to the courtrooms. She hated what she saw, what she heard.

"It was tough," she said. "There were all these people crowding around. There was just no place for me. I didn't like what they were saying to him. It pissed me off. I was ready to go off. It was hard to be a lady sometimes. So I just stayed back."

She would go to the court sometimes and just stay in the car. She felt better that way. Her job, she figured, was to help her man stay strong.

"I'm with you," she told him. "The Muslims are with you. They believe in you. They have your back. Any time you know someone has your back, you don't have to fear, you don't have to be afraid of nothing."

The background during this interlude—from the moment Belinda's father agreed to the marriage until the news was made public with the ceremony in August, no more than three months—was a country troubled by racial upheaval. Half the ghettos in America seemed to be on fire at one time or another. Atlanta. Cincinnati. Tampa. Buffalo. Birmingham. Newark, New Jersey. Plainfield, New Jersey. Rochester, New York. Minneapolis. Detroit. Milwaukee. Washington, D.C. The list seemed to have names from every part of the map, 159 race riots recorded during what became known as the long, hot summer of 1967.

The Newark riots made the most headlines because they were the most noticeable, directly across the Hudson River from New York City and the major media outlets. They ran from July 12 to July 17,

1967, and when they were finished sixteen civilians, eight suspects, a police officer, and a fireman were dead. In addition, 353 civilians, 214 suspects, 97 policemen, 55 firemen, and 38 military personnel were injured. More than 1,500 people had been arrested. Property damage was estimated at over $15 million. Three-quarters of the city was under a blockade for four days.

The Newark troubles followed a path that was present in most of the disturbances. An incident with police occurred—in this case the arrest of African American cabdriver John Smith for tailgating and driving in the wrong direction on a one-way street—which inflamed the population. It did not matter in this case that the rumor that Smith had died in police custody was untrue; the trouble already had started. In response, another incident occurred—in this case the death of twenty-nine-year-old Rebecca Brown, a mother of four, who was killed by National Guardsmen shooting bullets into her second-floor apartment. This increased the activity. Gunfire everywhere. Molotov cocktails. The continued presence of the National Guard. The entire community seemed in revolt.

Predictable responses came from predictable directions. New Jersey governor Richard J. Hughes called the rioting "open rebellion," a "criminal insurrection," and "un-American." Roy Wilkins, executive director of the National Association for the Advancement of Colored People, decried the "indiscriminate spraying of apartments with bullets." The standoff didn't end until all parties were stopped by exhaustion and inertia.

In Detroit, the numbers were worse. The 12th Street Riot left forty-three dead, 1,189 injured, thousands arrested, and more than two thousand buildings destroyed. The incident with the police was a raid at an after-hours club where an attempt was made to arrest eighty-three black men who were celebrating the return of two soldiers from Vietnam. In Milwaukee, there was a fight among teenagers that the police tried to stop. Four people dead, including a policeman, 1,500 arrested. In Minneapolis, there was mistreatment of an African American woman in a parade. No fatalities, but three days of wildness that featured eighteen fires, three shootings, twenty-four injuries, $4.2 million in damages . . .

The level of black frustration never had been higher. New, angry leaders had appeared, all of them finished with the nonviolent approach of the civil rights past. H. Rap Brown. Stokely Carmichael. Eldridge Cleaver. Angela Davis. The Black Panthers had begun to rise. "Black Power" was a chant in all confrontations. The time had come to confront "The Man," that white-bread character who controlled the police and the government and the money and everything else, the mechanics of daily life.

In an instant search for instant heroes for this explosion of rage, Muhammad Ali was moved to the front. Was anyone getting screwed more by The Man than Muhammad Ali? His situation was another example of the white man's injustice. Even though he never campaigned for violence, his moral pronouncements about the importance of the black man, the importance of self-worth, fit well with all marching orders for insurrection. Ali's picture, after the events of Houston, fit high on the wall of role models for black rebellion. He was a definite part of this long, hot summer.

On July 23, at a Black Power Conference in the symbolic, burned-out city of Newark, almost a thousand delegates gave approval by voice vote to a number of proposals. A refusal to accept birth-control programs because they seek to exterminate Negroes. Yes! Paramilitary training for all Negro youths. Yes! A national holiday for all black people on May 19, the birthday of Malcolm X. Yes! A refusal by all black Americans to serve in the armed forces and a declaration to oppose the war in Vietnam. Yes! A condemnation of the people who stripped Muhammad Ali's title. This drew the biggest cheer of all. Yes!!!

Ali was not actively involved with any of these groups or any of these people, but on August 13, 1967, less than a month later, he did return to Los Angeles to serve as the grand marshal of a thirty-block parade through the center of Watts to commemorate the two-year anniversary of the riot of 1965. He made no pronouncements, didn't do a press conference, but his presence drew cheers of "Muhammad" and "Cassius." Parade chairman Billy Joe Tidwell said that "he epitomizes a new era in the history of the black man in America."

Five days later, August 18, 1967, he was supposed to appear in Atlanta at the Ebenezer Baptist Church at the annual convention of the Southern Christian Leadership Conference. This would have been a scene. Dr. Martin Luther King in the keynote speech seemed to take a lesson from Ali's presentations when he said that he had consulted an English language dictionary and found that 60 of 120 synonyms for the word "black" were offensive. All 124 synonyms for "white" were favorable. Maybe a new word for "black" should be applied to African Americans.

Ali was not around to hear any of this. He did not appear, because he was back in Chicago.

Getting married to Belinda.

The formal wedding was held at the small brick house at the corner of East Eighty-Fifth Street and South Jeffery Boulevard that was given to them by Herbert Muhammad. The story Herbert told reporters was that he was fixing it up for his daughter, who was getting married, but she didn't need it. The story he told Belinda was that he was fixing it up for his mistress, but the relationship fell apart.

At any rate, there was a screen door that had a large Gothic *M* in wrought iron on the front. This didn't even have to change. It worked for either Herbert Muhammad or Muhammad Ali. Herbert said Ali could live there.

"I'm just going on what Herbert said to me, that he was fixing it up for his girlfriend," Belinda said. "It was fine. Louis Farrakhan and Jesse Jackson lived right near there."

"I didn't want to build a home because I might be going away for four, five years and I wouldn't have wanted to leave without seeing it through," Ali said to the *Chicago Tribune,* a few inaccuracies in his words. "Herbert had this house built for himself and it was just right so I bought it from him."

The champ in absentia and his bride were like a lot of young couples starting lives together. They had plans, dreams, hopes for kids. They also were pretty much broke. The money was gone.

Ali could itemize a lot of the missing cash. The divorce from Sonji was expensive. He had to post the $50,000 bond, had to pay $1,200 per month in alimony, had to pay $25,000 for his lawyer, $18,000 for her lawyer. He gave his mother the Cadillac, his father a truck, gave both of them a $29,000 house and $15,000 to furnish it. He had paid Hayden Covington $60,000 and now was being sued for $287,000 more. The public saw grand numbers for his fights, but the Louisville Sponsoring Group and then Main Bout took their shares and Uncle Sam took a bite and the actual numbers were a lot less than appeared in the papers.

"You can't say that I spend my money foolishly, that I waste it," he said. "I don't drink or smoke and you never see me with women or going out to have a good time. I haven't made any bad investments. I don't throw money away. I spend about three dollars a day on myself."

Belinda did bring a small bag of money into the relationship. This was her college savings, which she always did keep in a bag rather than a bank. Since she wouldn't be going to college now, she could use the money for daily living. She thought about how crazy the situation was. Here was a man who could make a fortune if he simply went to the Middle East to fight in a boxing ring. Countries would fall over themselves trying to make him rich. The U.S. government, by taking away his passport, eliminated this possibility. By taking away his license and titles, the boxing commissions had completed the job.

She spent her money without even telling him, buying essentials on her own. She worried about negative feelings that he might have, that he might not feel as if he was a good husband if he couldn't provide. The negative feelings were never far away.

"My wife is a great cook," Ali said to Herbert Muhammad one day, detailing all the meals she had made.

"Where's she getting the money for all this food?" Herbert asked. "I know she's not getting it from you, because you're not getting it from me."

This was a good point. Ali asked his wife where she was getting the money.

"Allah gives you what you need," Belinda said. "Just you don't worry about it."

Two months after the marriage, Robert Markus, a columnist for the *Tribune,* paid a visit to see the house and get a picture of Ali's new life without boxing. The house was easy to describe—the twin crystal sconces with electric candle-shaped bulbs, the plush couch, the inlaid color television set—but the champ proved to be a bigger problem. Markus struggled with Ali's talk about religion.

"It is not always easy to follow what Ali is saying," Markus wrote. "He shuffles notes he has made from a book to which he constantly refers. The book is 'Message to the Blackman' and it is written by Elijah Muhammad, the Muslim leader. Several passages are underlined and if you ask the champ a question about his religion he will scan thru the book until he finds what he considers an appropriate passage. Sometimes it is relevant. Sometimes it is not.

"If you listen hard enough you will get the idea that Ali wants to be remembered as a great man, a martyr. He went into a soliloquy: 'If they come for me tomorrow morning with 15 guards, I'll just say, "I'm ready." I'll kiss my pretty wife good-bye and tell her things to do and I'll go with them. They can do what they want with me. They can pull out my fingernails.'

"Ali began to act out the imagined horrors. He pulled at his nails, one by one. 'They'll say, "Renounce Allah."' His face contorted in pain, 'Noooo.' 'Renounce Allah.' 'Noooooo.' The champ relaxed. 'The next morning people in Ethiopia and Ghana and everywhere will say to the United States, "You did a bad thing."'"

The discussion of NOI doctrine was now a bigger part of Ali's life than it had been before marriage. Belinda was the master of the doctrine after her years at Muhammad University. She had the approved words for all situations. Ali was learning. He was the late convert. She taught. He listened and adopted the words as his own. He was very good at this.

The future was uncertain. The husband in this new couple could be sent to jail and just about any time. He had few job prospects, but a lot of attention. The wife's job was to keep him moving through this bad stretch. There was no prediction about when it would end.

"You have to realize that back then it was important to keep him uplifted, to keep him from being depressed," Belinda said years later. "Keep him from worrying about whether he made the right decision or not. I'd tell him, 'You made the right decision and because of your decision you will be the greatest man of all times. Just be patient.'"

Patience would be necessary for the next three years.

11

Colleges

He couldn't fight, but he still could talk. That was the answer to his money problems. A man didn't need a license to talk. There were no state commissions of talk. The speeches at Howard and a few other colleges had gone well. The youth of America, increasingly united against being called for the draft, would listen to the foremost figure who had defied the draft. There was money to be made out there on the college lecture circuit.

Not a lot of money, perhaps, not Astrodome money from Astrodome crowds, but enough to survive. Muhammad Ali would bring his message to the kids.

"Do you miss boxing?" people would ask.

"I'm too busy to miss boxing," he would reply. "I'm giving lectures."

Three days before his trial in Houston, he had tried to make some money fighting an exhibition in Detroit. He wore headgear and sixteen-ounce gloves as he boxed three desultory rounds apiece against Alvin (Blue) Lewis and Orville (Baby Boy) Qualls. The show was a bust, a crowd of 3,523 rattling around Cobo Hall, gate receipts of $5,000. Exhibitions did not hold out great promise.

Lectures were the answer.

He and Belinda worked out a plan at the start. She wrote letters to a few colleges to see who was interested. She plotted out a half-dozen speeches with him. He practiced. He tape-recorded what he said and played the words back to see how he sounded. He wrote out notes in the big letters to get himself rolling in the proper directions.

These would not be shuck-and-jive routines, make the young white man laugh. These would be serious. They would make the young white man squirm in his little khaki pants or his tattered jeans and his tie-dye shirts. Make the coeds' heads hurt inside that headband or under that cheerleader helmet of hair. This was Nation of Islam material.

Belinda, with her lifetime of listening to the Honorable Elijah Muhammad, could recite the leader's speeches as well as the leader could. She went through the routines, many that her husband already knew. He was a sponge. He would hear, remember, and repeat. That was his gift. His presentation was loud and passionate. Perfect.

Ali always liked to think of himself as a modern Wyatt Earp, the gun-slinging marshal of his television youth, played by actor Hugh O'Brian. Now he was Wyatt Earp, himself, pushing open those saloon doors a couple of times per week and finding a large room filled with wiseass college students. Sometimes there could be trouble.

"Go home, you draft-dodging nigger," someone shouted in one of those early speeches.

"I ain't doing this," Ali told Belinda when he came off the stage.

"Yes, you are," she replied. "This is our livelihood. A chance for us to make money. This is a chance, too, to get your license back. This is a campaign as well as speeches."

They worked out a plan for the next confrontation. The unseen character in the audience would say the draft-dodging-nigger stuff. What would Ali say?

"Ladies and gentlemen, that reminds me," he said the next time. "A long time ago when I was a little boy I used to take a rock and throw it at this donkey. I kept throwing rocks and my mama said to me, 'Cassius, you stop throwing rocks at that donkey because you are going to kill that donkey and one day that donkey is going to come back and haunt you.' [Dramatic pause.] Ladies and gentlemen, I do believe that ass is here tonight."

Life became a series of road trips. The young bride and her still-young husband were newlyweds off on this different adventure.

The rest of the immediate world had dropped away pretty suddenly. Members of the grand entourage went back to their previous lives. Bundini Brown went to run a bar in New York City. Angelo Dundee went to train Jimmy Ellis, Ali's former sparring partner, who was one of the eight contestants in a tournament to replace Ali as the WBA heavyweight champion. Bob Arum and Mike Malitz, the two white partners in Main Bout Inc., now were partners in Sports Action Corporation, which was promoting the tournament. Herbert Muhammad, the prime black partner, was back doing his father's business.

"We were like two time bombs walking the street," Belinda said. "I was as close to him as his jugular vein at this time. He didn't want to go anywhere without me. We were a team. Going out to conquer the world. We did it together. There wasn't no sitting back."

He would get $500, $1,000, maybe $1,500 for a speech. There would be money spent for gas, money for food, money for lodging. Even the $1,500 wasn't a lot of money sometimes. They would borrow money for gas, then pay it back when they cashed the latest check. The Cadillac would swallow a big piece of that check by itself sometimes.

He taught her how to drive. Took her to a parking lot and taught her because she had to get her license. They hurtled back and forth across America in the middle of the night and in the morning sun. They told each other jokes. They fought over the radio. They had an eight-track cassette player. He liked the old soul groups, James Brown and the O'Jays and, of course, Sam Cooke and Lloyd Price. She somehow always liked white music. Crooners. Folk singers. The Kingston Trio.

"Shit," Ali said.

They went to colleges they never knew existed. They went to places they knew by reputation, word of mouth. Belinda mostly rode shotgun with the maps for the local region. She was the one with the sense of direction. She fell asleep one time, told Ali to "take it." She awoke. They were really lost.

"I was only asleep for an hour," Belinda said.

"I was only lost for an hour," Ali said.

When they reached the appointed buildings at the appointed colleges, he gave the kids the whole boilerplate show. He talked about how the color white was always nice, the color black was always evil, about how the giraffes should stay with the giraffes and the sheep with the sheep and how he didn't hate a lion, say, but he stayed away from the lion because he knew what hurt a lion could bring. Same way with white people. He didn't hate the white man, but the black man had seen the hurt a white man could bring.

"Man, I go places where only the professors went before," he told Dave Kindred of the *Louisville Courier-Journal* at another stop, the

Boat, Sport and Vacation Show at Freedom Hall. "Harvard. UCLA. California State. Tennessee State. Me, a boxer, I'm doing this.

"I give them hour and a half lectures. Like 'The Negro Must Clean Himself Up Before Anyone Will Respect Us.' And on how we should treat our women. Women are the fields that grow nations. A farmer puts up a scary crow to protect his crops. We have to protect and respect our women.

"That's what I'm saying. I don't go on marches or throw rocks through windows."

These were adventures. The demand had grown so great, he signed with Richard Fulton Inc., a lecture bureau from Pleasantville, New York, that also handled newscaster Edwin Newman, actor Gary Collins, actress Bess Myerson, and baseball manager Billy Martin. Fulton sent out circulars to colleges around the country.

"We're in Alabama somewhere," she said. "I think it was Alabama. I'd never been to Alabama. We get off the highway because we need gas. It was like 'Deliverance,' little boys on the porch with banjos and shit. Then some rednecks come out with little beards, hair all over them. Like Neanderthals. I'm thinking this is a real hick town and we can get lynched down here and no one will ever know."

Ali pumped the gas, then went to the bathroom, which was an outhouse. One of the hillbillies came to the car.

"How the hell are you?" he asked.

"I'm just fine, brother," Belinda replied.

"Let me tell you something. That boy with you? Is he Cassius Clay?"

"Yes, that's Muhammad Ali."

The hillbilly went crazy. He screamed, "Jesus Christ, Jesus Motherfucking H. Christ, Jesus H. Christ, I got Muhammad Allah here!" Belinda had never heard such swearing. The hillbilly shouted for Ali to come out of the bathroom and sign a piece of paper.

People seemed to come from everywhere. They asked Ali to sign everything from magazines to toilet paper. They asked Belinda to sign, too. A woman came with a plate of homemade cookies for the road. A man came with water. Another woman came with some Southern-fried chicken, wrapped in paper towels and stuffed in a shoe box. For the road.

"I wish I had it all on camera," Belinda said. "Because what you think you see is not necessarily what you get."

There had been changes in Ali's legal team as well as in his entourage. Hayden Covington was gone. The defender of the Jehovah's Witnesses, the most successful lawyer of all time in cases decided by the Supreme Court, had resigned before his most celebrated case ever reached that final destination.

Reporters heard shouting from a conference room at the hearing in Houston when Ali's passport was denied in August 1967. Ali was in the room with his three lawyers—Hayden Covington, Quinnan Hodges, and Chauncey Eskridge. The broad subject was money. The specific subject, brought up by Covington, was an expense account.

"I did, too!" Ali was heard to shout.

"You did not!" Covington shouted in return.

The discussion lasted twenty minutes.

"What was all that shouting about?" Covington was asked when the door opened.

"Nothing that could be publicized," the lawyer replied.

It was publicized now. Covington had submitted a bill for $284,615. Most of that was for expenses, with a $75,000 retainer fee for the lawyer. Ali didn't have the money. Covington resigned and sued.

"He's the heavyweight champion of lawyers," Ali said. "But I don't have the money. I'd have to be allowed to fight for $300,000 just to pay my legal expenses."

Covington's major legal contention, the idea that Ali was a minister by vocation, a boxer by avocation, never had worked the way it did in the Jehovah's Witnesses cases. In the trial in Houston, U.S. attorney Mort Susman simply entered into evidence the first form Ali filled out for Selective Service. "Professional Boxer" was entered for "Occupation." End of argument.

Covington always thought the appeals court—judges, not juries—would recognize that Ali was, indeed, a lay minister. The amount of time the heavyweight champion of the world had spent in what could be called religious matters was definitely larger than the amount of time he spent on boxing. The appeals court, somewhere in the United States, would not be caught up with the politics, not be caught up with the fear the public seemed to have about the Nation of Islam. Muhammad Ali would become a free man.

"If the law is not good enough for him," Covington always said with his lawyer's flourish, "it is not good enough for any of us."

His replacement was thirty-eight-year-old Charles Morgan Jr., head of the American Civil Liberties Union in Atlanta, another lawyer with experience before the Supreme Court. Chauncey Eskridge had approached him when the end with Covington was in sight. He asked Morgan to work for a considerably lower fee.

"Would you do it for $35,000?" Eskridge asked.

Morgan replied that he would do it for free. The ACLU took clients of means and no means. He said he would throw his allegiance to Ali the same way he would if Ali were a private client. The deal was done.

This was another attorney who did not fit into the Nation of Islam's view of the world. He was another white man. He was another drinker. He was a two-pack-per-day smoker. He was a big man, overweight, and there was little doubt that many pork products had contributed to his size. He also was a longtime proponent of integration, equal rights, civil rights.

As a young attorney, liberal, a graduate of both undergraduate and law school at the University of Alabama, he opened an office in Birmingham. He was outraged when the 16th Street Baptist Church was firebombed by four members of the Ku Klux Klan on September 15, 1963, and four little girls were killed, twenty-two people injured. This was an incident that shook the entire country. The next day he gave a speech at the Young Men's Business Club in Birmingham.

"We are a mass of intolerance and bigotry, and stand indicted before our young," he said. "We are cursed by the failure of each of us to accept responsibility, by our defense of an already dead institution. . . . Every person in this community who has in any way contributed during the past several years to the popularity of hatred is at least as guilty as the demented fool who threw the bomb. . . . Who did it? Who threw that bomb? The answer should be, 'We all did it.'"

The speech changed Morgan's life. A cross was burned on his lawn.

He and his family received death threats. His secretary received death threats. He left Birmingham and in 1964 accepted an offer to open an office of the ACLU in Atlanta. His record was filled with various civil rights cases, many that involved gerrymandered voting districts and segregated jury pools and prisons.

He recently had been the antiwar attorney for Captain Howard Levy in a celebrated court-martial trial at Fort Jackson, South Carolina. Levy, a dermatologist in the army, had been ordered to teach dermatology to medics in the Special Forces. He refused because he said they were "killers of peasants and murderers of women and children."

Levy was found guilty, taken from the courtroom in handcuffs, but the Special Forces had been put on trial as much as he had been. Morgan even called Robin Moore, author of the best-selling book *The Green Berets,* to the stand. The silent, secret, undeclared war in Laos and Cambodia was brought into the courtroom. Levy's loss was still a win for antiwar forces.

Morgan attacked Ali's case. He had undergone knee surgery, so he wrote his brief from his bed at home in Atlanta, surrounded by his law books. He restructured the appeal to fit more within his experience, emphasizing the biased composition of draft boards. He mentioned the ministerial exemption, brought back the conscientious objector argument, too. He underlined how surprised he was that Judge Grauman's decision had been overturned by the Justice Department.

The appeal contained all the transcripts from the hearing with Grauman, plus a package of hate mail sent to the Louisville draft board. ("You still cowards, eh?" one letter began. "Send that nigger away.") The brief was filed in Atlanta the day before Christmas in 1967. The case was heard by the three judges from the Fifth U.S. Circuit Court of Appeals on February 19, 1968, in Houston.

Morgan basically asked five questions in his brief:

1. Was the Selective Service induction order to appellant invalid because of alleged systematic exclusion of Negroes from draft boards?
2. Did the District Court err in refusing to grant appellant's request for the production of certain documentary and other evidence?

3. Was there a basis in fact for the denial to appellant of a ministerial exemption?
4. Was there basis in fact for the denial to appellant of conscientious objector status?
5. Did the proceedings as a whole, Selective Service and Judicial, constitute a prohibited bill of attainder?

"What was there in this record to show that he would have escaped military service if he was a white registrant?" Judge James P. Coleman asked at the hearing. "I can't see where there would be any difference if he were your son or mine."

Morgan said the hundreds of anti-Ali letters to the draft board influenced its decision. He also said the board was not responsive to the petitions signed by thousands of Muslims who claimed Ali was a minister of their faith. The arguments lasted seventy minutes. Ali was in the courtroom.

"You've been quoted as saying you have no white friends," a television reporter asked as Ali and Morgan left to catch a cab. "Is that true?"

"Yes, that's true," Ali said.

The reporter looked at Ali, looked at Morgan.

"Your lawyer's white," she said. "What about him?"

"He's not my friend," Ali replied. "He's my lawyer."

The Court of Appeals announced its decision two and a half months later in New Orleans, on May 6, 1968. The answers to all of Morgan's questions were "no." The court pointed out the fact that Ali now had been classified 1-A through seven different processes. The only appeal left was to the Supreme Court. This did not seem to be a very good prospect.

"I'm surprised they didn't render a favorable decision on the Muslim ministerial thing," Hayden Covington said when contacted at his home. "I didn't expect him to win on those other charges, but that's all his lawyers seemed to have on their minds, instead of concentrating on the ministerial appeal. They used bird shot instead of a rifle bullet."

He said he didn't think the Supreme Court would look at the case now. Disappointment could not be heard in his voice.

—

The reports of this latest rejection, the next-to-last stop on the legal road map for the former heavyweight champion of the world, were not treated as major news. Even though the possibility that he would go to jail had increased, the *New York Times* ran its story on page 9. The *Boston Globe* ran its story on page 29. The *Louisville Courier-Journal,* the hometown chronicler of all Muhammad Ali moments, dropped the story back to page A5.

He was not front-page news anymore.

The daily grind turns all news into old news, usually sooner than you think, the shock headlines of yesterday becoming faded, worn-down, dated. That is the attention-span norm. The grind of 1968 was unrelenting. Nothing could stand in front of the events that unfolded, one after another.

The USS *Pueblo* was captured by the North Koreans in January. Martin Luther King was shot dead, assassinated, on the second-floor balcony at the Lorraine Motel in Memphis in April. Riots broke out everywhere. Two months later Robert Kennedy was shot dead, assassinated, in the kitchen at the Ambassador Hotel in Los Angeles. The Democratic convention in Chicago was an unbelievable collection of scenes of lawlessness and protest in August, and the Tet Offensive was killing American boys in record numbers in Vietnam throughout the year, and . . . there never seemed to be a moment to rest. Andy Warhol had been shot by Valerie Solanas? Right. The Russian tanks had returned to crush the Prague Spring? Right. Nixon or Humphrey? What?

Ali became a B-level villain at best. How could his situation be compared to the treachery of James Earl Ray or Sirhan Sirhan? Take a look at the unrest in the ghettos in Washington, Chicago, Baltimore, Kansas City, riots in 110 cities across the country. Take a look at smug Mayor Richard P. Daley and the head-knocking taking place during the Democratic convention in Chicago. Take a look at the news every night from Southeast Asia. Ali was smaller potatoes.

The lecture circuit made him a tame version of a radical. He wasn't involved in the strikes and sit-ins and protests, the newest news. He certainly wasn't involved in the violence, the unrest in the cities. He was off in this legal limbo, a convicted felon for evading the draft, but out on bail. Prison would make him interesting again, but he wasn't in prison yet. He was a rent-a-celebrity, guaranteed to bring edgy remarks and an entertaining evening to the residents of your local institution of higher learning. He could re-create that speech at Howard, but without the front-page urgency, the oomph that it once had.

"He spoke to a crowd conspicuous in its scarcity of blacks," Mike Miihalka wrote in the student newspaper, *The Tech,* when Ali appeared at the student union at the Massachusetts Institute of Technology on April 18, 1968, in Cambridge. "He bewitched the audience. He held them in the palm of his hand, brought them to the edges of their seats and pushed them back again with a shove of words. He scolded them, spanked them, made them laugh. And they left the hall wondering about what he had said."

That was the show. He began with, "I want to give all my fans a chance to see a world champion in person, live and in living color." He ended with a Dick Gregory joke about the black man who goes to a restaurant and is told, "We don't serve Negroes." ("That's fine. I don't eat Negroes. I just want a hamburger.") In between, he handed out enough Nation of Islam boilerplate and speeches about separation of the races to make the kids' heads grow dizzy.

"The 'so-called Negro' needs a program for open housing, not a program for shooting and looting, but the black men of America need a program for self-development," he said. "The Honorable Elijah Muhammad teaches us that we just cannot depend on the white to forever do for us that which we can do and should be doing for ourselves."

What was that?

"You should remember that when the Jews came to Miami Beach they were met with signs shouting 'No Jews and dogs are allowed,'" he said. "Now they own the place."

What?

This was two weeks after Martin Luther King was killed. A manhunt was taking place across the country. There was no grand remembrance from Ali, no mention at all except "Martin Luther King was a great black man . . . we [the NOI] didn't agree with his approach." He stuck with the message.

Three nights earlier he had been in New York on the couch of *The Merv Griffin Show* with comedian Jack E. Leonard and singer Brenda Lee. One night later he would talk to the members of Mosque No. 12

in Roxbury, the ghetto for Boston. He would follow that with a half-hour interview with Bud Collins of the *Boston Globe* that would be shown on public television stations around the country.

"I know blacks and whites cannot get along," he told Collins. "This is nature. It just gets worse every day. The latest government fact-finding committee just said that things are becoming separate, two societies, black and white. That's what we've been telling you all along. White women have got gun clubs all over the country, learn how to shoot at black targets. I understand they've got guns that will shoot through brick walls just to get Negroes. . . . Mayor Daley in Chicago, or somebody, ordered helicopters just for these riots, rotating machine guns on them, all these dogs that attack just black people and banana slick, and spray and mist."

In another week, he would be at the University of Wisconsin, where he would be cheered at first, then quickly booed when he talked against interracial marriage, called it "a trick to keep us with the white man." In San Francisco, a day after that, he was booed when he said that "no intelligent so-called Negro" would allow his daughter to marry a white man. The shout, at an antiwar rally, was "Ali go home."

He took questions, engaged his detractors at the end, sometimes face-to-face. He had the practiced answers of a true believer to all arguments. Hayden Covington's old Jehovah's Witnesses clients could not have been more prepared. The kids shouting in his face seldom knew the subject as well, whatever it was.

He talked to six hundred people in Louisville who were part of the Poor People's March on Washington. He said he didn't believe in marching "because I don't believe in turning the other cheek." He talked about the separation of the races and Nation of Islam theology to a sold-out crowd at the University of Notre Dame. He was back on the *Merv Griffin Show* with Burt Lancaster, James Brown, New York mayor John Lindsay, and the band Spanky and Our Gang. He was on the *Mike Douglas* show with Maureen Reagan, daughter of Ron and Nancy. He was on *The Tonight Show.* Johnny Carson had the night off. Woody Allen was the guest host.

He told everyone that as a Muslim, he wasn't involved in politics, but if he did vote in the November election he would vote for George Wallace. This was not a civil rights agenda.

"Governor Wallace, he tells the truth," he told Bud Collins. "I see him telling the truth. I don't believe in everything nobody says, but I like when he says Negroes shouldn't push to get into a white neighborhood and whites don't want to sell. Whites shouldn't have to move out if one Negro moves in. . . . That makes sense. If I don't want you, why do you push yourself on me? Wallace is admitting that isn't right and we should let the people do what they want to do, decide what they want to do in their own communities. Just don't make some northern so-called liberal come in and bust the neighborhood up and they all have to pack up."

On October 24, 1968, he went to Union College. He told the brothers at Phi Sigma Delta over dinner that this was the second stop on a sixty-eight-college tour. He walked with some of them across the Schenectady, New York, campus to a sold-out Memorial Hall. His fee here was $3,000, plus hotel and expenses.

"Santa Claus is white," he said. "Jesus is white. Even Tarzan, king of the jungle, is a white man swinging around with diapers on. . . ."

A few student leaders had been allowed to sit on the stage, allowed to ask prepared questions at the end of the lecture. Joel Blumenthal was one of them, a senior representative of WRUC, the campus radio station. His planned question was, "How do you ask for a conscientious objector deferment when you're involved in a violent sport where you try to beat up people?" After answering a couple of other questions, Ali called on Blumenthal. The radio man stood and froze.

He couldn't speak. He simply stared.

"This was the most perfect human being I'd ever seen," he said years later. "There wasn't a mark on him. He was an Adonis. He was the most charismatic figure I'd ever seen."

Blumenthal mumbled and fumbled.

"You afraid of me?" Ali said. "Don't worry. I'm not going to hit you."

Silence from Blumenthal. More silence.

"I understand," Ali said. "It's not often a champ like me comes through a one-horse town like this."

Applause.

Life had become a traveling form of suspended animation for him. Another audience. Another town. Belinda had to curtail her time on the road because on June 19, 1968, she had their first baby, Maryum, a seven-pound, six-ounce girl who soon was called "May-May." Belinda said Ali loved his new daughter, but after twenty minutes of baby talk was ready to hand her back to her mother. He traveled now sometimes with Robert Fulton, the speakers-bureau guy, or with someone else from the bureau or with a friend like Gene Kilroy, a white guy from Philadelphia who had been part of his entourage, or with assorted Muslims.

On October 16, 1968, six days before Ali went to Union College, Tommie Smith of the USA won the 200-meter race at the Olympics in Mexico City. Teammate John Carlos finished third. The buildup to the Games had been filled with a lot of talk about a boycott or certainly protests by black athletes to dramatize their dissatisfaction with racial relations in the United States. A lot of that talk was by Harry Edwards, a black professor at San Jose State. Under a sign in his office that read "Happiness by Any Means Necessary . . . St. Malcolm X," he counseled black athletes to stand up to the U.S. government.

Smith and Carlos, who both had attended San Jose State, became the lead protesters. Both appeared shoeless at the victory ceremony and wore black socks to represent black poverty. Smith wore a black scarf to represent black pride. Carlos wore a set of beads to commemorate black people beaten or lynched, tarred and feathered throughout American history. Each man also wore a single glove, Carlos on the left hand, Smith on the right. (They had planned to each wear two gloves, but Smith forgot his gloves back at the Olympic Village. They each used one of Carlos's gloves.) When "The Star-Spangled Banner" was played, each athlete thrust his gloved hand into the air in protest. The picture was dramatic, perfect, appeared on the front page of newspapers around the world.

The reaction was predictable back home.

"Smith and Carlos brought their world smack into the Olympic Games where it did not belong and created a shattering situation that shook this international sports carnival to its very core," Arthur Daley wrote in the *New York Times*. "They were also divisive."

"Smith and Carlos looked like a couple of black-skinned storm troopers . . . ," Brent Musburger wrote in the *Chicago American*. "Carlos ran looking like a trinket shop, beads and badges and the medallions bouncing as he dashed toward the finish line."

"I'm sick of Tommie Smith and John Carlos," John Hall wrote in the *Los Angeles Times*. "I'm sick of their whining, mealy-mouthed, shallow view of the world. I'm sick of apologizing and saying they are trying to improve things."

These were the stories that had been written about Ali. This was the same sort of patriotic disgust. How could these guys desecrate the moment? Weren't they supposed to be Americans? This was the issue of the day, the news.

Two days later, Bob Beamon rolled up his sweatpants to show his black socks while he was on the victory stand after setting the long jump world record at 29 feet, 2½ inches, almost two feet longer than the previous mark. Ralph Boston, who finished third, wore no shoes at all, just the black socks. This was to protest the suspension of Smith and Carlos from the U.S. team. The pair had left the Olympic Village.

"I think the way to have done it was to sit down and talk with Carlos and Smith and hear their side of the story before taking some punitive action against them," Ralph Boston said. "I think this was wrong. I think this was what was done with Cassius Clay."

Ali was precedent. Ali was history.

He was yesterday's news.

The year of living somewhat quietly ended on a curious note. He went to jail. Not the big jail, the federal jail where reservations had been made for a while now. No, this was local jail in Miami. The sentence was ten days. He went to jail for a traffic ticket.

"Joe Blow, who nobody knows, he's got to do his 10 days," he told reporters. "So the judge has got to uphold the law for me."

The traffic offense went back two years. He was stopped for making an improper turn and found to not have a license. He was fined $270 . . . but he never paid the fine. He was picked up again in Miami in May 1967, released on bond, and did not appear for his hearing three weeks later. That was when he was sentenced in absentia to ten days in prison in addition to the fine.

The sentence began on December 16, 1968. He began with a press conference, posing next to the barred gate of the Dade County jail as he said, "Oh, so this what a jail is like, huh?"

"Maybe this will be good for me," he said. "I've never suffered. I've enjoyed the luxury of America and I've had a good time. . . . I might have five for the Army thing. So this will be conditioning for me. I've never been in jail."

Only six nights earlier he had made a surprise return to his old life, back at a big-time fight for the first time in almost two years, since he fought Zora Folley. He appeared at a fight between Joe Frazier and Oscar Bonavena at the Spectrum in Philadelphia, causing a stir when he sat down at ringside.

The fight was for a portion of his old heavyweight empire. Frazier was the New York Athletic Commission heavyweight champion for the states of New York, Massachusetts, Maine, Illinois, Pennsylvania, Texas, and Mexico. Frazier had won that title with an eleventh-round TKO over Buster Mathis. The WBA champion now was Jimmy Ellis, who had survived the eight-man elimination tournament that Frazier didn't enter. Ellis had won a unanimous decision over Jerry Quarry in the final. The WBC, the third boxing board, still ranked Ali as champion but said it would withdraw recognition in the next year unless he was able to fight.

There was little doubt Frazier was the class of the field. Ali already was setting the stage for whatever might happen in the future.

"Here comes the champ!" he sometimes would shout at various appearances in a newscaster's voice that sounded very much like Howard Cosell. "Straight from Alcatraz, weighing 225 pounds, a little overweight, Muhammad Ali. There's $15 million in the house. Can Ali do it? Can he come back from Alcatraz? Can he whup Joe Frazier?"

"You don't feel no excitement, do you?" he shouted in the Spectrum when Frazier came into the ring. "When a champion comes out, you're supposed to feel excitement."

The fight plodded to a fifteen-round unanimous decision, making Frazier's record a perfect 22-0. Ali was not impressed, called him "a disgrace to the human race." He said the world knew who the real heavyweight champion was.

That would be the guy heading for jail.

"I hate to go to jail, because it upsets too many people on the whole planet, even in Asia and Africa," he said as he began his term in Miami. "Just for a traffic ticket."

He was given trustee status in the jail, assigned to work in the kitchen. The pay was forty cents per week, which made him say, "They've got a million-dollar champion working for 40 cents a week." He talked with black prisoners, tried to sell them on the benefits of the Nation of Islam. His sentence was shortened by two days, part of a general Christmas amnesty. Forty-nine other prisoners also were released.

Belinda met her husband at the gate.

"I told him when he went to just go in there and teach the brothers, educate the brothers," she said. "That's what he did. He shook that place up! All those people stopped eating pork, eating pig. They started going to the mosque. The man was too powerful, too strong. He had all them niggers stop smoking, stop drinking, stop taking drugs. Everything stopped. Them black brothers got smart. Half of them got out just because Ali was there. He had shook up that jail so much they kicked him out. The nigger wasn't there a week."

"I was shaking up the prison," Ali said as they were driven away from the jail. "I was shaking up the world. . . .

"I'm a baaaad man," he said.

The best part about the quiet year was home. Belinda was his buddy. Home was their Mecca. He told her everything that happened. There were no secrets. He had no money. The women weren't lining up to tempt him. He was an NOI crusader, off to convert the world. He told Belinda how he would go into nightclubs and tell women to put some clothes on. Stop showing your titties and ass! Put some clothes on!

"The man was immaculate," Belinda said. "He was good. That was beautiful then. That was the Muslim man I married."

12

Stirrings

W e are at a point now, where we must fight Communism everywhere it is detected," Arkansas state senator Milt Earnhart of Fort Smith wrote in a letter published in the *Arkansas Traveler* on March 12, 1969, the day Muhammad Ali's speaking tour took him to the University of Arkansas. "And if you believe a character like Clay is not encouraged by Communists, you are more naïve than I believe you are!"

Oh, my.

As Ali's perpetual lecture trip continued, another college town, another set of fresh, mostly white faces looking up from the audience, there still were awkward moments. The trip to Fayetteville, Arkansas, featured a bunch of them.

Ali was scheduled to speak as part of an extended program called "Symposium '69," which featured senators Mark Hatfield, George McGovern, Daniel Inouye, Ed Muskie, and fellow Robert Fulton client Edwin Newman, the broadcaster. Ali was the one controversial character in the mix. He was paired with Floyd McKissick, chairman of the Congress for Racial Equality, for this appearance.

The Pulaski County Businessmen's Association in Little Rock had protested this "un-American" speaker at the state university. The thought was that Ali was being allowed to subvert young minds. Arkansas president David Mullins blasted the businessmen's group in return, a move applauded by the *Arkansas Gazette* that called Ali "essentially a comic figure," but someone the students had a right to hear.

Senator Earnhart joined the fray here, proposing a resolution to condemn Ali's appearance at the school. The proposal was approved by the thirty-five-member State Senate by a voice vote, but not without some contentious debate. Senator W. D. Moore, who said he detested "Clay as an individual," was still vigorous in arguing that the detestable individual's views should be heard. Senator Moore proceeded to battle the anticommunist diehards.

"Are you saying indoctrination by the Russians is wrong, but indoctrination by the University of Arkansas is right?" he asked fellow senators Mutt Jones and Dan Sprick.

"Are we indoctrinating them?" Sprick asked.

"You're not letting them hear the other side."

"There is no other side."

"You've answered my question," Moore said. "There is no side but yours."

Ali gave the basic speech at the appointed time, still unsettling if you never had heard it. He decried the demonstrations across the country and all attempts at integration. The black man should live with the black man, the white man with the white man. The government, in payment for all that slave labor it used over the years, should donate some land—land "rich with water and minerals" at that—to the black man to start a new state. If it didn't do this, and do it soon, the end of days was approaching, Allah would bring "death and destruction" onto the planet. You could count on that.

Alice Davis Butler, one of the few black students on campus, was part of the crowd of four thousand at sold-out Barnhill Field House. She had gone to the speech ready to be uplifted, exalted by this famous man's words. She sat with friends in the first few rows. The more he talked, the more different he was from what she expected. He said black students should attend only black colleges. The black students also should patronize only black businesses, live only in black areas of town. He said he couldn't understand why black students would want to go to the University of Arkansas.

Butler and her friends were stunned. Being black students on the Fayetteville campus wasn't easy. They had to overcome a cultural and often an academic deficit from segregated high schools to survive. They suffered social indignities, had to battle against incivility daily. The football team, number one in the country, still did not have a black player. And now this famous black man, this champion, someone they respected, tells them what they are doing is wrong, if not worthless?

Butler left early, unable to listen anymore. Some of her friends left at the same time.

In one of those strange moments that happen on college campuses, though, she soon heard that she had a second chance to see Ali. He had invited the few black students at the school back to his motel. They could have an informal discussion. She decided to go. In her mind she decided she would ask him how he could say the things he did.

"When we arrived in his room, Mr. Ali jumped from the couch where he was sitting and said, 'Women,' and began to approach me hurriedly; I was the first woman to enter the room," Butler said years later in *Remembrances in Black,* an oral history of black students at the University of Arkansas. "The young man who was my date for the evening jumped back when Mr. Ali approached. I remember saying to my date, 'Some date you are.' And, he quipped, 'If he wants you, he can have you.' Nothing happened. Mr. Ali said he was only joking. But with bodyguards stationed all over the suite holding loaded guns, my nerve to take him on about his segregationist views was lost. Instead, we listened to him talk about his life and watched as the student body representative came to the room to pay him in cash. He spread all of the money out on the table for us to see. The whole scene was so unreal and yet it did happen. I have never forgotten it."

There were no riots, as one legislator had predicted. ("There always are riots when these things take place," he said.) No sign-up sheets for the Communist Party were passed around the room. A follow-up conference about the event was held six days later at the school with four legislators, two of whom had been for the speech and two against. This was advertised as part of the educational process.

"The Chinese say they are going to take over the world and the Russians say they are going to take us from within," Mutt Jones, still stuck on the Red Menace, said on the con side. "They say they are going to do it through college students and through professors."

Representative Herbert Rule of Little Rock, on the pro side, noted that the American Legion Post in Little Rock had called for a bill to be passed that no convicted felon could speak on the grounds of the university. He said that if that was the case, Gandhi never could have come to the campus, nor could Socrates or Jesus Christ.

The *Arkansas Gazette* had the last word in an editorial. The newspaper also noticed that Ali was different from what was expected.

"When the speaker was not advocating separation of the races, he was praising George Wallace to the sky, both of which stands seem to accord with the plurality of voting opinion in the state," the *Gazette* said. "One wonders again what the advance fuss was all about."

The day before Ali appeared at the University of Arkansas (and didn't recruit any young Communists), his name was linked with the name of a genuine spy for the Soviet Union in a case decided by the United States Supreme Court in Washington. This would turn out to be a good thing.

The case involved thirty-nine-year-old John W. Butenko of Orange, New Jersey. He had been an employee of the International Electronic Company, which did communications work for the Strategic Air Command. Butenko, in a publicized trial, had been found guilty of selling top-secret information about the SAC to members of the Soviet Union's diplomatic delegation to the United Nations in New York.

The FBI had tailed Butenko when he drove his 1961 blue Ford Falcon, license plate AVV871, to various New Jersey locations to meet with the diplomats. The meetings were held at places like Lou's Hitching Post, the China Chalet Restaurant, the Gold Key, the Old Hook Inn, and the parking lot of a Finast supermarket. As many as ten FBI agents watched the various participants at a single time.

When the arrests were made at a railway station, Butenko in the blue Falcon, the Soviets now with Butenko's brown leather briefcase filled with secrets in their green Ford sedan, his guilt seemed undeniable. Also found in the green Ford were a copier, a briefcase with a radio transmitter built inside, a mini camera designed to look like a pack of cigarettes, and another camera built to look like a transistor radio. After the government presented this evidence and called thirty-seven witnesses, Butenko was sentenced to thirty years in prison. Codefendant Ivan Ivanov, a chauffeur in the green Ford, was given twenty years. Three diplomats pleaded immunity and were shipped back to Russia.

The arrest happened in 1963. The trial took place in 1964. By 1969, an appeal filed by lawyers for Butenko and Ivanov reached the Supreme Court. The appeal was paired with an appeal by Willie Alderman, who was an underworld figure from Las Vegas. Called "Ice Pick Willie" for his alleged use of that tool during numerous strange deaths, Alderman had been convicted for conspiring to commit murderous threats through interstate commerce. The complaint in both cases was that illegal government wiretaps had been made of the plaintiffs and that the plaintiffs never had been allowed to hear or read the information the government discovered.

On March 10, 1969, the Supreme Court on a 5–3 vote sent both cases back to district courts for review. Illegal wiretaps could not be used for convictions. Period.

A change in the law, making it easier for the FBI and other agencies to obtain warrants for wiretaps, meant the decision had little effect on present and future cases, but a long list of past cases that involved illegal wiretaps now might be subject to review. Included were convictions of Teamsters president Jimmy Hoffa, now in prison on an eight-year sentence for jury tampering, Dr. Benjamin Spock, H. Rap Brown and other leaders of civil disobedience, and, yes, Muhammad Ali.

His attorneys were told there were five instances when he had been wiretapped illegally. In none of the instances was he the principal whose phone was tapped, but that did not matter. The government had information the attorneys did not. This was a Fourth Amendment situation, protection of an individual from unreasonable searches and seizures.

The ACLU's Charles Morgan filed a petition for a rehearing for Ali. This was a common filing, but rarely successful. Between 1961 and 1967, the Supreme Court had received one thousand petitions. It granted only ten. After the latest ruling, the Justice Department, through Solicitor General Erwin Griswold, asked that this ratio stay the same. It cited "security reasons."

On March 24, 1969, two weeks after the Butenko decision, the Supreme Court sent the cases of both Ali and Jimmy Hoffa and thirteen other defendants back to the lower courts. This essentially reopened Ali's case. The rehearing for Ali was only to examine the wiretap evidence, to decide whether it hurt him in his trial, but this was, at the very least, a foreign object stuck into the gears of the American justice system. His case had reached the end—almost certainly a dead end—at the Supreme Court. All the court had to do was refuse to hear his case and he would have been on the next train to Leavenworth. Prison had been imminent. Now it was not.

Promoter Bob Arum, also a lawyer, told Herbert Muhammad to get Ali back into the ring because he could be fighting again very soon. First, this new appeals process would take at least a year, probably more, to play out. Second, there was a chance the government, unwilling to say what particular people had been bugged while they talked with Ali, might simply drop the case. Either way, boxing could be part of the near future.

Arum was excited. There would be no need for preliminaries and tune-ups. Ali's career simply could be resumed at the top level.

"He's in good shape," the promoter said. "He's working with a heavy bag in some garage in Chicago, I hear. We don't think there's any point in putting him in a tune-up. We look ahead for him to knock the block off of these fellows who are claiming the championship. He thinks he can do it and the suspense of seeing whether he could come back after a layoff would make for the biggest fight of all."

Morgan, the ACLU lawyer, the actual lawyer, was not as optimistic. He was positive but warned that Ali would not be fighting "in 60 days." Things take time. He still hadn't received a transcript of the Supreme Court's decision.

"The government has admitted it bugged five separate Ali conversations," Morgan said. "They regard only one of those sensitive to the national security, but I feel all of them are vital to the case. I will demand to look at the record of the four other conversations and am prepared to raise all manner of hell as to the illegality of those tapes."

Ali was euphoric. He was in Denton, Texas, to open the Black Arts Festival that night at North Texas State. After the Supreme Court decision was announced, an afternoon press conference was set up in the Speech and Drama Building. He gushed about the news.

"I'm just thankful, thankful," he said. "It is all in the hands of Allah and if the decision goes against me, I'll take it."

The questions about his boxing career were immediate. He said he hadn't been in a gym for two years (so much for Arum's reports about hitting the heavy bag) and was twenty pounds overweight. Reporters noted that his face seemed pudgy and his blue suit seemed tight. He said he hadn't paid much attention to boxing, but that he might return.

"I would have to consult with my manager and business advisers," he said. "It would be a matter of debt and not prestige that would get me back in the ring. It would be to pay off a lot of needless debt."

As if he were exercising some hyperbolic muscles that had not been used for a while, he went through a quick rundown of the heavyweight situation. (So much for his claim that he hadn't been paying attention.)

"The people look at Jimmy Ellis and they know he is not a champion," Ali said. "They look at Joe Frazier and they see how short and slow he is and they know he is not the real champion. People see these guys fight and they look out in the crowd, see me and comment, 'Isn't that Muhammad Ali?'

"You can't watch a fight now and feel like it's for real. The boxing game is just like wrestling. It's phony."

He said that if his conviction was overturned and Frazier offered a fight, he would take it. He thought he could lose the weight and be ready by September. He said his philosophy had not changed.

"I believe in standing on your religious beliefs regardless of where they lead you," he said. "I have faith that we will win out in the end."

The joy did not last long. Ali flew to Philadelphia the next day, picked up his black Cadillac at the airport, and drove back to Chicago, where he was summoned to the home of the Honorable Elijah Muhammad. The news was startling: the most famous convert to the Nation of Islam had been suspended from the Nation of Islam.

The Honorable Elijah Muhammad, seventy-two years old now, not in the greatest health, did not like those comments about a return to boxing. His dislike would be printed for the world to read in the April 4, 1969, edition of *Muhammad Speaks,* the Muslim newspaper. This was an edict, almost a legal word from God:

> I want the world to know that Muhammad Ali has stepped down
> off the spiritual platform of Islam to go and see if he can make

money in the sport world. His plans were announced through-out the week beginning Monday, March 24, 1969, on radio and television.

Mr. Muhammad Ali plainly acted the Fool to the whole world.

The first reason Allah (God) came to us is to give us money. That is the first blessing Allah mentioned. (Meaning that Allah would provide money without the pursuit of irreligious goals.)

Mr. Muhammad Ali, in his answer to the moderator of the tele-vision program stating that he intends to return to the boxing ring.

Put us out of the corner of Mr. Muhammad Ali. Any man or woman who comes to Allah (God) and then puts his hopes and trust in the enemy of Allah (God) for survival, is underestimating the power of Allah (God) to even help them.

Mr. Muhammad Ali has sporting blood, this plainly shows it.

Mr. Muhammad Ali desires to do that which the Holy Quran teaches him against.

The Holy Quran teaches that this world is nothing but sport and play and Mr. Muhammad Ali wants a place in this sport world. He Loves It. We have seen it on television. We see it is in his blood.

This statement is to tell the world that we, the Muslims, are not with Mr. Muhammad Ali in his desire to work in the sports world for the sake of a "leetle" money.

Allah (God) has power over the heavens and the earth. He is sufficient for us.

In a second article, in the next issue of the newspaper, one week later, the Honorable Elijah Muhammad expanded on his thoughts. Ali had responded to the Devil's wink, had gone running toward boxing at the first chance. He had chosen the idea of money over principle. Tempta-tion had won his soul. There was a price to pay.

"MUHAMMAD ALI IS OUT of the Brotherhood of the followers of Islam under the Leadership and the Teachings of Elijah Muhammad for one (1) year," the Leader wrote. "THIS MEANS that Mr. Muham-mad Ali is not respected in the society and circle of Islam for the next year, from the date of this statement and this issue of MUHAMMAD SPEAKS newspaper.

"THIS IS THE LAW, which Allah (God) gave to me which to punish my followers. MR. MUHAMMAD ALI shall not be recognized by us, even under the holy name, MUHAMMAD ALI. We will call him Cassius Clay with us. We take away the Name of Allah (God) from him, until he proves himself worthy of the name. THIS IS THE RULE OF ALLAH (GOD) to me."

In a final line to the statement, the Leader wrote to his followers: "LET THIS BE A LESSON TO YOU WHO ARE WEAK IN THE FAITH." Ali was an example. If the U.S. government could make him an example, the Nation of Islam could, too.

This was quite a development. Ali was the most prominent face the religion had to offer, certainly more well known than the Leader himself. He had changed the entire arc of his life for the religion, chosen the sackcloth instead of the palace. He had divorced his non-Muslim wife, stepped away from a fortune. He had preached, won converts, traveled the country. He had lived the perfect Muslim life . . . until now. The terms seemed harsh.

Ali was chagrined. He answered one phone call from John Crittenden, columnist for the *Miami News*. He was apologetic toward the Leader.

"He's got a right to spank all of us," he said. "I'm his humble servant. What I said was out of place. . . .

"Boxing is temporary. I will be a Muslim until the day I die. I only pray that he will forgive me and let me back. We have a saying there are no big i's, only little u's—that it's all in the religion. When I'm wrong, I must pay like everybody else."

The rest of the media phone calls and invitations went unanswered. Talking from the top of his head had brought trouble again. He did travel to Atlanta to speak at Georgia Tech, where he was confronted by reporters. He was short with his answers, contrite again.

"I'm retired," he said. "I'll never climb into the ring or go into an arena again. I don't want to talk to you guys. I'm not here to talk sports. It was talking sports that got me in trouble a few weeks ago. I'm through with sports.

"How would it look if, when the case had turned in my favor, I suddenly returned to the ring and turned my back on the ministry? It would look like I did it to get out of the draft. I'd look like a hypocrite. That's not the way it is. My life is my belief."

Nobody in the outside world, especially the boxing world, believed this was the end of his career. Cynicism about his religion ruled most thoughts. Something would be worked out if the possibility to fight arose. The government might put an end to Ali's career, but the Muslims wouldn't. Would they?

The immediate problem for people who called him by his Muslim name (and many still did not) was what to call him now. Was he still Ali? Should Cassius be substituted? He *hated* Cassius, didn't he? Stan Isaacs, columnist for *Newsday* in New York, tried to clear up the confusion. He called lawyer Chauncey Eskridge in Chicago. Eskridge, remember, was not a Muslim.

"What about the business of the name?" Isaacs asked. "What do you call him?"

"I call him 'Muhammad Ali,' just like before," Eskridge said.

"But what about the edict from Elijah Muhammad? He said he's to be known as Cassius Clay for a year."

"That's what the brothers will call him. But to the rest of us, he's Muhammad Ali."

"If I don't believe in the Muslim religion, then I call him by his Muslim name of Muhammad Ali?"

"That's right," Eskridge said.

"And if I were a Muslim, then I wouldn't call him by his Muslim name but would call him Cassius Marcellus Clay, the name he once renounced as a slave name?"

"That's right."

"Well, let's suppose I was walking down the street with a friend of mine who was a Muslim in good standing. If we bumped into the fighter, then I would say, 'Hello, Muhammad,' and the Muslim brother would say 'Hello, Cassius.' Is that correct?"

"I would say that's about the way it is," Eskridge said.

Somewhere Bud Abbott and Lou Costello smiled.

—

The Honorable Elijah Muhammad was a prominent character in absentia when the rehearing for Ali arrived in June in the same Houston courtroom where he had been sentenced to the maximum five years and $10,000 fine two years earlier. Judge Joe McDonald Ingraham, yes, him again, heard the new evidence about the five FBI wiretaps that involved Ali.

One was from the phone of the late Dr. Martin Luther King, another was from the phone of an undisclosed foreign caller, and three were from the phone of the Honorable Elijah Muhammad. The information gained from the wiretaps seemed no more than the usual drips and drops of normal conversation, but the effort involved to obtain that information was eye-opening.

This was one of the first cases brought to retrial after the Supreme Court ruling. FBI agents were forced to testify about their illegal work in this rare situation. Illegal surveillance sounded as if it had been a nine-to-five job, good benefits, a chance for promotion.

C. Barrett Pickett, twenty-eight, described listening to the Leader for eight hours a day, five days a week during a four-year period from 1962 to 1966. No perspiration-filled van, no secluded rented room were involved. He listened from the air-conditioned FBI office in Phoenix to conversations from a hidden microphone in the Honorable Elijah Muhammad's house and a tap on his phone. A signal would alert the agent to turn on the recorder when the phone was engaged. The microphone was voice activated.

"Five or six" other people shared the job. They were listed on the FBI payroll as clerks. Pickett said he had been promoted this year to special agent. He said he didn't know much about the equipment he used. He couldn't describe it very well.

"The inside?" he said. "It was just a bunch of tubes. I am not an electronics expert. It was a Magnavox recorder."

One of the tapes from the Leader's phone was a call from Herbert Muhammad to Ali filled with simple gossip. Another was a call from John Ali to Ali. More gossip. The third call was from Ali to the Honorable Elijah Muhammad. The date was March 24, 1964.

"Elijah took the call from C. Clay," the log read. "Elijah asked the time there and then said it was only 1 hr. faster than here. Elijah said he wanted to see Clay as he was going to make a minister out of him when he quit thinking of fighting all the time. Elijah said he would make a better minister than a fighter anyhow. Elijah then said he would contact him when he had time to talk to him. Elijah also told him to keep quiet."

The message had historical interest because it came four days after Ali flunked his physical exam for the army, a month after he beat Liston to win the title in Miami, but it didn't reveal anything that would have affected his draft case. It did show that the Leader's views on fighting and being a minister had not changed in five years.

Ali's lawyers made some convoluted attempts to say the wiretaps had hurt his chances at deferments at different points in the legal process, but Judge Ingraham wasn't listening. A rumor circulated that the judge surely would reduce Ali's sentence, but again he wasn't listening. On July 24, 1969, he resentenced Ali to the maximum five years, $10,000 fine.

"Do you have anything to say for yourself?" the judge asked before he pronounced sentence.

"No, sir," Ali said. "Except I'm sticking to my religious beliefs. I know this is a country that practices religious freedom."

The appeals process now would begin. It was expected to last for a year, probably longer. The next stop would be the Fifth Circuit Court of Appeals in New Orleans. The final stop would be the Supreme Court.

The decision that he wouldn't box again sounded firm, and he repeated it at every chance he could. He was retired. How many times did he have to say it? The truth was that he was boxing again. A few days after the resentencing, he boxed every day. He fought seventy one-minute rounds against retired champion Rocky Marciano in the strangest heavyweight title bout ever conceived.

Okay, maybe it wasn't real boxing, but it had the feel, the smell, the sweat of real boxing. The shorts, the shoes, the Ali Shuffle. In a ring in a television studio in Miami, Ali and Marciano filmed the assorted jabs and feints, left hooks and uppercuts, the celebrations and knock-downs needed for the Super Fight, an imaginary fifteen-round battle that would be decided inside a National Cash Register 315 computer.

The final Cadillac. The procession through Louisville for the seventy-four-year-old boxing icon, almost a state funeral, a celebration of his inspirational life. June 10, 2016.

The renamed Muhammad Ali always has been close to his mother, Odessa, but his conversion to the Nation of Islam religion becomes a hurdle in their relationship. His father, Cassius Clay Sr., standing on the porch with Ali's brother, Rahman, also is disappointed with Ali's choice of faith. Rahman is as committed to the NOI as his brother is.

This was the apology that never arrived. Appearing before the Illinois Athletic Commission on February 25, 1966, Ali is expected to retract his comments about the Viet Cong and the war and the military draft. Instead, he underlines the words he had said. His fight against Ernie Terrell is canceled.

Three days after he refused to apologize to the Illinois Athletic Commission, Ali is at the Nation of Islam's Founder's Day observance in Chicago.

The climb through the courts begins as Ali arrives at Local Draft Board No. 47 in Louisville on March 17, 1966, to file his first appeal. There will be changes in lawyers, changes in venues, changes in the facts of his case over the next five years.

A nap at the GPO Tower in London, the city where Ali will fight Brian London in 1966. This will be his third straight foreign defense of his title while the United States is off-limits after his Viet Cong remarks.

Ali works on the heavy bag in preparation for Brian London.

Ali works on Brian London on August 6, 1966, at Earls Court in London. The preparation on the heavy bag paid obvious dividends. London was dispatched in three rounds.

Muhammad Ali's one public appearance with Dr. Martin Luther King Jr. in Louisville on March 29, 1967. The two men differ greatly on thoughts about integration, but Ali's case does help bring Dr. King into antiwar demonstrations.

Hayden Covington, Muhammad Ali's lawyer from the Jehovah's Witnesses, files a sixty-seven-page petition at the U.S. District Clerk's Office in Houston on April 25, 1967, in an attempt to delay his client's appearance for induction three days later. The appeal fails. His client is drafted but refuses to be inducted into military service. The long battle begins.

There had never been a meeting of top American athletes like this before, and there has never been one since, as football great Jim Brown gathers assorted African American stars in Cleveland to offer guidance to Ali. Seated, front row, were Bill Russell, Ali, Brown, and Lew Alcindor. In the back row were Carl Stokes, Walter Beach, Bobby Mitchell, Sid Williams, Curtis McClinton, Willie Davis, Jim Shorter, and John Wooten.

Ali watches with rapt attention as the Honorable Elijah Muhammad delivers another lengthy sermon. The Honorable Elijah Muhammad had become the most important person in the young champion's life.

The champ marries seventeen-year-old Belinda Boyd on August 18, 1967, in his home in Chicago. Presiding is Dr. Morris H. Tynes, minister of the First Church of the Master. Herbert Muhammad, Ali's business manager, is his best man.

Major Benjamin Coxson—con man, convicted felon, gadfly, mayoral candidate, drug dealer, and, ultimately, murder victim—is the man who brings Ali and family to Philadelphia. Coxson hands Ali a house and then another house in Joe Frazier's hometown. Ali hands Coxson notoriety and friendship.

Ali on Broadway. He makes his entrance in *Buck White* at the George Abbott Theatre in a preview on November 17, 1969. The play, a serious musical about race and protest, was a bomb. It closed after seven performances.

The Supreme Court for the spring session of 1971—the court that decides Ali's fate. Seated, from the left, are Associate Justices John M. Harlan and Hugo L. Black, Chief Justice Warren E. Burger, and Associate Justices William O. Douglas and William Brennan Jr. Standing, from left, are Associate Justices Thurgood Marshall, Potter Stewart, Byron R. White, and Harry A. Blackmun.

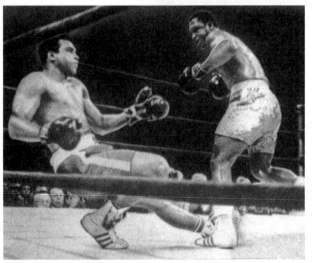

A hard left hand sends Ali to the canvas in the twelfth round of his Fight of the Century collision with Joe Frazier on March 8, 1971, at Madison Square Garden in New York City. Although Ali stands after three seconds, the knockdown cost points on all three judges' scorecards, leading to a unanimous fifteen-round decision.

The wait for the decision at the end of the Fight of the Century lacks the excitement of the fight itself. Frazier is a winner by unanimous decision, but Ali, in succeeding days and months, would make it sound like he was the true winner. This would lead to two more confrontations with Frazier.

Lawyer Chauncey Eskridge leaves the U.S. Supreme Court in Washington, D.C., on April 20, 1971, after making his last-chance appeal to keep Ali out of jail.

College speaking engagements become the major source of income once Ali is banned from boxing. He travels across the country, applauded at some stops, booed at others. Here he is at Boston University.

The addition of Maryum (left) and the twins, Jamillah and Rasheda, complicates life for Muhammad and Belinda. Gone are the freewheeling husband-and-wife trips to the colleges.

A free man. Muhammad and Belinda pose for pictures outside the 50th on the Lake Travelodge in Chicago after he heard the news of his Supreme Court victory. They are staying at the hotel while he trains to fight Jimmy Ellis, his first opponent after the loss to Joe Frazier.

A program with 129 variables would be fed into the NCR 315. The machine would whirr, hum, and decide, step-by-step, punch by punch, how the fight would evolve. The filmed punches and pieces then would be spliced together to match the computer results, and at the end there would be a winner and a loser. The fight would be shown, one time only, at an estimated five hundred locations in the United States, countless more around the world.

Old questions became new. Could the five-foot-ten, 185-pound Marciano crowd the six-foot-three, 211-pound Ali into a corner or against the ropes and pound away at his body to wear him down before finishing the job with a knockout bomb to the chin? Could Ali dance away from the trouble, unleash rapid combinations that would accumulate to leave the Rock a bloody mess? This was a barroom argument about men and eras put into a different form with this hard-to-understand computer stuff. Rocky was 49-0, 43 knockouts. Ali was 29-0, 23 knockouts. Rocky was Italian, white. Ali was Nation of Islam, black. There were selling points to the promotion.

"I would fight him like I fought everybody else," the forty-five-year-old Marciano said. "I more or less had one style that I used at all times. I started low, making myself a smaller target, and stayed in close. I learned how to punch inside and I tried not to be at long range. Instead of being in the middle of the ring, I liked to get my man up against the ropes where he could be an easier target and couldn't move."

"Rocky would admit himself that he was a good, strong mauler, a slugger type fighter, and I was scientific, creative and artistic," the twenty-seven-year-old Ali said.

The television event, the television show, the television fight, whatever it was, came from the active imagination of forty-four-year-old disc jockey and entrepreneur Murray Woroner of Miami. Actually, it was an extension of an idea he had pursued two years earlier on *radio*.

What would happen if the great heavyweight champions, from John L. Sullivan at the beginning to Muhammad Ali at the present, were matched against each other in a single tournament? That was the original radio concept. Each fighter would be at his physical prime. His attributes and statistics would be typed into the NCR 315, this much-bigger-than-a-refrigerator computer. Whirr, hum, "Hello from Madison

Square Garden . . ." This would be great radio. A script would be written; then read by Guy LeBow, a big-time radio announcer. Woroner
would do the color. Sound effects would be added.

Sixteen radio bouts would be held in the first round. Joe Louis and
Jack Dempsey and James J. Corbett would be involved. Old men would
be young again. Dead men would be alive. There would be a grand
series of shows. Radio. Anything can happen on radio if imagination is
involved.

"A couple of years ago Stan Freberg cut some commercials for Radio
Month, promoting radio listening, you know," Woroner told William
Johnson of *Sports Illustrated* in a buildup to the tournament. "In this
one bit, Freberg was arguing with a guy about radio versus TV, and
the other guy said, 'All right, tell me what radio can do that television can't do better.' Freberg says, OK, here's what I'm gonna do. First
I'm going to drain all the water out of Lake Erie.' And then there are
these gurgling, down-the-drain sounds—burble, burble, glug, glug, you
know. Then Freberg says, 'And I'm gonna fill Lake Erie with whipped
cream.' The sound goes spllssshhhhshsh. Now Freberg says, 'And I've
got this 40,000-ton cherry sitting in a field in Ohio and I'm gonna
call out the whole Air Force to fly up there and get it.' So you hear
zzzzzzzzzzzzzzz—the roar of a million airplanes. Freberg says, 'OK, they
got that big cherry up in the air now and they're carrying it toward the
whipped cream in Lake Erie; zzzzzzzzzzzzzzzzzzz.' The planes are working hard now and Freberg says, 'They're over the lake and now I'm going
to order them to drop that 40,000-ton cherry into that whipped cream.
OK, boys, let'er GOOOOO-OO-o-o-o!!!' Then you hear a gigantic
sppppplllllssssshhhhlllllooooooppp!!! The cherry has fallen square into
the whipped cream in Lake Erie—you've just seen it in your mind's eye,
and Freberg says, 'Now lemme see TV do that.'"

The radio tournament was a success. Woroner sold his version of the
whipped cream and the airplanes to 375 stations that carried the action
as Marciano climbed through the brackets and stopped Jack Dempsey
with a thirteenth-round knockout in the final. The number of stations
jumped to 650 when the promoter returned with a middleweight championship tournament in 1968. (Sugar Ray Robinson won a decision
against Stanley Ketchel for the title.) The possibilities for computer
matchups seemed endless. Elections . . . could Abraham Lincoln beat

John F. Kennedy? Wars . . . Nazi Germany versus the Roman Legions? Anything, really.

Television wasn't a consideration until a million-dollar defamation lawsuit arrived from Ali's lawyers. Ali had been ousted in the quarter-finals by Jim Jeffries in a fifteen-round decision. (Jeffries even dropped him in the ninth with body punches.) Ali was outraged. How could he lose to a ninety-two-year-old fighter who had been dead for the past twenty-four of those years? Not to mention that Jeffries was the first Great White Hope, brought back to fight (and lose) against Jack Johnson.

"Jeffries was the flat-footedest champion they ever had," Ali complained. "He was slow, but for 15 rounds [on the computer] he outpunched me. It made me mad and I know it must have knocked a lot of confidence out of people as far as these imaginary fight things are concerned."

The lawsuit gave Woroner the idea for the television fight. He convinced Ali to settle for a dollar, then added a $9,999 payment for filming the Super Fight with Marciano. Ali accepted. Marciano, retired now for almost fourteen years, also accepted and immediately went on a diet. He had lost fifty pounds and wore his everyday toupee when he came to the first film session. He looked very much like the fighter who last fought Archie Moore on September 21, 1955.

"Rocky Marciano was the sweetest man," said Ali's wife, Belinda. "I always wondered why white people pull Marciano out of their ass all the time. Now I saw why. He was undefeated. I sat in a room with him and he told me that Ali would never go undefeated because Ali had the fever. He would have to fight until someone stopped him. Rocky said that's what boxers had, the fever. It was hard to walk away from that."

Ali said in his autobiography that he felt closer with Marciano in the filming than he ever did with any other white fighter. They did what they were supposed to do, threw the fake punches and grimaced the fake grimaces and, in Marciano's case, wore the fake blood, but they knew they were working at nonsense. This was total nonsense.

"This is bullshit," Marciano said.

Ali agreed.

Seven different endings were filmed. The computer would pick one. Neither of the fighters would know the result until they watched the finished product on January 20, 1970, with the rest of America. Marciano had sat with Dempsey in a Los Angeles restaurant listening to the final radio fight, nervous, happy at the end. Maybe that would be the finish here, two nervous fighters in the same room. They both were contracted to go on trips, promote the fight. They would be linked together for a while.

Except three weeks later Rocky Marciano died.

On the night of August 31, 1969, the eve of his forty-sixth birthday, he was a passenger in a Cessna 172 that crashed in a field in Newton, Iowa, on a flight from Chicago to Des Moines. The pilot; another passenger, twenty-eight-year-old Frankie Farrell; and Marciano all were killed. A surprise birthday party awaited him in Des Moines.

Ali was stunned. The fight had just happened.

"For a guy his age he was in just as good shape as me," he said. "He was slimmed down and didn't have any fat that I could see. When he got tired, I was tired. Most of the time we pulled our punches, but once in a while one landed.

"For a week after that, I couldn't lift my arms because the body punches were for real. They say that's the way he beat his opponents when he was fighting, and I can believe it."

Two days before he died, Marciano was asked about the Florida meeting with Ali. He gave an honest reply.

"From what I've seen of Cassius Clay, he's as good or better than anybody I fought," he said. "I really don't know if I could have beaten him. I would like to have fought him. Even if I lost I'd have known that I fought the best. I always liked to fight the best."

He died before knowing the computer result.

The thought that Rocky had left with Belinda, that her husband had "the fever" for boxing, no different from most other boxers, seemed to ring true. The imaginary boxing seemed to have brought back the feelings for real boxing. There began to be signs, murky plans for a boxing future.

Ali was in Miami two weeks later, and Jimmy Ellis, friend and former sparring partner, was getting ready to defend his piece of the heavyweight championship against the ever-present Henry Cooper in

London. Jimmy could use a sparring partner and Ali could use the $100 for the day, and there the two old friends were, back in the old 5th Street Gym wearing sixteen-ounce gloves and headgear. There was no air-conditioning and Angelo was watching all movements with a director's eye and it all seemed very familiar.

The idea of a real fight did not go away. Thoughts were shared. Hazy thoughts, but thoughts.

"If I go to jail for five years," Ali said at the end of the workout, "I'll be 32 or 33 when I get out, and then maybe it's you and me, James."

"Well, I'll be 34 then," Ellis said. "And I'll either have made a lot of money or else I'll be so mad at not making it I'm going to be looking to hurt somebody. I may give you a return match clause and beat you again."

"Tell you something about money, James," Ali said. "Between the tax and what you pay your help and one thing and another—like my $1299 a month alimony—you can't keep much. Maybe money talks, but all it ever says to me is 'good-bye.'"

Money always was a question. Money was a lure. The quotes from Ali when he first heard that he might be able to fight again were the quotes that were remembered. Money would get him back in the game. The quotes after the ruling by the Honorable Elijah Muhammad were sentimental, but not his true feeling. The money was out there. He would fight again. That was the thought.

A small story came out of Macon, Georgia, that an attempt had been made to rent the nine-thousand-seat local coliseum for an Ali fight in the fall, but the proposal had been rejected by the city council. A bigger story soon came out of Mississippi. Frank Chambers, chairman of the state athletic commission, announced on October 11, 1969, that a license had been issued to arrange an Ali fight. The state had not held a boxing match "in at least 15 years" and was not tied to any of the organizations that had taken away Ali's titles. Mississippi seemed like a good bet.

The proposed promoter was Major Coxson, a flamboyant forty-year-old character from Philadelphia who had become Ali's friend. The Major had an extensive history with the American judicial system—arrested seventeen times, convicted ten times, two years in Lewisburg federal prison—but that had done nothing to dim his style. He owned eleven luxury automobiles, a collection that included a Rolls-Royce, a Jaguar, and assorted Lincoln Continentals and Cadillacs. He had charm, style, and no visible means of support.

Ali met him at a Philadelphia event. The Major had arrived in his black-and-silver Rolls—bulletproof glass and a list of other accessories including a chauffeur—and Ali was impressed.

"Take a ride with me," the Major said.

The friendship was born.

The Major had been a hustler all his life. In his senior year at Benjamin Franklin High School he stole enough money from his job as a car hop to buy a Cadillac, which he rode to school every day. He ran for president of his senior class and won in a landslide with three hundred more votes than there were members of the senior class.

After a failed attempt at college, he took over the daily operation of a center city parking lot. He convinced the owner of the lot to let him wash cars while he was watching the lot. Within a year he had extended that agreement to ten parking lots and employed a hundred people washing cars.

With his profits, he became involved in the used-car business and branched out from there. He was reputed to be a friend and business associate of Philadelphia Mafia capo Angelo Bruno. Philadelphia police suspected he was the largest drug dealer in the black community.

Ali was another addition to his luxury lifestyle. Ali gave him class, increased stature. The deposed heavyweight champion still said in public that he was retired, but the Major decided that maybe that idea could be changed.

"I wanted to see if I could take on the challenge of getting him a fight," Coxson told Maury Levy of *Philadelphia* magazine a few years later. "I called every governor in the country. I got a lot of bullshit. I figured I'd go down south. At least I'd get a straight answer. I contacted John Williams, the Governor of Mississippi. He had one arm. He didn't know if I was black or white. I went down there with Gene Kilroy. Gene is white. He was selling telephones in briefcases. . . .

"We went down to Mississippi and we got into the governor's office because they thought Gene was me. Anyway, we set up a fight and came back to Philadelphia and called a press conference at the Bellevue to announce it."

(Levy, the writer, said that Coxson heard he was writing an Ali story, so Coxson called and asked to be included. This was the Major's public relations style.)

The fight was dead just about the time the press conference had finished. The three-man Mississippi Athletic Commission said it could not sanction a bout involving someone who was "not in good standing" with any national boxing commission. The Major said the federal government had intervened, which may or may not have happened.

The important part was that Ali and the Major were friends. Ali appeared at the press conference. He seemed ready to get back into the game. He already was spending a lot of time on the East Coast visiting the many college campuses. Philadelphia was a central location. The Major had a house with twenty-two telephones, bedroom walls covered with mirrors, and bathtubs the size of small swimming pools. Philadelphia was a place to stay.

An added bonus was that the city was the home of Joe Frazier. There was no doubt now that Frazier was the opponent Ali was destined to meet if he ever was allowed to climb back into the ring. Jimmy Ellis might be the champion recognized in most states around the country by the commissions, but Frazier was the champion of New York and Massachusetts and the public mind. His unbeaten record had been extended to 24-0 after he stopped Jerry Quarry in June. The true debate about heavyweight champions had become Frazier or Ali.

Ali now tweaked the rivalry in fits and starts whenever he could with disparaging words about the so-called champ. Frazier had said some harsh words in response. Ali always seemed to have mischief in his messages. Frazier mostly was mad. He said the world was sick of "Clay" with his "fussin' and fumin'."

"What kind of man is this who don't want to fight for his country?" Frazier said. "If he was in Russia or someplace else, they'd put him up against the wall. He walks around like he's one kind of a big hero, but he's just a phony, a disgrace. Everybody wants to say what I'm saying. Some people can't, but I can."

Philadelphia made confrontation easy. Ali could increase the promotional heat. That was what he did on the afternoon of September 23, 1969.

He would claim in his suspect autobiography that the events of that day were all a show, that he promoted a fight at the PAL gym where Frazier trained to get people talking. He said Joe was part of the plan. Ali went on local radio that morning and announced he was going to show up at the gym. Joe promised he would be around. It all went from there. . . .

Frazier said that he was surprised by what happened. He said he wasn't really part of a plan. He heard Ali on the radio, on WHAT, shouting about how he was going to show up at the gym and Frazier was a coward and they could fight right there. What happened was just Ali doing what Ali did. . . .

Planned or not, the show was very good. Ali and an entourage arrived at the gym. He was full of bluster. He wanted to fight, wanted to fight now. He started taking off his clothes. Frazier, ready for training, said that he was right there and more than willing to take part. News of this confrontation had spread around the North Philadelphia neighborhood, and the gym was filled with more than a thousand people, at least twice as many as fire laws allowed. Police arrived. This was an event. This was a happening.

Before an actual fight began, as the cramped logistics kept the two men from each other, the police intervened. They said there would be no fight here. The two men could "take it to the park" if they wanted to fight. That would be Fairmount Park, where Frazier did his roadwork.

Ali put on his clothes and was off to the park in a hurry in a red convertible. Frazier started to follow, but was stopped by trainer Yank Durham, who talked some sense into him. Why fight in the park for nothing? Fight in the ring somewhere for millions of dollars. Frazier agreed.

That left Ali with the stage.

"He wants to show he can whip me," Ali shouted to a crowd, estimated at between two thousand and six thousand, that had convened in the park. "Let him prove it in the ghetto, where the colored folks can see it.

"Here I am, haven't had a fight in three years, 25 pounds overweight and Joe Frazier won't show up," he said. "What kind of champ can he be?"

Frazier, at the gym, complained about Ali's arrival in Philadelphia.

"He came here to run me out of my home town," he said. "If I don't take him on, he'll try to run me out of my own house next."

Frazier repeated that thought the next day when the two fighters appeared on the syndicated *Mike Douglas* show. The host sat between the two of them, looking very white and small. He asked Ali if he, indeed, would like to run Joe Frazier out of Philadelphia.

"The town's not big enough for two heavyweight champions," Ali said with his serious Wyatt Earp look.

"This show might not be big enough," Mike Douglas said.

Ali waited for Frazier on the street after the show. When Frazier came out of the studio, Ali stopped signing autographs on the top of his car and charged across the street. As friends tried to hold him back—and friends tried to hold Frazier back—Ali was able to land one soft punch that landed on Frazier's shoulder. The two fighters then were separated.

News at eleven.

13

Media

The change in the country had become noticeable. The tilt in public opinion against the war in Vietnam grew by degrees. Lieutenant William Calley went on trial for atrocities in My Lai. The Chicago Eight went on trial for the demonstrations at the 1968 Democratic convention. The Weathermen staged a Days of Rage protest about the Chicago Eight trial. A moratorium against the war was held across the country. A march on Washington was held. President Richard Nixon called for help from "the silent majority." Vice President Spiro Agnew complained about "the nattering nabobs of negativism." The first troop withdrawals were made.

Surprise. The mainstream was not such a turbulent place for the draft-resistant heavyweight champion of the world anymore. Maybe he had picked the right side, after all. Just maybe. Next-door neighbors now said worse things about the war than Muhammad Ali said. Or at least their kids did.

His trip back into public acceptance had begun. The possible return to boxing was accompanied by a definite return to the public consciousness. He was on more shows, in more publications, was a marketable product again. His exile to the margins of American life seemed to be winding down. The chance of jail still stood very much in his future as his appeals once again went through the courts, but his public presence was more livable. There was no doubt about that.

He showed up in more and more interesting places with more and more interesting people. . . .

—

Firing Line—The excitement of the matchup on the December 12, 1968, installment of *Firing Line* could be seen from the beginning. If the world could not have Muhammad Ali versus Joe Frazier inside the ring, it would have to settle for Ali versus William F. Buckley outside the ring. Adjectives and invectives would replace jabs and haymakers. No one would be saved by the bell. The three-knockdown rule was not in effect.

Buckley, forty-four, was the obvious favorite. He was the host, the erudite intellectual, the founder of the right-leaning *National Review,* known on the show for his polysyllabic takedowns of assorted guests. This was what he did for a living. Ali was Ali, the underdog here, but a man still well conditioned for argument, especially on familiar subjects. This also was what he had done for a living for a while.

To begin, Buckley went through a longish introduction of his guest, licking his tongue the way he did for emphasis, relishing the argument, the words delivered from some Ivy League, Yale University, Skull and Bones production line, well formed and specific, scholarly to the tenth degree. He could have been describing a troubled character from an Elizabethan drama about boxing and the Powers That Be. His familiar clipboard rested on one knee, ready to go. He had a red-and-white pen in his right hand to take notes. School was in session. Listen up. That was the first impression.

Except . . .

Except, heading toward the end of the introduction, William F. Buckley quoted his guest.

"I am the greatest," Buckley said in that same cultured voice, repeating Ali's longtime boast. "They all must fall in the round I call."

"I was the onliest boxer in history people asked questions like a senator," he said in a second quote, same voice.

The effect was not good. The words sounded silly the way he said them, as out of character as if Ali tried to use one of the host's multisyllabic tongue twisters outside its proper context. The idea arrived in the viewer's head that this would not be a rout. Buckley had one voice, for sure, powerful and intimidating, but Ali had another voice, also powerful, also effective. Ali hadn't said a word, but he was in the game.

His answers might not conform to Buckley's rules of exaggerated grammar, but they were well presented and smart. All those exchanges in all those colleges had removed the rough spots from his arguments. He was the master of his favorite subject: himself. Buckley was only a well-spoken visitor.

An early example came when the host said that Joe Louis had never been treated unfairly by white America, that Louis showed that a black man could be the heavyweight champ and white America would applaud. Why should Ali have so much trouble while Joe Louis did not? Why would white America persecute him?

Ali quickly said he was different from Joe, a man he called "a good red-blooded American boy," as champion. They were from different times, different circumstances. Joe did not become a Muslim. Joe did not rattle sensibilities. Ali said his problems were not with the white public, but with the people who ran his sport and with the government. The reason the boxing commissions of America had taken away the title here was for religion, not race. Boxing people had been gunning for him from the minute he became a Muslim.

"I did make the statement that many people in authority in boxing were trying to get me out of the way and they couldn't do it physically, so they did it legally," Ali said. "The only way they could take the title and make it justifiable to the public was to say that he wouldn't serve his country. Twice, you'll recall I was denounced by the draft . . . but as soon as I became Muhammad Ali, as soon as I announced I was a Muslim, then all of a sudden I became smart."

He continued with his point that the government was out to get him. Buckley's eyes rolled dramatically. ("Buckley had a red-white-and-blue flag on his face, didn't he?" a member of his staff said.) Ali kept pushing. The government treated him differently because of who and what he was.

"I have to be cool and not savagely radical when I see the white boys, our future leaders, see them leaving the country by the hundreds," he said. "When I see the teachers breaking into draft board houses in Wisconsin and Baltimore, tearing the files out of the walls, making a bonfire out of 5,000 draft cards, pouring blood on them. And then I see them go to court and the judge says two years and I get five years for legally doing what I'm doing."

Four months earlier, Buckley had been involved in a celebrated joust with writer Gore Vidal, his political opposite. ABC had hired the two men to provide some conflict to its coverage of both the Republican and Democratic conventions, the literate conservative pitted against the literate liberal in a series of eight mini debates. On August 28, 1968, in the seventh meeting, with the chaos of the Democratic convention and the riots in Grant Park as a backdrop, the debate spilled over its civilized boundaries.

Moderator Howard K. Smith posed the question of whether raising the Viet Cong flag, as the demonstrators had done, was akin to raising a Nazi flag during World War II. Vidal defended the demonstrators, criticized the police and the Chicago politicians. Buckley interrupted, even after Vidal told him to "shut up for a minute." Buckley's point was that Nazi sympathizers during World War II had been treated fairly, but ostracized by society. He thought this should be the case here, too. These were the same kind of demonstrators.

"The only sort of pro- or crypto-Nazi [today] I can think of is yourself," Vidal quickly interjected.

"Now let's not call names," said moderator Smith, located in another studio.

The word "Nazi"—Vidal later said he meant to use "fascist"—made Buckley rise in his chair. He came back with his own name. He attacked Vidal's homosexuality.

"Now listen, you queer, stop calling me a crypto-Nazi or I'll sock you in your God damn face and you'll stay plastered," Buckley said. "Tell him to go back to his pornography and tell him to stop making allusions of Nazis to someone who served in the infantry in the war."

This was tougher stuff than Ali's televised confrontations with Joe Frazier. There wasn't a fistfight, of course, no trip to Fairmount Park, but the exchange was candid and notable television. Buckley continued to sputter. Vidal derisively called him "Mr. Infantry," and mentioned that he never had heard a shot fired in anger. It all drew great publicity.

There was none of that here.

"Mr. Buckley liked Muhammad Ali," said Agatha Dowd, the host's major research assistant for the show and at the *National Review.* "He did think he was being manipulated by Elijah Muhammad. That was the basis for a lot of his questions. He was trying to point that out, trying to help him, but Mr. Ali wouldn't listen to it."

Indeed. Buckley tried to demean the theology of the Nation of

Islam, called it "a curious mixture of Calvary and the OK Corral," but Ali brushed past in a flurry of accolades for Elijah Muhammad. He defended his leader's role in the death of Malcolm X, extolled Elijah Muhammad's effect on the lives of ordinary black men. He presented himself as exhibit A.

"I barely got out of school," Ali said. "I mainly got out of school because I was champ and actually didn't pass. Now you are a wise man. You are an intelligent man. And if I was not a Muslim, a follower of the Honorable Elijah Muhammad, I couldn't talk to you for two minutes. I believe I can hold my own in an intelligent conversation. And it all comes from the Honorable Elijah Muhammad."

Wherever it came from, Ali's performance was terrific. He fought to no less than a draw with the heavyweight debate champ of the right-wing world. He was self-assured, logical. There were no histrionics, no jokes. If he didn't know a big word, he asked the meaning and went from there with his measured response. In many ways, this was a more shocking performance than his win over Sonny Liston in Miami. He was a bigger underdog here. He did great.

Four young people asked questions in the final minutes. One was Jeff Greenfield, who later became a political commentator on various networks. Another was Vere Gaynor, a student at Columbia University. ("I was the only conservative college student in New York City at the time," he later said. "That got me on the show. I mean, they'd shut Columbia down in those protests.") The final question from one of the young people was how Ali could return to fight as a boxer if he ever had the chance, while he refused to fight in Vietnam.

"Boxing cannot be compared with war," he said. "We have gloves on. We have cushions. We have judges. We have ambulances. The intention is not to kill. We don't have bullets. We don't have mama kill, baby kill. It is a sport. We are not there to kill. So boxing in no way can be compared with machine guns and bombs and—"

"Fair enough," Buckley said, thanking everyone and wrapping up the questions and the night.

Ebony—"Noon rush hour pedestrians did a double take at the boyish looking, dapper brown giant who had just stepped out of a mid-

Manhattan hotel lobby into the street," began the article by Hans-Jürgen Massaquoi. "His mischievous eyes, set deeply into a broad, clean-cut face, seemed to challenge the crowd to recognize him. He was not to be disappointed."

This was the April 1969 issue of *Ebony* magazine. No other magazine in America would have described the dapper brown giant exactly this way. Since November 1945, *Ebony* was the black man's monthly answer to *Life* magazine, filled with stories about black celebrities, black businessmen, black issues.

"Before I started *Ebony*," publisher John H. Johnson once said, "you'd never know from reading other publications that Negroes got married, had beauty contests, gave parties, ran successful businesses or carried on any normal living activities."

You did now. Johnson, twenty-eight years old when he began the magazine, had built it into a black media powerhouse. The magazine boasted that it sold more than a million copies per month that were read by as many as 4,750,000 people. These were people who spent money. Each issue usually ran over 150 pages, filled with ads directed at the black-folk demographic.

"Because they rarely have a chance to buy handsome homes, they tend to furnish the homes they have handsomely," an *Ebony* advertisement on the back page of the *New York Times* declared to other advertisers about its circulation. "Because they are not sure of their reception in public entertainment places, they entertain bountifully at home. And because they have a healthy vanity, they spend more on personal grooming products than do white families of the same income."

Ali was on the cover, dressed in a white shirt and red tie, blue suit pants, holding Maryum on the diving board of a swimming pool. Belinda, wearing a head scarf, watched. The title of the story was "The Unconquerable Muhammad Ali." The other two stories headlined on the cover were "A Year of Homage to Dr. Martin Luther King" and "Black Astrologers Predict the Future." Belinda looked nervous in the picture, as if Ali might drop the baby. Ali looked relaxed.

There was no doubt that he knew his audience in the magazine. In the eight pages of text, weaving through all those ads for all those products, he talked to the people in the barbershops and the salons in the ghettos who would take this issue of the magazine off the pile and begin to read while they waited for haircuts. These were people he knew.

He talked about his religion, about how black men put up the moon sixty-six trillion years ago, about how the black man is "the original man," about how "God, Himself is a black man." He talked about how he could get his title back even if he went to jail because he was twenty-seven now and would be only thirty when he came out, two years off the five-year sentence for good behavior. He talked about how prosperous he still was, which perhaps was an expedient stretch of the truth.

"I just bought this last week for $10,000—I mean cash, baby . . . ," he said, pointing at a new Cadillac limousine. "Shoot! I ain't worked for two years and I ain't been Tommin' to nobody and here I'm buyin' limousines—the President of the United States ain't got no better one. Just look at it! Ain't it purty?"

The message was different from the one he delivered at colleges because any small filters he might use on campus had been removed. This was how he could talk when he was just talking. He was on the street corner, selling the NOI, looking for converts, fishing. This was a chance to go fishing on a grand scale. Why was he still so happy, despite all his problems? He could tell you.

"The reason I can still be happy is because the Honorable Elijah Muhammad has taught me the truth," he said. "When they wanted me to denounce him and asked me, 'Which do you want—the Muslims or the $20 million, all kinds of white women and a big home in Hollywood?' I said, 'Give me the Muslims,' and I haven't regretted it yet."

How strong was his faith?

"The white man has stopped me from boxing and I have more Muslim brothers than I ever could dream of havin'," he said. "Every city I go to, the Muslims are waitin' with open arms and offer to share what little they have with me."

Massaquoi, the writer, was the managing editor at *Ebony*. He had a unique background. The mixed-race son of a Liberian diplomat to Berlin and a German woman, he was raised in Nazi Germany during World War II. He was seen as a non-Aryan second-class citizen, never persecuted, but unable to join the Nazi Party or even the army, which he wanted to do very much. After the war, he wound up in Liberia for a few years, then immigrated to the United States, where eventually he joined the U.S. Army as a paratrooper. Following his army tour, he graduated from the University of Illinois with a journalism degree.

If he talked about these experiences with Ali—and his wife, years later, said that he did—they didn't put any pause in Ali's fishing. There was no doubt that he stood with Elijah Muhammad on matters of race.

"No intelligent black man or black woman in his or her right black mind want white boys or white girls comin' to their homes, schools and churches to marry their black sons and daughters to produce little, pale half-white, green-eyed, blond-headed Negroes," Ali said. "And no white mind wants black boys and black girls comin' around their homes, schools and churches to marry their white sons and daughters and in return introducin' their grandchildren as little mixed-up, kinky-headed, half-black niggers."

If that wasn't clear, he expanded.

"White women are the most dangerous," he said. "They smile at you, and the next thing you know, you let your guard down. But that'll never happen to me.

"What hurts me more than anything is when I pick up the newspaper or turn on the television or go to the movies and see black men huggin', kissin', and makin' love with white women, pretendin' to be in love with our 400-year-old enemy and brainwashin' black boys and girls into believin' that white women are prettier and better than our beautiful black sisters."

He also included the NOI view of women as second-class citizens. Women should be loved, but they never should be treated as equals. He said he didn't "take any sass" from Belinda.

"Allah made men to look down on women and women to look up to men," he said. "It don't matter if the two are standin' up or layin' down. It's just natural."

Massaquoi did not object in the article to any of these racial conclusions that sometimes seemed to come straight from some tract from the Third Reich. He liked Ali. He liked him a lot. He finished with great praise for Ali's stand against the boxing establishment and the dictates of a white-dominated government. Ali was a model of defiance for young black men.

This was the final article of the issue. The back cover was an ad for Salem cigarettes. Over a picture of a green-and-white package of the product and the admonition that "You can take Salem out of the country but . . . you can't take the 'country' out of Salem," a handsome black man and a handsome black woman smoked their cigarettes on a handsome path in a handsome park.

"Whenever you light up a Salem, you get a menthol taste that's country soft, country fresh," the advertising copy read. "Because Salem gently air-softens every puff. Take a puff . . . it is springtime!"

Commerce—unlike other parts of American society—was color-blind.

The Joe Namath Show—On October 13, 1969, three months after he had been resentenced in Houston, three weeks after the Fairmount Park confrontation in Philadelphia, no news from the Supreme Court, Ali appeared on *The Joe Namath Show.* Namath, the twenty-six-year-old quarterback of the New York Jets, was the one athlete in the country who caused almost as much generational debate as Ali did. Cocky, stylish, outspoken, seen with beautiful women late into the New York nights, he had "guaranteed," then produced a 16–7 Super Bowl III win over the Baltimore Colts in January in the Orange Bowl. He was seen by slouch-shouldered white youth everywhere as the epitome of cool behavior with his white football shoes, his long hair, his playboy attitude. Older observers pretty much thought he was an overconfident blowhard. The fact that he was 4-A for the draft, bad knees, did not help his image with this group.

The television show, a local New York production that ran for thirteen weeks, was an easy-money reflection of the quarterback's post–Super Bowl notoriety. Sportswriter Dick Schaap, who had coauthored Namath's easy-money biography *I Can't Wait for Tomorrow . . . 'Cause I Get Better-Looking Every Day,* was the cohost. Schaap had known Ali for a number of years, had introduced eighteen-year-old Cassius Clay to Sugar Ray Robinson in Harlem on the way to the 1960 Olympics in Rome. He also had seen him a few weeks earlier in Chicago, where he had introduced him to another famous New York athlete.

"In the fall of 1969, when the New York Mets finished their championship baseball season in Chicago, Muhammad and I and Tom Seaver had dinner one night at a quiet restaurant called the Red Carpet, a place that demanded a tie of every patron except the dethroned heavyweight champion," Schaap would write in a 1971 article for *Sport* magazine. "The conversation was loud and animated, dominated by Muhammad as always, and about halfway through the meal, pausing for breath, he turned to Seaver and said, 'Hey, you a nice fella. You a sportswriter?'"

Dinner was followed by a trip in Ali's Cadillac. This was the car with the pink-and-white upholstery and the two phones. Knowing now who Seaver was—the dominating right-handed pitcher for the Mets—Ali insisted on calling Seaver's wife from the car. Seaver gave him the number.

"This is the baddest cat in the world," Ali shouted into the car phone when Seaver's wife, Nancy, answered. "And I'm with your husband and five hookers."

The hope was that some of this looseness would be repeated on *The Joe Namath Show*. This did not happen. Both Namath and Schaap would admit later they had no idea what they were doing in television at this stage of their lives, so they mostly ad-libbed their way through the thirty minutes. The shows were amateurish, painful to watch.

The show with Ali was as painful as any of them.

"Well, Muhammad, really, in all seriousness, how's it feel to be with a star?" Namath began, crossing his legs, rubbing his hands together.

Namath was the star. That was the joke.

"I'd have known if I had taken that flight with the astronauts," Ali replied. "They got pretty close to 'em [the stars] . . . oh, you're talking about yourself?"

Namath and the audience didn't seem to understand the response. Astronauts? Stars? What? The interview bumped forward from there.

Ali was dressed in a black suit, white shirt, dark tie. He had a pocket handkerchief sticking out of his jacket. Hunched down in his seat, he was less animated than usual. He read a poem that he used often at paid appearances—"I like your show, I like your style, but your pay is so cheap I won't be back for awhile"—repeated how badly he wanted to fight Frazier. He recounted the meeting at the gym and the craziness in the park. He said, "10,000 people came out to watch the showdown" and "50 police cars showed up to cool the crowd." The possibility of the Mississippi license still was dangling when the show was taped, so he challenged Frazier to show up in Mississippi for a bout. Frazier, he said, already had turned the idea down.

"He said he wouldn't fight in Mississippi," Ali said. "Said the Greyhound doesn't even go down there."

Namath asked if Ali thought he could be as good as he ever was if he returned to the ring. Ali handed the question back, asked if Namath thought he could take two years off and come back the same.

"No," the quarterback said.

"Well, I could," the boxer said.

The audience cheered.

Two guests were featured in each week's Namath show. One usually was from the sports pages, one from the entertainment/celebrity section of the newspaper. This approach created such unusual pairings as Tom Seaver and Yaphet Kotto, O. J. Simpson and Maxmilian Schell, Weeb Ewbank and Ben Gazzara, and Rocky Graziano and Truman Capote.

The guest for the second half of Ali's visit was actor George Segal, thirty-five, who had become a prominent leading man in both movies and television. Segal recently had signed a contract to star in *The Owl and the Pussycat* with Barbra Streisand. This, he said, had made him nervous. He would have to film nude scenes with Streisand.

"I'm going to be naked a lot of the time, it turns out," he said. "I'm embarrassed about that."

He said he was running laps in his shorts around Central Park every day to lose weight and feel better about himself on the big screen without clothes. There was byplay conversation with Namath and Schaap about nakedness and Barbra Streisand. This did not seem to interest Ali. He shrunk lower in his chair, became even less animated. Namath tried to coax him back into the conversation. Ali refused.

"You're talking about all of that naked stuff," he said. "I don't take part in conversations like that. Civilized people don't take part. I don't take part."

Namath and Schaap tried to joke their guest back into a happy mood. Their guest wasn't moving. Not that way.

"Maybe I should get out of here," he said.

He was convinced to stay for the final few minutes of the show, but was reserved. There was no more talk about nakedness. After the show, Namath and Schaap made semi apologies for the topic. They said they were surprised, didn't know Ali would be offended. He made a semi apology in return.

"I gotta act like that," he said. "You know, the FBI might be listening, or the CIA, somebody like that."

Esquire—The photograph on the cover of *Esquire* for the November 1969 issue gave an indication of how much liberal clout had formed behind Ali. Standing in a boxing ring was a disparate group of twelve intellectual and entertainment notables of the day, each pointing at the camera under a headline that read "We believe this: Muhammad Ali deserves the right to defend his title." Ali, the subject of a long article in the magazine, was not in the picture.

Author Truman Capote was in the front row of the group, right arm extended, left posed akimbo as if he were impatient, same as everyone else, waiting for action. He tried to make a tough-guy face, but didn't really succeed. A slight smile sneaked out the edges of his lips. Author Budd Schulberg, Senator Ernest Gruening, and Howard Cosell stood in a second row, grim and determined, followed by playwright Sidney Lumet, singer/actor Theodore Bikel, former boxer José Torres, artist Roy Lichtenstein, actors Richard Benjamin and James Earl Jones, and writers George Plimpton and Michael Harrington. It was quite a group.

"I can't remember how we decided to call each of these people," *Esquire* art director George Lois said years later. "I do know that the first one I wanted was Senator Ernest Gruening. He was 80-something years old, the first member of the Senate to be against the war. One of only two senators to vote against the Gulf of Tonkin Resolution. He was with Ali from the beginning."

Nineteen months earlier, Lois had staged an iconic cover shot with Ali as Saint Sebastian, the martyr, with the stick-on arrows and fake blood. (Ali called the Honorable Elijah Muhammad for permission to be in the shot.) This was a different approach now. The martyr had more and more people on his side. Lois could feel it. Ali might be going to prison—the art director thought this would happen soon, probably in the next few months—but there would definitely be a bigger ruckus than there would have been nineteen months earlier.

The ring for the cover shoot had been constructed in photographer Ira Mazer's studio in Manhattan. The mood was pleasant, the subjects gathered around cocktails and hors d'oeuvres for a start. The famous people seemed proud of what they were doing. They were making a public stand, not only for Ali, but against the war and against the government. They were part of a protest in their own celebrated way.

"I stayed out of the civil rights protest," James Earl Jones later said. "I didn't think I was very good at carrying a placard, and I was hoping to find some other way to serve."

The mood, alas, had slipped a bit by the time the picture was taken. The planned centerpiece in the shot in George Lois's mind was supposed to be Lew Alcindor, the seven-foot-two basketball center, fresh out of UCLA and three consecutive NCAA championships, the number-one draft pick of the Milwaukee Bucks for the coming 1969–70 season. Lois envisioned Alcindor as the most dramatic figure of them all, exploding out of the middle of the picture. Big man. Big presence. Big issue. Bam. The art director had talked once with the basketball player, secured his consent, gave him the date and place for the shoot. There had been no subsequent conversations because Alcindor had not answered his phone. This made Lois nervous. Now Alcindor hadn't appeared.

While the other luminaries waited, the art director kept trying to contact the basketball player. Nothing. He called Alcindor's mother, whom he knew a little bit. She had no answers. Nothing. Finally, he decided they would have to take the picture without Alcindor. The other people were looking at watches, talking about conflicts in their schedules. Theodore Bikel, a big man but nowhere near as big as Alcindor, was moved into the center as everyone assembled in the ring.

Everything was fine. Except then the ring collapsed.

"One end buckled," Lois said. "Everyone started to slide toward that end. They fell like bowling pins. It was like you were scraping a plate."

Finally, after apologies were made, nobody injured, the ring repaired, the cover shot was taken. The participants were proud again.

The story inside the magazine was written by Irwin Shaw, who had recently finished his six-hundred-page novel *Rich Man, Poor Man.* He mostly retold Ali's tale in a sympathetic fashion here, noting how the government had made him a special case, no doubt because of his religion. Inequities abounded. He spelled them out.

"Among other figures in the world of sports there has been no noticeable rush to the flag, and even among those few professional athletes who have been trapped into some form of military service there has been no case, to my knowledge, of a halfback or pitcher or even a Boxing Commissioner who has fallen in action or even heard a shot fired in anger. I am not suggesting that a regiment be formed of boxers and fullbacks, to be dispatched immediately to the Mekong delta, thereby depriving me of the pleasure of watching them throw a left hook or go off tackle, but to the ordinary American, especially the black American, it must seem that one man has been singled out and hounded down where hundreds of his more cautious colleagues have been allowed to drift off safely."

The title of the article was "Muhammad Ali and the Little People." An illustration across three pages by Jean Lagarrigue showed Ali as a modern Gulliver, tied to the ground in boxing trunks and work boots, while various Lilliputians dressed as groupies, families, soldiers, policemen, boxers, and television crews ran busily around and over his body.

The final piece of art was an enlarged version of the petition that was begun on the cover. Lois had recruited ninety more names.

"We just called anyone we could think of to add them to the list," George Lois said. "It was easy. Like I said, people felt good about doing this."

Under pretty much the same demanding headline—"We believe that Muhammad Ali, Heavyweight Champion of the World, should be allowed to defend his title"—the group again was eclectic and interesting. It included Elizabeth Taylor, Peggy Lee, Kurt Vonnegut, Jim Morrison, Leontyne Price, Jackie Robinson, Norman Mailer . . . all in large, aggressive type. This was the list:

George Abbott, Isaac Asimov, John Barth, Orson Bean, Harry Belafonte, Richard Benjamin, Theodore Bikel, Dirk Bogarde, Father Henry J. Browne, Kenneth Burke, Richard Burton, Truman Capote, Diahann Carroll, John Cassavetes, Dick Cavett, Shirley Chisholm, Jordan Christopher, Sybil Christopher, John Ciardi, William Sloane Coffin Jr., Henry Steele Commager, Howard Cosell, Harvey Cox, Sammy Davis Jr., James Dickey, Robert Downey, Fred Ebb, Ralph Ellison, Jules Feiffer, Leslie A. Fielder, Richard Fleischer, Henry Fonda, Robert Forester, Al Freeman Jr., Allen Ginsberg, Joel Grey, Herbert Gold, Paul Moore Jr., Senator Charles E. Goodell, Paul Goodman, Ernest Greuning, Michael Harrington, Mary Hemingway, John Hersey, John Huston, William Inge, Jasper Johns, James Earl Jones, John Kander, Elia Kazan, Neal Kenyon, John H. Knowles, MD, Peggy Lee, Roy Lichtenstein, Joe Louis, Robert Lowell, Allard K. Lowenstein, Myrna Loy, Sydney Lumet, Dwight Macdonald, Ali McGraw, Norman Mailer, Frank Mankiewicz, Elaine May, Roddy McDowall, Marshal McLuhan, Marianne Moore, Jim Morrison, Robert Motherwell, Patrick O'Neal, Gordon Parks, Mario Pei, George A. Plimpton, Norman Podhoretz, Katherine Anne Porter, Paula Prentiss, Robert Preston, Leontyne Price, Hal Prince, David Riesman, Jackie Robinson, Robert Ryan, John Schlesinger, Budd Schulberg, Robert Sherrill, Tom Smothers, Edward Steichen, Igor Stravinsky, Elizabeth Taylor, Virgil Thomson, Jose Torres, Rear Admiral Arnold E. True, Louis Untermeyer, John Updike, Jack Valenti, William J. vanden Heuvel, Gloria Vanderbilt, Kurt Vonnegut Jr., Eli Wallach, Roger Williams, Karen Wyman, Fred Zimmerman, Father Malcolm Boyd, Mike Nichols.

One name that was missing was Lew Alcindor. Lois finally contacted the twenty-two-year-old basketball star a few days after the shoot. Lois said Alcindor apologized and said he withdrew because he was afraid of "retribution." Retribution? From the FBI? The NBA? White America? None of the above.

"He told me that he had become a Muslim, but in a different sect from Ali," the art director said. "He said there had been threats from the Nation of Islam. He couldn't be seen with Ali."

A year and a half later Alcindor would change his name to Kareem Abdul-Jabbar as a member of the Hanafi sect of Sunni Muslims. The leader of the Hanafi sect was Haamas Abdul Khaalis, a onetime national secretary of the Nation of Islam who had broken away from the Honorable Elijah Muhammad, much as Malcolm X had. Alcindor's reservations were well founded. Future sad events would prove that he was right to worry.

14

Buck White

The singing was energetic and somewhat tuneful. The acting seemed a bit stiff. Those were the first thoughts of Peter Wood, a thirty-eight-year-old freelance writer assigned by the *New York Times Magazine* to watch the efforts of the newly ordained leading man on the stage of the George Abbott Theatre at 152 West Fifty-Fourth Street in the first rehearsals for the new musical.

Imagination was required by Wood to make judgments. The stage was almost empty. The curtains had been pulled back and sets still had to be constructed and actors held printed scripts while they spoke. A three-piece combo supplied musical accompaniment instead of the full orchestra. Wood sat in an aisle seat in the front row of the mostly empty theater and took notes.

He was no drama critic. His last story for the magazine had been about a tuna tournament in Galilee, Rhode Island.

"I was what I would call 'a journeyman writer' at Time-Life books," Wood said years later. "I also wrote some sports stories for the *Times* magazine, but not the usual sports. I wrote about ice fishing, about racquet sports, things like that, the different sports. That was why I got this assignment, I guess. This wasn't really a sports story. It was different."

Muhammad Ali on Broadway.

Very different.

The play was called *Buck White* and Ali was the title character, aka Big Time Buck White. The timing and the parameters of the script and the money, short as it was ("$300 and something a week" to start, according to his wife), all seemed right. There would be a generous raise if the play was a hit.

Clauses in the contract knocked out all "objectionable" language and allowed Ali to leave with two weeks' notice if the Honorable Elijah Muhammad ordered him to quit or if his appeal on the wiretap evidence was denied by the Fifth Circuit court of appeals and then denied by the Supreme Court and he had to begin to serve his prison sentence. The possible trip to prison always was included in his plans. There also was a clause that permitted him to leave for two weeks to engage in "a so-called major heavyweight fight" if that possibility arose.

"Nothing's changed," Ali told reporters. "I'm just doing what I always did, talking the truth . . . but getting paid for it here."

A little more than a year earlier, *Life* magazine had invited him to New York to see a performance of *The Great White Hope,* starring James Earl Jones as Jack Johnson. Ali loved the play, told Jones backstage he thought "this is about me . . . Jack Johnson is the original me." He even went onto the stage after the audience left to say a couple of Johnson's lines about coming back from Europe to fight Jess Willard in Cuba.

"Here I is," Ali said in the empty theater, speaking for Johnson, speaking for himself, maybe speaking just to hear his own voice. "Here I is."

Now he had his own empty theater.

His role required him to sing four songs. His character was a fast-talking radical speaker, arrived at the headquarters for the Beautiful Allelujah Days (BAD) organization to answer questions and rally the troops. A bit of typecasting might have been involved.

The first act was filled with anticipation of Buck White's arrival. Ali didn't even appear until he made a grand entrance just before intermission. He dominated the second act as he delivered pronouncements, answered questions, and sang those four songs. The song he sang now was called "Mighty Whitey," the showstopper, the money number. He sang with great enthusiasm.

You've had us in your lock
Tight as any cage.
And now you're acting shocked
Cause we are in a rage.
Us on the bottom with you on the top
That's just the game that we aim to stop.
Yeah, that's all over now,

Mighty Whitey.
All over.

The cast was gathered around him. He stood on a soapbox to be seen. Wood, the writer from the *Times,* noted that his subject liked the song, sang it to himself during breaks in the rehearsal. Ali seemed relaxed, natural with the message. He sang about the National Guard, about the police, about how there would be no peace.

In the middle of the song, not in the script, he stepped down from the soapbox and moved to the middle of the stage. He stared straight at Wood. He pointed his finger at him. There was no doubt about whom he meant to single out because no one else was in the nearby seats.

If you're expecting us to Uncle Tom
You might as well get your bomb
Cause it's all over now Mighty Whitey
All over now.

Here Ali bounded across a bridge that was stretched over the orchestra pit, landed in the aisle, bent down, and put the writer in a headlock. The writer didn't know what to think. Ali laughed.

"Was you scared?" he said, releasing his grip. "Supposing you were from out of town—Akron, Ohio, say—just here in New York for a day or two, and caught this play. Would I have scared you?"

"You're damn right," Peter Wood said.

Sometimes there are stories that write themselves.

The play had a history. Though the idea of Ali as an actor seemed far-fetched, this was no slim piece of musical-comedy froth put together to showcase a famous name and sell tickets. This was a political play in a political time, an all-black cast delivering challenging words from the ghetto to the rest of America. There was an edge here. On opening night, Oscar Brown Jr., the singer, poet, political activist who had written all the songs, would become the first black man to direct a musical on Broadway.

Both a straight version and a musical version had been produced in different cities around the country, and both had been successful. The straight version had run for 169 performances off Broadway in New York a year earlier at the South Village Theatre on Vandam Street. Critic Clive Barnes of the *New York Times* called it "a great evening in the theater."

"Suddenly the audience is brought from the happy world of the melon-grinning shoeshine boy to the real world of black aspiration and revolutionary black power," Barnes wrote. "The fact that this transformation is achieved with no loss of the smiling ironic atmosphere makes it all the more impressive."

Joseph Dolan Tuotti, a white man from the Bronx, who had moved to Los Angeles, was given credit as the writer, but pretty much the only part of his work that remained was the title. As the cast of black actors in LA rehearsed and performed the play in the beginning in various storefront surroundings, virtually every word of dialogue had been changed. One actor would say "Nobody would say this in Watts" and another would say "Nobody would do that in Harlem," and words and actions were bent into street-familiar syntax.

Elgin Baylor, the basketball star from the LA Lakers, and Jack Haley Jr., the television executive whose father played the Tin Man in *The Wizard of Oz,* became early backers when a first few good reviews appeared. A first real home was found in a theater built in the burnt-out husk of the Safeway supermarket at Imperial and Holmes, which had been at the epicenter of the 1965 Watts riot.

Ron Rich, who was an actor in the cast, also was the producer. He had wanted to find a theater in Watts and one day drove past the "smelling and stinking" carcass of the supermarket, which had been left abandoned and untouched since the riot. Perfect. All he needed was some benefactor to turn a carcass into a theater.

Early in his career, Rich had heard old stuntmen, veterans from the Roy Rogers and Gene Autry movies, talk about the vast holdings and capabilities of Warner Bros. Studios. Warner Bros. could build anything and build it fast. The actor/producer called the office of Jack Warner, the head of Warner Bros. Studios, a notorious no-nonsense, bottom-line curmudgeon, a Hollywood titan. Would Mr. Warner be available? There was a pause while a secretary checked. Rich realized how crazy his idea was. What was he thinking? Then, good Christ Almighty, Jack Warner Himself came on the phone. He had a big voice.

Rich, who was nervous, outlined what he wanted to do. The theater would be good for Watts. This would be part of the healing. There would be a workshop for actors and playwrights. He mentioned that Budd Schulberg, the famous writer of *On the Waterfront,* wanted to be involved. There was this play *Big Time Buck White* that would get everything moving. This was a chance to make a social statement for Warner Bros. Blah, blah.

Warner turned him down. Rich laid out a few more great things the theater would do. Blah, blah. Warner turned him down again. Big voice.

"Well, maybe you should reconsider," Rich said, mad at the direction of the conversation, moving into his own big voice.

"Why would I do that?" the executive said.

"Because if you don't, there'll be hundreds of black people surrounding your offices in the morning and they won't leave. Nothing will move."

"You do that," Jack Warner said, "and I'll lock up every nigger you send in my jail back there."

Rich laughed at the audacity of this. Certainly nervous no more, he mentioned that Warner didn't have a real jail, just a prop jail for movies. Warner laughed at Rich's audacity. They hung up. A few hours later, Warner's secretary called. She asked Rich if he could be at the Safeway store at eight o'clock the next morning. She said no more.

At eight a.m., he stood at the husk of the store as the trucks started pulling in. An army of workers and equipment appeared. By lunchtime, the theater had been built. The stage. The dressing rooms. The seats. The offices. Everything.

"It was amazing," Rich said. "There was a first class theater in the middle of Watts. By noon of that day."

This was now the Frederick Douglass Theatre. (Rich called Jack Warner to thank him. Warner did not take the call.) *Big Time Buck White* became the first production. *Time* magazine did a story. Vice President Hubert Humphrey called and told Rich that if a theater could be built in the middle of Watts, all things were possible.

In search of a broader audience after a while, white people leery of journeying to Watts after the assassination of Martin Luther King in the spring of 1968, the play eventually was moved to the more traditional Coronet Theatre on La Cienega Boulevard. A memorable opening night started another successful run, the house filled with celebrities attracted by personal invitations from Marlon Brando. Steve McQueen was there. Warren Beatty was there. James Coburn sent the all-black cast a statue made from licorice.

Oscar Brown, who wrote more than a thousand songs in his life and already had tried and failed to mount a production of another counter-cultural Broadway show, saw the play and asked to turn it into a musical. That version, featuring fourteen songs, opened in San Francisco on February 12, 1969, at the Committee Theatre. It also was successful.

Five months into the run there was a move to take the show to New York. This was June 1969. Zev Buffman was a Los Angeles–based producer, already involved with both the straight play and the San Francisco production. He recently had staged the musical *Jimmy Shine,* featuring the emerging actor Dustin Hoffman on Broadway. Buffman wanted *Buck White* to be his next show. He also wanted Muhammad Ali to be the star. In the LA original, Dick Williams, a powerful, politically committed thirty-year-old actor with a large Afro and a larger stage presence, had played Buck White. In the musical, a conga drummer named Big Black, another powerful character, played Buck. Neither man had a name that would stand out on a New York marquee. Ali did.

The problem was getting in touch with him. Oscar Brown, though he had grown up in Chicago, did not know the boxer. He looked for help. Ron Rich, still an actor and producer in the production, said he didn't know Ali, but knew Howard Bingham, Ali's close friend and confidant. Rich called Bingham, went to Chicago to meet Ali, then took him to see a version of the straight play. Ali liked it. He also liked Rich. They became friends.

After the usual false starts and stops attached to any production, contracts were signed and the first rehearsal was held at the George Abbott Theatre on October 29, 1969. Oscar Brown said he was "honored" to have Ali as his star.

"He is a historical figure," the director said. "He ranks with Samson, David, the champions of old. He has remarkable mental capacity. He stood up for what he believes in—at great sacrifice. When he spoke out on the Vietnam War, he stood virtually alone. He had the courage of his convictions."

Most of the rest of the cast was imported from Los Angeles and San Francisco. The feeling of great adventure associated with any production scheduled to open on Broadway was backed here with some realistic hope. These people already had appeared in the play in other places and it had been well received.

"I'd been in the play in San Francisco, but then I took a role in 'Hair,' also in San Francisco," actor Charles Weldon said. "Oscar Brown came to me and said, 'Hey, Man, you want to come to Broadway?' I'd never been East in my life. When I went to the airport to go to New York, the entire cast of 'Hair' came to see me off. They sang me all the way from the ticket counter to the plane. 'The Age of Aquarius.' 'When the moon was in the Seventh Heaven . . .'"

A great adventure, indeed.

The actors settled into the Wellington Hotel on Fifty-Fifth Street and Seventh Avenue. Ali had a suite with Belinda and Maryum. He was his usual hyperactive self, bouncing, bouncing, one thing to another, but the speed was increased with New York. He was a perfect match for the place that advertised that it did not sleep at night.

He would bounce through the rehearsals during the day, talking all the time, always moving. He would tap other actors in the back of the head and threaten to "knock you out." Then he would tap someone else on the opposite shoulder, make him turn the wrong way, then laugh at the result. He could have been the star of some high school production. The bouncing would continue after the rehearsals ended.

"He wanted me to go everywhere with him," Ron Rich said. "I couldn't keep up. He took catnaps, something I never could do. He'd wake up and be ready to go. Any time, day or night. He'd call my room."

Rich would try to explain to Ali he was tired. Ali would tell him to get moving. Rich would wonder, "What was that noise in the background?" Oh, Ali would say, he already was outside the hotel, calling from a pay phone. People had gathered. How many people? Rich could hear sirens in the background, the police arriving to control the sudden crowd. The police? Rich would say he would be right down.

"Ali never minded a crowd," the actor said. "Years later, I was with him and he shut down the Pennsylvania Turnpike. Someone had given him a $12,000 bicycle from France. We were driving on the Pennsylvania Turnpike and he decided he wanted to try the bike. He pulled the car to the side of the road, pulled out the bike and started to ride it. On the Pennsylvania Turnpike.

"People saw him, Muhammad Ali on a bike, and slowed down and stopped. Got out and asked for his autograph. People on the other side of the road did the same thing. All traffic stopped. Eventually a couple of state troopers showed up. They asked for Ali's autograph, too."

Learning the lines was a problem. Ali learned the lyrics to the songs fine, but the spoken lines were an ongoing struggle. He would practice all the time, then falter on the stage. Sometimes Rich, who had learned all of Big Buck's lines as well as his own, would try to mouth the words to get him started. Sometimes that was not enough.

"Hey, Rubber Band Man, what's my line?" Ali would say, right in the middle of the play.

"Here's your line," Charles Hudson, playing Rubber Band Man, would say in return, then deliver the line.

The official opening was scheduled for December 2, 1969, but previews began in the middle of November. Ali's best moments would come during a question-and-answer period that was part of every performance. Two actors planted in the audience would get things started, then actual members of the audience would ask their own questions. (One of the plants played a white bigot, scripted to ask antagonistic questions. This threatened to be a problem in LA when the entire theater was rented out to the Black Panthers for a performance, but to everyone's relief the Panthers figured out quick enough the antagonist was an actor.) Ali handled the questions the way he did on the college lecture circuit, with ease and humor.

"Why can't I just ad lib all the time?" he asked Rich all the time. "I wouldn't have to learn any lines."

"Because then it wouldn't be a play," Rich said. "It would be something else."

Ali wore a large Afro wig and a fake beard and mustache for the role. He also wore a leather kind of smock that made him look like a cross between a biblical character and the village blacksmith. There was no mention of boxing in the play unless one of the questioners in the audience brought up the subject. Ali would frame his answer in character, say, "This is what Buck White would do in that situation." The one glimpse of the boxer under the makeup came in the middle of a scene called "The Riot." Ali would begin to shadowbox while saying his lines, then go into his shuffle. The other actors would feel the power and back away.

"I'm not going to let him knock me out," one said.

The boxer/actor Clay/Ali did make a small move toward getting in shape. Bundini Brown proclaimed that the champ would need three months to harden his body, six months to be ready to fight again if the possibility arose. Running seemed to be a good beginning. James Earl Jones had said that he ran in Central Park all the time when he was playing Jack Johnson. That was how he survived playing the role. Ali took Ron Rich to Central Park for a first workout.

"Ali hated running with a passion," Rich said. "Just hated it. I'd been a long-distance runner all my life. I'd been a runner and a boxer in the Marines. But Ali didn't know that."

They started running. The pace was not very fast.

Rich talked while he ran. Ali did not. He told Rich after a while that good runners did not talk while they ran. It used up energy. Rich said he understood. He wouldn't want to use up energy. Then he took off, running much harder, much faster, off into the horizon. He looped back, came up from behind the still-plodding Ali, and grabbed his butt.

"And then the motherfucker ran off and left me," Ali said from that moment, delighting in telling the story. "This faggot-ass can outrun me."

The rehearsals often were open to the public. The part of the public that seemed to attend most was female. Charles Weldon would look out from the stage and see a hundred, a hundred and fifty women, all there because they wanted to see and maybe meet Ali. After the show, many of them would stand outside and wait for him to exit.

"The thing was, his wife always was with him, so he'd leave," Weldon said. "That would leave the 150 women for the rest of us. We had carte blanche, something I've never seen at another play. It was a very good situation."

Sometimes an actor, accompanied by one of these women, would run into Ali back at the hotel. The meeting would be remembered. The next day Ali would corner the actor to hear how he made out with the different women, what exactly happened. A large part of his daily conversations always was about the women.

"He definitely had a roving eye," Weldon said. "He'd say, 'Tell me what happened, if you don't tell me I'm gonna knock you out.' All of it was the Sixties, remember. Free Love. Everyone was a bit more misogynistic then."

There was no misogyny in the play. There was no free love. There were no women. Ali always had said he never would make a movie in Hollywood because the scripts all called for him to make love to a woman, most often a white woman. He would not do that on the screen and he would not do that in the theater. He wouldn't even dance.

"I'd never do a love scene," he told reporters. "Not only with a white woman, any woman. I'm a religious person. Get Billy Graham to play a love scene. Or the Pope. It's the same thing."

Belinda came to the theater often. She saw the women, saw how they looked at her husband, but did not worry. She was confident in herself, in the marriage. She did not mind that Ali was a flirt. She thought that was a part of his nature. He always would be a flirt. She considered herself a flirt, too, someone who could make people like her.

She brought Maryum, who was seventeen months old now, walking, and let her prowl around the seats during the rehearsals. The writers who came to do stories on Ali were intrigued by the domestic scene, intrigued by Belinda. Here was this partner of this controversial character, this female Black Muslim. She seemed mysterious, exotic. She still was only nineteen years old.

"She is a big-boned, handsome woman, graceful in a totally unsophisticated way," Peter Wood wrote for the *Times* Sunday magazine. "The day I saw her she had her hair tied back and was wearing a voluminous pants suit out of black silk, becoming to her, but in no way 'revealing.' She laughed at Ali's jokes and horsing around and was not above making fun of him herself. Her whole comportment and style expressed a fine compromise between the strict letter of the Muslim faith and the necessity of being human."

"She is tall and slender and shy to the point of aggravation," wrote another *Times* reporter, Leticia Kent. "She wears no make-up, not even lipstick. . . . Her straight black hair is fastened in a pony tail. She has on a green plaid sleeveless wool maxi-suit. Ali disapproves of miniskirts."

Things were happening. She felt it, too. The possible five-year prison sentence that had hung low over her two years with Ali was still there, maybe lower than ever, but windows seemed to be opening on the sides, light allowed to enter. Opportunities were arriving. Talk was more positive. She had not been around for any of his fights, but this time on Broadway was a look at the excitement that must have existed.

An example. She and Ali went to see H. Rap Brown one night. Brown sent word that he would like to meet Ali. Would Ali like to meet with Brown? Sure. Brown, still the chairman of the Student Nonviolent Coordinating Committee, was in hiding. He was on the FBI Ten Most Wanted List, charged with inciting a riot and carrying a gun across state lines. His most famous quotes later in life, when he also was the minister of justice of the Black Panther Party, were "Violence is as American as apple pie" and "If America doesn't come around, we're gonna burn it down."

There was some risk involved in the meeting. If Ali and Belinda were found to be associating with a wanted felon, they could be sent to jail. Someone picked them up, asked them to put black bags over their heads, and drove them to the apartment house where Brown was staying. The bags were removed. Belinda and Ali were led to see Brown. Belinda noticed that his hiding spot was almost across the street from a police station.

"Something had just blown up and they said he was behind it," Belinda said. "We're sitting there next to this terrorist, this criminal, this revolutionary. Radical! Nicest person you ever wanted to meet. He became a friend of mine. But he was serious about blowing up shit."

Things just happened in New York. Belinda would go shopping to pick up fruits and vegetables. One day, in the middle of her mission, she ran into singer Richie Havens. She ran into comedian Dick Gregory another day. She brought them both with her to the theater to see her husband. Wilson Pickett, the singer, was a visitor.

"That Clay's singing is going to put us out of business," Wilson Pickett said to reporters.

"Hear what one of the greatest singers says about me?" Ali asked. "Wilson Pickett. Was I good? How was the show?"

Frank Sinatra came to one of the preview performances. There was a part in the play where the actors in the cast—not Ali—went into the audience with plates and baskets to ask for donations for BAD, their organization. People threw in spare change or a buck or two. The money was divided by the actors after the show, drinking money, another small perk.

Charles Weldon, Rubber Band Man, held a basket in front of Sinatra and shook it. The audience watched. Sinatra didn't move. Weldon shook the basket again. "Tap the plate. Feel so great. If you donate." People laughed. Sinatra finally pulled out his wallet. He dropped a $50 bill into the basket. He did not seem happy about it. This was the biggest donation ever received.

"Fifty dollars," Weldon said. "I think it's the smallest bill he had in his wallet."

Sinatra came backstage. The singer was a big boxing fan, an Ali fan. He had his own legal troubles, fighting a court order to appear before a New Jersey commission that was investigating organized crime, but New York always was his playground. He had appeared in the past month with Coretta Scott King, Harry Belafonte, and Woody Allen at the Felt Forum in a reelection benefit for Mayor John Lindsay. New York was the place where people like that could be gathered into one room. Sinatra had an invitation for Ali and Belinda. A night on the town.

"He wanted us to go to this exclusive place, Toots Shor's, where all the white stars went," Belinda said. "He sent a limo to pick up Ali and me. We had steak and lobster and the whole whoop-de-doo. All of a sudden, Sammy Davis Jr. and Dean Martin were there, too. The whole Rat Pack. Now, I'm in love with Frank Sinatra. Always have been. That's the kind of music I used to listen to! Sammy Davis Jr. Dean Martin. I'm just sitting with all these guys and I don't know what to think. And then we all get into the limo to go some place else."

Somewhere in the night's travels, someone in the limo spotted two men in the shadows drinking from bottles inside brown paper bags. The limo driver was told to pull to the curb. The two drinkers noticed the limo. One of them noticed one of the occupants, who had lowered a window for a better look.

"Hey, Frank Sinatra is in that limo," the drinking man exclaimed to his friend.

"You better stop drinking that Old Irish Rose," the friend said. "You better cut it out."

The friend looked. He also saw Sinatra.

"Now *I* saw Frank Sinatra!" he said. "You got me seeing that shit. What are we drinking here?"

Ali poked his head out of a window and asked the two guys if drinking was what they did all day every day. Muhammad Ali? Then Sammy. Then Dean. The two drinkers were befuddled. Belinda stuck her head out of the window.

"This is all real," she said. "That's Frank Sinatra and that's Muhammad Ali and that's Dean Martin and that's Sammy Davis."

"Now there's an angel in the car," first drinking man said. "The angel is talking to us."

"It's all real," Belinda said.

Sinatra gave each of the drinking men $100. The men stared as the limo disappeared into the Manhattan night.

The play, sadly, was a bomb. Opening night was December 2, 1969. Closing night was December 6, 1969. A couple of reviews contained kind, reserved words for Ali, but the reactions to the play overall mostly were negative. Some were very negative. The play lasted for only six real performances.

"'Buck White' pretends to be furious, pretends to be a scowling face, pretends to be arranging for black/white confrontation tonight," Walter Kerr said in the *New York Times*. "But 'Buck White' is only saying 'boo!' and saying it in such a painfully artificial way that not even the champion of the dispossessed, the sincere and urgent Cassius Clay, can breathe any fire into it."

"The evening comes to a close without getting anywhere in particular and it certainly fails to be theatrically arresting," Richard Watts Jr. of the *New York Post* said.

"I have a suggestion to make," George Oppenheimer said in Long Island's *Newsday*. "Lift the ban against Ali-Clay's fighting and substitute one against his acting."

Zev Buffman, the producer, had announced great plans for the future before the play opened. Ali had been signed for the entire 1969–70 season, could make as much as $5,000 a week if all went well. A script already was being written for a *Buck White* movie that would be filmed concurrently with the run of the play at a budget of $2.75 million and a cast album would be released and, and . . . all that disappeared when the critics spoke.

"I don't care what the critics say," Ali told United Press International. "I know the play was good, the people were real. Everybody up there on the stage can act and sing and dance better than any critics, so who are they to criticize?"

The postmortems from the people involved did not blame Ali. The play shouldn't have opened on Broadway; should have opened in Harlem or definitely off Broadway. That was a basic thought. This was a counterculture show trying to interest a conservative old-line crowd and conservative old-line critics. The publicity was all wrong, aimed at the wrong people. This was a play that should have attracted liberals, college kids, the young audience. Never happened.

Ron Rich had one other idea.

"I think the FBI shut it down," he said. "There were some things that happened, that didn't feel right. Even with the reviews the play should have run for at least a month. The FBI always was around. They didn't want Ali to make money. J. Edgar Hoover wanted to keep him down."

A final performance was held on January 18, 1970, on *The Ed Sullivan Show*. The appearance had been booked in advance with the idea that the play still would be on Broadway. Ed was Ed in his introduction. He took care of the name problem by stringing all the names together, "Muhammadalicassiusclay." Ali made a big entrance through the studio audience, then sang "We Came in Chains" and "Mighty Whitey" with the cast. Everyone applauded. June Allyson and Buddy Greco also sang on the show. Minnie Pearl told jokes. Bill Dana told more jokes as the character José Jiménez. There was a magician.

Ali talked with Ed after he sang his songs. He used the occasion to pitch the computer fight with Rocky Marciano, which would be shown across the country and around the world in the coming week.

"Who wins?" Ed asked in a stage whisper.

"I don't know," Ali said.

That was that.

Twelve days earlier he had announced his newest career venture. In the offices of Random House at 201 East Fiftieth Street, he was handed a ceremonial first check of $60,000, part of a $200,000 advance to write his autobiography with collaborator Richard Durham, a former editor of the *Chicago Defender.* Doors definitely had begun to open.

"Writing is as good as fighting," the boxer turned actor now turned essayist said. "I'm gonna tell it all just like it is—and I can't wait to get started. I believe that this book will outdo all of them that's been written."

Things were happening. The musical *Buck White* never would be staged again.

15

New York

The first steps to return Ali to a real boxing ring for a real fight in front of real people in New York were taken during the midst of this commercial revival. At the same time those public rehearsals for *Buck White* were being held at the George Abbott Theatre on Fifty-Fourth Street with all those women in attendance, an appeal was filed quietly on November 8, 1969, in Foley Square at the United States District Court for the Southern District of New York to have his boxing license reinstated by the New York State Athletic Commission.

A thirty-three-year-old attorney for the Legal Defense Fund of the NAACP, Michael Meltsner, was in charge of the case. One of the few white lawyers in the office, drawn to the profession by watching the 1954 Army-McCarthy hearings on black-and-white television while he was a student at Stuyvesant High School in Manhattan, Meltsner was earnest, smart, wore some serious horn-rimmed glasses, and had helped make life miserable for assorted segregationist holdouts in the South. He wanted now to make a few people miserable back home.

It had been 132 weeks and a day—925 days, total, more than two and a half years—since Ali refused to take that one step for the draft oath in Houston. April 28, 1967. That was when New York State chairman Edwin Dooley immediately announced the champion's boxing license had been withdrawn, an action seconded by state boards across the country. That ended Ali's career, shut down his livelihood. No one knew when the Supreme Court would decide, yay or nay, to hear his final appeal. That could be tomorrow. That could be a year from now. Nobody knew.

From the beginning, Meltsner had wanted to fight what he saw as a grandstand maneuver by Dooley and the New York commission, but had been held back by Ali's lawyers in the criminal case. Until now.

"I went first to Jack Greenberg, who was the head of the LDF, right after the ruling, and I said, 'there's something here. We ought to consider bringing a case on Ali's behalf because what the state athletic commission did doesn't begin to comport with due process,'" Meltsner said. "He sent me to Chauncey Eskridge [Ali's business lawyer], who said, 'Well, maybe, but we've got other things we're worried about, like the criminal case, and we're not ready for this now.'"

Eskridge and the string of criminal lawyers thought a quick return to the ring would increase the fire directed at their client. How many times was the question asked, "How can this guy fight in the ring if he can't fight for his country?" If Ali did fight in the ring, the worry was that the coast-to-coast animosity that already existed would be amped up even higher. Every American Legion post, every chapter of the Disabled American Veterans would scream that much louder when his case arrived in front of a judge. The public pressures would be enormous. Ali could wind up in jail for a long time.

This opinion had been repeated to Meltsner on a number of occasions. Every time he found himself in the same room as Eskridge, he had brought up his idea. Eskridge always said "it's not timely." This decision had lasted for those 132 weeks and one day, those 925 days.

"Now, two and a half years later, a lot of things combined to change Chauncey's mind," Meltsner said. "The biggest one was that the Vietnam War looked a lot worse now to a lot of people and Muhammad Ali looked a lot better."

On November 3, 1969, five nights before Meltsner filed his case, President Nixon had addressed the nation about Vietnam. He had promised to end the war when he took office in January, but eleven months had passed and the fighting continued and the protests had become much louder. A Gallup poll in October said 58 percent of all Americans now thought it had been a mistake to send U.S. troops to Vietnam. Four years earlier the numbers had been reversed, 61 percent of Americans in favor of the war.

Woodstock had been held during the late summer. Henry Kissinger had attended his first secret peace talks in Paris in August. The U.S. Army had brought murder charges in September against Lieutenant

William Calley for the massacre of Vietnamese civilians at My Lai. The trial of the Chicago Eight had begun in early October with three days of demonstrations organized by the Weathermen faction of the Students for a Democratic Society. Its slogan was "Bring The War Home." Much had changed.

On October 15, a "Moratorium for Peace" was held across the country. This brought out the largest demonstrations yet against the war. A crowd of 100,000 people filled Boston Common. Teach-ins were held on college campuses. In Washington, a group of black militants carried black crosses and a coffin and a Viet Cong flag and tried to bring them onto the White House grounds. In Chicago, at the trial of the Chicago Eight, all the defendants wore black armbands and Abbie Hoffman tried to drape a Viet Cong flag over the defense table. David Dellinger, another defendant, stood and tried to read a list of names of Illinois soldiers who had died in the war. In Bloomington, Indiana, Clark Kerr, the former president of the University of California, was hit in the face with a custard pie when he tried to give a speech.

Four nights later, in a speech in New Orleans to Republican donors, Vice President Spiro T. Agnew called the organizers of the Moratorium "an effete corps of impudent snobs who characterize themselves as intellectuals."

"The young, at the zenith of their physical power and sensitivity, overwhelm themselves with drugs and artificial stimulants," he said. "Subtlety is lost and fine distinctions based on acute reasoning are carelessly ignored in a headlong jump to a predetermined conclusion."

With all this as background, President Nixon addressed the nation in what would become known as his "silent majority" speech. His hound-dog face stared into the camera as he read his serious words from the teleprompter.

"In San Francisco a few weeks ago I saw a demonstrator carrying signs reading, 'Lose in Vietnam. Bring the Boys Home,'" he said. "Well, one of the strengths of our free society is that any American has a right to reach that conclusion and to advocate that point of view. But as President of the United States, I would be untrue to my oath of office if I allowed the policies of this Nation to be dictated by the minority who hold that point of view and who try to impose it on the Nation by mounting demonstrations in the street.

"For almost 200 years, the policy of this Nation has been made under our Constitution by those leaders in Congress and the White House elected by all of the people. If a vocal minority, however fervent its cause, prevails over reason and the will of the majority, this Nation has no future as a free society. . . .

"And so, tonight, to you, the great silent majority of my fellow Americans, I ask for your support."

Two weeks later, on November 15, 1969, a windy, thirty-degree Saturday, the Mobilization March was held from Arlington National Cemetery to the Washington Monument. The estimated 250,000 participants were part of the largest antiwar demonstration in United States history. Signs included "Silent Majority Condoned Hitler" and "I'm An Effete Intellectual Snob for Peace." Two thousand policemen patrolled the parade route. Army and Marine units were massed on side streets, ready for action. Paratroopers stood guard around important Washington buildings. A twenty-four-block area around the White House had been cleared before the march began. A row of fifty-seven parked buses made the demonstration impossible to see from inside the building, where aides said the president worked all day and possibly took some time to watch the Ohio State–Purdue football game on television.

A return to the ring for Muhammad Ali clearly was much lower on any list of national worries than it once had been. The country was scratching at itself so hard that wounds and irritations appeared everywhere. The judicial fate of a boxer, even this boxer, did not matter so much. Eskridge and the legal team from the criminal case did not need to have any more reservations.

There was another reason, too, why it seemed important to move Muhammad Ali back into the ring.

"I had a strong feeling from everyone concerned that Muhammad was broke," Michael Meltsner said. "If he was going to go to jail, it was important that he made some money before he went."

The case was oddly personal to Meltsner. He didn't know Ali, never had met him, had gleaned opinions of the fast-talking man from newspapers and television, same as pretty much everyone else in the country, but the combination of the politics and the boxing made the lawyer think very much of his father. Ira Meltsner, dead now for fourteen years, was part of the motivation.

"My father and I would listen to the fights on the radio when I was growing up," Michael Meltsner said. "Every Friday night. Always the radio. Not television at all. Always the radio in my house. The Gillette Cavalcade of Sports. Don Dunphy would broadcast from the Garden. He had a partner. They were marvelous at how they created the excitement. The crowd reactions. They put it on television eventually, but my father and me, our experience was on the radio."

Meltsner was an only child. The family first lived in Queens, then moved to an apartment in Manhattan. His father was liberal, political, ran once for office and lost, then settled into a career as a salesman of novelties. One of Ira Meltsner's proudest moments was when he signed Jackie Robinson to a first endorsement deal for calendars that would be given to body shops and car dealerships in black neighborhoods. Ira Meltsner, along with his liberal politics, along with the fact that he was a constant reader of books, periodicals, anything, was a baseball fan, a Dodgers fan, a boxing fan. He was not afraid to bet a few dollars on the possible Friday night outcome.

"Here's the question you have to remember when you bet on a fight," he told his son. "What result will make the next fight worth more money for the promoters, the fighters, everyone involved? Look at it that way and you can predict boxing."

He seemed to be right a lot of the time.

Sugar Ray Robinson and Rocky Marciano and Chico Vejar and Chuck Davey and Sandy Saddler and Willie Pep and Carmen Basilio and Jersey Joe Walcott and Gaspar Ortega and a never-ending string of battlers, bombers, dancers, stylists, punchers, winners, losers, and victims of the occasional draw entered the apartment and fought each other around the living room. Ira Meltsner knew their records, their tendencies, their life stories. He told them all to his son.

In looking back, there was an underlying sadness about these Friday nights that neither father nor son suspected. Ira Meltsner not only died when his son was nineteen, but had been dying the entire time they listened to those fights. He had been diagnosed with Hodgkin's disease back while his son still was in utero. Doctors said Ira wouldn't live more than five more years, but they said it to his wife, not him. He never knew he had the disease. His son never knew. The secret stayed with his wife as long as Ira lived. She went to the draft board during World War II and told them that her husband should be 4-F because he had Hodgkin's disease and would be dead before the war ended. The nineteen more years he lived turned out to be a surprise, a gift, ultimately a memory.

"I don't think it's an accident that I wound up with Muhammad Ali's case, that it came out of my thoughts, out of my dreams," Michael Meltsner said. "There's a Freudian expression: 'it's over-determined.' There's all kinds of vectors in this. I've handled all kinds of cases in my time. Some of them very significant—I think, significant. I handled a case that desegregated all the southern hospitals. I handled a capital case when I was 26 years old in the Supreme Court. But this one rang all the bells for many reasons."

The appeal Meltsner filed on November 8, 1969, was built the way most appeals are built. He laid out a buffet line of grievances before Southern District of New York judge Marvin Frankel. Anything that possibly could invalidate the New York Athletic Commission's ruling was included. Was Ali's race a factor in the commission's ruling? Was his religion a factor? Did the commission have the power to make the ruling in the first place? Was the ruling too strict? Was Ali denied "due process"? Was this "cruel and unusual punishment"?

Frankel could pick one of the above. Pick any one. That was all that was needed for Ali to be back in business.

In preparation for the hearing, the client had reapplied on September 22, 1969, for a New York license. His lawyers in the past had been so afraid of the bad publicity, they never even challenged the original decision to revoke his license, never requested the hearing that would have been granted by law. That original license had lapsed at the end of a year.

If he received this new license, then none of the court proceedings, of course, would be necessary. He would be back in the ring as soon as possible. The New York State Athletic Commission, of course, quickly shot down that possibility.

"The Commission has the power and the duty to inquire into the conduct of those who hold or apply for licenses," the agency announced three weeks later in its unanimous denial. "Your refusal to enter the service and your conviction in violation of Federal Law is regarded by this Commission to be detrimental to the best interests of boxing or the public interest, convenience or necessity."

This left the decisions to the court, to Judge Frankel. Meltsner was happy with that possibility. Frankel was forty-nine years old, liberal, appointed to the bench by Lyndon Johnson at the urgings of Robert Kennedy. A personal friend of LDF head Jack Greenberg, he was known to have an ear for the pleas of the underdog. He had grown up in Newark, left home early to work in the Civilian Conservation Corps, had served in the army in Africa during World War II, then put himself through Queens College by driving a taxi and working in the Garment District. He had made his name as a lawyer by winning a First Amendment libel case in front of the Supreme Court for the *New York Times* that centered on statements in an advertisement that sought contributions for Martin Luther King and other civil rights leaders.

If Meltsner could have picked any judge from the Southern District, he would have picked Frankel. The situation seemed perfect.

Except Frankel ruled against just about the entire buffet line of appeals.

"The peculiar mix of mystique and big business characterizing the world of professional sports is nowhere more complex and bemusing than 'the boxing game,'" the judge wrote in his December 24, 1969, decision. "Even judges have some awareness of the brutal, corrupt and dirty chapters in the history of this subject. On the other hand, the blood, sweat and smoke of the fight arena have been the ingredients for producing folk heroes, enshrined as models for the young as well as shrewd investments for others. All such diverse things are reflected in the broad mandate of the Athletic Commission, which is required to watch out for 'fixes,' for sharp managerial practices and for other corrupt devices while it strives to follow the loftier and still cherished ideals of a simpler age reflected in the notion of 'a clean sport.'"

The commission was a necessary governing body. The commission simply was doing what it was supposed to do, regulate the sport. No, it had not discriminated by race or religion. No, it had not extracted "cruel and unusual punishment." No, it had not violated "due process." No, no, and no.

Only one of Meltsner's arguments gave Frankel pause. In the lawyer's buffet approach, he had included the thought that Ali was being singled out for special treatment here. Hadn't other boxers convicted of felonies been allowed to continue to fight? This was where the memories of those Friday Night Fights returned. Ira Meltsner's stories contained any number of characters who had wound up on the wrong side of the law and then found a new life in the ring. The legal phrase here was "equal protection under the law." Why should Ali be treated differently from these other boxers?

Hurrying to put his case before the court, Meltsner hadn't included any examples in his brief, only made the broad statement that the other fighters with felony convictions had been allowed to continue to fight. Frankel, in his dismissal of the case, noted that Ali and his lawyers would be allowed to refile their appeal if they included specifics. This was a rare exception, an open door left after a negative decision. Meltsner took quick advantage. He didn't even have to do much research. The famous names, obvious examples, were found easily in the Friday night past. In a rush, he typed and filed an amended paragraph to the original appeal.

"Defendants have arbitrarily, capriciously and invidiously refused to renew plaintiff's professional boxer's license in violation of plaintiff's right to equal protection of the laws guaranteed by the Fourteenth Amendment," he wrote. "Although defendants have denied plaintiff a boxer's license on the basis of his refusal to submit to induction and consequent conviction, defendants have on other occasions licensed professional boxers who had been convicted of crimes involving moral turpitude, to wit: (1) Jeff Merritt, who currently holds a New York State boxer's license, has been convicted on robbery; (2) Joey Giardello, who was granted a New York State boxer's license on August 4, 1965, had been convicted of assault; (3) Rocco Barbella, also known as Rocky Graziano, who was licensed to box in New York State from approximately 1942 to 1947, and from May, 1949, to an unknown date, had been twice convicted of petty larceny and in addition was court-martialed while serving in the United States Army and convicted of being absent without leave and disobeying orders and sentenced to one year of hard labor and a dishonorable discharge. In addition, on October 3, 1962, defendants recognized Sonny Liston, who had been convicted of armed robbery and of assault with intent to kill, as heavyweight boxing champion in the State of New York. On information and belief, defendants have in their possession of all professional boxers licensed in New York State which reveal other instances in which individuals convicted of a crime of moral turpitude have nonetheless been licensed to box in the State of New York."

Less than a month later, Judge Frankel ruled that the case would be heard again to listen to this argument. Meltsner had another chance, a better chance. He now had time to fill in the specifics.

The research assistant on the case was Ann Wagner, a recent graduate of NYU Law School. An ad on a bulletin board when she was still in school had led her to LDF to gain some experience as a law clerk. She was another white person in the LDF office and felt a little strange about the fact, tensions inevitable in a place where race seemed to be a part of every discussion, large or small. She liked the job well enough, though, and now was on the verge of being hired full-time.

One of her assignments as a clerk had been sifting through records in New York courts to determine whether alleged criminals had sufficient ties to their communities to allow them to be released on low bail. This was dirty, musty work, which required patience and an acquired facility in looking at old court records. She had done well, learned the legal language necessary to make sense of the files, which made her a perfect choice for this case.

Almost perfect.

"I thought boxing was quite abhorrent," she said. "I didn't have the slightest interest at all. I was also skeptical about Ali. I wasn't a big fan. In fact, in the beginning I kept calling him Cassius Clay. I was much more in line with Martin Luther King's thinking than anything the Black Muslims had to say."

She held her nose to begin her research. She went to the public library and began to read through a pile of biographies and autobiographies of boxers, looking for criminal records in their pasts. She also went to the office of *Ring* magazine, known as the "Bible of Boxing."

She read back articles. She talked with Nat Fleischer, the venerable publisher and editor. Without much effort she found maybe half a dozen fighters who had rolled through the criminal courts.

This gave Meltsner enough material to gain a court order to have her allowed to examine the files of the New York State Athletic Commission. The commission had refused earlier requests, but now was forced to comply.

"I hired my sister, who was in need of work, who I knew to be very capable," Wagner said. "I created this form and for a week to 10 days, my sister and I went into the basement of the state boxing commission and combed through every file and filled out this form which related every instance where they had licensed somebody with any kind of criminal conviction."

This was summer when they did their research. Wagner and her sister wore shorts. The older men in the commission office treated the women with disdain. Here they came again, these two girls in shorts. The whole thing seemed like a joke. What could these girls know about boxing? The girls mostly smiled and returned to the basement.

What they found kept them busy. The pile of completed forms grew high.

"We emerged at the end with a very, very long list of people who had been licensed as boxers, as trainers, as everything," Wagner said. "The Commission had licensed people with convictions for murder, rape, armed robbery, and they had licensed people at every stage. So they had licensed people who were on parole or probation and on and on it went. So we created this document of all the people they had licensed."

The document, nine typewritten pages filled with names and statistics, was submitted to the court on August 18, 1970. More than ninety convicted felons' names were on the list. Fifteen boxers convicted of crimes while in the military were on the list. Meltsner saw the list as nothing but discrimination, Ali singled out for being black, for being a Muslim, for being a big pain in the ass for the Selective Service and the government of the United States.

"It's all right to be a rapist or a robber," the lawyer told the *New York Times*. "As long as you're not political."

He wrote in his brief that his client's "swaggering both within and without the boxing ring evoked in many either veneration or abhorrence. These emotions were intensified by Clay's declaration that he is a member of the Black Muslims, which were as controversial then as the Black Panthers are today."

The New York State Athletic Commission's lawyers—the office of Louis Lefkowitz, the New York attorney general—were given a chance to rebut the findings, but offered little proof. They claimed that Ali's case was different because his appeal had not been heard. Even if he were allowed to fight, he might not be available because he might be in jail. They asked that the case be dismissed. This was denied.

A different judge, the Honorable Walter R. Mansfield, was selected to decide the case. The fortunes of an alleged draft dodger would be determined by a bona fide war hero. Mansfield was fifty-nine years old, another LBJ appointee, the son of a former mayor of Boston. As a U.S. Marine during the Second World War, he had been a member of the Office of Strategic Services, the forerunner of the Central Intelligence Agency. He parachuted behind the lines in both Yugoslavia and China to work with partisan troops.

His name had been in the newspapers during the summer for a ruling he made in the Southern District that struck down the ban on women drinking in McSorley's Old Ale House. No woman had been served in the establishment at 15 East Seventh Street in its 116-year history. As long-standing biases and traditions were challenged everywhere, Mansfield had overturned a big one.

Though—as the *New York Times* reported—not without reservations:

There was a trace of wistfulness in the ruling by District Court Judge Walter R. Mansfield ordering the doors of the tavern to both sexes. "It may be argued that the occasional preference of men for a haven to which they may retreat from the watchful eye of wives or womanhood in general, to have a drink or pass a few hours in their own company, is justification enough: that the simple fact that women are not men justifies defendant's practices." However, the judge concluded, "The answer is that McSorley's is a public place, not a private club, and that the preference of certain of its patrons is no justification under the equal-protection clause of the United States Constitution."

On September 14, 1970, Mansfield made his decision in the case of *Muhammad Ali, Plaintiff, v. The Division of State Athletic Commission of the Department of State of New York and Edwin B. Dooley, Albert Berkowitz and Raymond J. Lee, as Chairman and Members Thereof, Defendants.* There was no wistfulness involved.

Mansfield's ruling made it sound as if this were one of the most lopsided cases he ever had heard. He clearly was overwhelmed by the statistics Ann Wagner and her sister had put together.

"The fruits of this investigation are rather astounding," the war-hero judge wrote. "The Commission's records reveal at least 244 instances in recent years where it has granted, renewed or reinstated boxing licenses to applicants who have been convicted of one or more felonies, misdemeanors or military offenses involving moral turpitude. Some 94 felons thus licensed include persons convicted for such anti-social activities as second-degree murder, burglary, armed robbery, extortion, grand larceny, rape, sodomy, aggravated assault and battery, embezzlement, arson and receiving stolen property. The misdemeanor convictions, 135 in number, were for such offenses as petty larceny, possession of narcotics, attempted rape, assault and battery, fraud, impairing the morals of a minor, possession of burglar's tools, possession of weapons, carrying concealed weapons, automobile theft and promotion of gambling. The 15 military offenses include convictions or dishonorable discharges for desertion from the Armed Forces of the United States, assault upon an officer, burglary and larceny."

The requested injunctive relief for Ali was granted. The state commission was enjoined from "denying him a license to box because of his conviction for refusal to serve in the Armed Forces of the United States." The state had a chance to appeal, but Attorney General Lefkowitz quickly made it known that this would not happen. Ali was free to reapply for a license, which easily would be granted.

"Wait long enough," a *Boston Globe* editorial said, "and some wrongs will be righted—or so most of us go on hoping, anyway."

Meltsner was ecstatic. Thoughts of his father came back in a rush.

"He was the kind of Dodgers fan who would carry a transistor radio around in the old days when games were being played," Meltsner said. "This was not a tiny little thing like a Walkman; this was the size of a shoe box. There was a large seafood place called Lundy's that he would take my mother and me to for dinner. He would put the radio right on the table and listen through dinner. Nobody minded. The waiters would come around and ask, 'what's the score?'"

The score this day was perfect.

Muhammad Ali was not in court for the decision. He hadn't been involved in any of the planning, any of the proceedings, really hadn't been involved personally in any part of the case. His fate was handled again in the courts as if he were an abstraction, a story, a situation, his life a legal study instead of an actual, physical, day-to-day, continuing existence. The charm here was that at last the political arguments against him had been wrung out of the decision. He was a winner in a U.S. courtroom for the first time since he was in Louisville at the start of it all in the hearing with Judge Grauman when he won and then lost. His physical, day-to-day, continuing existence was going to change for the better.

"I think it's good, really, really good," Ali said from Miami when he heard the news. "I just hope I'll be in shape when the time comes for me to earn a living again.

"The other day I was parting my hair, greasing my scalp, and I counted 10 gray hairs that sort of scared me. And then it scared me more when I watched Floyd Patterson beat Charlie Green on television. If he's that rusty and been off only two years, I hate to think what might have happened to me in 3½ years.

"It just made me rush to the gym that much faster to get into shape. But it's hard to tell what's left and what's missing from working in a gym."

The appeal, from beginning to end, had taken eleven months. The decision on September 14, 1970, was the end of a long process. A lot had happened during that time. Ali had been a busy man on a bunch of fronts. There was much to tell.

Why was he in Miami?

He already was back in the boxing business. He was in training. He was scheduled to fight in forty-two days in Atlanta.

16

Return to the Ring

The phone call from Georgia had come to the house in Philadelphia in the second week of August 1970, a month before the New York decision. This was the house with the mirrored walls, the chandeliers in the bedroom and the garage, with the bathtubs the size of baby swimming pools. The house with the twenty-two telephones. The former house of the flamboyant Major Coxson. This was now Muhammad Ali's house.

The phone Belinda answered was in the kitchen.

She was making dinner. Ali was eating a salad.

"Mrs. Ali, you got your wish," the voice said on the other end. "Mrs. Ali, I'm Leroy Johnson. I'm here with Jesse Hill and . . . Muhammad Ali got his license."

Belinda was staggered. She was pregnant again, twins, though she didn't know it at the time. The news was unbelievable. She was happy and pregnant—sick and overwhelmed all at once. Ali could see that some momentous thing had occurred.

"What's the matter?" he asked.

"Take the phone," she said.

"What's the matter?" he repeated with more concern.

"You got your license, baby," Belinda said in a whisper.

Her husband was the one who was staggered now. This was news he could not believe. There had been so many false starts and sudden stops, so many rugs pulled at the last minute. How could this be true? He started spouting. Belinda tried to keep him quiet so Leroy Johnson would not hear on the other end of the phone.

"You lie!" Ali said. "Don't tell me that. You lie! I don't know what's more exciting, you having a baby or somebody over here on the phone telling you crap!"

"You got your license," Belinda repeated in a whisper. "You can't keep the man on the phone waiting. Sit down, though."

Ali sat down and took the phone and heard the news that he had been granted a license to fight in the state of Georgia and he started to cry. The forced exile, the crisscrossed wandering across America for three years, was finished.

"This ain't no joke," he told Belinda. "My God, I got my license."

The proposed fight was for October 26 at the five-thousand-seat Municipal Auditorium in Atlanta. The proposed opponent was Joe Frazier. All the political hurdles had been cleared by Johnson, a powerful Georgia state senator. Even Governor Lester Maddox, the old-line segregationist rabble-rouser, apparently had been handled. If Frazier couldn't fight, someone else would be found.

On August 14, 1970, a few days later, Ali was the surprise guest at a press conference at the Atlanta Marriott Hotel to announce the fight with Frazier or with some other suitable opponent. The last bit of skepticism had disappeared when he listened on the phone in his hotel room to various politicians make their pronouncements in the function room. He was happy, satisfied, when he joined them across a head table.

One week later his twin daughters, Jamillah and Rasheda, the names chosen from words he made up during his college speeches as good Muslim names, were born three months prematurely at the Medical College of Philadelphia, each weighing less than three pounds. Twelve days after that he was fighting three exhibition fights at Morehouse College in Atlanta, his first time in the ring before a paid crowd in three years and seventy-two days.

Things were happening in a hurry.

"Major Coxson got us to move to Philadelphia," Belinda said. "He loved Ali. He was a little gangster, but he loved Ali. He said to him, 'I got a house for you right here in Philadelphia. You can have it. You and your family can come here. You don't have to pay nothing, a nice house right off City Line Avenue and we can help you do all the colleges.'

"So we moved to Philadelphia. We got there and I got pregnant with the twins. Then things started rolling. Ali got people starting to take him to organizations and camps for boys. Then we had a staff and people would come to Ali and bring up things. So we had a little money coming in and we could pay the bills. So things got a little better right there. And furniture . . . some of the furniture was there already and Major Coxson got us big beds. Big round beds with velvet."

The house was at 1835 North 72nd Street, not far from the corner of Haverford and City Line avenues in the Green Hill Farms section of Philadelphia. Part of the Main Line. An article in *Jet* magazine quoted the Major about the transaction. He claimed he had been the first person of color in the all-white neighborhood. He said he had sold the house to Ali for $90,000 although he had bought it two years earlier for $115,000.

"Ali paid $60,000 down and will pay the remainder," the Major told *Jet* magazine. "I'm losing money on the deal. But what the hell is money between friends?"

The significant factor here was the neighborhood. The move to Philadelphia was more than just a move to Philadelphia. There was a change here in philosophy. Ali was living in a predominantly white neighborhood.

Hadn't he always denounced successful black men who did that? Make some money . . . marry a white woman . . . move to a white neighborhood? Weren't his speeches always about how black people should live with black people, how black people should patronize only black stores? Didn't he question those kids at the University of Arkansas about why they ever would go to that school? Wasn't living on the Main Line in Philadelphia, predominantly rich, predominantly white, something like going to the University of Arkansas? Worse?

This was pointed out to him loudly when he gave a lecture at Muhlenberg College in Allentown, Pennsylvania, on January 30, 1970, just after the move. Black militant students in dashikis knew all about his new Main Line address. They shouted that if he really cared about black people he should live with black people. Wasn't that what he always preached?

"Do you want me to buy a home in the ghetto?" he asked. "Why do I want to live in a rat bin and have a rat bite my child?"

This did not make the students happy. One kid stood and challenged the idea. Ali, pacing the stage, also was not happy.

"Sit down!" he said. "You're nothing but a nigger! Be quiet, boy, before I knock you down! You niggers give me more trouble than the whites!"

More than a hundred students now walked out. The rest jeered and hooted.

Life was definitely different for Ali on the East Coast. The yearlong suspension from the Nation of Islam continued. Religion did not dominate his conversation anymore. Boxing was important again. Deals were important. Deals were everywhere. He had edged away from the Honorable Elijah Muhammad and back toward the secular world.

Three years out of boxing had wrecked his finances. Everybody seemed to have another story about how he had borrowed $100 here, $200 there, never paid it back. Bills had gone unpaid. The college lectures were not big moneymakers. He needed something more, and now he was starting to get it.

There was the book deal with Random House at the start of the year to work on his autobiography, *The Greatest: My Own Story,* for the advance of $250,000. (The night at Muhlenberg would not be mentioned when the book finally appeared.) Then he signed a deal with Brut aftershave. He used Brut, same as Wilt Chamberlain, Mickey Mantle, and Joe Namath. Yes, he did.

He had another deal when he went to the closed-circuit showing of the unification bout for the heavyweight title, Frazier against Jimmy Ellis. As the action played out on the screen at the packed Philadelphia Arena, as Frazier dismantled Ellis for a fifth-round TKO, Ali gave his running thoughts to a writer from *Esquire* magazine for $8,000. That was a deal. There were no comments for other reporters who noted that he drove home to the Main Line in a lavender Cadillac with a white roof.

Herbert Muhammad, Elijah's son, was back on the scene as Ali's business manager now that there might be business to manage. Herbert had come back during the play on Broadway and stayed. The yearlong suspension from the Nation of Islam, for wanting to return to boxing (which nobody mentioned anymore, not even the Leader), seemed moot as moves were made to actually make this return happen.

Herbert had allowed a line of promoters to try to obtain a license, arrange a comeback fight, get the job done. The Major in Mississippi had been a candidate. Murray Woroner—remember him?—tried and failed in Florida. Bob Arum failed in Las Vegas. Then Arum tried again and failed again in Toronto. (That attempt went to the Supreme Court, which denied Ali's request to travel to Canada. The decision also knocked out a possibility in Montreal.) The state of Washington declined an offer. Detroit declined. Tulsa, Oklahoma. Ali went all the way to Charleston, South Carolina, for exhibition bouts that were canceled at the last moment by city authorities.

Atlanta was the real deal. Atlanta was the big deal. A thirty-year-old guy from New York, Robert Kassel, was one of the promoters who had spun through their Rolodexes trying to find a place that would grant Ali a license to fight. Frustrated, he called his father-in-law, Harry Pett, a businessman who lived in Atlanta. Was there any chance that Ali could get a license in Georgia? Pett said he knew a man, Leroy Johnson, who would know the answer.

Johnson, an attorney, was the first African American elected to the Georgia senate. He was a politician's politician, a schmoozer, a backslapper, a deal maker. He said he would check. What he found was very interesting. Cities had jurisdiction over boxing in Georgia, not the state. The state would be a problem with Lester Maddox as governor. The city would not be a problem. Johnson had favors he could collect in Atlanta.

The mayor, Sam Massell, who was white, had received 90 percent of the black vote when he was elected. Johnson was responsible for much of that. The Board of Aldermen also had to approve the license. Most of the members of the board also had received 90 percent of the black vote. Johnson was responsible for that, too.

He formed a promotional group with black businessmen Jesse Hill and Harry Pett called House of Sports. Robert Kassell gave the group the rights to the live gate while he concentrated on television rights. Bingo. The mayor and the Board of Aldermen gave their blessings. Atlanta was the real deal.

"I called Bob Arum [Ali's longtime promoter, who also would be part of the operation] and said, 'Bob, I think I have put this together in Atlanta,'" Kassell told *Atlanta* magazine years later. "He said, 'That's ridiculous. It's not going to happen.' Then I called Angelo Dundee.

Same thing. They all said, 'That can't be.' Nobody believed the fight was going to happen because nobody had been able to pull it off."

Until now.

"I've never tried to get a fight," Ali said. "It was the promoters. I never pushed. I said 'if you get one, I'll take it.' Now this . . . This is more than a fight, it's a victory for justice."

The exhibitions came in a rush. Belinda had the babies early in Philadelphia and, whoosh, there he was in the ring at the gym at Morehouse College. The place was filled, maybe three thousand people, and the indoor temperature on a hot night had to be over a hundred degrees. The Reverend Ralph Abernathy and the Reverend Martin Luther King Sr., father of the slain civil rights leader, were in the front row. Dundee and Bundini Brown were in his corner once again. Whoosh. The pieces were back together.

He fought a total of eight rounds against three different opponents. They wore headgear, but he did not because he said he wanted to feel the force of any shots that he might receive. He was heavy, twenty pounds overweight, his face puffy, but he certainly still could move. He danced around each of his opponents, stayed out of trouble. In the eighth and final round, he brought back the Ali Shuffle. The place went crazy.

"That's the first time I've done that since Ernie Terrell," he said in the locker room. "Of course I've rehearsed it a few times in my bedroom."

He said he was out of shape, predictable, but could be in fine condition in eight weeks. Frazier seemed out of the question, already scheduled to fight light heavyweight champion Bob Foster in Detroit in November, so someone else apparently would be the first real opponent. That was fine. Eight weeks and Ali would be ready for Frazier, for whoever was in the ring.

The men in his corner also thought he could be ready. Dundee said that "all the bricks are in place. All we need is there to work on." The work was what was important. Get to Miami. Get back in the gym. Bundini Brown said the same thing. In a different way.

"You can't become a soldier until you go to basic training," Bundini said.

There was no evidence that he saw the irony in his words.

—

The opponent was brawler Jerry Quarry, twenty-five years old, three years younger than Ali. Frazier was out. Quarry was in. He was the number-one-ranked heavyweight contender according to *Ring* magazine, number three according to the World Boxing Association. The contracts were signed nine days after the Morehouse exhibitions at a press conference at the Hotel Belvedere in New York. Ali would receive a guarantee of $200,000 against 44.5 percent of the net income, Quarry 22.5 percent. Quarry was more than happy with the arrangement.

"I've always wanted to fight him," he said, sitting next to Ali. "He's quick, but he's not a big puncher and I can punch with either hand. I can take a lot out of him. I don't know if he'll be as good as he was. That remains to be seen. But he better be."

Quarry was six feet tall, 194 pounds, with short arms and a history of being cut easily. His record was 37-4-4, and while he had won his last four fights in a row, they were against average heavyweights. He had lost a decision to Jimmy Ellis and technical knockouts to both Frazier and George Chuvalo. If Ali was close to the fighter he had been when he left, there should be no problems.

"I'll fight both Frazier and Quarry on the same night," he had suggested as the match was considered.

Quarry routinely was called "a good-looking Irish guy" or "an Irish brawler," which was boxing shorthand that meant he was the latest version of the Great White Hope. He had grown up hard with his three brothers and four sisters in a string of migrant-worker camps around Bakersfield, California. Their father, Jack, had been an amateur boxer at one time, one of many occupations. He had the words "Hard" and "Luck" tattooed underneath the knuckles of each hand, the message "A Quarry Never Quits" somewhere else on his body. Jack was known as a tough man to please.

"My heritage was 'The Grapes of Wrath,'" Jerry Quarry once said.

He started boxing when he was three years old. Before he turned professional in 1965, he had fought over two hundred amateur fights. He was an oddity in what largely had become a black man's sport, a throwback to other generations, a Depression-era sort of character, a tough white man coming into a tough business to put food on the table. You expected him to arrive at most fights in a boxcar.

"Did you find his style awkward?" he was once asked after he dispatched an opponent with a knockout.

"Well, he sure fell awkward," Quarry replied.

The last white man Ali had faced in the ring had been, well . . . did Rocky Marciano count? That fight, the computer fight, the imaginary fight, finally had been shown in January. Ali watched with Belinda and some other people in a packed theater in Philadelphia. The result was not good: Rocky in a knockout in the thirteenth round. Ali felt embarrassed at first and then angry.

He called the production "phony" and "a sham" and "a Hollywood fake" a few nights later on the *Dick Cavett Show*. Murray Woroner sued him for $2 million. Pro forma stuff. That was pretty much the end of the computer boxing game.

Atlanta would be the real attraction, not cut from the imagination. Atlanta signaled the real return of a heavyweight great from the past. The fight would be shown in 206 closed-circuit locations around the country. The live attendance would be limited in the five-thousand-seat Municipal Auditorium, but most expectations were that closed-circuit would make this the most lucrative fight in boxing history.

"It's like a dream for so many people . . . ," Ali said at the 5th Street Gym, embarking on his training. "Like an old boxer of Sugar Ray Robinson's caliber being put in a time machine and suddenly being a contender again. Or like you could bring Joe Louis back for one day of fighting. Many people said I was finished and it was all over for me. It's like a dead man rising. I tell you. There are young people who didn't get to see me six years ago. It's like stepping back in time."

Boxing was on his mind. He wouldn't answer questions about his draft status or his ban from the Nation of Islam. He didn't even want to say much about Joe Frazier. Jerry Quarry was the subject. Boxing.

"I've got Quarry on my mind and winning on my mind," he said. "I've got six weeks to get ready. Old fighters like Joe Louis, Rocky Marciano and Jack Dempsey would have said a year was too long to lay off and then fight again. I've been gone three years."

Things happened around him as he pounded sparring partners and ran in the Miami mornings. The New York license decision was announced. That was cause for celebration. On the other side, it was announced that his draft case had been sent once again to the Supreme Court for a final appeal. The Fifth Circuit Court of Appeals in New Orleans had rejected his plea about the wiretaps. The Supreme Court once again was his last chance to stay out of jail. That was not cause for celebration.

Ali simply kept boxing. The contract stipulated that the two fighters had to hold their workouts at the Sports Arena in Atlanta for the last twelve days before the fight. On the final day in Miami, weight almost what he wanted it to be, Ali lay against the ropes, one arm down, and let sparring partner Al (Blue) Lewis unload body shot after body shot. He said the astronauts always ran tests on the ground before they left on a spaceship.

"Why don't you smile any more?" a reporter from London asked.

"I don't play in training," Ali said. "This is serious business."

"No more poetry?"

"There is no time," Ali said.

(Pause.)

"To rhyme."

He stayed in Leroy Johnson's cottage on a lake fifteen miles outside Atlanta. In his autobiography, published three years later, he would talk about gunfire coming from the woods, racial threats from the local Ku Klux Klan, but there was no mention of any of this in the press. Visits were made, almost nightly, to the cottage of singer Otis Redding in the neighborhood. These were mentioned.

The phone did ring one time at four o'clock in the morning. Ali answered. Belinda was at the other end. The twins finally had come home from the hospital, healthy, their weight increasing daily. She said they looked like two Navajo Indians.

"What do you want?" Ali asked. "It's four o'clock in the morning."

"That's what I wanted to tell you," the mother at home now with three little girls under the age of two, busy already in her day. "It's four o'clock in the morning."

Lester Maddox, the controversial and almost comical governor, a talk show character on the national stage, came back into the game, late, to encourage people from Atlanta to boycott the fight. He didn't have control over the event, one way or the other, power over boxing ceded to municipal governments in Georgia, but that didn't stop him from saying that he "would hope that Clay gets beat in the first round and he's flattened for a count of 30." He called for "a day of mourning" on the day of the fight.

"I don't know what that word means," Ali said, when asked about Maddox's comment.

"It means it will be a black day," a sportswriter explained.

"Oh, yeah, there'll be a lot of my folks here," Ali said.

The racial matchup was downplayed. The tickets had been sold. This definitely would be a black event in a black city. The Lester Maddox voters would not attend, but they never had made plans to attend. This, more than any unsegregated event in American sports history, shaped up as a celebration of blackness.

Quarry admitted he felt overwhelmed by it all. The three promoters were black. Everyone around the arena seemed to be black. All the politicians. All the visitors. Ali had black bodyguards. (Not the Muslims he had in the past. These were paid law enforcement officers.) All the attention was focused one way. Black and more black. The two doctors who gave the physical exams were black. That was the final layer of blackness for Quarry.

"If there are two black doctors handling the fight, I'm not going in," he said. "Screw it. They want equal rights and all that? Well, I want it, too."

His trainer, Teddy Bentham, who noticed a lot of pencils moving while his fighter talked, tried to change the subject. He figured he would give the sportswriters a different angle.

"You can say that when Jerry hits that big son of a bitch, he'll break his neck," Teddy Bentham interjected.

"And if you want to say big BLACK son of a bitch, you can say that, too," Jerry Quarry said.

The writer George Plimpton, famed for his accounts of playing quarterback for the Detroit Lions, sparring with Archie Moore, and taking participatory stabs at different occupations, was allowed into Ali's dressing room before the fight. He hunched himself in the corner and recorded what he saw. Ali's argument with Angelo about whether to wear a mandatory protective belt consumed some time. (Ali didn't want to wear it because he thought it made him look fatter than when he wore his normal metal cup.) Ali changed his shorts at the last minute, deciding to wear white shorts with a black stripe from his brother Rahman's gym bag. ("Brings your ass down just right," someone said.) Ali threw some jabs at the Reverend Jesse Jackson's extended right hand. Ali embraced actor Sidney Poitier. ("Sidney's here!" Ali said. "I'm really ready to rumble!") Ali seemed relaxed, ready to go.

"A knock sounded at the door," Plimpton wrote in his final paragraph. "It's time," a voice called. "Muhammad Ali gave one last peek at himself in the mirrors and he went out into the corridor, his people packed around him."

He was back in business.

This had become an electric night in the old, beaten-down auditorium, dedicated in 1909 with a possum dinner for President William Howard Taft. People had gathered first at the new Regency-Hyatt House, marveled at the grand atrium, then shuttled to the fight in an assortment of limousines, many of them painted in psychedelic colors. Furs and top hats and evening dress, miniskirts and maxiskirts and all manner of jewelry were on display. One man wore a floor-length mink coat and a mink hat and smoked a foot-long pipe. Sequins were everywhere.

"Off on the periphery of the bright lights, carrying the golden-faced $100 ringside tickets, came the Negro Americans who have succeeded and mean to enjoy it," white *Atlanta Constitution* columnist Reg Murphy wrote. "Put a magnificent athlete like Ali in the ring, give him the benefit of the doubt about whether he should be fighting, and bring this glittery crowd of success stories together. This probably is an event unparalleled in Negro history."

"It was the greatest collection of black money and black power ever assembled until that time," white boxing historian Bert Sugar later wrote. "Right in the heart of the old Confederacy, it was 'Gone with the Wind' turned upside-down."

Coretta Scott King received the biggest ovation, but Sidney was there, Jesse was there, Bill Cosby, Whitney Young, Adam Clayton Powell, Hank Aaron, Donn Clendenon, Clarence Williams, Al Hirt. Diana Ross was there, as were the Supremes. Diana wore a see-through shirt. The Temptations were there. Curtis Mayfield sang the National Anthem.

The fight lasted nine minutes.

"The way to a man's chin is through his stomach," Quarry had said during the promotion.

"If he gets close enough to hit me in the stomach, he'll be close enough for me to hit him on the jaw," Ali had replied.

The latter was the case.

Quarry could not get to Ali. Too fast, too fast, too fast. Ali could get to Quarry. No problem. There was a first round to sort of get loose, a second round for Ali to show his domination, a third round of devastation. Two left hooks and a right opened a large cut over Quarry's left eye. Ali proceeded to hit the cut twelve times by actual count before the round finished. Someone noticed that the cut was bleeding from four different places. Dundee had written the number three and TKO inside one of Ali's gloves, a prediction for the final round. The prediction came true when Teddy Bentham in the other corner signaled for referee Tony Perez to stop the fight.

Quarry objected to the decision, tried to struggle free to fight a fourth round, but was restrained. The cut would need fifteen stitches. The medical staff, it should be noted, had been doubled to four doctors, two black and two white.

"I'm stronger and I hit harder than I did three and a half years ago," Ali said in his press conference. "I'm still two years short of my prime at 30. I could go again in six weeks."

A presentation was made. Reverend Ralph Abernathy and Coretta Scott King gave him a trophy from somebody for something.

"You are a living example of soul power," Reverend Abernathy said. Mrs. King added that he was "not only our champion, but a champion of justice and peace."

There had been no demonstrations against the fight, no trouble of any kind. The great worries of almost three and a half years seemed silly. Why had this man not been allowed to work? Silly. The actions of the organizations that controlled boxing, plus the actions of the boxing commissions in every state in the country, looked shortsighted and dumb. Leroy Johnson and his friends showed them all how easy it could have been.

The one strange part of the evening came later. Many of those well-dressed people at the fight were handed invitations to a grand after-party at 2819 Handy Drive SW in Atlanta. The occasion was supposed to be the birthday of someone named Tobe. The party was supposed to start on Monday night and end sometime Wednesday.

Over a hundred of the fight fans, probably many more, a group that allegedly included Cassius Clay Sr., rode out to Handy Drive. The party turned out to be a surprise party with a scary surprise. Eight men with hoods and shotguns escorted the partygoers into the house. All wallets, jewelry, fur coats, anything of value, were taken and thrown into bags. The people, forced to disrobe, were taken to the basement and forced to lie on the floor. When the entire basement was filled, new people were told to lie on top of the first layer of bodies.

Many of the victims disappeared once the robbers left. They wanted nothing to do with law enforcement. Some of the victims had longer arrest records than any of the robbers did. This concerned the police.

"These people don't accept a thing like this too lightly," Lieutenant J. D. Hudson of the Atlanta police said. "They will have men out searching, too. And if they get there first, there won't be an arrest and trial."

Belinda Ali, back in Philadelphia with the kids, also reported some weirdness. The phone rang and someone said, "Ali won, you lose. The bomb goes off at midnight." She figured it was a hoax, decided that if someone was going to plant a bomb it would already have exploded, but she called Ali anyway and he called the Major.

"So Major Coxson's bodyguards, all these hit men that I found out later, they came and took us out of the house and put us in the Iroquois Apartments right on City Line Avenue," Belinda said. "I knew they were gangsters, but I didn't know they were hit men. They took care of us."

The city bomb squad checked the house the next day and found nothing. There never were any more threats. Belinda thought this was because her husband was back in the game, out in public, looking good. The *New York Times* and other news outlets had even begun to call him by his proper name. The attached "aka" now was "Cassius Clay." Roles had been reversed.

"Ali Scores Third-Round Knockout Over Quarry in Successful Return to Ring," read the headline in the New York newspaper of record. There you go. The name was right even though the headline was wrong. Ali had scored a TKO, not a knockout, over Quarry.

—

The goal now was to fight Frazier. That would be a fight so big it would make people's heads explode. Ali was working inside a window that could close at any moment, nobody sure what the Supreme Court would do. The fight should happen soon, before the window shut.

Frazier, alas, still had the matchup with Bob Foster on November 18 in Detroit to get out of the way. That meant any fight between Ali and Frazier would not take place until sometime after Christmas because promotion of such a large event would take time. This would be just about the biggest rocket in American sports history sent into the air.

Ali did not like the idea of such a long wait. He wanted another fight before Christmas to make some more money in case the Supreme Court issued a fast ruling and he had to go away for five years. Another fight also would be good because three rounds with the overmatched Quarry was not a great comeback test. So nine days after the first fight, Ali announced the second. . . .

Oscar Bonavena.

December 7, 1970.

Madison Square Garden.

"This is no tune-up for Frazier," Ali declared about this obvious tune-up for Frazier. "This is a real serious fight. A big one. If I lose, I lose everything."

The announcement brought Ali back into the Garden, back into New York (not as an actor), back into the hustle and the bustle. He posed for pictures with New York State Athletic Commission chairman Edwin Dooley, that long battle finished. Bonavena missed the press conference at Les Champs restaurant due to a family emergency in Argentina.

A five-foot-eleven, 206-pound native of Buenos Aires, he was, indeed, a rugged customer. He had a 46-6-1 record, which included victories against Chuvalo, Mildenberger, and Folley, all victims of Ali. Two of the losses were to Joe Frazier, but they were both rugged affairs, both decisions. His worst loss was in a decision to Jimmy Ellis in the heavyweight elimination tournament. Nothing went right that night. He was a straight-ahead, no-nonsense brawler. Presumably, like Quarry, he would not be hard for Ali to find.

Then, again, he might.

"Bonavena doesn't stand straight up, a target for Clay's jabs," said Gil Clancy, hired to be the Argentine fighter's American trainer. "He fights low, crouched over, and he bobs and weaves all the time. He's hard to hit and a lot of punches roll off his heavy neck."

The idea that this was a fight to mark time did not leave. Frazier's fight with Foster came and went in a hurry. The 209-pound heavyweight knocked out the 185-pound, six-foot-three light heavyweight forty-nine seconds into the second round. Foster was knocked down once in the round, climbed to his feet, went back down. One half of the matchup was now ready to go. Ali had to fill in the other bracket.

He watched the Frazier fight on a closed-circuit screen at the Municipal Auditorium in Atlanta, the place where he dispatched Quarry. As Bob Foster went down for the second and last time, Ali stood up.

"I want Joe Frazier!" he said. "I want Joe Frazier!"

He shadowboxed in the aisles. The crowd whooped. Imaginary lefts and rights flew through the air.

"Is Joe Frazier this fast?" Ali asked. "Can he do anything about this?"

The Bonavena fight came two weeks later. The visitor trained in the Catskills at Grossinger's, the training spot of boxers from previous generations. Ali trained in New York City at the Felt Forum, the arena attached to the new Madison Square Garden. Both men tried to sell tickets.

"He is a black kangaroo," Bonavena said through translators when first asked about Ali. "He jumps all around a lot. I will punish him. I will hit him and hit him and hit him."

The visitor persisted in referring to Ali as "Clay." He also said that "Clay" smelled, that he didn't use enough deodorant. In keeping with the barnyard theme, he also talked about "Clay's" military situation when the two men met for the first time at the weigh-in.

"Why you no go in the army?" the Argentine asked. "You chicken. You chicken. Cluck. Cluck. Cluck."

"Say that one more time and I'll hit you right here," Ali said.

"You chicken. Cluck. Cluck. Cluck."

Ali predicted he would dispose of Mr. Bonavena in nine rounds, maybe much sooner if this chicken and deodorant business continued.

The Garden was full on the chosen night, 19,417 people. A lot of the furs were back, no doubt a lot of them worn by people who were robbed at that fake birthday party in Atlanta. Ali and his entourage came to the action on the subway, which dropped them right in Penn Station, an escalator ride away from the Garden. Ali said he wanted to be with his people, that he had to be the first to do this, that he made history all the time. He was not the only one who said this.

"The reappearance of Muhammad Ali to a New York boxing ring is something more than merely the reappearance of a young man who may be the greatest heavyweight ever," columnist George Frazier wrote in the *Boston Globe*. "It is also, and perhaps more significantly, the gladsome termination of a holy crusade, the confirmation of a person's privilege to ply his trade, and a giving of the indecent lie to the New York State Boxing Commission, which, like boxing commissions everywhere except in Georgia, is an absolute disgrace."

The fight did not unfold the way it was supposed to unfold. The visitor, nicknamed "Ringo" because of his Beatles haircut and "The Bull" because he was from Argentina and every fighter from Argentina is nicknamed "The Bull," turned out to be one tough package.

Ali started the fight talking, the way he had with Terrell and Patterson in the old days. He would punish Bonavena for all that "Clay" business. The talking was finished by the fourth round. Bonavena was harder to hit than predicted, faster than predicted. He was wild with his punches—George Frazier had said, "Bonavena couldn't hit Clay with a 30-30"—but he was busy. This was the toughest fight in Ali's professional career.

For the first time, the added years seemed to have taken some of the dancing out of his game. He wore a new pair of white shoes with red tassels that he called his "shuffle shoes," but there was no shuffle. The tassels, in fact, fell apart as the rounds progressed, splotches of red spread on the canvas. Bonavena took whatever punishment Ali gave. The fight slowed so much in the later rounds there were boos from some of the fur coats.

In the fifteenth round, easily ahead on all the scorecards but sure to be faced with some new and different questions in the postfight interviews, Ali suddenly broke through the dull haze and connected with a big left to Bonavena's jaw. The man had never been down in his career and now he was down. Now he was up. Now he was down again. Now he was up. Now he was down for a third time, finished under the three-knockdown rule in New York. For emphasis his trainer threw a white towel from his corner. Fifty-seven seconds were left in the fight.

Done.

"This is the champion," Bonavena said. "Frazier never win him. He no coward. He no chicken. Cheep. Cheep. Cheep."

"I'm satisfied for three reasons," Ali said. "I proved I had the stamina to go 15 rounds against the toughest man I ever fought. I proved I can take a punch by taking more punches in one fight than I have in all my others. And I proved I could punch by stopping a man who'd never been stopped."

Both sides of the brackets now were filled.

The inevitable was free to happen.

On December 30, 1970, unbeaten heavyweight champion Muhammad Ali and unbeaten heavyweight champion Joe Frazier signed a contract to fight each other on March 8, 1971, at Madison Square Garden. Each fighter would receive $2.5 million for his efforts.

17

Joe Frazier

I been through all this stuff," Muhammad Ali said. "I'm used to it. It's something big every time. There was the time somebody was going to assassinate me. And the racial issue and the religious issue. I fight in Georgia and the governor declares a day of mourning. I've been through all this. But Frazier just jumped into it.

"It's like climbing up the Empire State Building. If you go up step by step, looking back down every time you take a step, it doesn't bother you. But if you've never seen it and somebody blindfolds you up on top and whips the blindfold off, when you look down you get dizzy. That's what's happening with Frazier."

And so it began.

The elevator in this version of the Empire State Building left from the ground floor, taking everyone with it, and began to climb, heading for levels of hyperbole never seen in the American sports skyline. This was the Fight, the Fight of the Century, whatever exaggerated term a man wanted to use. Everyone was going to be a little dizzy at the end.

"In the first 70 years of this 20th Century, man has conquered disease, pestilence and space with varying degrees of success," sports editor Cooper Rollow wrote in the *Chicago Tribune*. "He has flown thru the heavens and walked on the moon. But for a few vivid and suspenseful moments [on March 8] he will take a backward trip thru time to the days of the ancient Roman gladiators, when two men came to center court and locked in mortal combat."

There you go.

Life magazine announced that Frank Sinatra would take the pictures from ringside and Norman Mailer would write the words for its coverage of the grand event. Budd Schulberg would be there for *Esquire.* William Saroyan would be there for *True,* another men's magazine. There would be a cutoff at 760 press credentials for writers and broadcasters from twenty-six countries.

The money for the fighters, the unprecedented $2.5 million apiece, was already in the bank, held in escrow, backed by a $4.5 million letter of credit from the Chase Manhattan Bank for promoter Jack Kent Cooke. Tickets for the live gate at Madison Square Garden had gone in a hurry, the $150 high-end seats now being scalped for as much as $700. The closed-circuit production, the true moneymaker for the event, would be beamed into an estimated 350 locations across the country. Coverage would also be extended to thirty-five foreign markets, described in twelve different languages.

Tickets were more expensive than they ever had been for the closed-circuit shows in theaters and arenas, some as high as $30. There would be no radio coverage, no free television. A reporter asked Cooke, the promoter, if this bothered him. Did he wish more people could see the fight? Hadn't the landing on the moon been shown for free on television? Why couldn't the fight be free?

"I wish a lot of things," said the millionaire owner of the Los Angeles Lakers, the Los Angeles Kings, and the Fabulous Forum in Los Angeles. "I wish everyone drove a Cadillac. I wish everyone was employed and there were no childhood disease. But we can't have everything perfect in an imperfect world."

Money flowed everywhere. Shelly Saltman, hired to come east from Los Angeles to help with public relations, shared a room at the St. Regis Hotel with one of the booking agents for the closed-circuit production. There was a knock at the door. A large man from New Orleans entered. He was carrying a briefcase.

"He puts it down on the bed, talking to the booking agent," Saltman said. "He opens it up and there is a million dollars in cash inside. It was just like the movies. I had never seen anything like this. He wanted the rights to all of Louisiana. The booking agent said he couldn't help him!"

Ali was back at the 5th Street Gym to train. Frazier went to the Concord Hotel in the Catskills, a place where he had prepared for big fights in the past, but left after three weeks because a large snowfall made roadwork impossible. He returned to his own gym in Philadelphia, did his roadwork in Fairmount Park. Yank Durham described the Philadelphia weather as "balmy."

The words flew back and forth from long distance.

"I'm hot and disturbed about the reference to Frazier taking a shot at the title, my crown," Ali told the workout audience in Miami. "I've never wanted to get at a man so bad. . . . And when I whip him they'll be just as interested in Red China and Russia as they are here."

"You tell Clay I'm real and ready," Frazier said from Philadelphia. "C-L-A-Y, that's right—Clay. Write it in big letters. He say he punish people who call him Clay. Well, I don't want him to take it easy. Give me his best."

Ali, of course, unleashed his psychological arsenal against Frazier early. He said he wanted fifteen different referees from fifteen different countries to work the fight because each of them would be tired out after only one round. That was how fast the action was going to be. He said he had three informers watching Frazier's workouts. He said he received reports every night at ten thirty.

"They tell me that all Frazier's got is a left hook," he said. "What have I got? I got a jab, a hook, a punch and lightning footwork, that's what."

He had taunted Frazier in interviews for years, demeaned him at every chance. Frazier was an Uncle Tom. Frazier was ugly, a symbol of the "dese" and "dose" typical of fighters. Ali did impersonations that were not kind. He said anything he could about Frazier because he knew it drove Frazier crazy.

"Maybe Nixon'll call him if he wins," he said. "I don't think he'll call me."

Ali broke down the fight for anyone who would listen. Frazier had no idea what he was going to experience. Those short arms would get him in trouble. Ali had a six-inch advantage in reach. Frazier, who loved to work inside, never would be allowed to get inside. He would be frustrated. Ali would dance. He also would pound with hard punches. He was older now, stronger. He knocked out Bonavena. He would knock out Frazier, too.

The people—the people who mattered, the black people—would all be for Ali. He said so. Ninety percent would be cheering for Ali. It would be embarrassing. They knew he was their representative, not

Frazier. Think about it. Frazier was in big trouble. Frazier was the white man's surrogate. Frazier had no chance. Think.

> Yes [Ali told Norman Mailer one day at the 5th Street Gym], you think of a stadium with a million people, 10 million people, you could get them all in to watch, they would all pay to see it live, but then you think of the hundreds of millions and the billions who are going to see the fight and if you could sit them all down in one place, and fly a jet plane over them, why that plane would have to fly for an hour before it could reach the end of all the people who will see this fight. It's the greatest event in the history of the world, and you take a man like Frazier, a good fighter, but a simple hard-working fellow, he's not built for this kind of pressure, the eyes of that many people upon him. There's an experience to pressure that I have had, fighting a man like Liston in Miami the first time, which he has not. He will cave under the pressure. No, I don't see any way a man like Frazier can whup me, he can't reach me, my arms are too long, and if he does get in and knock me down I'll never make the mistake of Quarry and Foster or Ellis of rushing back at him. I'll stay away until my head clears, then I begin to pop him again, pop! pop! [a few jabs] no, there is no way this man can beat me, this fight will be easier than you think.

> The dizziness had begun.

The Ali who said all this, the Ali who entertained visitors daily, was a far different character from the Ali who had arrived eleven years earlier at the 5th Street Gym to begin his career. Eleven years? He celebrated his twenty-ninth birthday on January 17, 1971. He wasn't the bug-eyed kid with a gold medal, ready to conquer the world, energy and excitement crackling out of his pores. This was a different stage of life. He knew what he knew.

A line of man fat hung above his shorts now, noticeable during his workouts. He promised that it would disappear, but didn't seem all that worried. Weight would not be bad against Frazier. Weight would be power. His workouts were show as much as exercise. He talked to the people who paid a buck to climb up the stairs and watch, talked to the always-assembled press. Hey, there's LeRoy Neiman, the artist. Hey, there are the reporters from England. Hey. He talked while he sparred, talked while he hit the heavy bag. The show seemed more important than the exercise.

His roadwork wasn't across the causeway anymore, alone and in combat boots. He ran next to his own Cadillac, driven by Reggie Barrett, his friend/chauffeur/valet. His route took him around the manicured grounds of the Bayshore Golf Course off Dade Boulevard. When he was finished—and after he picked up a quart of freshly squeezed orange juice at Wolfie's delicatessen on Collins Avenue—he went to his rented apartment fourteen stories up in the Florida sky in Octagon Towers, a Jewish retirement home. This was a long way from 4610 NW 15th Court in Brownsville, where he stood in the dusty yard in front of those neighborhood kids and first said he didn't want to go to war. A signed picture from Diana Ross, "To Ali, my champion," sat on the dresser.

The ban still seemed to be in place from the Honorable Elijah Muhammad, so there was little talk about the religion, little talk about the draft. Herbert Muhammad was still around, yes, still important. He had negotiated the deal with Jack Kent Cooke, had laid out the $2.5 million figure that Cooke alone among a half-dozen bidders had matched. The rest of the NOI Muslims, the stern characters who stood behind Ali at earlier fights, had been replaced by the freelance cast of advisors and hangers-on, associates he had collected through the years. Bundini was there. Ali's father, Cassius Clay Sr., was back, more important than he had been. This, again, was a different time, a different stage of life. Maybe their son hadn't come back to the Baptist church, but Cassius Sr. and Odessa could take comfort in the fact he was attached to the family again.

His home was now in Cherry Hill, New Jersey, outside Philadelphia. He had moved to a larger, more expensive house at 1121 Winding Hill Drive in the Voken Tract section of Cherry Hill just before training camp started. Major Coxson again was the reason for the move. He lived in the same neighborhood, secured a very good deal—Belinda said he gave them this house, too—and could be even closer to his friend. The Major said he saved Ali some money in other ways, too. He said he felt Ali was like his brother.

"I saw where the City of Philadelphia was going to take 90-some thousand dollars in city wage tax out of his purse because he lived in Philadelphia," the Major told *Philadelphia* magazine's Maury Levy. "So I saw a way for him to move to Cherry Hill to beat the city out of some money."

"We could use the extra room with the twins," Belinda said. "We had some money now. I had these little credit cards for Bamberger's, Wanamaker's. I could go and buy stuff."

This new life was not necessarily a better life. Not for Belinda. It was funny that this fight, this return to the spotlight, had been the goal for those three and a half years, scraping along, scuffling, hoping that Ali would get his license. Now that it was here, this moment that had been a dream, bigger in reality than the dream ever had been, it seemed a lot more downbeat than she ever expected.

Ali was running around with other women. There was no other way to say it. She knew it and he knew she knew it and nothing ever would be the same. The NOI Muslim couple, joined at the hip, was not joined anymore. Not the way it was.

The promoters in Atlanta had noticed that he "certainly was a red-blooded young man." One of the reasons they wanted him at Leroy Johnson's cottage in the woods was to keep him under control. They instituted a curfew.

"It's kind of sad," Belinda said. "You stay with somebody, have fun with them for a long time, then all of a sudden, you know, you're trying to deceive a person, lie all the time, you know. . . . I could read him. I could read him real good. That's why it hurt me. I'm right up there, next to the man 24-7. Only your wife knows your actions. Your wife would know something that nobody knows. These women, they think women [at home] don't know? Women always know. It's impossible. It's sad."

The fame and the money were at fault. That was her thought. Herbert Muhammad, who had girlfriends, was at fault. He told Ali that whatever he wanted to do was fine. Women wanted him. Go ahead. The guys, the assembled support staff, were at fault. They covered up for him. They were good guys, helped him in a lot of ways, but they were guys. Go ahead. She understood. Men did that.

Then again, no one was at fault except Ali. He made his own decisions in the end, and they were the wrong decisions. He was weak. Women were his weakness.

"Didn't nobody put a gun to his head and tell him to do that," Belinda said. "He was weak by not knowing stuff in the first place. He didn't have a foundation. He had a father that went around with different women. Like father, like son. He didn't see the power in being strong. He could see it in my father's family. He saw my father, my mom. He called my father 'Nassau Daddy.' He'd say, 'here's Nassau Daddy.' He loved him. He respected him. He was on his best behavior when he saw my mother and father."

The idea became stuck in her head that Ali was going to lose to Frazier. She hadn't been around him when he was a fighter in the first half of his career, so she hadn't seen him work. She had been impressed when he came back, when he worked hard to fight Quarry. He worked then with a purpose. He was a master of speed, a big guy who danced on his feet. She wasn't impressed by how he worked now.

The reports were all bad. He wasn't giving Frazier respect. He wasn't driving himself, pushing. He thought he was going to win easily. He was training like he thought he would win easily.

"Ali would fall into a gap," Belinda said. "If the people around him would say 'you're bad, man,' he'd get lazy. Wouldn't train. If he had it in his mind he could whip somebody, that's when he falls weak. I saw all these people telling him he was going to do this, going to do that, you're bad, man. I could see this. All day long. He wouldn't get up, wouldn't run. I said, 'whoa, wait a minute. This is opportunity.' I'm not going to support Ali. He was screwing around with every Tom, Dick and Harry's woman. Bad."

She said she told him this.

Many times.

There was no reason for Joe Frazier's wife, Florence, to have these kinds of conversations in Philadelphia. He had cut out the frills of daily life and paid no attention to other women, men, or children, to the colossal whine of attention around him. There were no lingering press conferences with Joe Frazier every day. There were no snappy anecdotes. He wasn't selling tickets, he was preparing for the fight of his life.

His gym on North Broad Street was a no-nonsense athletic office, remodeled and painted, clean and utilitarian. His workouts were the same. He turned up his music—Otis Redding, James Brown, soul classics—so loud that nobody could talk or think. That was just fine. He would punch and move, punch and move. Always forward.

The one time he talked at length before the fight was in a first-person article for *Sports Illustrated* for a fee. He talked with writer Mort Sharnik and said this was the fight he always had wanted. Not for the money, really, but for the opportunity to shut "Clay's" mouth.

All the conversation through the years by "Clay" about him being an Uncle Tom was an insult. All that conversation about being "the white man's champion." "Clay" was the one with a white trainer, the one who was backed by "those rich plantation people" at the start. "Clay" was the one who had a white lawyer to get him out of jail. This was a fight about all that. This was serious.

"When I go to training camp, I go to training camp," Frazier said in the article. "Nothing gets in my way. I've always pushed myself. Like most of my strength came to me before I began to box. If something was hard, why I'd just make it a little harder, more complicated, so I'd put in more and get more out. That's how I've always trained for fights. . . .

"I'm going to be in shape for this fight. I'm going to be ready and I'm going to whup him. That's what this fight is all about—conditioning. And there's no way he's going to be better than me. Conditioning. That's my thing. But for him to win he'd have to be in much better shape than me, because he has to do two things: 1.—move backwards, 2.—fight. Me, I only have to fight. It's that simple."

Frazier's life story told more about the black experience in America than Ali's untroubled childhood in Louisville did. One of thirteen kids of sharecroppers in Beaufort, South Carolina, he had to leave town due to a racial situation. He fought with a white youth, then angered a white farmer. Trouble was coming. His mother told him that if he couldn't get along with white people—get along meaning say "yessir" and "nossir"—then he should head north.

He stayed with his married older brother, Tommy, in Harlem for a while, but when he couldn't find any better job than stealing cars, he gravitated to Philadelphia, where he worked in a kosher slaughterhouse shoveling remnants off the floors. He decided after a while he had grown heavy and sloppy in the north, hanging around a lot, and would try to get in shape.

"He came into the Police Athletic League Gym to reduce his weight," manager/trainer Yancey Durham said. "I was a boxing instructor there. I trained some amateurs and some pros."

The rest was a straight progression upward on any graph on any chart. Frazier remembered that he had wanted to be a fighter in Beaufort, where he hit a homemade heavy bag in the backyard. The gym felt like home to him from the moment he walked through the door. He began a steady eight-year climb through the amateurs to the Olympic gold medal to an unbeaten professional record and now the Fight of the Century.

There were no frills to his style. He stepped inside and tried to hit a man. Sometimes he was called "the black Marciano." There were no frills to his life. He had known Florence since they were teenagers in Beaufort and now at the age of twenty-seven he had five kids. Their names would be embroidered on the back of the robe he would wear into the ring. Florence's name would not because you knew kids would be around you for the rest of your life, but you never could tell about a wife. Not that he had plans.

He had worked hard, survived, succeeded. He didn't have to apologize to anyone. He had brought along the people to this fight whom he met in the beginning. The effects of fame and money didn't seem to have done much to him. The guy he was now, the guy who wore better clothes, lived in a better house, drove better cars, sang with his own group, the Knockouts, instead of in the shower, was pretty much the same guy he always had been.

"What kind of shape is he in?" a reporter asked Durham.

"Joe's always in shape," he said. "I can't rate it. He's no better, no worse, than he was for Buster Mathis or Manuel Ramos or Jerry Quarry or Dave Zyglewicz or Jimmy Ellis or Bob Foster. Joe is always in shape."

Durham did much of the talking for Frazier. He was an easy interview, often talking in the first person for his fighter, the way trainers and managers did in the past. He said he wished that Frazier would retire after this fight, money made, mountains climbed. He could join Rocky Marciano in the clubhouse of the undefeated.

"I will encourage him to get out," the manager/trainer said. "Yes, even though it would mean more money to me if he stays. He means more to me than money. Suppose I encourage him—and I could do it—to fight just one more fight. And something happened. That would be on my conscience."

Durham was a military veteran. His life had been changed forever when he was run over by a jeep at an air base in England. Both of his legs were broken. That ended his boxing career right there. Someone asked him—as a veteran—what he thought of Ali's decisions about the military draft.

The manager/trainer's quick answer was that he was against them. Then he thought about what he said.

"You know what my IQ was when I went in the Army?" he asked. "It was 20. That's the truth. I'm not kidding you. It was 20 because I wanted it to be 20. Everything they asked me to do, I did it backwards. But it didn't work. They said 'you're in the Army.' So I was in.

"Clay was willing to lose his life for his beliefs. I wasn't. The things he gave up, I would never have done that—the fame, the glory, the money; he gave it all away. It takes a lot of courage to give up those things, I think."

The fight was on a Monday, March 8, 1971. Ali and Frazier both arrived on Saturday. Ali had fifteen rooms reserved for his people at the New Yorker Hotel, across the street from the Garden. ("I bet Joe Frazier doesn't have that many rooms," he said.) Frazier had six at the City Squire.

The last few days had been a swirl of activity. Both fighters appeared, but not together, for physicals on Wednesday. After both men were judged healthy by Dr. Harry Kleinman, an elevation in both pulse rates determined as normal, Frazier returned to Philadelphia and Ali returned to Miami. Ali had wanted to stay in New York, but simply going through crowds to get to the Felt Forum for the physical had been torture. Angelo convinced him to return to Miami. The final line in Angelo's argument was the fact that the airline had promised to prepare two special steaks, not airline steaks, for the ride.

"He shoots his mouth off a lot, but he's a human being and he's fighting for the heavyweight championship of the world," Angelo told reporters who were distressed that the quote machine would be broken in the last days before the fight. "He needs privacy. He deserves a calm atmosphere. You can't get off a merry-go-round and fight for the heavyweight championship."

The little stories took hold with the fighters absent. Frazier was a 7-5 favorite in Las Vegas, but Ali was an 11-8 choice in London. The Brits just loved him. Frazier was upset at the green-and-gold brocade robe that had been delivered for the big night, felt it was too short and too loose. Lew Magram, the New York tailor who made the robe for $300, balked and then consented to do alterations. Frazier's robe and Ali's red velvet shorts and everybody's shoes and everything else they wore in the ring, it turned out, belonged to the promoters. The promoters would put the pieces of the production up for bid.

The blow-by-blow voice on the closed-circuit broadcast would be sixty-two-year-old Don Dunphy, who had called all those Friday Night Fights on the *Gillette Cavalcade of Sports.* Howard Cosell, the modern voice of boxing, allegedly had priced himself out of the job and was mad at many people. The color commentator was movie star Burt Lancaster, hero of swashbuckling features but never known for anything to do with boxing. A lot of people were mad that he had this job. He was a friend of Jerry Perenchio, one of the promoters.

The New York Police Department and the Garden announced there would be as many as five hundred security people working the event. Between the live crowd and closed-circuit crowds in the area and just general traffic, as many as forty thousand people could be around the Garden at the same time. The police warned about pickpockets and the perils of buying counterfeit tickets.

The three Apollo 14 astronauts—Alan Shepard, Stuart Roosa, and Edgar Mitchell—would be in attendance, back from the moon for less than a month. (Talk about being dizzy at the top of the Empire State Building.) Everybody who was anybody was supposed to be there, from

Marcello Mastroianni to Woody Allen to Ted Kennedy to Joe Namath to Peter Falk to Diana Ross to Miles Davis. Everybody. Hugh Hefner. Colonel Harland Sanders. Everybody.

Ali had written out his prediction, placed it in an envelope to be opened on TV before the fight. (He predicted that he would win by a knockout in the sixth.) Frazier predicted that *he* would win with a knockout in less than ten rounds. He did not put the prediction in an envelope, just said it. Woody Allen picked Ali. Walter Matthau picked Frazier in seven. Edward Villella of the New York Ballet picked Frazier. Casey Stengel picked Ali. Everybody had a pick. Mae West picked Frazier. Zsa Zsa Gabor picked Ali. Rocky Graziano, Sugar Ray Robinson, Ezzard Charles, and Henry Armstrong picked Ali. Joe Louis, Archie Moore, Willie Pep, and Tony DeMarco picked Frazier. Everybody. Comedian Flip Wilson said he picked Ali, but his character, Geraldine, picked Frazier.

"I'll crawl across the ring and tell him, 'You're a bad nigger,' if I lose," Ali said in a last promise.

"He's all psyched up," Frazier said. "I'm afraid he'll have a heart attack before the fight comes."

The pieces of the production were almost put together. People began to arrive, ready to see what there was to see. Frazier wanted it known that he planned to show up for the advertised Joe Frazier Victory Party at the Statler Hilton Hotel after the fight. There were questions about whether he would sing with his musical group, the Knockouts.

"I'm going to be there, but I don't know if I'll sing or not," he said.

"That will depend on what happens in the fight, how I feel, how I look."

Belinda came to the fight from Philadelphia with the kids a day early and met her parents. They were all part of the fifteen rooms at the New Yorker. She still thought Ali was going to lose, still said so. She had asked for a blue ticket, way in the back of Madison Square Garden where no one could see her. She also said she was going to wear a black dress because that would be the appropriate color for defeat.

She went looking for her husband the day she arrived. She wanted to find out where she would get that $25 ticket. She asked around the lobby of the hotel, but the various members of the entourage, Bundini and the rest, said they didn't know where the champ was. She found this odd. The way they talked seemed different.

She decided to call the room of Gene Kilroy, the longtime aide to Ali, part of the entourage, often the only white man in the group. She would ask Kilroy. The phone rang. She said a woman answered.

"Is Gene Kilroy there?" Belinda asked.

"Who?" the woman answered.

"Is Gene Kilroy there or not?"

There was a pause. A male voice could be heard in the background.

"Tell 'em Gene Kilroy's not here."

"He says, 'Gene Kilroy's not here.'"

Belinda recognized the male voice. She told the woman to put her husband on the phone. Now. The woman stammered. She told Ali that his wife was on the phone, and Ali told the woman she was lying. Belinda repeated her demand. Now. Understand? The woman told Ali that his wife sounded very mad. Ali took the phone.

"What the fuck are you doing with this chick in the room the night before the fight?" Belinda said. "This is what I'm talking about. I'm coming to that room and kick you out so you can lose this fight. But you ain't going to be in that room on my watch, you stupid idiot."

Belinda said she knew Kilroy's room number so she went right there and pounded on the door. Then she pounded some more. She screamed a little bit. She screamed more. Ali finally opened the door. He wasn't wearing any clothes. That was "how stupid and scared" he was. Belinda said she asked where the woman was. Ali said she was gone. Belinda went to the bathroom and pulled back the shower curtain. There was the woman. She was wearing clothes.

"I'm sorry, I'm sorry," the woman said.

Belinda said she picked up a knife that for some reason was on a table. She announced she was going to kill both the woman and Ali. Then she said she was going to kill only the woman "because she was so ugly." How could her husband be with such an ugly woman? Belinda said he just sat and watched this all play out in front of him.

"This is just business," the woman pleaded. "He gave me $40. Please don't kill me."

Belinda threatened some more, then put down the knife and let her go. This was a "$40 hooker with a heroin habit," an ugly $40 hooker at that. Belinda made her promise never to talk about what had happened. She also made Ali promise.

"I'm tired of these shenanigans," she said. "I really am. I'm tired of this. I'm so embarrassed about this because she's ugly and you're stupid. You've got a fight tomorrow night."

"I understand," she said her husband said. "I'm sorry."

Belinda said she left the room and went to the bank of elevators. There was a small hassock where people could sit to wait. She said she sat down and cried.

It should be noted that Gene Kilroy said years later that this never happened, that he thought Ali stayed at his parents' home the night before the fight. Belinda insisted that it all was true.

She said she dried her face, went back to her room where her parents were visiting. The next night she put on her black dress and went to the Garden, where she sat in the $25 blue seats "next to some white girl." She waited for what she thought was inevitable.

"Introducing, from Louisville, Kentucky, he's wearing red trunks. . . .

"His opponent, from Philadelphia, Pennsylvania, he's wearing green trunks. . . ."

Deep breath.

Roar.

The fight actually began.

"In the first round, Ali did what he should—jab and move, landing the right hand rather easily," Joe Flaherty would report for the *Village Voice*. "Frazier, too, was predictable—a crab with a souped-up governor trying to envelop an elusive prey. Round two followed the same pattern with Ali successfully keeping Frazier off stride with combinations and jabs, but the lunacy was beginning to show its quirky head. Both fighters were giving running verbal critiques of each other's performance, each waving disgustedly at the end of every round."

Neither fighter was following the script. That was a first thought. Frazier, the classic body puncher, the windup toy that never wound down, blasting away at the nether regions to make the opponent slow down for the later rounds, was trying to hit Ali's head. Ali, after a first turn around the ballroom in the opening round, had decided he didn't want to dance. The butterfly was gone . . . and the bee seemed to have changed its point of attack. Ali was blasting at those nether regions.

He refused to sit down at the end of the second round. Showbiz? Frazier moved to the center of the ring before the bell sounded to start the third. More showbiz? They settled into the business at hand.

"Already there were signs that this would not be one of Ali's easy nights," Shirley Povich would report in the *Washington Post*. "He wasn't finding Frazier with those stiff, textbook jabs because Frazier's bent head was not staying put. And already Frazier was showing what was for the former Cassius Clay a distressing habit of being able to bull him into a corner and slug away."

By the fifth round, Ali was taking the full sixty-second break. There were no second thoughts about that. The hijinks, the back-and-forth messages between the two men that they wanted to kill each other, had been replaced mostly by grunts.

Ali seemed to have a strategy that he would make Frazier tire himself out by throwing so many punches. He had practiced the strategy in Miami, remember, before both the Bonavena fight and this fight, letting his sparring partners pummel him in the midsection. The invitation was extended here. Frazier was more than happy to pummel.

In the fifth round, Frazier seemed as if he had caught the hit-me-first disease that Ali had contracted. He stuck out his chin—stuck it out more than once—and theatrically offered to let Ali hit him right there. Ali obliged.

"The Emperor [Ali] had held him off and patted him with his long cat-like paw. 'There, there, why so hot little man?'" Alistair Cooke would report in the *Guardian* of London. "Then Frazier did a monstrous thing. He put out his tongue and he grinned. Since Frazier looks like Sammy Davis cast in concrete, it was as if one of the gargoyles of Notre Dame had come down and cackled an obscenity in the middle of divine service. The Emperor winced in a spasm of rage and Frazier dropped his guard and flapped his arms waggishly around his thighs as if to say, 'Well, pretty boy, what are you waiting for?'"

This was a stretch of time when scoring the fight was not easy. In the wire room at the *Washington Post,* a small crowd had gathered to watch the round-by-round reports delivered straight from the machines by the Associated Press and the United Press International. The UPI apparently was pro-Ali and the AP favored Frazier. After seven rounds the UPI had Ali ahead, 5–2. The AP had Frazier ahead, 4–2, with one round even.

In the ninth round, Ali made his move. The UPI reported that he landed "eight straight solid shots." Then again, maybe Frazier countered the move. The AP said Ali landed "a series of light jabs, half of which Frazier blocked." Whatever happened, the round ended without either fighter landing on the canvas.

The general perception was that Frazier was ahead, simply by his dogged industry, but at the same time Ali seemed to be waiting for a moment to explode, to land that big punch the way he did against Bonavena. The fight was still a fight.

In the eleventh, the balance tipped. Eddie Futch, the assistant trainer in Frazier's corner, had noticed on film that Ali liked to drop his right hand before he threw an uppercut. He did this to load the punch with extra power. Part of the plan was that Frazier would look for this drop and explode a left hook over Ali's right hand.

There had been occasions in the fight when Ali did his part, but Frazier had been too slow or off the mark with his hook. Ali dropped that hand this time for the load-up with thirty seconds left in the round. Frazier exploded the left hook. It landed flush on the right side of Ali's jaw, the biggest punch of the fight. Ali clearly was hurt.

"Ali was entranced, his body shivering and out of control," Bud Collins would report in the *Boston Globe.* "He tried to pull himself together in his numbness and Frazier pursued, but not wildly. Joe was always in control of himself. He socked Ali with a few more hooks in the remaining 30 seconds, but he couldn't put him down."

The twelfth, thirteenth, and fourteenth rounds passed, two tired fighters working on fumes. Ali made sporadic attempts in the fourteenth to unload a big shot, but Frazier countered. A grim march to the finish seemed ensured. Ali, in his own mind, thought he was winning the fight. Most people—and referee Arthur Mercante and judges Artie Aidala and Bill Recht were included—thought Frazier was winning.

The fifteenth seemed to follow the same pace. The click of time was all that mattered. Then Ali lowered his right hand again, ready to throw the uppercut. Frazier exploded the left hook again to the same place on Ali's jaw. Ali went down, ker-plunk. He landed on his bottom side with a truly surprised look on his face. This could happen to me? He was standing at the count of three.

"There was a minute and a half to go in the round," Bob Waters would report in *Newsday*. "Ali made it. His eyes were silver-dollar wide. His toes pointed in and sometimes the head didn't seem to want to go where the body was going. But when the bell rang, Ali's face was even with Frazier's and both of Ali's feet were flat on the canvas.

"Frazier curled his lips at Ali. 'I told you I'd get you,' he said. He had gotten him."

The knockdown would be shown sixteen times on the closed-circuit broadcast before Burt Lancaster said good night and headed back to Hollywood. Someone counted. Every newspaper in America would run a picture of the knockdown. Maybe not every newspaper—the right-wing *Manchester Union Leader* would not even mention the fight per orders of publisher William Loeb—but most.

The decision was announced without any great protests. Referee Mercante, who said that he never had seen harder punches thrown in all his career in the ring, scored the fight 8–6, one even, for Frazier. Artie Aidala had it 9–6, Frazier. Bill Recht had it 11–4, Frazier. (UPI had it 7–7, one even, a draw. AP had it 9–5, one even, for Frazier.)

Ali's jaw was swollen to lopsided, cartoon proportions. He looked like Popeye after a bad night on the town. There was no detour to a press conference. Ali was packed into a black Cadillac and taken to Flower Fifth Avenue Hospital. Bundini went to the conference. He said that "he [Ali] just want you to know it was a hard 15 rounds," but much was made about Ali's absence. The man who talked so much could not talk now. The irony was noticed.

Frazier did talk for a few minutes. His face also did not look nice, covered by bumps and contusions, a topographical map of the Appalachian Mountains running across his forehead. There was an exhausted joy in his comments, but also a hard tone. He still was not happy with his opponent.

"I want him to apologize to me," he said. "I want him to say that he's sorry for all of those things he said about me. I didn't make him crawl across the ring on his hands and knees like he promised."

The champion—no doubt about it now, the heavyweight champion of the world—also was not happy with the people gathered in front of him.

"What are you guys going to say now?" he asked. "You've been writing about the great Ali and what he was going to do to me. I can read, you know. Now let me go and get my face straightened out."

The fight had been as exciting as everyone had imagined it would be. Except in those places where the closed-circuit broadcast had coughed and sputtered, there would be no requests from people for their money back. The metaphors attached to the night, Ali as the martyr, the angry black man, the draft protester, against Frazier, the conservative choice, the honest workman, the mow-your-lawn black American, all seemed a bit foolish when the shouting stopped. That is the way it is with these big events. A more subdued eye views the results.

"I suppose it will be taken in some quarters as a victory for hot dogs and apple pie, the Fourth of July and moonlight on the Wabash," Jim Murray would report in the *Los Angeles Times*. "And it's safe to belong to the American Legion again, pack up your troubles in your old kit bag—but actually it was just a fist fight."

X-rays determined nothing was wrong with Ali's jaw that wouldn't heal naturally. He was back at the hotel within a couple of hours after the fight was finished. Belinda was there.

"His jaw was swollen," she said. "His face was swollen. He shook his head. He says, 'it's all your fault. You said I was going to lose, that's why I lost.'"

This wasn't the truth.

He knew this wasn't the truth.

"You lose, you lose," he told a group of reporters who gathered in his suite at the New Yorker the next day. "I don't cry. I don't cry because I lose. The world will still go on. A plane can crash with 45 people, black and white. Is my losing as bad as 45 people dying, and that's forgotten?

Having Presidents die and Martin Luther King die and that's forgotten. How many people in Vietnam are dying? What I'm saying is, I'm just another person."

The great march back to the big time had been completed. There simply wasn't the sound of trumpets at the end. That was the truth.

"You lose, you lose," he said again. "I've studied life. People have accidents, people die. My wife and my babies and my house is waiting. The sun is still shining."

18

Supreme Court

The decision to award the fight to Joe Frazier at the end of the night was a worry to Jonathan Shapiro. He was one of the 20,455 eyewitnesses stuffed inside the Garden on that March 8, 1971. He went with some people from work, sat high in the blue seats, roared along with everyone else at the fifteen rounds of action. Ali lost? Ali really lost? The decision just sat there, strange and ugly after the long, long days and months and years of buildup. Ali lost.

"I hope this doesn't foretell what comes next," Jonathan Shapiro said to the people from work.

He was Ali's newest lawyer. The people from work were mostly colleagues from the Legal Defense Fund.

A date now had been set, April 19, 1971, one month after the Joe Frazier fight, for that last appeal before the Supreme Court. Win and Ali would be a free man, ready to pursue a career that now was focused on a solitary goal: a rematch with Frazier. Lose and that rematch could be as many as five years in the future as federal marshals would come to his door in Cherry Hill, or wherever he was, to take him to a very different situation.

Shapiro's job was to try to make the good result happen. He was young, thirty-one, only two years older than Ali. He never had argued a case before the Supreme Court, but certainly thought he could. He wanted to try.

"You're 31," he said years later. "You think you can do anything."

His employer, the Legal Defense Fund of the NAACP, also employed Michael Meltsner, the lawyer who had led the successful appeal to return Ali's New York boxing license. Chauncey Eskridge, Ali's longtime general lawyer, had come to the group months earlier for help when the Supreme Court became the final chance for appeal. He was not satisfied with Charles Morgan, the veteran civil rights lawyer from Atlanta, and wanted to make a change.

Shapiro was the change. He was a cum laude graduate of both Columbia University and Harvard Law School, another one of those bright, long-haired activist lawyers from the North who had gone to the South to work on the struggle for civil rights. His plan at the start had been to leave for a summer from his job at a well-appointed New York law firm, do good works, then return to a fine, button-down life in the fall. The return never came.

Work for the Lawyers' Committee for Civil Rights Under Law in Jackson, Mississippi, was scary, meaningful, exciting, kind of fun. He was young and married, living in the middle of headlines.

"Schwerener, King and Goodman, that happened in '64," he said. "This was '65. It was a frightening place. Lawyers were threatened. Lawyers were shot at, beaten up. . . . We lived in a black subdivision of Jackson. This was a time when churches and synagogues were being bombed fairly regularly. We thought the safest place to live was with the only people we could deal with, the only people who would have anything to do with us, the black community. Our first child, our daughter, was born in Mississippi in 1967. A blonde, blue-eyed Southerner."

The Legal Defense Fund, where he now worked in New York, handled the same issues on a wider stage. The LDF had brought *Brown v. Board of Education* to the Supreme Court in 1954, the legal decision that desegregated the nation's schools. LDF lawyers still challenged hundreds of school districts across the country on desegregation issues. The organization also had tackled segregated hospitals, restaurants, parks-and-recreation facilities, public buildings of any kind. It had defended leaders and participants in arrests after sit-ins, marches, protests.

The decision to take Ali's case was not automatic. The fight for the return of his boxing license had been a far easier legal issue. For an agency that worked relentlessly for integration, the Nation of Islam was a troubling presence. The death of Malcolm X, the accompanying violence of the NOI, was a definite consideration. The debate about representing violent clients grew every day.

"One of the interesting things about Ali's case was how many of these issues were affecting society and government at the time," Shapiro said. "They came together in this case. There was the war, the civil rights movement, the rise of the Nation of Islam, sort of the whole Black Power movement. During this time when the Southern Nonviolence Coordinating Committee and Eldridge Cleaver were creating the Black Panthers, there was a real division about whether we should represent these people or stick with the traditional."

Notoriety won the day. The LDF would become involved again. The thought was that Ali's case had become iconic, symbolic of all fights against racism and the war. Shapiro watched with Eskridge in New Orleans when the Fifth Circuit Court turned down the appeal seven months earlier, on August 19, 1970. That was a week before Ali's twin daughters were born, two weeks before he fought those exhibitions at Morehouse College. Shapiro then began work on the final appeal to the Supreme Court, which was made a month and a half later, October 1, 1970, as Ali prepared for Oscar Bonavena.

The fragmented approaches by the list of lawyers during almost four years had created a curious file. Edward Jacko, the first attorney, Jacko the Giant Killer, had filed immediately for a conscientious objector classification on the basis that Ali was opposed to war. Hayden Covington had neglected this appeal and concentrated on the idea that Ali was a minister, that all members of the NOI were ministers, the same as the Jehovah's Witnesses. Charles Morgan had worked the wiretap argument, especially the fact that Ali had not been able to hear one classified tape that might have played a part in the guilty verdict by the court. A couple of other issues also had been noted.

An appeal to the Supreme Court is a request for a writ of certiorari, which is a decision that the Court will listen to arguments for the case. The denial of the writ would mean that the case would not be heard and would end at that moment. The federal marshals would knock at Ali's door. Only eighty cases out of seven thousand applicants were heard every term.

"Our cert petition was 56 pages," Shapiro said. "The main issue that we dealt with, 34 to 36 pages, was the wiretap issue. . . . We spent 10 pages arguing that he had the right to have his draft status determined by a Selective Service board from which members of his race had not been systematically excluded. . . . We argued, too, that the denial of his CO claim may have been based on a finding that his objections to participation in war were political and racial rather than religious. Then we also did raise the ministerial exemption. We spent just one page on that."

All the history, all the arguments were stuffed into this one document. That is normal legal procedure. The Supreme Court justices could choose whatever aspect or aspects of the case they found interesting. They could discard whatever ones they didn't. If they discarded all of them, as often happens, that would be the end.

On January 11, 1971, two months before the Frazier fight, the Court issued the writ. The majority of the judges originally were against this. Justice William Brennan, a liberal, was very much for it. He thought the Court would be seen as cowardly if it did not address such a famous case about such a famous person that had been in the public consciousness for so long. How could Ali be sent away without a final day in court? The public would be upset.

Brennan's argument won the day with a twisted-arm majority, but limits were set. The writ would be granted only within the narrowest boundaries.

Gone were the claims that Ali was a minister of the Nation of Islam. Gone was the claim about the illegal wiretap. Gone were the claims about the illegal all-white draft board in Louisville, the illegal all-white jury in Houston. The only appeal that the Court would hear was the original appeal for exemption from the draft as a conscientious objector, the original appeal by Jacko the Giant Killer.

The case, in many ways, had been distilled to the two hours Ali spent in front of retired judge Lawrence Grauman in the beginning in Louisville. The rest had been a long judicial dance that no longer counted for anything.

Ali heard the news in Philadelphia as he arrived at a gym in a new Rolls-Royce for a photo session with Joe Frazier to publicize the Fight of the Century. He was scheduled to leave the next day to begin training at the 5th Street Gym in Miami. He was in a hurry, didn't have much time to talk.

"I am glad about the court's decision," he said. "The one thing on my mind right now is Joe Frazier."

Anything else?

"Don't anyone touch the car," he said. "You'll scratch it."

The case was not scheduled to be heard in Washington until April 19, 1971, a month after the fight was due to take place. That assured everyone involved that the Fight of the Century actually would happen. Ali, indeed, was able to concentrate on Frazier and the general hoo-ha of the event. Very few questions were asked about his legal situation and his questionable future. A fat velvet curtain was drawn in front of all that as the big show grew bigger and bigger.

"Do you ever think about what comes next in court?" one intrepid reporter did ask during one 5th Street session.

"Yeah," Ali said. "Not all the time, but sometimes I'll be lying there, resting or dozing off, and I'll wonder about the appeal. What if it fails? When it does come up, what I tell myself is that I'll just go to jail, and you have to get out some time."

Four months passed, three of them in an exaggerated hurry with the Fight of the Century. The fourth and final month, six weeks actually, was dragged out as the swelling in Ali's chin receded and he edged back into the world. His old spirit returned, better than ever. He had beat Frazier! Of course he had. Uncle Sam and other white men had taken all his money from the fight! Of course they had. His voice came back just fine.

Ali had bought another bus, reminiscent of the old Big Red that he drove north for the Sonny Liston fight in Maine back in 1965. He also had bought another car, a new Oldsmobile, specially built with $7,500 worth of solid gold trim added. The car was the crazy stuff fighters do when they make money. The bus had a purpose. He now could travel to those weird college towns and speaking engagements in style.

He was spotted in the bus when he appeared at a charity variety show in Detroit on March 29, only three weeks after the fight.

"The loss to Joe Frazier seems to have made me more popular than ever," he told the crowd. "The people really believe I won that fight. That's why I'm on top. They're the judge. . . . I'm still the champ as far as they're concerned."

He was spotted in the bus in Milwaukee when he spoke at the University of Wisconsin–Milwaukee the next night before a crowd of 1,500 at the Student Union. . . .

"Boxing introduced to me the real fight of freedom, justice and equality for 20 million black people . . . ," he said before spending the night in the bus, which was parked behind Mitchell Hall. "I wouldn't mind going to jail because I'd be with my brothers. I'm ready to die for my people now, but not for somebody else [in Vietnam]."

The bus was back in Chicago the next night. He told his audience at Chicago State that Uncle Sam, the white man in Washington, took $1.5 million of that $2.5 million from the Fight of the Century the day after the fight. . . .

"New York State then puts a lien of $389,000 on each of us," he said. "That left me $620,000. Then I had to pay my trainer, sparring partners, expenses, hotels, airplanes and everything, so I came out with about $450,000. Then I had to buy my home, furnish it, landscape it and take care of my mother, father and brother . . . and when I break it all down, I'm busted."

On April 18, 1971, two weeks later, a nineteen-year-old kid named Louis Diamond was halfheartedly hitchhiking his way out of Chicago. This was a Sunday. He had spent the day in a park on the North Side, listening to music, maybe drinking a little wine, maybe smoking a little smoke, maybe just being part of the scene, people passing out leaflets for different causes, everything political. He lived with his parents in the suburbs, so he was going home. He was at the bus stop, waiting for the city bus, but he also had his thumb out. Just in case.

It was a hot day and he saw this different kind of bus, an RV, really, come down the street. The thought went through his mind that it would be really cool if this thing stopped for him. This thing stopped for him.

"Would you like to meet the Champ?" asked the well-dressed black man who opened the door.

Diamond looked into the RV/bus. Muhammad Ali was lying on a bed in the back.

"Well, sure," the kid said.

The story—told years later to vice.com—went from there. Ali was headed to Northwestern University, in Evanston, Illinois, to give another speech. He sat up and asked for directions to the Triangle fraternity on campus. The kid gave the best directions he could, and Ali kept talking about life and choices and the fact that "we are all brothers and sisters." The bus stopped again to pick up some girl who was hitchhiking, then stopped five minutes later to let her off. Louis Diamond was amazed.

"I was agog at the idea that here is this man who is hated in America and there's no one who seems to be his bodyguard and he's stopping and picking up stray hitchhikers on the way to speak at this public event."

Diamond was long gone when the former champ arrived at the Triangle fraternity and spoke later at the public event at McGaw Hall on the Northwestern campus. He had developed some new speeches that he gave now, more general in nature, more upbeat and philosophical.

"Every intelligent person sooner or later asks 'what purpose is there to life?'" he said. "When you did this, you have taken the first step toward wisdom. The secret of life is the desire to accomplish something. God is so just he puts everything here for a purpose. The wise man is he who knows his purpose.

"Many people confuse happiness with pleasure. Pleasure is only the shadow of happiness. Most people spend a lifetime seeking pleasure and deluding themselves. Like alcohol and drugs. What does it give them? A couple of hours of feeling high and then a hangover and cramps."

His talk started at seven thirty and was done an hour later. He apologized for being brief, but said he had a long trip ahead of him in the bus. He was due in the morning in Washington, D.C., where his case was going to be heard in the Supreme Court.

"Usually my lawyers show up for me," he said. "But they said I should be there this time. Must be something important."

The bus with New Jersey license plate UWT830 pulled out of the parking lot in Illinois a few minutes after nine. The plan was to drive for twelve, thirteen, fourteen straight hours to cover the 695 miles to D.C. There were six drivers to share the work.

Somehow he never made it. Wrong turn? Trouble with the bus? Not enough time allotted? Something. A chair had been saved for Ali at the hearing the next morning, but it remained empty as his future was being debated.

—

Jonathan Shapiro had done the preparation. The law can be a shifting line in shifting sand at this level. A couple of Supreme Court cases had come along in only the past year that might have a bearing on Ali's case.

The first was *Welsh v. the United States* in June 1970, a ruling that Elliot Ashton Welsh II, an atheist, should be classified as a conscientious objector, that an objection could be made on "philosophical, political, sociological beliefs, or merely a personal code." That seemed to open the categories for conscientious objector much wider than they had been when Ali's request was heard.

The second case was *Gillette v. the United States,* which was front-page news on the same morning readers of the *New York Times* studied the result of the Fight of the Century. Guy Gillette called himself a humanist and objected to serving in an "unjust war." Not all wars, this war. In an accompanying case, Louis Negre, a Catholic army reservist, had fought being sent to Vietnam because St. Thomas Aquinas and other Catholic scholars said believers should not participate in an "unjust war." The Court had ruled against both men, saying that American citizens could not choose between wars to fight. They had to fight all wars or none.

The argument for Ali had to account for these decisions. Had the draft board rejected him because he objected on political rather than religious grounds? (His conviction should be overturned.) Was he objecting to this war or all wars? (If it was all wars, his conviction should be overturned.) For days, weeks, Shapiro framed the argument . . . then handed it to Chauncey Eskridge at the end. Eskridge reviewed it, and liked it. Eskridge also decided Eskridge would deliver the argument before the Court.

Shapiro was not happy.

"I understand now," he said years later. "I would have liked to have argued. I certainly knew the case a lot better than he did. But I think the judgment was correctly made that a black man should be arguing the case. Not the young Jewish lawyer from New York."

So it was Eskridge who stood behind the lectern in front of eight Supreme Court justices. (Justice Thurgood Marshall had recused himself because he had been solicitor general of the United States when the case began, part of the prosecutorial team against Ali.) Eight judges would decide the defendant's fate. Eskridge had thirty minutes to convince them his client should be found not guilty. There were two lights on the lectern. A white light would tell the lawyer when five minutes were left. A red light would tell him he should be done.

Eskridge began by detailing the background to Ali's objection to war. Ali's conversion to the teachings of the Nation of Islam. Ali's public statements about the draft. Ali's appeal after his classification as 1-A. The hearing with Judge Grauman was highlighted. The number of witnesses. The FBI report. Ali's lengthy testimony. The result. Didn't Judge Grauman recommend that Ali be given a conscientious objector classification? The letter from the United States Justice Department to the draft board in Louisville was discussed in detail. How could the Justice Department disregard Judge Grauman's decision? How could it recommend that Ali be inducted into the service?

Questions from the judges bounced around the issues. Justice William O. Douglas seemed interested in the Quran and jihad. Justice Potter Stewart wondered about the differences between Islam and the Nation of Islam, which were many. Eskridge answered, said some more about the letter from the Justice Department to the draft board, and was done.

Edwin Griswold, the solicitor general of the United States, presented the government case. The former dean of Harvard Law School, Griswold was a conservative Republican who had been appointed by Democrat Lyndon Johnson and was retained under Richard Nixon. He had tried over one hundred cases before the Supreme Court.

"The petitioner just doesn't want to fight a white man's war, and I can understand that," Griswold said. "But that's not the same as being a pacifist."

The solicitor general spent a lot of time comparing Ali to Negre, the Catholic who was refused conscientious objector status for picking one unjust war to protest instead of all wars. He said the Welsh decision didn't matter, because religion had been part of Ali's situation; he wasn't a political or humanist candidate for conscientious objector. One of the questions put to Griswold by Justice John Harlan was whether the government questioned Ali's sincerity.

"No, Mr. Justice," the solicitor general said, "we do not."

Eskridge had a small chance at rebuttal. The hearing was finished.

Jonathan Shapiro thought Ali was going to jail. He had squirmed through Eskridge's presentation, thought of different things that should have been said. Arguing a case before the Supreme Court was a lawyer's version of the Super Bowl. Shapiro couldn't stop thinking it would have been better for Ali if he were on the field.

On the day after Ali's appeal was heard, the Supreme Court announced that it had affirmed a lower court ruling that forced busing could be used to desegregate schools. The case was *Swann v. Charlotte-Mecklenburg Board of Education.* It was one of those LDF cases. It had been argued in October 1970 by attorney Julius Chambers. He was thirty-three years old. A young man, it seemed, could argue and win a case before the highest court in the land.

Ali surfaced in Houston that Thursday for a strange bit of business. There were no explanations about why he missed the Supreme Court hearing. He was ready to announce at a press conference that he would fight mammoth basketball star Wilt Chamberlain on July 26 in the Astrodome. It would be one of those adolescent arguments—"What would happen if Superman had a fight with God?"—brought to life. Chamberlain never had boxed professionally, but stood seven feet two, weighed 275 pounds, and possessed unnatural coordination for a man that size. What if he slipped a good right hand through Ali's defense? What if he just pounded Ali, doink, on the top of the head? What if?

The fight would be shown on closed-circuit around the country, and Ali and Wilt each would receive a million dollars for his efforts. There had been rumors about this matchup for four years, since Ali first won the title from Liston. It was funky, different. The bet was that a profitable number of customers would follow the "what if?"

"This ain't no joke," Ali declared. "If he doesn't fall off his motorcycle or I'm not in jail, we'll fight."

A prediction?

"Timberrrrrr," Ali said.

The fight, alas, was canceled before it was officially announced. Instead of Chamberlain, his accountant arrived at the site of the press conference in a helicopter. The accountant went into immediate discussions with the promoters, laying out various new demands for his client. The promoters balked. The fight was done.

Speculation was that Chamberlain, brought to the realization that this event really was going to happen, decided that he didn't want it to happen. Better to battle Bill Russell of the Celtics in the low post than to be hit repeatedly in the face.

Ali, on the other hand, obviously was more than ready to get back into the ring. The campaign for a rematch with Frazier had begun in earnest. He said Chamberlain would have been a better opponent than the heavyweight champ.

"Frazier's only a puncher and a hooker," Ali said. "This man's the greatest and strongest athlete. A man with such height, power and reach don't have to get sharp. He just has to hit you once with all that power."

Frazier was in no hurry to get back to business. Troubled by blood clots after the Fight of the Century, he had checked himself into St. Luke's Hospital in Philadelphia for an extended stay. He was out now, recovered, but mostly taking a celebratory lap after his victory. There had been a parade in Philadelphia. He had addressed the South Carolina legislature, then visited his boyhood home in Beaufort.

The day before Ali's hearing, he also had been in Washington. Accompanied by his wife and three of his five children, he was at the White House to attend Sunday service as guests of President Nixon. The champ, dressed in a gray suit with a pink-and-white shirt and a striped tie, said he enjoyed the day although he thought the sermon ran a bit long. The president had opened the service with a quote from Frazier.

"Nothing comes easy in life," Nixon said, quoting Frazier. "Not everyone can be a champ, not everyone can be an athlete. But everyone can do his best to try and make something of himself."

The president had become an expert in the "nothing comes easy in life" situation. The war in Vietnam was a constant, barking presence.

He had followed through on his election promise to start withdrawing troops, but two years had passed and 284,000 soldiers were still in the country, still at war. He had announced that 100,000 more troops would be withdrawn by December, over 14,300 men per month, but even that pace was now considered too slow by the general public.

The country was sick of the war. The entire week after Ali's hearing—and Joe Frazier's visit to the White House—was filled with protests. For a start, an estimated one thousand Veterans Against the Vietnam War rattled around the city, camped on the esplanade, and made themselves heard. On Friday, seven hundred of them took off their Silver Stars and Purple Hearts, their many combat medals and awards, and threw them over a fence to land in front of the Capitol at the feet of a statue of the first Supreme Court chief justice, John Marshall.

Joseph Bangert, a twenty-two-year-old former Marine, told the *New York Times* that he had wanted to give his six medals back while he still was in Vietnam. He said that was when he learned that "'the political force' they were fighting was the people."

"We were taught, 'Don't trust the kids, don't trust the old women, they'll kill you,'" Bangert said. "It's the people's struggle against the aggressor, but we're the aggressor."

On Saturday, the veterans were joined by 200,000 to 500,000 people, depending on who did the estimating. Another protest of 165,000 people was staged in San Francisco. Protests now seemed natural, part of life after four years. The protest in Washington was the fourth since Nixon took office.

"Your presence here today means that you're going to force the Congress to undeclare war," Congresswoman Bella Abzug told the protesters.

A Harris poll in May said that "the tide of American opinion has now turned decisively against the war in Indo-China." For the first time, a majority of the American public, 59 percent, felt that it was "morally wrong" to be fighting in Vietnam. Only 29 percent felt that it was right. By 60 to 26 percent, most Americans favored a continual troop withdrawal "even if the government of South Vietnam collapsed." Also for the first time, a narrow plurality, 42 percent to 39 percent, said it would agree to a coalition government if Communists were in it.

Nixon tried to stall for time. That was all he could do.

"If the United States should announce that we will quit regardless of what the enemy does, we would have thrown away our principal bargaining counter to win the release of American prisoners of war," Nixon replied to the protesters. "We would remove the enemy's strongest incentive to end the war sooner by negotiations. And we will have given enemy commanders the exact information they need to marshal their attacks against our remaining forces at their most vulnerable time."

The war was done. There was little doubt.

—

The real story of what happened in the Supreme Court on the way to its decision on June 28, 1971, would not be known until the 1979 publication of *The Brethren,* a book by Bob Woodward and Scott Armstrong that described the workings of the Court under Chief Justice Warren Burger. One thing was certain—the twists, the turns, and the byzantine path each of the eight judges (Thurgood Marshall still recused) followed to a verdict was quite different, and quite strange. These events would later be put into an HBO movie called *Muhammad Ali's Greatest Fight,* first shown in 2013.

The basic facts of the verdict were as follows:

1. Ali's conviction was overturned.
2. The vote was 8–0.
3. The score—in a phrase from the sports page—was no indication of the way the game was played.

"Naturally I was elated over the decision," Eskridge said on the day the ruling was announced. "It means finally somebody agrees with you. We went through the District Court twice, the Circuit Court of Appeals twice and then we briefed our case in the Supreme Court twice. Finally we got a breakthrough when the court agreed with us. You can't help but be elated.

"We tried every opportunity we got to convince our opponents that they were wrong in characterizing Ali's religious beliefs as racial and political."

Not so fast. Eskridge didn't know what had happened, only the celebratory result. Jonathan Shapiro did not know. He would be "fascinated" when he read the Woodward book. Nobody but the judges, and a few of their clerks, really knew.

A first vote had found Ali guilty, 5–3. That meant he was going to jail. There was no doubt. The court was in transition. The liberal leftovers from the years with Chief Justice Earl Warren were being replaced by the more conservative selections of President Richard Nixon. Chief Justice Burger was one of them.

Three liberals, Justice Brennan, Justice William O. Douglas, and Justice Potter Stewart, voted for Ali. The rest of the judges voted against. Burger, who hadn't wanted to issue the writ of certiorari in the first place, was pleased to move along to other, meatier issues.

The task of writing the opinion was handed to Justice John Harlan, seventy-two years old, the senior member of the Court in service, already in treatment for the spinal cancer that would kill him in three months. Harlan instructed his clerks to do the typing, covering certain points. The decision would be released on a Monday morning in June and that would be that. Next to Nelson Mandela in South Africa, Ali would become the most famous political prisoner in the world. Maybe even more famous than Mandela.

Harlan's clerks were recent law school graduates, most of them familiar with the deferments and angles to stay clear of the military draft, young guys who also figured they had nothing against those Viet Congs. Their sympathies were mostly on Ali's side. One of the clerks, twenty-six-year-old Tom Krattenmaker, a graduate of Columbia Law School, a self-described "pest," couldn't get the idea out of his head that something was wrong with this decision.

He had read *The Autobiography of Malcolm X* by Malcolm X and Alex Haley and found it fascinating. The Nation of Islam was well described in the book. It was a real religion, wasn't it? There was nothing in that book to make Krattenmaker think that the NOI encouraged wars of any kind. He went ahead, on his own, and read *Message to the Blackman in America,* the Honorable Elijah Muhammad's book, the bible of the religion. What did it say on the subject? The only war that was discussed was Armageddon, the end-of-the-world reckoning. Even in Armageddon the conflict mostly consisted of God against the white devils. This was war in the abstract.

Krattenmaker found a precedent for the NOI doctrine, a 1955 decision in *Sicurella v. United States.* This was one of those dozens of cases Hayden Covington had pleaded successfully on behalf of Jehovah's Witnesses in the Supreme Court. (Hayden Covington. The lawyer who still was looking for the rest of his money from Ali.) Anthony Sicurella, a Jehovah's Witness, had applied to be a conscientious objector due to his religious belief that forbade participation in unjust wars. His application had been turned down in the lower courts because they said the Witnesses did not condemn all wars, only certain wars. Covington argued successfully that this religion, the Jehovah's Witnesses, sanctioned only a war like Armageddon, a hypothetical end-of-the-world war. This was the same thought the Nation of Islam had.

Krattenmaker presented this information to a skeptical Harlan. ("When I decide on a case I walk away from it," actor Laurence Harvey as Harlan said in the movie.) In a surprise, Harlan read the material and agreed. He changed his vote. There was now a tie, 4–4.

Burger, the chief justice, reportedly was apoplectic. (Frank Langella as Burger in the movie lamented that this opinion would open the door for all black men to join the Nation of Islam to escape the military draft.) Assorted other members of the Court also were uneasy. Ali would still go to jail with a 4–4 vote, the rule, but now would become an even more sympathetic character. No opinion was written for a tie vote. He would go to jail in silence from the most important court in the land.

Justice Potter Stewart, one of the original three justices who voted for Ali, thought this would be awful. America would not react well to a decision by nondecision. He set out to find a technicality, a route that would allow the Court to vote unanimously, 8–0, to free this famous man, yet set no precedent.

His answer came from that long-ago letter from the Justice Department to the Kentucky Court of Appeals, the letter that rejected Judge Grauman's decision and asked the board to reject Ali's plea. The letter said Ali, among other faults, was not sincere in his belief and that his request was political and racial rather than religious. These opinions were obviously wrong. Solicitor General Griswold had admitted in front of the Court that Ali was both sincere and religious. Draft Board 47, in rejecting Ali's plea, had not spelled out the reason for the rejection. If it had been either of these wrong reasons, the decision should be reversed.

Good enough.

Fine.

The technicality was sold at a general meeting of the court. (Frank Langella/Burger grudgingly gives his vote to make the total unanimous.) Ali was a free man. The legend would go forth that in the end he was freed on a unanimous vote by the Supreme Court. Eight to zip. He had been right all along. The truth was much murkier.

This was celebrity justice at work. If he hadn't been Muhammad Ali, famous boxer, his case never would have been heard by the Supreme Court. If he hadn't been Muhammad Ali, famous boxer, his conviction never would have been overturned. A normal citizen with normal resources probably would have been convicted, sentenced, and served at least three years of his jail time already. He never could have climbed twice through the court system of the United States.

Then again, if Muhammad Ali hadn't been Muhammad Ali, maybe none of this would have happened at all. Maybe he was picked out, persecuted because he was Muhammad Ali. The important part was that he was free in the end.

"He lost a unanimous decision the last time out," trainer Angelo Dundee said, talking about the Fight of the Century. "I'm glad he won a unanimous decision this time."

A footnote to the crazy turns taken to reach the verdict was a concurring opinion written by Justice William O. Douglas. He began a convoluted discussion of the Quran and jihad and the Gillette/Negre case with the sentence "I would reverse this judgment of conviction and set the petitioner free." This was a dissent to the first 5–3 verdict. He was the most liberal justice on the court, known for his dissents on most verdicts. This was another one, a dissent that was changed to a concurring opinion. In context, it was a hoot.

"If you read it, it seems clear that it's a dissent," Jonathan Shapiro said. "Just the language. What probably happened, everybody knew that Douglas would go away to his summer home in Washington state early, before the court had formally adjourned. It looks as if this decision, which came out on the very last day of the term, must have been a last-minute thing and he had already filed his dissent."

A hoot.

Ali was back in Chicago when the decision was announced. He had signed to fight Jimmy Ellis on July 26, 1971, in Houston at the Astrodome, same date and place where he was supposed to fight Wilt. He had been training in Chicago for the past two weeks.

The time was a quarter past nine in the morning. He knew the decision was going to be announced sometime during the day, but thought it would be later, maybe even at night. He was in his green-and-white Lincoln Mark III with Eugene Dibble, a longtime Chicago friend, and they stopped at a little store on Seventy-Ninth Street on the South Side for some fresh-squeezed orange juice.

"I was coming out of the store," Ali reported. "I had an orange in my hand and the fellow who owned the store, a little black fellow, he came running out. He said, 'I just heard on the radio, the Supreme Court said you're free on an 8–0 vote.' And he grabbed me and held me."

"I'm so happy for you," the little man said.

Ali might have whooped. He said he did. He might have gone back into the store and bought a round of orange juice for the half-dozen customers. He said he did.

Praise be to Allah. That was his first reaction. Praise be.

"I thank Allah and the Honorable Elijah Muhammad," he said. "I thank the Supreme Court for recognizing the sincerity of my belief in myself and my convictions. I'll try to live better, that's all. I have been living right and clean, and I'll continue to try to do good."

The people with the cameras and notebooks caught up with him at the motel where he was staying, the 50th on the Lake Travelodge. He talked with them in the lobby. Belinda came down for a bit, posed with him for pictures, and returned to the room. He was quiet. The furious pace of a furious life did not fit the moment. He was wrung out, dry, thankful.

"I just want to sit one day and be an ordinary citizen, go to the hardware store, cut the grass," he said. "Don't be in no more papers, don't talk to nobody, no more lectures. Just rest. But a man told me the other day, he said, 'you're marked,' he said. 'You'll never be free, young man. From here on out you'll be called for something.'"

He would not sue anybody. He would not gloat.

"I can't be mad because what they did they thought was right," he said. "I got to ask them to respect the rights to my beliefs. But if I'm going to ask that, then I got to respect the rights to their beliefs."

His most descriptive quote would come more than a week later in *Sports Illustrated.* There would be time to sort out the sensations that the news brought, time to adjust without the television cameras in his face. How did he feel? He didn't feel. That's how he felt.

"Blank," he said. "Blank. It's like a man been in chains all his life and suddenly the chains taken off. He don't realize he's free until he get the circulation back in his arms and legs and start to move his fingers. Then all at once he knows the chains gone and he can move around freely again. I don't really think I'm going to know how that feel until I start to travel, go to foreign countries, see the strange people in the street, then I'm gonna know I'm free. But it ain't meant that much to me yet."

In Philadelphia, Joe Frazier had mixed thoughts about the news.

"What makes everybody think what happens to Clay means anything to me?" the champion asked. "Sure, I'm glad he doesn't have to go to jail. I don't want to see anyone in jail unless they hurt someone or steal something. Clay didn't do that. The guy's had nothing but trouble, but it ain't going to make it any easier for him the next time we fight—if we do fight."

In the afternoon, Ali worked at Johnny Coulon's Gym in Chicago, a cramped and ancient sweatbox at 1154 East 63rd Street, tucked into the third floor next to the elevated train tracks. He had trained for the first two weeks at the Fire Department Gym on the Navy Pier, but it was too big, too active, too noisy. It was like boxing in an airplane hangar. Two thousand people per day came to watch. This was better. Only the press was allowed. The proprietor, Johnny Coulon, was a long-ago bantamweight champion of the world, a pallbearer at Jack Johnson's funeral. He celebrated his birthday every year by walking the length of the gym on his hands. This was like 5th Street in Miami. This was boxing.

News reports said that Ali wore white satin shorts with a light blue rubber shirt for his workout. He skipped rope, hit the heavy bag, but did not spar. The day was hot and the windows of the gym had been nailed shut long ago so boxers would not be bothered by drafts at the end of workouts. He was sweating when he came out of the ring at the end to talk one more time. The cameras and notebooks had followed.

"What will you do to celebrate?" a television man asked.

"I'll say a prayer to Allah," Ali said. "I've said one already. This one will be longer."

Done.

Finished.

He also would go out to dinner with Belinda.

The strange forced march through the halls of this country's bureaucracy had ended. The rest of his life could now begin. Two nights later he would be in Charleston, South Carolina, for two three-round exhibition fights.

Epilogue

MUHAMMAD ALI

The return to his sport brought a long line of celebrated moments for the emancipated man, working now in the mainstream, freed from the threat of imprisonment. Almost twenty-nine years old, heavier, a bit shopworn from his time on the shelf, Ali was no longer the fastest heavyweight ever seen, that unique combination of size and speed that made him famous in a hurry, but he still was fast enough, good enough to do some wonderful things in a boxing ring.

He fought twenty-nine fights over the next ten years, finished with a career 56-5 record when he finally retired thirty-seven days before his fortieth birthday. Take away the three losses he suffered in his final four fights when his skills clearly had diminished, and Ali lost only once after that first bout with Joe Frazier. The loss came on the last day of March 1973, on a split decision when his jaw was broken in the second, third, or eleventh round (depending on who told the story) by Ken Norton in San Diego, a result Ali avenged in a rematch six months later in Los Angeles.

The Norton bouts were part of a climb that spanned thirteen fights over almost three years—toward a return match with Frazier on January 28, 1974. Ali won that fight by unanimous decision in twelve rounds over his nemesis, back at Madison Square Garden, the event advertised as Super Fight II. That win set up the grand drama of the rope-a-dope win in eight rounds over George Foreman in Kinshasa, Zaire—the Rumble in the Jungle—on October 30, 1974, to reclaim the heavyweight title. The Foreman win, in turn, set up the final epic third fight with Frazier on October 1, 1975, the Thrilla in Manila, which ended with the exhausted Ali's fourteenth-round TKO over the exhausted challenger in the Philippine Coliseum in Luzon City.

Ali's presumed shortened career turned out to be the opposite of that, a long, full ride in the end. A debate always will exist about how good he could have been and what he could have done if he had not missed those three prime years, but the results were still terrific. He often has been cited as the greatest boxer of all time, many times by himself.

BELINDA ALI (KHALILAH CAMACHO-ALI)

The marriage lasted for five more years. There were some good times, some fun, especially when she encouraged him to build a training facility in Deer Lake, Pennsylvania. They created a unique site, boulders with names of boxing greats painted on the sides, fresh air, spartan living. Elvis Presley showed up one day, Andy Warhol on another, John Gotti on a third. The world showed up.

There also were some bad times, especially involving women. The door to extracurricular activity had been opened wide. Another woman soon lived on the site with a love child Ali acknowledged was his. Yet another woman presented yet another child. Women were everywhere. Ali would disappear with women into the showers right there at Deer Lake. Everybody saw.

"He had women on the side, had babies, there was just no end to it," Belinda said. "He was weak. He would always tell me everything. I was always aware of what was going on. It wasn't like he hid it from me. He brought it right in my face. I was in Cherry Hill one day and he asked me to go to the store and he had hid this girl in the house. I felt something was wrong. Had a feeling. So I left my wallet and I come back and she's in my bed. . . . He had a real problem."

There were women troubles at the George Foreman fight in Zaire that Belinda said she will detail sometime in her own book. ("The worst time in my life," she said.) She had wanted Ali to retire after he beat Foreman. He already had beaten Frazier in the rematch. This would have been the perfect time to walk off the stage, to reconnect, to raise a family. It never happened.

The ostensible end of the marriage came in Manila, the Philippines, at the third Frazier fight. Ali had started his affair with model Veronica Porché at the Foreman fight and she had been around him ever since as his mistress, often introduced as "Belinda's cousin" or "the babysitter." Now she was with him in Manila. Belinda was back in Chicago at the new home, a mansion in Hyde Park. Reports came back about Ali and Porché, including a report that Philippines president Ferdinand Marcos had complimented Ali on his "beautiful wife" at a reception and Ali did nothing to correct him. Belinda decided to go to Manila.

She traveled straight from the airport to Ali's suite at the Manila Hilton. Behind closed doors, she cursed him, maybe trashed the place, maybe not, maybe scratched his face, maybe not, told him what a fool he was making of himself, then went back to the airport. The legend was that she boarded the same plane that had carried her across the Pacific, now refueled, cleaned and ready to make the trip in reverse.

When she returned to the Hyde Park mansion, she eventually took her four kids (a son, Muhammad Ali Jr., had been added to the three girls) and went to live in a brownstone on the South Side. She filed for divorce on September 2, 1976. When Ali married Veronica Porché a year later, his new wife was pregnant with their daughter, Laila, and they already had a daughter, Hana.

"I left him because he wasn't what he said he was, because of his lack of morals and disrespect to the family . . . ," Belinda, now known as Khalilah, told *People* magazine after the divorce. "Anybody can have a son, but it takes a man to be a father. He wasn't even there when we were together. He's supposed to be a man, but did he prove it? He did with his fists and his mouth, but not with his other actions."

Belinda's first name was changed to Khalilah in 1975 by Wallace Muhammad, the Honorable Elijah Muhammad's son. She always wanted a Muslim name. Khalilah Camacho-Ali has been married and divorced two more times. She was on friendly terms with Ali later in life, able to smile about the good times in their "roller-coaster" marriage. She lives in Deerfield Beach, Florida.

THE HONORABLE ELIJAH MUHAMMAD

The image of the Leader had softened by the time of his death due to congestive heart disease at the age of seventy-seven on February 25,

1975, one day before Saviours' Day. His health had been a problem in recent years as he struggled against bronchial asthma, high blood pressure, and diabetes. His fiery rhetoric had declined along with his health. The Nation of Islam, as opposed to the Black Panthers and other militant groups, now seemed less threatening, a more familiar presence on the national landscape. Mayor Richard Daley proclaimed the day after Elijah Muhammad's death "Nation of Islam Day" in Chicago.

Muhammad Ali attended the funeral service two days later at Mosque No. 2, the Temple of Islam in Chicago. He entered with the Reverend Jesse Jackson, first sat in the press section, then was encouraged to sit on the rostrum. He wore a pinstriped suit and was the only person on the stage not in a blue Nation of Islam uniform. A funeral procession with over five hundred cars traveled from the temple to Mount Glenwood Cemetery, where the Leader was laid to rest inside a copper-lined vault in a $20,000 silver coffin.

The *New York Times* obituary quoted a 1959 appraisal of Elijah Muhammad by George Schuyler, a black conservative columnist from the *Pittsburgh Courier:* "Mr. Muhammad may be a rogue and a charlatan, but when anybody can get tens of thousands of Negroes to practice economic solidarity, respect their women, alter their atrocious diet, give up liquor, stop crime, juvenile delinquency and adultery, he is doing more for Negroes' welfare than any Negro leader I know."

"He turned alienation into emancipation," the Reverend Jackson said. "He concentrated in taking the slums out of the people and then the people out of the slums. He took dope out of veins and put hope in our brains."

THE NATION OF ISLAM

The American-based, race-centered religion that Muhammad Ali joined and followed through his controversial days of draft defiance was changed dramatically when the Honorable Elijah Muhammad died. The leader's son, forty-one-year-old Wallace D. Muhammad, aka Warith Deen Mohammed, replaced him and quickly abandoned the old teachings of the Nation of Islam and merged the group into the Sunni Muslim faith known around the world.

Gone were the declarations that NOI founder Wallace Fard Muhammad was divine and that Elijah Muhammad was a prophet. Gone were the black separatist views. Gone were the dress codes, the paramilitary groups, the talk about spaceships. Wallace's new title was Chief Imam. The NOI mosques around the country—as many as four hundred— were converted to traditional Muslim mosques.

Muhammad Ali and Khalilah both followed Wallace Muhammad into traditional Muslim belief. Muhammad Ali was a practicing Sunni Muslim for the rest of his life. Khalilah is today.

Louis Farrakhan, longtime associate of Elijah Muhammad, split with Wallace Muhammad after three and a half years and in 1981 revived the Nation of Islam name and faith. A number of mosques were returned to the new NOI. Farrakhan has remained in charge. He led the Million Man March on Washington in October 1995. A controversial character, he has been accused of being part of the plot to kill Malcolm X and has been accused of being a racist and an anti-Semite.

Major Coxson

The flamboyant forty-four-year-old racketeer, hustler, man about town who brought Ali to Philadelphia was murdered at four o'clock in the morning on June 8, 1973. He was found kneeling against his waterbed in his Cherry Hill, New Jersey, home, shot three times in the back of the head, hands and legs bound by neckties, a gag in his mouth. A stepdaughter also was shot and killed while his common-law wife and her son were shot and seriously wounded, but survived. Another stepson, fourteen years old, escaped by climbing out a window.

Ali lived only a few blocks away from the scene of the crime in the second house he had been given, or bought at a discount, from the Major. Less than fourteen hours earlier he had been with his friend at the corner of Sixteenth and Chestnut in Philadelphia, talking and standing next to the Major's Rolls-Royce. Their relationship always had been public.

Only a month earlier, Coxson had lost at the end of a colorful campaign for mayor of Camden, New Jersey. To establish residence in the city, he had bought a dilapidated second house in Camden that he rehabilitated, painted white, and called "The White House." He said the mayor's office in Camden was a first stop on becoming "the first black President of the United States." Ali had been part of the campaign. He dedicated his rematch TKO of Jerry Quarry to the Major and introduced him prior to the first Norton fight as "my unpaid financial advisor."

A drug deal gone wrong led to the Major's demise. He was under investigation for several misdeeds and felonies at the time of his death. The architect of the murder, convicted two years later, was Ronald Harvey, a member of Mosque No. 12 of the Nation of Islam. The Philadelphia chapter was known to contain many members of the alleged "Black Mafia" in the city.

Harvey also was convicted, along with four other members of Mosque No. 12, of the largest mass murder in Washington, D.C., history. Seven people were killed five months earlier on January 17, 1973, in a house rented by Kareem Abdul-Jabbar for members of the Hanafi sect of Sunni Muslims. The leader of the Hanafi group, Hamaas Abdul Khaalis, had written a letter disparaging the NOI and the Honorable Elijah Muhammad. Like Malcolm X, he was singled out for assassination by NOI members, but was not home when the attack occurred. Five of his children and his nine-year-old grandson were among the victims.

After the murder of the Major, police warned Ali that he was another potential victim, and they offered him protection. Ali declined. He said if anyone wanted to find him, the task would be easy because he was known all over the world.

"To me this [rumor] is a very bad joke," Ali said, training for his rematch with Norton. "Before all my big fights, they try to weaken me. Just before the Liston fight, Malcolm X was shot. But I'm not afraid of anything but the mighty Allah. I'm not hiding and my children and my wife aren't hiding. And the only contract I know about is the one with Norton. I got one out for him and he got one out for me."

This all sounded good, but within days of the Major's murder he moved Belinda and the kids back to Chicago. He did not attend his friend's funeral but sent a large floral display of red carnations and chrysanthemums. He never lived in the Philadelphia area again.

A postscript to the Hanafi murders occurred four years later on March 9, 1977. The grief-ridden Hamaas Abdul Khaalis was despondent over what he saw as a lack of justice in punishment of the murderers of his children and grandchild. Khaalis led a twelve-man group of Hanafis that took 143 hostages in three Washington buildings. This commenced a thirty-nine-hour standoff that resulted in one death. Among the demands, which included the delivery of the men responsible for the killings of Khaalis's family, was a request to see both Wallace Muhammad and Muhammad Ali. None of the demands were met.

Khaalis was sentenced to prison, where he died in 2003.

THE SUPREME COURT

Two days after the Ali decision, the Supreme Court announced that the *Washington Post, New York Times,* and other newspapers would be allowed to continue publication of the Pentagon Papers. Edwin Griswold, the solicitor general of the United States, who had argued Ali's case, also presented the losing government position that publication of these documents would harm the nation's security.

The Pentagon Papers were a definitive classified study of the U.S. involvement in Vietnam from 1945 to 1967. They were made public by Daniel Ellsberg, who had worked on the study, and detailed a long history of lies from the government to the American people about the war. The seven-thousand-page document was contained in forty-seven volumes.

Justices Hugo Black and John Harlan would retire from the Court during the summer of 1971, but the other seven justices would be part of the decision on January 22, 1973, in the landmark case of *Roe v. Wade.* This decision outlawed state and local restrictions against abortions.

THE MILITARY DRAFT

The draft remained controversial throughout the Vietnam War. College deferments, and other legal escape routes for many educated eligible males, left working-class white kids and minorities to carry a disproportionate share of the burden. In an attempt to change this situation, a draft lottery was instituted on December 1, 1969. An irony was that if Muhammad Ali had been two years older, his January 17 birthday would have ranked him number 235 in the draft. Only the first 195 numbers were called for physicals. He would not have been touched.

The draft was ended on January 27, 1973. Disparate voices have called for its reinstatement during the various conflicts the United States has faced since Vietnam, but no action has been taken. Since the Vietnam War, the U.S. armed forces have been composed solely of volunteers.

Vietnam

The Vietnam War ended on August 30, 1975, when North Vietnamese forces entered Saigon and South Vietnamese president Duong Van Minh unconditionally surrendered. Direct U.S. involvement had ended more than two years earlier under the terms of the Paris Peace Accords when most U.S. troops were recalled. The final death total for Americans in Vietnam was 58,315, with 153,303 wounded. This was from a total of 2,594,000 American troops who served in the war. An estimated 1.3 million combatants of all nationalities died. This was added to an estimated one million civilian deaths.

The disproportionate death total for African Americans, an estimated one out of every four U.S. combat deaths in 1965, was reduced to 13 percent at the end of the war, a more representative figure for a group that was 11 percent of the population. The domino theory that all of Southeast Asia would become Communist if Vietnam fell proved to be wrong. Vietnam fell and nothing significant happened.

Joe Frazier

He could never leave his role as the spurned suitor for the American heart. He could never let it go. Until November 7, 2011, the day he died of liver cancer at the age of sixty-seven in his home in Philadelphia, Frazier was locked into his rivalry with Muhammad Ali as if they were preparing for one last fight in the afterlife.

Though Ali made assorted movements toward a bygones-be-bygones adjustment in their relationship in the thirty-six years after their third battle, in Manila, Frazier never forgave him for the things he said, the things he did. For the no-nonsense workman from Philadelphia, the injustice of how Ali treated him and how the American public reacted—in love with the "dodge drafter" and the Black Muslim instead of the patriotic Christian—could not be forgotten nor forgiven. He never forgot being called "The Gorilla" and "Uncle Tom" on the public stage.

"Now people ask me if I feel bad for [Ali], now that things aren't going so well for him," Frazier wrote in his 1996 autobiography, *Smokin' Joe*. "Nope, I don't. Fact is, I don't give a damn. They want me to love him, but I'll open up the graveyard and bury his ass when the Lord chooses to take him."

Finished as a fighter at age thirty-two after he was destroyed by George Foreman in five rounds in 1976, his only bout after the Thrilla in Manila, Frazier spent the rest of his life in that awkward twilight that follows a leftover celebrity. He sang sometimes with his group, ran a gym, managed his son Marvis's boxing career while it lasted, signed a bunch of autographs, and played the role of the retired heavyweight champion of the world. A case could be made that there was not a single day when he did not hear the name Muhammad Ali or did not think one thought about him.

When Ali famously lit the Olympic flame in 1996, Frazier was one of the few people who did not cheer. "It would have been a good thing if he would have lit the torch and fallen in," Frazier said. "If I had the chance I would have pushed him in."

Fifteen years later, in 2011, Frazier died of cancer. "The world has lost a great champion," Ali said in a released statement. "I will always remember Joe with respect and admiration. My sympathy goes out to his family and loved ones."

BOXING

Ali always predicted that boxing, which he mostly meant as the heavyweight division, would die without him. The idea seemed preposterous as Larry Holmes came along, followed by Mike Tyson and Evander Holyfield, always some American fighter in the mix, always another big bout on the horizon. That is not the case any longer.

Interest has never been lower for heavyweight boxing in the United

States. In the 2016 Olympics in Rio de Janeiro, no American qualified for the superheavyweight, heavyweight, or light heavyweight division. This was a first. In the 2012 Games in London, the three Americans in those divisions all were eliminated in the first round of fights. American athletes with size and coordination now move toward basketball or football or mixed martial arts, the new gladiatorial phenomenon.

The success of the Klitschko brothers, Vitali and Wladimir, also switched attention in the heavyweight division to Europe. The Great White Hopes spoke foreign languages when they finally arrived. Starting on June 26, 1999, when Vitali knocked out Englishman Herbie Hide in two rounds for the WBO title, the Ukrainian brothers have dominated heavyweight boxing for almost two decades. Defensive fighters, never stylists, they took the various versions of the title to Europe and seldom brought them back. The Klitschko brothers' reign apparently is finished, but no charismatic American has stepped forward to take the crown.

Boxing does flourish somewhat in the lower weight classes, notably filled with Spanish-speaking contenders. The one person from Ali's protest years still involved in the sport is eighty-five-year-old promoter Bob Arum, CEO of Top Rank Inc.

MUHAMMAD ALI

Two of the big symptoms for Parkinson's disease are a shuffling gait and an expressionless face. Who would have thought during his youth that Ali would have been a candidate? He was the master of the Ali Shuffle, fast and balanced. He was the Louisville Lip, controversial and constant. Parkinson's?

The diagnosis came in 1984.

"It was a slowness of movement that was his limiting factor at the time," Dr. Stanley Fahn told CBS News years later. "I saw immediately he had a masked face, that is a decreased expression. He had decreased blinking and he had a typical Parkinson's tremor."

The rest of the story was the rest of his life. The fastest, noisiest car on the block moved slower and slower, the sound turned lower and lower until it couldn't be heard at all.

The easy explanation was that the disease was a result of all those punches over all those years. The truth is that nobody knows. Parkinson's research never has found a definitive cause for the disease. Belinda points out that Parkinson's often settles in hyperactive people like Katharine Hepburn and Michael J. Fox. Ali in his early life certainly was a hyperactive person, couldn't sit still.

He was divorced from Veronica Porché and married Yolanda (Lonnie) Williams in 1986, two years after the diagnosis. Fifteen years younger than Ali, a neighbor to his parents in Louisville, Williams first had met him when she was six years old and he was twenty-one. She, like Belinda, had a vision that she somehow would marry him. She, like Belinda, eventually did.

The marriage, far less turbulent than the others, lasted almost thirty years, until the end of his life. Lonnie became caretaker, confidante, manager, gatekeeper, final word. She shielded her man from hurts—Frazier's assorted comments that you only had to "look at him" to see who really won those fights—and promoted the good. The Ali she presented to the world became a force for good, a reasoned observer of life, the sainted, silent figure of peace and hope and inspiration who inspired others.

He became something like James Dean and Marilyn Monroe and Elvis, celebrities frozen in pictures of their prime by early death. The difference was Ali was still around, a quiet reminder of his old transcendent self. The general public accepted it all.

"We admire the man who never stopped using his celebrity for good," President Barack Obama said once, describing the champ. "The man who helped secure the release of 14 American hostages from Iraq in 1990; who journeyed to South Africa upon Nelson Mandela's release from prison; who has travelled to Afghanistan to help struggling schools as a United Nations Messenger of Peace; and who routinely visits sick children around the world, giving them the pleasure of his presence and the inspiration of his example."

The grand iconic moment in the second half of his life came at the 1996 Olympics in Atlanta when he lit the flame at the opening ceremonies on July 19. It was a surprise, a shock to people, when he came out of hiding and took the torch from swimming star Janet Evans. He held it high in his right hand while his left hand shook unabated from his disease. He then turned and lit the flame to open the Games. The stadium crowd, the television audience around the country, around the world, cheered at the picture, the man who had endured, still around, still something to see. The forever champion.

Ali died on June 3, 2016, of septic shock in Scottsdale, Arizona. He was seventy-four years old.

Notes on Sources and Acknowledgments

The first piece of business in writing a book about Muhammad Ali is to buy a book about Muhammad Ali. That book here is *Muhammad Ali: His Life and Times,* written by Thomas Hauser in 1991. It is an oral history of the man, 515 pages of interviews of many of the characters in his life, a baseline of information and anecdotes, many from people who no longer are with us.

The second piece of business is to buy another book about Ali. Perhaps it is *King of the World,* a chronicle of his early life by David Remnick. Perhaps it is *The Greatest: My Own Story,* by Ali as told to Richard Durham, a largely discredited but always readable 1975 autobiography. Perhaps it is, especially in this instance, *Muhammad Ali's Greatest Fight: Cassius Clay vs. The United States of America* by Howard Bingham and Max Wallace. Perhaps—no, surely—it is all of them.

The buying of books, once begun, does not stop for someone writing about the life of Ali. No sports figure has been dissected and trisected, examined more in print, than the talkative heavyweight champion who called himself "The Greatest of All Time." Small books of verse arrive at the house, followed by books about specific times or situations in his life, followed by compilations of columns written about him, followed by the biggest book imaginable. That would be *The Greatest of All Time,* a 650-page coffee-table extravaganza, called "the biggest, heaviest, most radiant thing ever printed" by publisher Benedikt Taschen. (The mailman was not happy about delivering "the biggest, heaviest, most radiant thing ever printed.")

The situations and controversies chronicled in these books, of course, open the path to many other books in many other fields. There are books about the Nation of Islam and the Honorable Elijah Muhammad that must be bought. There are books about Malcolm X, especially his grand autobiography, written with Alex Haley. There are books about the civil rights struggle, books about Vietnam, especially about draft resistance, books about promotion, marketing, books about crime in Philadelphia, books about boxing. There are books.

The writer of the new addition to this pile is caught in a tsunami of words. The bound volumes that soon fill a bookcase are exceeded by the stories from newspapers, magazines, blogs of all dimensions. More words. Many more words.

The *New York Times,* with Robert Lipsyte and Dave Anderson on the case, is another irreplaceable timeline. The *Louisville Courier-Journal* is the important hometown voice. The rest of the newspapers in the country, all of them, present the daily bits and pieces of Ali's life. He always was moving, one place to another, always talking, always doing something. He was news—Muhammad Ali, here in Little Rock!—when he stepped inside another set of city limits.

In addition, there are videos, sound bites, YouTube tapes, documentaries, movies, always another and another. Ali is Ali, then Will Smith is Ali, then Billy Crystal, then somebody else, then Ali is Ali again. The fights can be seen in their entirety, black-and-white, outrageous interviews at the end. The *Wide World of Sports* shows can be seen in their entirety, Muhammad and Howard, an enduring pair of comic-serious actors.

One interview off the Internet leads to the next and the next. Why didn't I see that one earlier? There always is another snippet of Ali sitting on a couch, talking with someone, often from the United Kingdom. His voice, his face, his style, quiet or agitated, happy or upset, become as familiar as if they belonged to a close relative, a member of the household.

A terrific resource for this book was a collection of thirty-four audiotapes made by *Sports Illustrated* writer Jack Olsen for a 1966 *SI* series that soon became a book, *Black Is Best: The Riddle of Cassius Clay.* Olsen interviewed not only Ali but also his mother and father, assorted backers and friends, then added his own observations. It was an intimate look at his subject at a time when all legal hell was breaking loose. Thanks to Nathan Georgitis, digital collections librarian at the University of Oregon Libraries, for his help in obtaining the tapes.

Another terrific resource was a personal book owned by lawyer Jonathan Shapiro of Shapiro, Weissberg & Garin LLP of Boston. Shapiro, who prepared Ali's case before the Supreme Court, had a bound record kept of all of Ali's court proceedings. This included the FBI report on Ali and the appeal before Judge Lawrence Grauman, never before made public. Thanks to Mr. Shapiro. Thanks also to another Boston attorney, Michael Meltsner, a distinguished professor of law at Northeastern University, for his explanation of the effort to regain Ali's boxing license in New York.

Khalilah (formerly Belinda) Camacho-Ali was candid and terrific in detailing her life with Ali. She said, early in the interviews, that she thought Ali had controlled the narrative of his story, simply by his charisma and colorful conversation, that writers never went beyond what he had to say, that he filled up notebooks. She was very good at filling up her own notebook. Thanks to her. Thanks to Ernest Downing for his help.

Thanks to Bob Halloran for his memories of the day Ali was reclassified. Thanks to Ron Rich and Charles Weldon for their memories of *Big Time Buck White*. Thanks to Lawrence Grauman's son, Lawrence Jr., for insights into his father. Thanks to writer Maury Levy for his memories of Major Coxson and Ali. Thanks to the late Philadelphia *Daily News* sports columnist Stan Hochman, a neighbor of Ali. Thanks to Dr. Nathan Hare for memories of the speech at Howard University. Thanks to Tony Tomsic, Joel Blumenthal, Vere Gaynor, Peter Wood, Ann Wagner, Shelly Saltman, Dr. Malachai Crawford. Thanks to Dan Durning for his writing and help on Ali's visit to the University of Arkansas. Thanks to George Lois for his memories of Ali at *Esquire*. Thanks to anyone who talked to me, also to anyone who didn't. Thanks to the many reporters who recorded the many words of Ali for the many stories that were written about him. All of that was invaluable.

On a personal note, thanks to my editor, Jason Kaufman, agent Esther Newberg, and anyone who listened to my complaints over the past three years. Thanks to my partner, Linda Finkle, to my children, Leigh Alan Montville and Robin Montville Moleux, and to my grandsons, Jackson and Colin Moleux.

Thanks, most of all, to Mr. Muhammad Ali. The Greatest.

Bibliography

Abdul-Jabbar, Kareem, with Peter Knobler. *Giant Steps: The Autobiography of Kareem Abdul-Jabbar*. New York: Bantam Books, 1983.

Ali, Muhammad, with Richard Durham. *The Greatest: My Own Story.* New York, Random House, 1975.

Arkush, Michael. *The Fight of the Century: Ali vs. Frazier, March 8, 1971.* Hoboken, NJ: John Wiley & Sons, Ltd., 2008.

Baldwin, James. *The Fire Next Time.* New York: Holt, Rinehart & Winston, 1962.

Bingham, Howard, and Max Wallace. *Muhammad Ali's Greatest Fight.* New York: M. Evans and Co. Inc., 2000.

Branch, Taylor. *At Canaan's Edge: America in the King Years 1965–68.* New York: Simon & Schuster, 2006.

Brown, Jim, with Steve Delsohn. *Out of Bounds.* New York: Zebra Books, 1990.

Brunt, Stephen. *Facing Ali: 15 Fighters, 15 Stories.* Guilford, CT: The Lyons Press, 2002.

Cashill, Jack. *Sucker Punch: The Hard Left Hook That Dazed Ali and Killed King's Dream.* Nashville, TN: Nelson Current Books, 2006.

Clegg III, Claude Andrew. *An Original Man: The Life and Times of Elijah Muhammad.* New York: St. Martin's Press, 1997.

Collins, Mark (editor). *Muhammad Ali Through the Eyes of the World.* New York: Skyhorse Publishing, 2007.

Dundee, Angelo, with Bert Randolph Sugar. *My View from the Corner: A Life in Boxing.* New York: McGraw-Hill, 2008.

Early, Gerald. *The Culture of Bruising: Essays on Prizefighting, Literature and Modern American Culture.* Hopewell, NJ: The Ecco Press, 1994.

Early, Gerald (editor). *The Muhammad Ali Reader*. Hopewell, NJ: The Ecco Press, 1998.

Evanzz, Karl. *I Am the Greatest: The Best Quotations from Muhammad Ali*. Kansas City, MO: Andrews McMeel Publishing, 2002.

Evanzz, Karl. *The Messenger: The Rise and Fall of Elijah Muhammad*. New York: Pantheon Books, 1999.

Ezra, Michael. *Muhammad Ali: The Making of an Icon*. Philadelphia: Temple University Press, 2009.

Fisher, Art, and Neal Marshall, with Charles Einstein. *Garden of Innocents: The Uproarious Inside Story Behind the Fight of the Century*. New York: E. P. Dutton, 1972.

Foley, Michael S. *Confronting the War Machine: Draft Resistance During the Vietnam War*. Chapel Hill, NC: University of North Carolina Press, 2003.

Foley, Michael S. (editor). *Dear Dr. Spock: Letters About the War to America's Favorite Baby Doctor*. New York: New York University Press, 2005.

Frazier, Joe, with Phil Berger. *Smokin' Joe: The Autobiography*. New York: Macmillan, 1996.

Frum, David. *How We Got Here: The 70's: The Decade That Brought You Modern Life—for Better or Worse*. New York: Basic Books, 2000.

Garrow, David J. *The FBI and Martin Luther King Jr.: From "Solo" to Memphis*. New York: W. W. Norton, 1981.

Gitlin, Todd. *The Sixties: Years of Hope, Days of Rage*. New York: Bantam Books, 1987.

Greenberg, Jack. *Crusaders in the Courts: How a Dedicated Band of Lawyers Fought for the Civil Rights Revolution*. New York: Basic Books, 1994.

Griffin, Sean Patrick. *Black Brothers Inc.: The Violent Rise and Fall of Philadelphia's Black Mafia*. Preston, United Kingdom: Milo Books, Ltd., 2005.

Griffin, Sean Patrick. *Philadelphia's "Black Mafia": A Social and Political History*. Dordrecht, The Netherlands: Kluwer Academic Publishers, 2003.

Gross, Michael. *My Generation: Fifty Years of Sex, Drugs, Rock, Revolution, Glamour, Greed, Valor, Faith, and Silicon Chips*. New York: HarperCollins, 2000.

Hampton, Henry, and Steve Fayer. *Voices of Freedom: An Oral History of the Civil Rights Movement from the 1950s Through the 1980s*. New York: Bantam Books, 1990.

Hauser, Thomas. *The Lost Legacy of Muhammad Ali*. Toronto: SportMedia Publishing, 2005.

Hauser, Thomas, with the cooperation of Muhammad Ali. *Muhammad Ali: His Life and Times*. New York: Simon & Schuster, 1991.

Heller, Peter. *In This Corner: Forty World Champions Tell Their Stories*. New York: Simon & Schuster, 1973.

Kindred, David. *Sound and Fury: Two Powerful Lives, One Fateful Friendship*. New York: Free Press, 2006.

King, Earl. *The Breeding of Contempt: Account of the Largest Mass Murder in Washington D.C. History*. Bloomington, IN: XLibris Publishing, 2002.

Kram, Mark. *Ghosts of Manila: The Fearful Blood Feud Between Muhammad Ali and Joe Frazier*. New York: HarperCollins, 2001.

Lincoln, C. Eric. *The Black Muslims in America*. Trenton, NJ: Africa World Press, 1961.

Lipsyte, Robert. *An Accidental Sportswriter: A Memoir*. New York: HarperCollins, 2011.

Lois, George. *$ellebrity: My Angling and Tangling with Famous People*. London: Phaido Press, 2003.

Lois, George (editor). *Ali Rap: Muhammad Ali, The First Heavyweight Champion of Rap*. Cologne, Germany: Taschen Publishers, 2006.

Lynd, Alice (editor). *We Won't Go: Personal Accounts of War Objectors*. Boston: Beacon Press, 1968.

Lytle, Mark Hamilton. *America's Uncivil Wars: The Sixties Era from Elvis to the Fall of Richard Nixon*. New York: Oxford University Press, 2006.

Marable, Manning. *Malcolm X: A Life of Reinvention*. New York: Penguin Books, 2011.

Marqusee, Mike. *Redemption Song: Muhammad Ali and the Spirit of the Sixties*. London and New York: Verso, 2000.

Massaquoi, Hans J. *Destined to Witness: Growing Up Black in Nazi Germany*. New York: William Morrow & Co., 1999.

Mee, Bob. *Ali and Liston: The Boy Who Would Be King and the Ugly Bear*. New York: Skyhorse Publishing, 2011.

Meltsner, Michael. *The Making of a Civil Rights Lawyer*. Charlottesville, VA: University of Virginia Press, 2006.

Miller, John, and Aaron Kenedi. *Muhammad Ali: Ringside*. Old Saybrook, CT: Konecky & Konecky, 1999.

Monaghan, Paddy. *Street Fighting Man*. London: John Blake Publishing, 2008.

Morgan, Charles Jr. *One Man, One Voice: A Crusading Southern Lawyer Recounts His Most Dramatic Cases—from Howard Levy to Muhammad Ali, from "One Person, One Vote" to "Impeach Nixon"—in the Continuing Struggle for Civil Rights and Honest Government.* New York: Holt, Rinehart and Winston, 1973.

Olsen, Jack. *Black Is Best: The Riddle of Cassius Clay.* New York: Putnam, 1967.

Pacheco, Ferdie (The Fight Doctor). *Muhammad Ali: A View from the Corner.* New York: Carol Publishing Group, 1992.

Paloger, Ronnie. *The Paloger Collection of Muhammad Ali Memorabilia.* Los Angeles: Christie's, 1997.

Reemtsma, Jan Philipp. *More Than a Champion: The Style of Muhammad Ali.* New York: Alfred Knopf, 1998.

Remnick, David. *King of the World.* New York: Random House, 1998.

Roberts, Randy, and Johnny Smith. *Blood Brothers: The Fatal Friendship Between Muhammad Ali and Malcolm X.* New York: Basic Books, 2016.

Schulke, Flip, with Matt Schudel. *Muhammad Ali.* New York: St. Martin's Press, 1999.

Schulman, Bruce J. *The Seventies: The Great Shift in American Culture, Society, and Politics.* New York: Da Capo Press, 2001.

Sellers, Cleveland, with Robert Terrell. *The River of No Return: The Autobiography of a Black Militant and the Life and Death of SNCC.* Jackson, MS: University Press of Mississippi, 1990.

Sneddon, Rod. *The Phantom Punch: The Story Behind Boxing's Most Controversial Bout.* Rockport, ME: Down East Books, 2015.

Taschen Publishing. *Greatest of All Time: A Tribute to Muhammad Ali.* Cologne, Germany: Taschen Publishing, 2010.

Tuotti, Joseph Dolan. *Big Time Buck White (A Play).* New York: Grove Press, 1969.

Wrest, David (editor). *The Mammoth Book of Muhammad Ali.* London: Constable & Robinson Ltd., 2012.

X, Malcolm, with Alex Haley. *The Autobiography of Malcolm X.* New York: Penguin Books, 1965.

Index

EVEL
The High-Flying Life of Evel Knievel: American Showman, Daredevil, and Legend

Evel Knievel, the father of extreme sports, was a high-flying daredevil. He was the personification of excitement and danger and showmanship, and represented a unique slice of American culture and patriotism. But behind the flash and the frenzy, who was this man in red, white, and blue? With characteristic flair and insight, Leigh Montville delves into Knievel's amazing place in pop culture, as well as his notorious dark side, exploring Knievel's complicated and often contradictory relationships with his image, the media, his own family, and his many demons. Montville has delivered another definitive biography of a one-of-a-kind sports figure.

Biography

TED WILLIAMS
The Biography of an American Hero

Still a gangly teenager when he stepped into a Boston Red Sox uniform in 1939, Ted Williams had a boisterous personality and penchant for towering home runs that earned him adoring admirers and venomous critics. In 1941, the entire country followed Williams's stunning .406 season, a record that has not been touched in over six decades. Then at the pinnacle of his prime, Williams left Boston to train and serve as a fighter pilot in World War II, missing three full years of baseball, making his achievements all the more remarkable. With unmatched verve and passion, and drawing upon hundreds of interviews, acclaimed bestselling author Leigh Montville brings to life Ted Williams's superb triumphs, lonely tragedies, and intensely colorful personality in a biography fitting of an American hero and legend.

Biography

THE MYSTERIOUS MONTAGUE
A True Tale of Hollywood, Golf, and Armed Robbery

John Montague was a boisterous enigma. In the 1930s, he was called "the world's greatest golfer" by famed sportswriter Grantland Rice. He could drive the ball 300 yards and more, or he could chip it across a room into a highball glass. He played golf with everyone from Howard Hughes and W. C. Fields to Babe Ruth and Bing Crosby. Yet strangely, he never entered a professional tournament or allowed himself to be photographed. Then a *Time* magazine photographer snapped his picture with a telephoto lens and police quickly recognized Montague as a fugitive with a dark secret. From the glamour of 1930s Hollywood to John Montague's extraordinary skill and triumphs on the golf course to the shady world of Adirondack rumrunners and the most controversial, star-studded court trial of its day, *The Mysterious Montague* captures a man and an era with extraordinary color, verve, and energy.

Biography

THE BIG BAM
The Life and Times of Babe Ruth

Leigh Montville chronicles a thoroughly original, definitively ambitious, and exhilaratingly colorful biography of the largest legend ever to loom in baseball—and in the history of organized sports. Based on newly discovered documents and interviews—including pages from Ruth's personal scrapbooks—*The Big Bam* traces Ruth's life from his bleak childhood in Baltimore to his brash entrance into professional baseball, from Boston to New York and into the record books as the world's most explosive slugger and cultural luminary.

Biography

ANCHOR BOOKS
Available wherever books are sold.
www.anchorbooks.com

CASEY STENGEL
Baseball's Greatest Character
by Marty Appel

For more than five glorious decades, Casey Stengel was the undisputed, quirky, and beloved face of baseball—revolutionizing the role of manager while winning a spectacular ten pennants and seven World Series Championships. For a man who spent so much of his life in the limelight—an astounding fifty-five years in professional baseball—Stengel remains an enigma. Acclaimed New York Yankees' historian and bestselling author Marty Appel digs into Casey Stengel's quirks and foibles, unearthing a tremendous trove of baseball stories, perspective, and history. Weaving in never-before-published family documents, Appel creates an intimate portrait of a private man who was elected into the Baseball Hall of Fame in 1966 and named "Baseball's Greatest Character" by MLB Network's *Prime 9*.

Biography

HIS OWNSELF
A Semi-Memoir
by Dan Jenkins

Dan Jenkins takes us on a tour of his legendary career as a sportswriter and novelist. We see Dan hone his craft, from his high school paper to his first job at the *Fort Worth Press* to the glory days of *Sports Illustrated*. Dan was always at the center of it all—hanging out at Elaine's while swapping stories with politicians and movie stars, covering every Masters, U.S. Open, and British Open for over four decades. The result is a knee-slapping, star-studded, once-in-a-lifetime memoir from one of the most important, hilarious, and semi-cantankerous sportswriters ever.

Autobiography

MESSI

A Biography

by Leonardo Faccio

Admired around the globe for his athleticism, skill, and fierce competitiveness, Lionel Messi has already shattered records at FC Barcelona, one of the most storied clubs in the world. As a talented youth player in Buenos Aires, Messi left his home for Spain in search of the medical help his family could not afford to treat his rare hormone deficiency. Small of stature but possessing tremendous natural gifts, Messi developed into a star at Barcelona's famed La Masia soccer school. Leonardo Faccio has written a biography of an enigmatic celebrity and a meditation on athletic genius, drawing on interviews with Messi himself, as well as with everyone from his family, teammates, childhood friends— even his favorite butcher. In-depth and intimate, soccer fans who enjoy watching Messi come alive on the field will delight as he comes alive on the page.

Biography

OPEN

An Autobiography

by Andre Agassi

Andre Agassi had his life mapped out for him before he left the crib. Groomed to be a tennis champion by his moody and demanding father, Agassi had won the first of his eight grand slams and achieved wealth, celebrity, and the game's highest honors by the age of twenty-two. But as he reveals in this searching autobiography, off the court he was often unhappy and confused, unfulfilled by his great achievements in a sport he had come to resent. Agassi writes candidly about his early success and his uncomfortable relationship with fame, his marriage to Brooke Shields, his growing interest in philanthropy, and—described in haunting, point-by-point detail—the highs and lows of his celebrated career.

Autobiography

THE LEGENDS CLUB

Dean Smith, Mike Krzyzewski, Jim Valvano, and
an Epic College Basketball Rivalry

by John Feinstein

On March 18, 1980, the Duke basketball program announced the hiring of Mike Krzyzewski, the man who would restore glory to the team. The only problem: no one knew who Krzyzewski was. Nine days later, Jim Valvano was hired by North Carolina State to be their new head coach. The hiring didn't raise as many eyebrows, but the two new coaches had a similar goal: to unseat North Carolina's Dean Smith as the king of college basketball. And just like that, the most sensational competitive decade in NCAA history was about to unfold. In the skillful hands of John Feinstein, *The Legends Club* captures an era in American sports and culture, documenting the inside view of a decade of absolutely incredible competition. Feinstein pulls back the curtain on the recruiting wars, the intensely personal competition that wasn't always friendly, the enormous pressure and national stakes, and the battle for the very soul of college basketball.

Sports

INSTANT REPLAY

The Green Bay Diary of Jerry Kramer

by Jerry Kramer and Dick Schaap

Instant Replay takes readers inside the 1967 season of the Green Bay Packers, following that storied team from training camp to their dramatic victory in Super Bowl II. Candid and amusing, Jerry Kramer describes from a player's perspective a bygone era of sports, filled with blood, grit, and tears. No game better exemplifies this period than the classic "Ice Bowl" conference championship game between the Packers and the Dallas Cowboys, which Kramer, who made the crucial block in the climactic play, describes in thrilling detail. Vivid and engaging, *Instant Replay* is an irreplaceable reminder of the glory days of pro football.

Sports

THE LAST HERO
A Life of Henry Aaron
by Howard Bryant

Henry (Hank) Aaron retired from professional baseball in 1976, but his reputation has grown in magnitude; his influence extends beyond statistics. Here, at long last, is the first definitive biography of one of baseball's immortal figures. Based on meticulous research and extensive interviews, *The Last Hero* reveals how Aaron navigated the upheavals of his time—fighting against racism while at the same time benefiting from racial progress—and how he achieved his goal of continuing Jackie Robinson's mission to obtain full equality for African Americans, both in baseball and society, while he lived uncomfortably in the public eye. Eloquently written, detailed and penetrating, this is a revelatory portrait of a complicated, private man who through sports became an enduring American icon.

Biography

ANCHOR BOOKS
Available wherever books are sold.
www.anchorbooks.com